District Gazetteers of India Series 181

PUNJAB DISTRICT GAZETTEERS

MONTGOMERY DISTRICT

Owing to the antiquity and rarity of this book, certain pages are regrettably absent, and readability is compromised due to the blurring of the original text. If you possess any insights regarding the availability of these missing sections, kindly inform us. Your assistance is crucial in ensuring the completion of this significant work for the benefit of future generations.

District Gazetteers of India Series 181

PUNJAB DISTRICT GAZETTEERS

MONTGOMERY DISTRICT

BY

P. J. FAGAN

36 VOLUMES (IN 37 BINDINGS)

(VOL. 24th)

GYAN

Published by

Gyan Publishing House
5, Ansari Road
Daryaganj, New Delhi-110002
Phone: 011-47034999, 9811692060
E-mail: books@gyanbooks.com

Distribution Network
gyanbooks.com
India, USA, Canada, UK, Australia, France

ISBN: 978-93-6208-248-0 (Set) 36 Volumes (In 37 Bindings)
978-81-212-5643-8 (HB)

First Published, 1900

2nd Impression 2024

Printed at: Gyan Press, Delhi.

PUNJAB DISTRICT GAZETTEERS (VOL. 24th)

Author: P. J. FAGAN

LIST OF VOLUMES

S. NO.	ISBN NO.	VOL.	TITLE	AUTHOR	PRICE	PAGES
			ASSAM DISTRICT GAZETTEERS			
1	9788121286046	1st	Cachar	B. C. Allen	1200	300
2	9788121286039	2nd	Sylhet	B. C. Allen	1500	378
3	9788121286022	3rd	Goalpara	B. C. Allen	800	203
4	9788121286015	4th	Kamrup	B. C. Allen	1370	344
5	9788121286008	5th	Darrang	B. C. Allen	1450	364
6	9788121285995	6th	Nowgong	B. C. Allen	1120	280
7	9788121285988	7th	Sibsagar	B. C. Allen	1370	343
8	9788121285971	8th	Lakhimpur	B. C. Allen	1380	347
9	9788121285964	9th	Naga Hills and Manipur	B. C. Allen	1170	294
10	9788121285957	10th	The Khasi And Jaintia Hills, The Garo Hills And The Lushai Hills	B. C. Allen	1350	363
11	9788121285940	11th	The Sadiya and Balipara Frontier Tract	B. C. Allen	760	190
			BENGAL DISTRICT GAZETTEERS			
12	9788121218665	1st	Angul	L. S. S. O'Malley	500	168
13	9788121259644	2nd	Bakarganj	J. C. JACK	1350	194
14	9788121218689	3rd	Balasore	L. S. S. O'Malley	675	228
15	9788121259606	4th	Bankura	L. S. S. O'Malley	1390	199
16	9788121218368	5th	Bhagalpur	J. Byrne	580	194
17	9788121218283	6th	Birbhum	L. S. S. O'Malley	450	150
18	9788121259668	7th	Eastern Bengal and Assam - Bogra	J. N. Gupta	1320	188
19	9788121218344	8th	Burdwan	J. C. K. Peterson	680	227
20	9788121259545	9th	Calcutta District Gazetteer - Statistics, 1901 - 02		480	68
21	9788121218306	10th	Champaran	L. S. S. O'Malley	610	205
22	9788121259620	11th	Eastern Bengal District Gazetters - Chittagong	L. S. S. O'Malley	1500	216
23	9788121259569	12th	Chota Nagpur Tributary		180	26
24	9788121259422	13th	The Cooch Behar Gazette: Statistics		2040	292
25	9788121218405	14th	Cuttack	L. S. S. O'Malley	740	248
26	9788121261364	15th	Eastern Bengal District Gazetteers Dacca	B. C. Allen	800	207
27	9788121218429	16th	Darbhanga	L. S. S. O'Malley	540	180
28	9788121204965	17th	Darjeeling	L. S. S. O'Malley	500	248
29	9788121259460	18th	Eastern Bengal District Gazetteers - Dinajpur	F. W. Strong	1250	178
30	9788121259408	19th	Faridpur	L. S. S. O'Malley	980	140
31	9788121218467	20th	Gaya	L. S. S. O'Malley	810	270
32	9788121214025	21st	Bihar and Orissa District Gazetteer: Hazaribagh	E. Lister	950	234
33	9788121218320	22nd	Hooghly	L. S. S. O'Malley	1020	340
34	9788121218184	23rd	Bengal District Gazetteer Howrah	L. S. S. O'Malley	590	199
35	9788121259309	24th	Eastern Bengal and Assam - Jalpaiguri	John F. Gruning	1250	178
36	9788121259286	25th	Jessore	L. S. S. O'Malley	1340	192
37	9788121259248	26th	Khulna	L. S. S. O'Malley	1540	220
38	9788121259224	27th	Malda	G. E. Lambourn	940	134
39	9788121297912	28th	Manbhum	H. Coupland	1250	313
40	9788121218481	29th	Midnapore	L. S. S. O'Malley	750	252
41	9788121218580	30th	Monghyr	L. S. S. O'Malley	840	280
42	9788121259163	31st	Murshidabad	L. S. S. O'Malley	1750	250
43	9788121259583	32nd	Bengal District Gazetteers - Muzaffarpur	L. S. S. O'Malley	1300	188
44	9788121259149	33rd	Mymensingh	F. A. Sachse	1340	192
45	9788121259125	34th	Nadia	J. H. E. Garrett	1500	214
46	9788121259101	35th	Eastern Bengal and Assam - Noakhali	J. E. Webster	800	115
47	9788121218443	36th	Feudatory States of Orissa	L. E. B. Cobdenramsay	1180	395
48	9788121259088	37th	Pabna	L. S. S. O'Malley	990	142
49	9788121218504	38th	Palamau	L. S. S. O'Malley	570	190
50	9788121218627	39th	Patna	L. S. S. O'Malley	750	250
51	9788121218528	40th	Puri	L. S. S. O'Malley	980	328
52	9788121218740	41st	Purnea	L. S. S. O'Malley	660	220
53	9788121258944	42nd	Rajshahi	L. S. S. O'Malley	1500	216
54	9788121256674	43rd	Bihar and Orissa District Gazetteers: Ranchi	M. G. Hallett	1950	278
55	9788121258920	44th	Eastern Bengal and assam - Rangpur	J. A. Vas	1250	178
56	9788121218542	45th	Sambalpur	L. S. S. O'Malley	730	242
57	9788121214049	46th	Santal Parganas	L. S. S. O'Malley	1250	308
58	9788121218603	47th	Saran	L. S. S. O'Malley	570	190
59	9788121218641	48th	Shahabad	L. S. S. O'Malley	570	190
60	9788121256698	49th	The Gazetteer of Sikhim	H. H. Risley	2280	481
61	9788121218566	50th	Singhbhum, Saraikela And Kharsawan	L. S. S. O'Malley	840	280
62	9788121259446	51st	Eastern Bengal District Gazetteers - Tippera	J. E. Webster	1020	146
63	9788121259040	52nd	24 Parganas	L. S. S. O'Malley	1990	284

S. NO.	ISBN NO.	VOL.	TITLE	AUTHOR	PRICE	PAGES
			CENTRAL PROVINCES DISTRICT GAZETTEERS			
64	9789362085474	1st, Vol. A	Akola (Descriptive)	A. E. Nelson, C. Brown	1740	436
65	9789362087232	2nd, Vol. A	Amraoti (Descriptive)	S. V. Fitzgerald, A. E. Nelson	2100	524
66	9789362085191	3rd,Vol. A	Balaghat (Descriptive)	R. V. RUSSELL	860	216
67	9789362085986	4th, Vol. A	Betul (Descriptive)	R. V. RUSSELL	1220	306
68	9789362082039	5th, Vol. A	Bhandara (Descriptive)	R. V. RUSSELL	1170	292
69	9789362087713	6th, Vol. A	Bilaspur (Descriptive)	R. V. RUSSELL	1740	434
70	9789362084255	7th, Vol. A	Buldana (Descriptive)	A. E. Nelson	2170	543
71	9789362082107	8th, Vol. B	Chanda (Descriptive)	R. V. RUSSELL	940	234
72	9789362084576	9th	Chhattisgarch Feudatory State	E. A. De Brett	1760	440
73	9789362084873	10th	Chhindwara (Descriptive)	R. V. RUSSELL	1100	274
74	9789362086426	11th, Vol. A & B	Damoh (Descriptive and Statistical Tables 1891-1901)	R. V. RUSSELL	1660	414
75	9789362080240	12th, Vol. A	Durg (Descriptive)	A. E. Nelson	930	232
76	9789362080448	13th, Vol. A	Hoshangabad (Descriptive)	R. V. RUSSELL	1720	430
77	9789362080028	14th, Vol. A	Jubbulpore (Descriptive)	A. E. Nelson	1900	474
78	9789362088079	15th, Vol. A & B	Mandla (Descriptive and Statistical Tables 1891-1901)	R. V. RUSSELL	740	186
79	9789362086693	16th, Vol. A	Nagpur (Descriptive)	R. V. RUSSELL	1580	394
80	9789362085221	17th, Vol. A	Narsinghpur (Descriptive)	R. V. RUSSELL	1030	257
81	9789362086501	18th, Vol. A	Nimar (Descriptive)	R. V. RUSSELL	1200	299
82	9789362082145	19th, Vol. A	Raipur (Descriptive)	A. E. Nelson	1580	396
83	9789362085948	20th, Vol. A	Saugor (Descriptive)	R. V. RUSSELL	1140	285
84	9789362080318	21st, Vol. A	Seoni (Descriptive)	R. V. RUSSELL	930	232
85	9789362089625	22nd, Vol. A	Wardha (Descriptive)	R. V. RUSSELL	1210	302
86	9789362088468	23rd, Vol. A	Yeotmal (Descriptive)	R. V. RUSSELL	1110	277
87	9789362083500	24th, Vol. I, Pt. I	Gwalior (Text and Tables)	R. V. RUSSELL	1960	489
88	9789362081667	24th, Vol. I, Pt. II	Gwalior (Maps)	R. V. RUSSELL	790	198
89	9789362087478	24th, Vol. I, Pt. III	Gwalior (Village List)	R. V. RUSSELL	1620	406
90	9789362089731	24th, Vol. I, Pt. IV	Gwalior (Photos)	R. V. RUSSELL	2790	698
91	9789362088956	25th, Vol. II	Indore (Text and Tables)	C. E. Luard	2100	524
92	9789362088543	26th, Vol. III	Bhopal (Text and Tables)	C. E. Luard	1090	272
93	9789362082732	27th, Vol. IV	Rewah (Text and Tables)	C. E. Luard	1000	250
94	9789362087065	28th, Vol. V, Pt. A	Western States - Malwa (Text)	C. E. Luard	3050	762
95	9789362080707	29th, Vol. VI, Pt. A	Eastern States - Bundelkhand (Text)	C. E. Luard	1850	463
96	9789362086273	30th, Vol. VI, Pt. B	Eastern States - Bundelkhand (Tables)	C. E. Luard	1670	417
			GAZETTEER OF THE BOMBAY PRESIDENCY			
97	9788121283458	1st, Part I	History of Gujarat	Ed.: James M. Campbell	4500	644
98	9788121285599	1st, Part II	History of the Konkan Dakhan and Southern Maratha Country	Ed.: James M. Campbell	5870	840
99	9788121285575	2nd	Gujarat, Surat and Broach	Ed.: James M. Campbell	4150	598
100	9788121285551	3rd	Kaira and Panch Mahals	Ed.: James M. Campbell	2370	339
101	9788121285537	4th	Ahmedabad	Ed.: James M. Campbell	2600	372
102	9788121285513	5th	Cutch, Palanpur, and Mahi Kantha	Ed.: James M. Campbell	3330	478
103	9788121285490	6th	Rewa Kantha, Narukot, Cambay, and Surat States	Ed.: James M. Campbell	2030	290
104	9788121285476	7th	Baroda	Ed.: James M. Campbell	4550	652
105	9788121285452	8th	Kathiawar	Ed.: James M. Campbell	5300	758
106	9788121285438	9th, Part I	Gujarat Population - Hindus	Ed.: James M. Campbell	4450	636
107	9788121285414	9th, Part II	Gujarat Population - Musalmans and Parsis	Ed.: James M. Campbell	2120	304
108	9788121285391	10th	Ratnagiri and Savantvadi	Ed.: James M. Campbell	3500	501
109	9788121285377	11th	Kolaba and Janjira	Ed.: James M. Campbell	3550	513
110	9788121285353	12th	Khandesh	Ed.: James M. Campbell	4450	638
111	9788121285339	13th Part I	Thana	Ed.: James M. Campbell	2880	413
112	9788121285315	13th Part II	Thana	Ed.: James M. Campbell	2490	357
113	9788121285292	14th	Thana - Places of Interest	Ed.: James M. Campbell	4600	659
114	9788121285278	15th Part I	Kanara	Ed.: James M. Campbell	3250	468
115	9788121285254	15th Part II	Kanara	Ed.: James M. Campbell	2440	468
116	9788121285230	16th	Nasik	Ed.: James M. Campbell	4880	698
117	9788121285216	17th	Ahmadnagar	Ed.: James M. Campbell	5400	772
118	9788121285193	18th Part I	Poona	Ed.: James M. Campbell	4100	586
119	9788121285179	18th Part II	Poona	Ed.: James M. Campbell	3750	537
120	9788121285155	18th Part III	Poona	Ed.: James M. Campbell	3500	503
121	9788121285131	19th	Satara	Ed.: James M. Campbell	4840	692
122	9788121285117	20th	Sholapur	Ed.: James M. Campbell	3820	547
123	9788121285094	21st	Gazetteer of the Bomaby Presidency: Belgaum	Ed.: James M. Campbell	3590	514
124	9788121285070	22nd	Dharwar	Ed.: James M. Campbell	5880	841
125	9788121285056	23rd	Gazetteer of the Bombay Presidency:Bijapur	Ed.: James M. Campbell	4980	712
126	9788121285032	24th	Kolhapur	Ed.: James M. Campbell	3150	450
127	9788121285018	25th	Botany	Ed.: James M. Campbell	2850	408

S. NO.	ISBN NO.	VOL.	TITLE	AUTHOR	PRICE	PAGES
128	9788121284998	26th, Part I	Materials Towards a Statistical Account of the Town and Island of Bombay - History	Ed.: James M. Campbell	3525	504
129	9788121284974	26th, Part II	Materials Towards a Statistical Account of the Town and Island of Bombay - Trade and Fortifications	Ed.: James M. Campbell	3750	538
130	9788121284950	26th, Part III	Materials Towards a Statistical Account of the Town And Island of Bombay - Administration	Ed.: James M. Campbell	4840	702
131	9788121284936	27th	General Index	Ed.: R. E. Enthoven	2990	428
			MADRAS DISTRICT GAZETTEERS			
132	9788121258821	1st	Anantapur	W. Francis	1590	227
133	9788121258562	2nd	Malabar	C. A Innes & F. B Evans	4210	602
134	9788121258807	3rd	Bellary	W. Francis	2640	377
135	9788121258784	4th	Statistical Appendix For Chingleput		390	56
136	9788121258760	5th	Coimbatore	K. N. Krishnaswami Ayyar	4790	628
137	9788121232821	6th	Madras District Gazetteers District Gazetteer Cuddapah	C. F. Brackenbury	1950	285
138	9788121258722	7th	Statistical Appendix For Ganjam		510	73
139	9788121256759	8th, Vol. 1st	Godavari District Gazetteer	F. R. Hemingway	1280	320
140	9788121256797	8th, Vol. 2nd	Godavari District Gazetteer	F. R. Hemingway	340	83
141	9788121258685	9th	Statistical Appendix For Kistna		890	127
142	9788121258661	10th	Statistical Appendix For Kurnool		380	54
143	9788121258623	11th	Madura	W. Francis	2650	379
144	9788121258586	12th	Statistical Appendix For Madura		1040	148
145	9788121258647	13th	The Nilgiris	W. Francis	3060	437
146	9788121234283	14th	Madras District Gazetteers Gazetteer Of The Nellore District Brought Upto 1938			2110
386						
147	9788121258524	15th	North Arcot		830	118
148	9788121258500	16th, Vol. 1, Part I	Salem	F. J. Richards	2400	343
149	9788121258609	16th, Vol. 1, Part II	Salem	F. J. Richards	2520	360
150	9788121258463	17th	South Arcot	W. Francis	3360	480
151	9788121258487	18th	Statistical Appendix For South Canara		560	80
152	9788121258449	19th, Vol. 1st & 2nd	Tanjore: Main Volume and Statistical Appendix		2900	401
153	9788121258401	20th	Tinnevelly	H. R. Pate	3830	547
154	9788121258425	21st	Statistical Appendix For Tinnevelly		450	64
155	9788121258388	22nd, 1st & 2nd	Trichinopoly: Main Volume and Statistical Appendix	F. R. Hemingway	3410	487
156	9788121241960	23rd	Vizagapatam District Gazetteer	W. Francis	1520	385
			PUNJAB DISTRICT GAZETTEERS			
157	9788121255936	1st	Ambala District 1883-84		870	124
158	9788121255950	2nd	Amritsar		1650	236
159	9788121255974	3rd	Delhi		1820	260
160	9788121255998	4th	Ferozepore		1320	188
161	9788121256018	5th	Faridkot		490	70
162	9788121256032	6th	Gujranwala 1893-94		1780	254
163	9788121256056	7th	Gujrat	C. E. Luard	1590	228
164	9788121256070	8th	Gurdaspur 1891-92		1764	252
165	9788121256094	9th	Gurgaon 1883-4		1420	203
166	9788121256117	10th	Hazara	H. D. Watson	3200	458
167	9788121256131	11th	Hissar district and Lohar State		2570	367
168	9788121256155	12th	Hoshiarpur		1980	283
169	9788121256179	13th	Jhang		1490	213
170	9788121256193	14th	Jhelam		1410	202
171	9788121256216	15th	Jalandhar District 1883-84		750	108
172	9788121256230	16th, Vol. XIV-A	Jullundur District, with maps and Kapurthala		2786	398
173	9788121256254	17th, Pt. I	Kangra (Proper)		2030	290
174	9788121256278	17th, Pt. II	Kangra (Kulu, Lahual, Spiti)		2500	357
175	9788121256292	18th	Karnal		2700	386
176	9788121256315	19th	Kohat		2150	307
177	9788121256339	20th	The Lahore District 1883-84		1710	244
178	9788121256377	21st	Ludhiana and Maler Kotla		2350	335
179	9788121256391	22nd	Lyallpur		1029	147
180	9788121256414	23rd	Mianwali		1640	234
181	9788121256438	24th	Montgomery	P. J. Fagan	2230	318
182	9788121258357	25th	Multan (1901-02)	E. D. Maclagan	3360	480
183	9788121258692	26th	The Rohtak District 1883-84		1370	196
184	9788121258739	27th, Vol. III A	Dujana State 1904		600	16
185	9788121256476	28th	Shahpur District		2490	356
186	9788121256490	29th	Simla District		1110	159
187	9788121256513	30th	The Chamba State		2860	408

S. NO.	ISBN NO.	VOL.	TITLE	AUTHOR	PRICE	PAGES
188	9788121256537	31st	The Chenab Colony 1904		2170	310
189	9788121256551	32nd	Kalsia State		370	53
190	9788121256575	33rd	Suket and Mandi		1080	154
191	9788121256599	34th	Phulkian States, Patiala Jind And Nabha 1904		2898	414
192	9788121256636	35th	Simla Hill States		3100	443
193	9788121256650	36th	Sirmur		1280	183
			RAJPUTANA DISTRICT GAZETTEERS			
194	9789362089847	1st, Vol. I-A & B	Ajmer-merwara (Text and Statistics Tables)	C. C. Watson	1720	246
195	9789362088895	2nd. Vol. II-A & B	Mewar Residency (Text and Statistics Tables)	K.D. Erskine	2370	339
196	9789362087935	3rd, Vol. III-A & B	The Western Rajputana States Residency And The Bikaner Agency	K.D. Erskine	5000	718
			UNITED PROVINCES OF AGRA AND OUDH DISTRICT GAZETTEERS			
197	9789362080523	Vol. I	Agra	H. R. Nevill	3160	452
198	9789362084149	Vol. II	Aligarh	H. R. Nevill	1820	260
199	9789362081452	Vol. III	Allahabad	H. R. Nevill	2860	409
200	9789362085917	Vol. IV	Almora	H. G. Walton	2330	333
201	9789362089717	Vol. V	Azamgarh	D. L. Drake Brockman	2440	349
202	9789362089069	Vol. VI	Bahraich	H. R. Nevill	1970	281
203	9789362089670	Vol. VII	Ballia	H. R. Nevill	2450	350
204	9789362080974	Vol. VIII	Banda	D. L. Drake Brockman	2440	349
205	9789362082657	Vol. IX	Bara Banki	H. R. Nevill	2410	344
206	9789362089588	Vol. X	Bareilly	H. R. Nevill	2290	327
207	9789362088772	Vol. XI	Basti	H. R. Nevill	2250	321
208	9789362086556	Vol. XII	Benares	H. R. Nevill	3210	458
209	9789362089762	Vol. XIII	Bijnor	H. R. Nevill	2540	363
210	9789362087522	Vol. XIV	Budaun	H. R. Nevill	2650	378
211	9789362085665	Vol. XV	Bulandshahr	H. R. Nevill	2930	419
212	9789362080899	Vol. XVI	Cawnpore	H. R. Nevill	3090	442
213	9789362082237	Vol. XVII	Dehra Dun	H. G. Walton	2390	342
214	9789362089489	Vol. XVIII	Etah	E. R. Neave	2240	320
215	9789362086983	Vol. XIX	Etawah	D. L. Drake Brockman	1940	277
216	9789362081650	Vol. XX	Farrukhabad	E. R. Neave	2270	324
217	9789362083326	Vol. XXI	Fatehpur	H. R. Nevill	2640	377
218	9789362081018	Vol. XXII	Fyzabad	H. R. Nevill	2370	339
219	9789362086907	Vol. XXIII	Garhwal	H. G. Walton	1780	254
220	9789362085092	Vol. XXIV	Ghazipur	H. R. Nevill	2240	320
221	9789362083272	Vol. XXV	Gonda	H. R. Nevill	2310	330
222	9789362088185	Vol. XXVI	Gorakhpur	H. R. Nevill	2650	378
223	9789362082756	Vol. XXVII	Hamirpur	D. L. Drake Brockman	1940	277
224	9789362081780	Vol. XXVIII	Hardoi	H. R. Nevill	2350	336
225	9789362085641	Vol. XXIX	Jalaun	D. L. Drake Brockman	1650	236
226	9789362080998	Vol. XXX	Jaunpur	H. R. Nevill	2450	350
227	9789362088123	Vol. XXXI	Jhansi	D. L. Drake Brockman	2740	391
228	9789362081568	Vol. XXXII	Kheri	H. R. Nevill	2310	330
229	9789362088161	Vol. XXXIII	Lucknow	H. R. Nevill	2460	352
230	9789362081155	Vol. XXXIV	Mainpuri	H. R. Nevill	2440	348
231	9789362086839	Vol. XXXV	Meerut	H. R. Nevill	3040	434
232	9789362080400	Vol. XXXVI	Mirzapur	D. L. Drake Brockman	3400	486
233	9789362088666	Vol. XXXVII	Moradabad	H. R. Nevill	2660	380
234	9789362082213	Vol. XXXVIII	Muttra	D. L. Drake Brockman	3000	428
235	9789362083555	Vol. XXXIX	Muzaffarnagar	H. R. Nevill	3160	451
236	9789362080820	Vol. XL	Naini Tal	H. R. Nevill	2640	377
237	9789362087799	Vol. XLI	Partabgarh	H. R. Nevill	2180	312
238	9789362082022	Vol. XLII	Pilibhit	H. R. Nevill	2200	314
239	9789362085337	Vol. XLIII	Rai Bareli	H. R. Nevill	2250	322
240	9789362088901	Vol. XLIV	Rampur	H. R. Nevill	1640	234
241	9789362082664	Vol. XLV	Saharanpur	H. R. Nevill	3070	438
242	9789362088406	Vol. XLVI	Shahjahanpur	H. R. Nevill	2110	302
243	9789362089823	Vol. XLVII	Sitapur	H. R. Nevill	2220	317
244	9789362083913	Vol. XLVIII	Sultanpur	H. R. Nevill	1860	266
245	9789362081544	Vol. XLIX	Unnao	H. R. Nevill	2140	305

GAZETTEER

OF THE

MONTGOMERY DISTRICT.

BY

P. J. FAGAN, Esquire, C.S.,

Settlement Collector.

1898-99.

Revised Edition.

Compiled and Published under the Authority

OF THE

PUNJAB GOVERNMENT.

LAHORE: "CIVIL AND MILITARY GAZETTE" PRESS.

1900.

PREFACE TO THE SECOND EDITION.

The new edition of the Gazetteer has been prepared on the conclusion of the revision of the settlement of the district. The more valuable portions of the former edition, which consisted of extracts from Mr. Purser's classical Settlement Report, have been as far as possible retained intact, corrections and additions being made where needful. The remaining portions have been corrected, amplified and brought up to date. The appended tables, as a rule, contain the latest available information.

MONTGOMERY,
The 22nd February 1899.

P. J. FAGAN,
Settlement Collector.

TABLE OF CONTENTS.

CHAPTER I.—THE DISTRICT.

Section A.—Descriptive—

Subject. Page.

CHAPTER I.—THE DISTRICT—*continued.*

Section A.—Descriptive—*concluded.*

Section B.—Geology, Fauna and Flora—

SUBJECT. *Page.*

CHAPTER I.—THE DISTRICT—*continued.*

Section B.—Geology, Fauna and Flora—*continued.*

SUBJECT. | Page.

CHAPTER I.—THE DISTRICT—*concluded.*

Section B.—Geology, Fauna and Flora—*concluded.*

CHAPTER II.—HISTORY.

Subject. Page.

CHAPTER III.—THE PEOPLE.

Section A.—Statistical—

Section B.—Social and Religious Life—

Section C.—Tribes, Castes and Leading Families—

SUBJECT. *Page.*

CHAPTER III.—THE PEOPLE—*continued.*

Section A.—Tribes, Castes and Leading Families—*concluded.*

Section D.—Village Communities and Tenures—

SUBJECT. *Page.*

CHAPTER III.—THE PEOPLE—*concluded.*

Section D.—Village Communities and Tenures—*concluded.*

CHAPTER IV.—PRODUCTION AND DISTRIBUTION.

Section A.—Agriculture and Arboriculture—

SUBJECT.	Page.

CHAPTER IV.—PRODUCTION AND DISTRIBUTION—*continued.*

Section A.—Agriculture and Arboriculture—*concluded.*

Section B.—Domestic Animals—

SUBJECT.	Page.

CHAPTER IV.—PRODUCTION AND DISTRIBUTION—*continued.*

Section D.—Prices, Weights and Measures, and Communications—*concluded.*

CHAPTER V.—ADMINISTRATION AND FINANCE.

Section A.—General Administration—

Section B.—Land and Land Revenue—

SUBJECT.	Page.

CHAPTER V.—ADMINISTRATION AND FINANCE—*concluded.*

Section B.—Land and Land Revenue—*concluded.*

CHAPTER VI.—TOWNS AND MUNICIPALITIES.

Table No. I—showing LEADING STATISTICS.

1	2	3	4	5	6
		DETAIL OF TAHSILS.			
DETAILS.	District.	Montgomery.	Gugera.	Dipálpur.	Pákpattan.
Total square miles 1896-97 ...	5,586	1,749	1,525	986	1,326
Cultivated square miles (1896-97) ...	620	31	81	334	174
Culturable square miles (1896-97) ...	3,878	1,211	1,022	569	1,076
Irrigated square miles (1896-97) ...	693	18	52	407	216
Average square miles under crops (1892-93 to 1896-97) ...	773	77	107	371	218
Annual rainfall in inches (1892-93 to 1896-97) ...	37·4	10	7·0	10·1	9·4
Number of inhabited towns and villages (1891) ...	1,867	277	342	679	569
Total population (1891) ...	499,521	93,648	113,447	180,455	111,971
Rural population (1891) ...	480,350	80,999	113,447	180,455	105,449
Urban population (1891) ...	19,171	12,649	...	...	6,522
Total population per square mile (1891) ...	87	54	74	187	85
Rural population per square mile (1891) ...	83	47	74	187	80
Hindús (1891) ...	121,181	21,750	22,330	46,862	30,539
Sikhs (1891) ...	16,032	1,515	3,295	6,534	4,688
Musalmáns (1891) ...	361,923	70,301	87,822	127,056	76,744
Average annual land revenue (1892-93 to 1896-97)* ... Rs.	3,36,900	60,952	54,928	1,53,477	67,543
Average annual gross revenue (1892-93 to 1896-97)† ... "	7,25,996				
New assessment ... "	5,08,028	62,655	82,990	2,07,515	1,54,848

* Fixed, fluctuating and miscellaneous.
† Land, Tribute, Local rates, Excise and Stamps.

CHAPTER I.

THE DISTRICT.

SECTION A.—DESCRIPTIVE.

Chapter I. A

Descriptive

General description.

The Montgomery district, formerly known as Gugera, is in the Lahore division, and lies between north latitude 29° 58′ and 31° 33′, and east longitude 72° 30′ and 74° 11′. It is bounded on the north-east by the district of Lahore, on the north-west by the district of Jhang, on the south-west by the district of Mooltan, and on the south-east by the river Sutlej, which separates it from the State of Baháwalpur, and a small portion of the Ferozepore district. The shape of the district may be said to be a rough parallelogram, the sides running at right-angles to the rivers Sutlej and Rávi forming its breadth, and those running parallel to them its length. The river Rávi divides it into two unequal portions, of which that lying in the Bári Doáb includes about a third of the whole area. From Thatha Suratan on the Lahore border near Bucheke to Bub on the Rávi where it enters the Mooltan district, the extreme length is about 90 miles. The extreme breadth from Sahibewála on the Sutlej to the Mari road on the Jhang boundary is 74 miles. It is divided into four tahsils by two lines running roughly parallel with the sides of the parallelogram : of which that of Gugera lies to the north-east, Dipálpur to the south-east, Montgomery to the north-west, and Pákpattan to the south-west. Of the whole area of the district two-fifths is included within village boundaries, the remaining two-thirds constituting the great grazing grounds of the *bár*, and being the property of Government. But the whole of the *bár* tract north of the Rávi is being rapidly brought under cultivation by means of the Gugera and Buralla branches of the Chenáb Canal, and will shortly be removed from this district and incorporated in the new district of Lyallpur.

Some leading statistics regarding the district, and the several tahsils into which it is divided are given in Table No. I on the opposite page. The district contains no towns of more than 10,000 souls, Kamália with a population of 7,490 being the largest. The administrative head-quarters are situated at Montgomery, on the line of rail between Mooltan and Lahore. Montgomery stands fifth in order of area, and 23rd in order of population, among the 31 districts of the province, comprising 5·20 per cent. of the total area, 2·39 per

Chapter I, A.

Descriptive.

General description.

cent. of the total population, and 0·79 per cent. of the urban population of British territory. The latitude, longitude, and height in feet above the sea of the principal places in the district are shown below:—

Town.	N. Latitude.	E. Longitude.	Feet above sea-level.
Montgomery	30° 40	73° 10'	500*
Gugera	30° 58'	73° 21'	490*
Dipálpur	30° 40'	73° 42'	510*
Pákpattan	30° 21'	73° 25'	616

* Approximate.

The high central ridge, the Dhaya.

Almost in the middle of the district in the Bári Doáb a ridge of high land runs from north-east to south-west, the whole length of the district. This ridge is often called the Dhaya, though the term is more properly applied to the slope to the top of the ridge from the lowlands at its foot. This slope is generally gradual, and in places, especially on the northern or Rávi side of the ridge, almost imperceptible. The slope on the southern or Sutlej, side is more marked, and towards the Lahore border it becomes very abrupt, and is cut into deep chasms by the rain-water running down into the valley beneath. The edge of the high bank here bears a remarkable resemblance to the right bank of the Beás as seen at Phillour. The average breadth of this ridge is about 10 miles. The country slopes down from the top of it to the rivers, the slope to the Sutlej opposite Montgomery being about 40 feet, and to the Rávi half that. The Sutlej runs at an average distance of 25 miles from the centre ridge, the Rávi nowhere at a greater distance than 16 miles; while from Chíchávatni to the Mooltan district the ridge forms the left bank of the Rávi. It is generally supposed that at some period in the long past, the Beás ran close under the ridge to the south, and the Rávi to the north. The latter stream, following the usual course of the Punjab rivers, edged away to the west, while the Beás altered its course and fell into the Sutlej. This centre plateau is almost entirely uncultivated. The soil is generally inferior and saline; in places remarkably so. With a plentiful supply of water and good cultivation the greater portion of the land could be brought to bear fair crops. When the rains have been favourable, grass grows abundantly. But even in the best seasons there are vast stretches of land where not a blade of grass is to be seen, and where even the hardy *lána*, a salsolaceous plant, is unable to live. In other places the *lána* flourishes; while in the better parts of this arid region the *wán*,

Chapter I, A.

Descriptive.

The high central ridge, the Dhaya.

jand, and *karil*, relieved by a rare *farásh*, are the only plants found that can lay claim to be more than mere shrubs. Water lies from 60 to 70 feet below the surface; it is sometimes very good, sometimes so brackish as to be almost undrinkable. The quality seems better towards Mooltan and worse towards Lahore. The wisdom of our predecessors saw fit to locate the Sadr station of the district in one of the most arid and dreary spots to be found in the howling wilderness described above; in consequence whereof Montgomery has earned its unenviable but well deserved reputation of being the worst penal settlement for Europeans in this part of India.

The country below the ridge.

The country between the ridge and the rivers is of a more hospitable character. The soil is generally of good quality; saline tracts are comparatively rare, and of no great extent; water is generally sweet and nearer the surface; vegetation is more abundant; and a considerable portion of the country is under cultivation. The *kikar* is indeed rare, except along the rivers or canals; and the better classes of trees are, of course, still less commonly met; but the *farásh* grows in most places where there is a hollow in which the rain-water can lodge; and the trees mentioned in the preceding paragraph are more numerous and of fairer growth than is usually the case on the ridge. The *farásh* is the only tree that flourishes in the district; and the Rávi side appears to agree much better with it than the Sutlej side of the district. The vast extent of uncultivated land forming the north-western portion of Pákpattan, the southern tahsil of Montgomery, is, however, very little better than the ridge. The upland or Rechna Bár portion of the district on the right or northern bank of the Rávi differs considerably from that in the Bári Doáb, chiefly in the quality of the soil, which in the former is generally excellent. Vegetation is far more abundant, and the grazing much superior; the depth to water, however, is greater As already noticed, the whole of this tract is being rapidly brought under cultivation. Cultivation is chiefly confined to the land close along the rivers and the Deg *nala*, and the tracts irrigated by the inundation canals in the Dipálpur, Pákpattan and Gugera tahsils.

The bár and its divisions.

The uncultivated tracts of the district are known as the *bár*. They are thus described in Lieutenant Elphinstone's Settlement Report :—

"This waste is divided by the Jats of the Bári Doáb into four distinct tracts—the Rávi *bár*, or jungle traversed by the old Ravi; the Ganji *bár*, which occupies the crest of the ridge called Dhaya; the Beás *bár*, traversed by the bed of the old Beás; and the Nili *bár*, which intervenes between the latter and the cultivated lands adjoining the Sutlej. The Ganji *bár*, as might be expected from its elevated situation, is the most arid and naturally barren portion of the whole district. The other divisions of the *bár* jungle are chiefly composed of soil of good quality, which only requires irrigation to produce remunerative crops. The Rávi *bár* is at present remarkable for the dense forest with which it is clothed. This belt of forest known as the *farásh* jungle extends for about 40 miles from Chíchak, in *pargannah* Gugera, to Harappa. The jungle waste, which extends from the cultivation on the Rávi to that of the Chenáb in the Jhang district, is known by the name of Sandal *bár*. Its soil appears generally inferior to

Chapter I, A.
Descriptive.

that of the Bári Doáb; and water in this tract is said to be procured with some difficulty, and to be of inferior quality."

The upland of the Rechna Doáb.

In the Sandal *bár* the ground rises so as to form a high ridge similar to that in the Bári Doáb. It is thus described by Lieutenant Elphinstone:—

"The upland of the Rechna Doáb is neither so distinctly marked, nor apparently so elevated as that of the Bári Doáb. The latter rises abruptly from the plain to the height of about twenty feet; but the former merges so gradually into the lowlands, that in many places the changes of soil and vegetation alone indicate that the level of the Dhaya has been reached. Where abruptly separated from the plain, I have never seen the bank exceed five feet in height. I have already observed that in the Bári Doáb the Dhaya gradually approaches the Rávi, and at last constitutes the left bank of that river. But the upland of the Rechna Doáb preserves a uniformly parallel direction with the river, leaving an intervening space of about ten miles for the cultivation and lowlands."

The above descriptions are not quite accurate in all respects. The soil of the Sandal *bár* is undoubtedly markedly superior to that of the Bári Doáb, and in one part of the course of the Rávi in the east of the Gugera tahsil the uplands approach close to the river.

The rivers. The Sutlej.

The Sutlej, as before said, forms the south-east boundary of the district, separating it from the Mamdot *iláqa* and the Fázilka and Muktsar tahsils of the Ferozepore district, and from Baháwalpur. The Rávi intersects the northern tahsil of Gugera and Montgomery. A hill torrent—the Deg—joins it on its right bank at Gatta Phakni. These are the only natural streams of the district. Two tahsils adjoin the Sutlej—Dipálpur and Pákpattan. In the former the river is generally called the Sutlej, in the latter, it is more frequently spoken of as the Nili, or the "blue" river. It is not known as the Ghára; that term is applied to the upper portion of the Khánwah canal. The course of the river is tolerably straight. But it is very changeable. It is impossible to say where it may be any one year. This capriciousness is the cause of considerable expense in keeping open the heads of inundation canals, and sometimes leads to the failure of the water supply in them when most needed. During the rains the Sutlej is broad, deep and rapid, and often very destructive in its course. It has a mean velocity of about four feet per second. The discharge is about 100,000 cubic feet per second. The surface slope of the Sutlej varies much in short lengths, and has been found to range from 1 in 10,150 to 1 in 3,333. In the 19 miles from Ganda Singh to Betu, the average surface slope was found according to the last edition of the Gazetteer to be 1·03 feet per mile; again, in the 36 miles from Betú to Lálu Gudar, the slope was 1·13 feet per mile, the average over the whole 55 miles being 1·09 feet, or 1 in 4,844. Of late years the volume of floods has been small, and they have not caused much destruction to the villages. The inundations, however, have been during the last seven years on the whole more extensive than at the time of the last settlement. They

Chapter I, A.

Descriptive.

The rivers—The Sutlej.

are, however, very far from being always an unmixed blessing. Sometimes they score the ground so that it cannot be ploughed. This is called *khálmár*. Again, they cover the soil with a deep deposit of sand, and so convert fertile tracts into deserts. In short, the inundations of the Sutlej, though of great importance, vary so much in extent and quality of the soil deposited, that in an agricultural point of view they must be considered very inferior to those of the Rávi. The bed of the Sutlej is broad and sandy, and the bank generally abrupt, but not more than 10 to 12 feet high. Large islands are found in the river. These are known as *donás* in Dipálpur, and as *bilárás* in the lower part of Pákpattan. The volume of water in the stream in the cold weather is considerable; the minimum discharge being 4,003 cusecs per second. The river is not fordable in Montgomery. There is practically no boat traffic up or down the river now, though sailing boats are occasionally seen on it. The length of the Sutlej, conterminous with this district, is about 104 miles.

The Rávi.

The Rávi has a longer course than the Sutlej, but is a much smaller river. Its course in former days used to be exceedingly tortuous, but it is now straighter, and its whole length in Montgomery is now 139 as against 165 miles in 1882. Its banks are generally well defined. The bed is less sandy than that of the Sutlej, and the soil deposited by the floods is of exceedingly good quality. The volume of water in the flood season has during the last 20 years been far less than formerly, and its stream dwindles to a very small size in the cold weather. It is fordable in many places, and in not a few is less than 50 yards across. Of course, with such a small stream islands can be rarely formed. The average cold weather discharge at Shahdera for 5 years is 1,310 cusecs. The opening of the Bári Doáb Canal has naturally caused a great diminution in the amount of water in the stream during the cold season; but it may be doubted whether it could seriously diminish the supply when the river is in flood. The continued failure, in whole or part, of the inundations of the Rávi cannot, therefore, with certainty be attributed to the canal. The main cause is probably to be found in the straightening of the bed of the river; and the flow of the water being in consequence less checked by bends a smaller amount spills over the country. As the fall of the river is much less than that of the Sutlej, the volume smaller, and the soil of the banks of firmer quality, the adjoining villages are less liable to be completely annihilated than they are on the southern river. There is no boat traffic on the Rávi.

The Deg.

The Deg is a hill torrent, depending entirely on the rains for its water supply. It is supposed to rise at Parmandal, in the Jammu hills, and after flowing through Siálkot, a small portion of Gujránwála and Lahore, it enters the Montgomery district at Thatha Suratan near Bucheke. After a course of

Chapter I, A.

Descriptive.

The Deg.

about 35 miles it falls into the Rávi at Ghatta Phakni Hithár. It is about 60 feet broad and 11 feet deep. When heavy rain falls in the upper courses of the Deg, the stream overflows its banks and inundates the surrounding country. Irrigation is carried on from it by *jhallárs*; and water-courses are also used. But as the bed of the stream is much below the level of the country round about, the water is always liable to flow back into the river from the water-courses on the subsidence of the floods. There is comparatively little direct spill from the Deg. No alluvion or diluvion takes place on the Deg. The question of turning the water of the Rávi into the Deg has been several times considered. Ranjit Singh is indeed said to have done so; and the traces of the canal he dug for the purpose were visible some time ago at Sháhdera. The result appears to have been unsatisfactory. Mr. Morris, the Settlement Officer of Gujránwála, made proposals for a similar undertaking, but they were considered impracticable. The inundations of the Deg are said to be very fertilizing, and here, as in Lahore, the best rice in the district is grown on land irrigated by them, which is largely a hard clay soil. But the superior quality of the rice appears in a great measure due to a superior method of cultivation. As is the case in respect of the two large rivers, the floods of the Deg are no longer so extensive as they were. This is probably due to the increase of cultivation, and consequent greater demand for water than existed during the troublous times of the Sikh rule. At one time the stream is said to have inundated a tract of country nearly a mile in width; at present only a few hundred yards on each of its banks are irrigated from it, except at certain places, chiefly on the north bank, where the levels of the adjacent country allow of more or less extensive spills taking place, and also in the lower part of its course, where a large *band* across the stream near the villages of Pindicheri Kalán and Hassoke holds up the water in the flood season and throws it over an extensive area. Formerly the Deg ran along for a considerable distance further south. The country about Kamália known as Jhangar used to be irrigated by it, as was also the now upland tract between Pindi Sheikh Músa and Garh, called Deg Khádi, *i.e.*, the Khádar of the Deg. It is separated from the Rávi by an elevated belt of land. At the settlement of 1857 it used to suffer from over-inundation of the Rávi, but now it has shared the common fate, and suffers from want of water. The Rávi is said to have joined the Deg about the time of the downfall of the Mughal empire.

Creeks or river-inlets.

Along the rivers numerous inlets or creeks are to be found. Sometimes a branch of the river runs all the year round through these. But generally the entrance to these channels or creeks is higher than the cold weather level of the rivers. During the floods they are filled, and when the rivers fall they are transformed into lakes; a considerable quantity of water remains, which is used for irrigation by means of *jhallárs*. These inlets

Chapter I. A
Descriptive
Budhs, or river-inlets.

are known as *budhs*. They are the places most suited for the heads of the small water-courses the people sometimes construct. For as they are withdrawn from the main course of the stream, there is less chance of the head being swept away; and as the velocity of the water falls off when it enters one of these inlets, the sediment it brings down settles to a considerable extent in the *budh*, and so the silting of the water-courses is checked. Most of the fishing of the district is carried on in the *budhs*. As a rule, the water in them does not last till the rivers rise again. Indeed in many cases it does not last long enough to mature the spring crops.

Rávi canals

There are at present 6 inundation canals in the Rávi tahsíls which are under the control and management of the District Board, assisted by the professional advice of the Executive Engineer, Upper Sutlej Canals Division. They are the Deg, Nikkí, Sukhrawa, Wáh, Pindi Sheikh Músa, and Gharak Gharakna.

The irrigation from the first three is confined to the Gugera and that from the other three to the Montgomery tahsíl. The Deg canal is fed by the Deg *nala* and its head is at Bucheke. A regulator bridge over the *nala* holds up the water, and turns it into the canal. The idea of utilizing the water of the Deg *nala* was mooted by Messrs. Knox and Gladstone, Deputy Commissioners in 1883 and 1884. The construction of the regulator dam was completed in 1885 at a cost of slightly over Rs. 11,000. The canal, which was completed in 1888, cost Rs. 22,000. It was extended by means of a *rájbaha* from the tail a few years later, and it now runs to Sháh Biláwal. The total length is 22 miles.

The Nikkí.

The Nikkí was, as its name implies, originally a small canal, and is said to have been dug in Mughal times. It used to begin at Basti-kesa when the Rávi flowed near that village. In 1850 Major Marsden improved the Nikki by cleaning out the channel near its mouth and straightening it at Juta. It was cleaned out again in 1879, and several dams constructed on it, while the head was moved to Mangan. In 1883 Mr. Knox who took much interest in the Rávi canals, started a scheme for the extension of irrigation from the Nikki and Sukhráwa. Mr. Atkinson of the Canal Department was deputed to report on it. This resulted in the head and alignment ot the canal being improved. The head is now on an old river creek at Mangan. The total length of the canal is 23½ miles, and it ends at a *band* at the village of Aláwalke. There is a masonry regulator at Baránpur above which three *rájbahas* or distributaries have been taken out; there are two more lower down the canal. Irrigation is by *jhallárs*, and by flow from water-courses or *chhárs*.

The Sukhráwa

The Sukhráwa is a smaller canal than the two last. It appears to have been originally little more than a natural *nala*. Here again owing to the exertions of Messrs. Knox and

Chapter I A.
Descriptive.

Gladstone in 1883 and 1884 improvements were effected. A new head was constructed at the village of Uthwál, and the alignment was altered, and the canal was tailed into the dry bed of of the Nikki which extends below the *band* at Aláwalke. There are two small distributaries on it near Gugera, and its total length is 18 miles.

The Wáh and Pindi Sheikh Músa canals.

The Wáh and Pindi Sheikh Músa canals are small ones which irrigate small areas, cis-Rávi and trans-Rávi, respectively, in the eastern portion of the Rávi riverain of the Montgomery tahsil.

The Ghark Gharakna.

The Ghark Gharakna are two canals, or rather two branches of one canal, in the western part of the trans-Rávi riverain near Kamália. It was placed formally under the District Board in 1897, and has been considerably improved. The Deg, Nikki and Sukhráwa have been always more or less under district management, and in 1885 the proceeds of an 8-anna rate levied per acre irrigated were assigned to the District Board in consideration of its undertaking the management and improvement of the canals. In 1894 they were finally placed under its control, and it was authorized to collect a water rate of 8 annas per acre of canal-irrigated crop. The same arrangements are in force on the Wáh, Pindi Sheikh Músa and Ghark Gharakna canals.

The following statements show the average annual area irrigated by the Rávi Inundation Canals during the last few years and the average annual income and expenditure. Their proper working and management is of great importance to the agricultural prosperity of the Rávi tahsils :—

Chapter I, A.
Descriptive.
The Ghark Gharakna.

Statement showing gross area irrigated on Nikki, Sukhráwa, Pindi Sheikh Músa and Deg canals with their Distributaries from 1890-91 *to* 1897-98.

Name of Canal.	Culturable area.	One-third area to be irrigated.	Gross area irrigated. 1890-91.	1891-92.	1892-93.	1893-94.	1894-95.	1895-96.	1896-97.	Total.	Average.	Gross area irrigated in 1897-98.
1	2	3	4	5	6	7	8	9	10	11	12	13
Nikki Canal	...	...	2,130	783	2,068	2,467	2,321	734	823	11,326	1,618	6,255
Sukhráwa Canal	...	...	3,379	2,086	5,015	4,862	5,213	1,824	1,623	24,002	3,429	7,675
Pindi Sheikh Musa Canal	...	...	105	23	745	398	167	...	...	1,438	205	507
Deg Canal	...	...	3,666	2,321	3,106	3,135	4,025	4,465	7,551	20,169	4,167	7,790
	...	...	9,280	5,213	10,934	10,862	12,026	7,023	9,997	65,935	9,419	22,227
Average gauge of Rávi at Shahdara	...	...	...	...	...	...	74·2	60·6	47·8	...	...	59·1
Do. do. Chíchâwatni.	...	...	...	...	...	85·05	94·82	68·72	41·69	. .	...	63·9
Do. Deg Canal	...	...	9·96	9·63	...	5·96	19·05	10·58	4·85	...	...	4·80

Chapter I, A.
Descriptive.
The Ghark Gharakna.

Statement showing Assessments, Collections and Expenditure for the last seven years ending 1897-98 on Ravi Canals.

Year	Assessments.		Collections.	Remarks.	Expenses.				Remarks.
	Gross area irrigated.	Amount in rupees.			Establishment.	Repairs and silt clearance.	New work.	Total.	
		Rs.			Rs. a. p.	Rs. a. p.	Rs. a. p.	Rs. a. p.	
1891-92	5,213	2,703	4,501		609 9 11	...	9,994 0 0	10,603 9 11	Establishment charges from 1891 to 1895-96 *exclude* pay of the District Engineer and Lower Subordinates who managed the canals
1892-93	10,934	5,728	1,806		548 15 9	...	...	548 15 9	
1893-94	10,862	5,710	7,170		445 3 6	1,704 11 2	396 0 0	2,545 14 8	
1894-95	12,026	6,029	5,845		731 2 2	1,019 3 7	186 14 0	1,937 3 9	
1895-96	7,023	2,814	6,552		811 9 0	2,042 1 0	6,338 10 0	9,192 4 0	
1896-97	9,997	3,357	2,799		2,688 10 1	3,958 12 1	532 0 0	7,079 6 2	
1897-98	22,227	10,000	2,461		2,959 0 4	3,832 7 7	...	6,791 7 11	
Average	11,209	5,277	4,448		1,242 0 5	1,793 14 2	2,492 8 0	5,528 6 7	

Chapter I, A.

Descriptive.

The prospects of these canals have been much improved by the introduction in 1895 of a system under which the officers of the Canal Department afford professional advice in, and exercise some supervision over, their management.

Sutlej Inundation Canals.

The Khánwah, Upper Sohág and Lower Sohág-Pára canals form with the Katora the group known as the Upper Sutlej Inundation Canals. The Katora really belongs to the Lahore district, but affords some irrigation to the north-eastern portion of the Dipálpur tahsíl by means of an extension of the Chuniáu *rájbaha*. The heads of the Khánwah and Upper Sohág are also in the Lahore district, while that of the Lower Sohág-Pára, which is an improved and extended edition of a former canal known as the Kuhna or old Sohág, is at Lálu Gudar in this district. The irrigation from the Khánwah and Upper Sohág is mainly confined to the Dipálpur tahsíl, and that of the Lower Sohág-Pára to Pákpattan.

The Khánwah.

According to popular tradition the Khánwah, the Upper and the Kuhna-Sohág were all parts of one and the same hill stream called the Vein or Bein, which is said to imply an irregular stream with a clay bottom like a canal. There are two streams of this name in the Jullundar Doáb. The one flowing through Kapúrthala is said to have run in old days, before the Sutlej and Beás had changed their courses, between these rivers through the present Bári Doáb. The Sutlej, shifting to the west, cut this stream in two. The portion in Jullundar continued as before, while the other portion, which had been cut off and was consequently called Ghárá, became dependent for its water on the Sutlej. When the river was in flood water came down this channel as far as Hujra, and then ran through the Gandobár *nala* into the old Beás. When Mirza Khán, the Khán-i-Khánán, was governor of Lahore, he improved this water-course, chiefly by constructing an inlet or head on the Sutlej, connecting the *nala* with the river, about 20 miles above its former point of communication, and by erecting dams and embankments along the course of the canal. He is said, too, to have extended the canal, so that water went down it, as far as a *nala* in Pákpattan, probably through the local *nala* called the Ghuri.* The canal below Hujra was, after these extensions were made, called the Khánwah. After the Khán-i-Khánán nothing seems to have been done for a long time to improve the canal. It of course silted up, and it was only in heavy floods that any water came down. The flourishing " town of Dipálpur became depopulated, and the whole *taluka* of Hujra would have become as desolate as the region now traversed by the old Beás, had it not been

* The Ghuri *nala* rises in the low basin near the village of Rám Parshád about a mile north of Jindrán on the Khánwah, and runs nearly due west past Chishti Shams Din and Kila Sondha Singh, and falling into the old Beás near Rájgarh, about 4 miles north of Hujra. It is only 8 miles long. Thus the water of the Ghuri would have to flow for some 80 miles down the old Beás to reach the *nalla*.

Chapter I, A.

Descriptive.

The Khánwah.

for an occasional supply obtained at high floods by the old channel which previously formed the inlet of the *nala.*" If the Mughals did nothing, the Afgháns of Dipálpur and the Sayads of Hujra, who succeeded them, were not more energetic. It was not till after Ranjít Singh had occupied the country that any effort was made to restore the canal. In A.D. 1807 Diwán Rádha Rám, the *kárdár,* repaired the head and cleared out the channel. The canal after that flowed steadily during the rainy season till 1823. The next year it silted up. Jawand Singh, Mokal, then held *taluka* Dipálpur in *jágír,* but did nothing. Bába Bishen Singh was at Hujra: he did nothing. But in 1841 Fakír Chirágh-ud-din, under orders of Maháraja Sher Singh, had the canal cleared out, and a new head dug at Mámuki, still known as Sher Singh's inlet, but long since abandoned. Shortly after annexation the canal was made over to the Canal Department, and has since been greatly improved. It was lengthened, and now tails into the Pára *nala* at Mahmúdpur on the Pákpattan and Gugera road. In 1853 three *rájbahás,* or large distributing channels, were made—(1) the Northern Rájwah, from the bridge at Hujra to the bridge at Nathu Shah, sixteen miles long; (2), the Southern *rájbaha* from the bridge at Hujra to the bridge at Dipálpur, eleven miles long; (3), the Bháwal Dás *rájbaha* from the bridge at Dipálpur to the village of Bháwal Dás, five miles long. The second of these now runs into the third, and they form one continuous distributary. The lately constructed Kanganpur *rájbaha,* which takes out of the canal in the Lahore district, runs into this district, and gives irrigation to several villages. The banks of the canal are covered with trees of various kinds; while *sarr* (*Saccharum munja*) grows abundantly along the *rájbahas.* The Khánwah has at present (1898) two supply heads, the Khizra and the Nijábat, 8 and 2 miles long, respectively.

The set of the river decides which head can be used in any year. The canal proper commences near the village of Mattar; and its length thence to Mahmúdpur, where it tails into the Pára *nala,* is 86 miles, of which 59 lie in this district. For the first 43 miles, as far as Hujra regulator, the bed width is about 60 feet and the longitudinal slope 1 in 6,667. Below Hujra the bed width is about 40 feet, which is gradually reduced to 10 feet at the tail. From Hujra to Dipálpur the slope is 1 in 5,263, and thence to the tail 1 in 4,000. There are masonry regulator bridges at Hujra, Dipálpur and Kacha-pakka, also a masonry bridge at Nathu Shah. The discharge of the Khánwah ranges up to 2,600 cubic feet per second during high floods. The average discharge during the flow season for the 10 years ending 1896-97 was 956 cubic feet.

The Upper or new Sohág.

The two Sohágs formed one stream, and are said once to have been part of the Bein. The Sutlej first cut this river near Lálu Gudarke, a little to the south of Atári. Then, again, at Panjgiraian, a cluster of villages to the south of Mámuki. In fact,

Chapter I, A.
Descriptive.
The Upper or new Sohág.

the story is that the Bein ran in the shape of a printed S, and the Sutlej cut it first at the bend to the right, and then at the top over the bend. And there is no doubt that the upper Sohág *nala*, after leaving the river, runs in a curve and rejoins it. Still it is hard to see how the Khánwah and the two Sohágs could be part of the same stream. It may be that the Khánwah represents the Kapúrthala Bein, while the upper and lower Sohágs are continuations of the eastern Bein. It seems highly probable that the Sukhnye, which runs through Mamdot, and debouches into the Sutlej opposite Lálu Gudarke, is the connecting link between the Sohág and the Bein. It is quite evident that when the Sutlej changed its course to the north and joined the Beás above Ferozepore, it must have cut both the Beins in the upper and lower portions of their course. The upper Sohág does not seem to have been used as an irrigation channel till A. D. 1827, when Sardár Jawand Singh, Mokal, the *jágírdár* of Kangaupura, in Chuniáu, dammed up the Dhan *nala* at Jhang Abdulla Sháh, by which the water of the Sohág used to escape, and brought this water through the Bhus *nalla*, which joins the Sohág near Ghara Singh, into his lands. About 1840 the mouth of the new Sohág closed up. In 1854 the Canal Department took charge of it, and erected a dam near Jhang Abdulla Sháh, and cleared out the Dhan *nalla*, and extended it so as to carry the water of the Sohág into the Khánwah, near Bungi Gursa Singh. Next year the dam was pulled down, and the channel cleared out to Kaler Kalán, and continued thence to Táhir, a little to the west of Basírpur, on the Dipálpur and Fázilka road. In 1864 a further extension was made, and the canal carried down a new cut to Bunga Hayát, in the Pákpattan tahsíl, and thence alongside the Dipálpur and Pákpattan road to the Pára *nala*, into which the surplus water escapes. On account of so much of the canal being new, it used to be known as the new Sohág (*Sohág jadíd*). The upper Sohág canal has at present (1897) three supply heads varying from ¾ of a mile to 6 miles in length. The canal proper commences at Lola, and is divided into two portions—the upper (from Lola to Táhir) 32 miles long, and the lower (from Táhir to the tail at the Pára *nala*) 29 miles, or a total length of 61 statute miles. In the upper portion the bed width is 60 feet with a longitudinal slope 1 in 7,000. The width is gradually reduced to 10 feet at the tail with a slope of 1 in 4,000. The discharge of the canal ranges up to 3,000 cubic feet per second in high floods. The average discharge during the flow season for the ten years ending 1896-97 was 567 cubic feet. There are two masonry regulators at Gáman Waghra and Báháwal Dás; also a masonry bridge near Parma Nand. In 1865 two *rájbahas* were dug, one from Gáma Wagra to Bunga Saleh, five miles long, and the second from Bháwal Das to Bapparwál, seven miles in length. In recent years two more distributaries have been constructed. The Háji Chand minor, which runs as far as Tughrel, and the Kaler *rájbaha*, constructed in 1893, with its Wananwála branch, which ends at Rukanpura. The heads of both these distributaries are in the Lahore district.

Chapter I, A.

Descriptive.

The Lower Sohag Pára Canal.

The Lower Sohág-Pára Canal has superseded the Kuhna or old Sohág. The latter canal ran along the bed of the Sohág *nala,* whose head is at Lálu Gudar in the Dipálpur tahsíl. The capacity of the *nala* was estimated at 10,000 cubic feet per second. About 130 years ago, when the Sikhs were defeated at Kutabwála by the Diwan of Pakpattan, many of them were, according to popular tradition, drowned in the Sohag. About 80 years ago the *nala* had so silted up that but little water came down. About A. D. 1816 a dam was erected at Nandpur; and fifteen years later the energetic Jawand Singh, Mokal, ran up another at Jassoke Soház, and drew off the water by a cut called the *lakhi* into his *jágir* of Dipálpur. The first year's returns were said to be worth a *lakh*; hence the name of the cut. After two years the Haveli *kárdár* destroyed Jawand Singh's dam after a little fighting; next year Jawand Singh built it again, but two years later it was finally demolished by the *kárdár.* About fifty years ago Mahtáb Rái, the *kárdár* of Haveli, dug a new head near Lálu Gudar. By 1858 the supply of water had so diminished that irrigation was only possible by lift. Up to 1863 the canal remained in charge of the district authorities, but on its total failure then it was made over to the Canal Department. Its irrigating capacity was very small. The canal extended only as far as Haveli, where there was a dam across the *nala.*

The new lower Soház-Pára Canal follows generally the line of the old *nala,* but the alignment has been improved and convolutions avoided. There are two heads, one at Lálu Gudar and one a short distance lower down the river at Tahli Bágar, both in the Dipálpur tahsíl Near Kálewál in Pákpattan 37·58 miles from the head it divides into two branches, the Northern one called the Pára running to a point beyond Jiwan Shah, and the southern one or the Soház ending near Kaliána. The lengths of the branches are 31·8 and 26·41 miles, respectively. The Pára branch is so called from a *nala* of the same name the line of which it roughly follows, and which is itself a branch of the old Soház *nalla.* The bed-widths and slopes of the main canal and its branches are as follows:—

Main Canal.

For the first 15 miles the bed-width is 80 feet. Below 15 miles it is 75 feet, which is gradually reduced to 60 feet at Kalewál. The bed slope first $5\frac{1}{4}$ miles is 1 in 10,000; from $5\frac{1}{4}$ to 18 miles 1 in 7,000; 18 to 23 miles 1 in 6,000; $23\frac{1}{4}$ to 29 miles 1 in 5,000, and 29 to Kálewál regulator 1 in 4,545.

Pára Branch.

For the first 10 miles the bed-width is 33 feet. Below 10 miles it is 22 feet, which is gradually reduced to 7 feet at the tail. The bed slope is from head to tail 1 in 5,000.

For the first $3\frac{1}{2}$ miles the bed-width is 21 feet. Below $3\frac{1}{2}$ miles it is 17 feet, which is gradually reduced to 12 feet. The bed slope first $4\frac{1}{2}$ miles is 1 in 6,000, and from $4\frac{1}{2}$ miles to tail is 1 in 4,000.

Chapter I, A.

Descriptive.

Sohág Branch.

There are two masonry regulator bridges, one on the Dipálpur-Fázilka District road and the other on the Dipálpur-Haveli District road.

The average discharge of the canal during the flow season for the five years ending 1897 has been 954 cubic feet per second.

The distributaries (*rájbahás*) and minors from the canal are as follows:—

Distributaries from main canal.	Length in miles.	From Haveli rájbaha.	Length in miles.	From Sohág branch.	Length in miles.
1. Haveli rájbaha.	13·28	1. Jawáya Biloch minor.	1·8	1. Pákpattan rájbaha.	9·27
2. Mári Minor.	1·79	2. Pir Ghani minor.	1·35	2. Farídpur minor.	6·24
3. Bhuman Shah rájbaha.	4·15				
4. Músewál rájbaha	9·73				

The construction of two more distributaries is in contemplation. The canal was opened as far as Haveli in 1884, and was continued into the Pákpattan tahsíl in 1887-88. The total capital expenditure up to the end of 1896-97 was over Rs. 7,12,000. The canal was constructed chiefly with the object of bringing under cultivation the large extent of Government waste land in the central and eastern portions of the Pákpattan tahsil, which is now the area included in the Sohág-Pára Colony.

Other irrigation channels.

Besides these four canals there are some other irrigation cuts from the rivers. These are under the control of the people of the villages to which they belong. The most important of them are the *nala* Jherku, from the Rávi in the Montgomery tahsíl, and the Kamálwah, *chhár* Machhi Singh, and *chhár* Goláb Ali from the Sutlej in Pákpattan.

The *nala* Jherku.

The *nala* Jherku issues from the Rávi at Kund Kaure Shah, and rejoins it at Chakbandi Nathu Amir and Chakbandi Barkha. It is known by the same name from its mouth to Muhammadpur; thence to Giloi as the Chura, and after that as the Sukhráwa. A project is under consideration for taking the *nala* under the control of the District Board.

Chhars.

There are a good many water-courses or *chhars* on the right bank of the Rávi near Kamália which, when the river floods are favourable, give irrigation to a considerable number of villages. They are under zamíndári management.

The Kamalwah.

The Kamálwah near Pákpattan is said to have been dug by one Khán Kamál, the Governor of Dipálpur, in Akbar's

Chapter I, A.

Descriptive.

The Kamálwah.

time. Probably, he only improved it. In places the channel is deep and well defined, in places scarcely perceptible. For many years no water came down it, till in 1868 the people of Sádiq, Chhina and 23 other villages constructed a dam across the Malleke *budh* near Chak Dádu Ahloka, about six miles to the west of Pákpattan, and dug a water-course into the Kamálwah from this dam. The dam is at present no longer in existence, and in recent years the *budh* has received little water from the river, and has afforded very little *sailáb*.

Muhammad Mahdi Khan Canal

In 1882 an extensive grant of land was made to Muhammad Mahdi Khan, a retired Extra Assistant Commissioner, in the south-western part of Pákpattan. For the irrigation of his land he excavated a canal 19 miles in length, now known by his name. It gives water to his grant, and to another made subsequently to his sons, and to a considerable number of other estates through which it passes.

***Chhár* Golab Ali.**

A little further down the river is Goláb Ali's *chhár*, which irrigates five estates. It was dug about 24 years ago by Pir Goláb Ali, a man much respected in these parts. It leaves the river at the Tibbi *budh*, and runs as far as Sital Gand.

Drainage channels and dry *nalas*.

A glance at the map will show the remarkable manner in which the whole district between the central ridge and the rivers is cut up by old *nalas*. These are not only interesting to the antiquarian and student of history, but are also of considerable importance, as regards the extension of irrigation in the district, as most of the proposals to this effect make the utilization of one or more of these channels their basis. In some of these *nalas* bordering on the rivers, a precarious supply of water is even now obtained. The principal *nalas* are, between the Rávi and the ridge :—

The Wahni ; The Sukhráwa (1) ; The Sukhráwa (2).

between the ridge and the Sutlej :—

The old Beás ;
The old Soháq, with its off-shoots—
(*a*) The Pára ;
(*b*) The Dhadar :

The Khád ;
The Ding, with its branches—
(*a*) The Bhág ;
(*b*) The Dhingi ;
(*c*) The Kubrár ;

The Diwánwah ;
The Ghag ;
The Bakhílwah ;
The Bishárat.

***Nalas* of the Ravi.—Wahni.**

The Wahni leaves the river at Daúla, a little below Saiyadwála, in the Gugera tahsíl, and runs nearly due south past Satghara. The two Sukhráwás are thus described in the Settlement Report of 1858 :—

The Sukhráwá—(1) The smaller Sukhrawa.

(2) The large Sukhráwa.

"The name Sukhráwa is applied to two different *nalas* both running nearly parallel with [illegible], of four and eight miles. One of these passes near t[illegible] civil lines from the lands attached to the village of that name. It communicates with a *jhil* near that river, from which it obtains a supply of water during the rains; but this supply is so precarious that very little use can be made of it for irrigation purposes. The other *nala* has no communication with the river. It traverses the jungle which intervenes between the margin of cultivation and the Dhaya or high bank. Its course is remarkably winding and intricate, and it sends out branches, which intersect the plain in every direction. Both these *nalas* are said by the natives to mark the course of the Rávi at different periods. The width alone, however, of the first *nala*, which nowhere exceeds twenty yards, precludes every possibility of this belief regarding its being founded on fact. The second *nala*, on the other hand, has undoubtedly been at some former period an important water-course. It is

Chapter I, A.

Descriptive.

(2) The larg Sukhráwa.

about eighty yards across, and though its course is much more intricate than the present bed of the Rávi, the open ground in its vicinity, and extensive patches of sand near its banks, render it possible that the tradition of the natives in this instance may be correct. In that case the Dhaya, which skirts it at no great distance, would have formed the limit of the inundations, as it still does at present in a portion of the Harappa tahsíl. That both the old Beás and the Sukhráwa, especially the former, contained at one time sufficient body of water to admit of irrigation being conducted on their banks, cannot be doubted. The remains of abandoned villages and the ruins of brick buildings and forts, which show that some of these places must have had pretensions to importance, are still scattered over the whole of the desolate tract; and from the well known habits of the present population, we can assume with some confidence that only a total cessation of the supply of water in these ancient river-beds could have effected so remarkable a change.

The Sutlej *nalas*.—The old Beás.

The old Beás *nala*, after passing through a portion of the Lahore district, enters the Dipálpur *tahsil* near the town of Shergarh, and traverses the whole of the Montgomery District at a distance of about twenty miles from the Sutlej. The popular story is that till the end of last century the Beás, instead of joining the Sutlej near Ferozepore, flowed down this *nala*. Lieutenant Elphinstone doubted the correctness of this story, on the ground that the *nala* could not carry the volume of water in the Beás, which is a very convincing reason. As in the Ain-i-Akbari it is distinctly stated that the Beás and Sutlej united twelve *kos* nearer Ferozepore, the story may be dismissed as fiction. The subsequent change in the point of junction is due to the Sutlej, and not the Beás, having shifted its course; still it is a fact that water came down this *nala* till a comparatively short time ago. The year 1750 is fixed as the date it ceased to flow. There seems no reason to doubt that the *nala* was a branch of the Beás: there is nothing to connect it with the Sutlej. In order to ascertain what it originally was it will be necessary to determine whether, when the Beás river ran under the Dhaya, it was at such a distance from this *nala* that both could have been independent streams. This might possibly have been the case in Montgomery. The question is, could it in Lahore and Multan? If so, the old Beás may be simply the continuation of the Kapúrthala Bein, as the Sohág is of the Phagwára Bein. The *nala* is rarely more than 200 feet across; the depth is from 12 to 15 feet. Its carrying capacity is 3,400 feet per second. The Bakhilwah issues from the Sutlej at Ghulám, and falls into the Nikki, a branch of the lower Sohág at Dulla Náusbad. Formerly nineteen villages were irrigated from it—eight by direct overflow, nine by water-courses, and two by *jhallárs*. Many years ago water ceased to flow except in very high floods. The villages dependent on it suffered severely. The old Sohág has already been mentioned. Leaving Haveli, it runs nearly west to some distance past Pákpattan, and there turns due south. It gets lost before it reaches the river. But it evidently ends at Shekhoke, though the channel is not defined there. Its bed is sandy; the banks generally steep; it is about as deep as the old Beás, and from 200 to 400 feet broad. The name Sohág is said to mean a place where verdure and cultivation abound. The Pára is a branch of the old Sohág, which it leaves a little

The Bakhilwah.

The old Sohág.

The Pára

Chapter I, A.
Descriptive.
The Pára.

below Bunga Hayát, on the Pákpattan and Dipálpur road. The Pára is 500 feet broad at its mouth; after one mile the breadth falls to 350 feet, which is again reduced to 200 after five miles. This is maintained for forty miles. The average depth is 10 to 15 feet. A large branch then goes off to the Beás, called the Nawábbin, from a Nawáb of Multán, who is said to have dug it last century to enable his wife to come down by water to Multán. The width is here 100 feet, which gradually diminishes, till at the junction of the Pára and the Sukhnye it is only 15 to 16 feet; the depth is three feet. The banks are generally steep. The soil of the *kadhi*, or valley of the Pára, is of excellent quality.

The Dhadar.

The Dhadar branches off from the Sohág about 16 miles to the west of Pákpattan. It is a small rather shallow *nala*, but it once irrigated an extensive tract of country. It runs west for some distance, and then south to Jamlera. The Dhummuk *nala*, in Mailsi, seems to be the continuation of it. The Pára and the Dhadar are both Pákpattan *nalas*.

The Khád.

The Khád belongs to Dipálpur. It commences at Thakarke Mahmúd, about nine miles to the east of Haveli. It runs thence to Izzatke Kála. From there, one branch goes straight to Nama Jindeka, one *viá* Mulia Chishti, Núr Shah, Kanduwál, &c. From Nama Jindeka it goes into the Pír Ghanni *budh*. This *nala*, which is not more than 20 miles long, is known by no less than four different names in different parts of its course. To Maneka Nikkiwála it is called the Nikki; thence to Bukan Gudarke the Budhi, from there to Nama Jindeka, the Khád and after that the Warnál. This is a fine deep *nala* with very steep banks. *Jhallárs* are used on it, and sometimes there is fine *sailáb* from it. The soil on its bank is generally very bad, and impregnated with *kallar*.

The Chura.
The Khohárianwála.
The Kaluwah.

Among the tributaries of the Khád are the Chura, the Khohárianwála and the Káluwah *nalas*. The first is the most important. It commences at Mushifke Mahár, and passing Bulewála, Bhai Darsan, and other villages, joins the Khád at Kanduwál. This *nala* flows when there is heavy rain, and in heavy floods river water comes down it. The Khohárianwála is a small branch of the Khád, running from Pipal Sazawár to Izzatke Kála. The Kaluwah runs south into the Khád at *chak* Káluwah below Haveli. These last two *nalas* are mere rain-drainage channels.

The Bishárat.

The Bishárat is a more famous *nala* than the Khad, of which it is probably the continuation. It issues from the Pír Ghanni *budh*, and after a remarkably tortuous course, passing close to Pákpattan, it falls into the Sohag at Pakka Sidhar. It is said to have been excavated by one Bishárat Khan, about the beginning of the 14th century. This is clearly wrong. There are no signs of excavation, and it is incredible that any one would dig such a winding channel, even with the object of diminishing the velocity of the stream, and thereby increasing its irrigating capacity. It is from a ferry on this *nala* that Pakpattan derived its name. It is a shallow and generally narrow *nala*. It dried up about 100 years ago, though water has since occasionally been

Chapter I, A.

Descriptive.

The Ding and its tributaries.

found in it. Proposals have on several occasions been made to open it again, but they seem impracticable. The Ding is a continuation of the Kamalwah. At Bunga Bhai Khan the Ding divides. The southern arm joins the Bhag at the corner of Jajal Bhag and Khola Wali Muhammad. The northern arm joins the Kuhrar at Nebwal. In places this is a very fine, deep, clean-cut *nala*. Water used to come down it up to 1853. The remains of old *jhallárs* may still be seen on it at Shekheke. There is a dam on this *nala* at Sahu Biloch. The Dingi leaves the Sutlej at Haidar Malkana, and falls into the Ding at Bunga Bhai Khan. The Bhag is a fine *nala* of fair size. It leaves the river at Kadús, below Kot Bakhsha, and joins the Ding at Jajal Bhág; a dam is sometimes erected here. *Jhallárs* are used on this *nala*, but the irrigation is scanty. This was not always so. The name implies "being very beneficial." The Kuhrár leaves the Sutlej at Kot Bakhsha, and after passing Bhai Darsan at Bara divides into two branches; these re-unite at Jít Singhwála, and then appear to fall into the Sohág, near Pakka Sidhar, but neither on the map nor on the spot can any certain information be obtained of what becomes of this *nala*. It is broad, but except near the river, rather shallow. The Ding falls into the right branch of it at Nebwál, and some say the Kuhrár is only a continuation of the Ding.

The Dingi.

The Bhag.

The Kuhrár.

The Diwánwah is a cut dug by Diwán Sáwan Mal from Malik Baháwal to Bohar. It has been dry for many years. The Ghag has its mouth at Tirsangi, and runs into the Sohág at Hardo Mansura. *Jhallárs* are used on it, and some land is inundated from it. There are numbers of other *nalas*, but as they are of no importance as irrigation channels, they need not be noticed here.

The Ghag.

There are no marshes or lakes (*chamb, jhíl*) in this district except a *jhíl* at Kot Fázil, where the Deg enters the district. *Jhallárs* are used on them, but they are of little depth, and the water dries up soon. The tract traversed by the old Beás is remarkable for a chain of pools at distances of some three or four miles, which used to be filled by the surface drainage, and to be of the greatest value to the graziers of the *bár*. It appears, however, that they have dried up of late, owing to the scanty rainfall for so many years. Here and there depressions in the ground may be met with, where water lodges for some time after heavy rain.

Jhils.

There is nothing to show that the district was ever more densely populated than at present. But the changes in the course of the rivers, the drying up of such important water channels as the old Beás, Sohág and Dhadar, and the improvement of the Inundation Canals, have naturally caused a shifting of the population. In all parts of the district, mounds covered with remains of the earthen vessels and broken bricks are to be met, marking the site of what was once a village or town. These are known by the general name *theh, tibbá* or *khola*, but each mound has a further distinguishing name, to which the general name is prefixed.

Deserted villages. *Thehs. Kholás.*

Chapter I, A.

Descriptive.

Deserted villages. *Thehs. Kholás.*

The word *theh* seems more commonly used in the Rachná, and *khola* in the Bari Doab. These remains of former habitations are most frequent along the old Beas and the Dhadar, and in the country about Kamália. It should be remembered that these *thehs* are not necessarily the ruins of villages inhabited at the same time. If a village is once abandoned from any cause, it is considered unlucky to build a new village on the old site. So many of these mounds merely represent the same village at different periods of its existence. If the history of this part of the Punjab during the 18th century is considered, the perpetual wars, desolating famines, and the general state of insecurity, will be found to afford other and strong reasons, besides the drying up of the irrigating streams, why many cultivated tracts should have relapsed into their primitive state of waste. But to the last-mentioned cause must be attributed the fact that the land has not been again brought into cultivation. Not only has the stoppage of the water-supply necessarily led to the abandonment of land irrigated by flow, but it has been accompanied by a serious fall in the level of the water in the wells in the vicinity of the old *nalas*. Numerous old wells exist all over the district; but in the *bár* tracts the water is much below the brick-work, and if it is intended to work any of these wells, an interior cylinder has to be sunk.

Old wells in the *bár*.

Government jungle. Scattered wells. *Kasht Khám tahsil.* Grazing leases.

The area of lands included within village boundaries is 1,452,407 acres. The remaining 2,114,953 acres are owned directly by the Government; but a large part of this in the Sandal Bar north of the Ravi, is being brought under cultivation by means of the Chenab Canal. It has long been the custom for the people to apply to the ruling power for leave to occupy portions of the jungle; and since the introduction of the British rule these applications have become very numerous. The area of the grant is often small—50 acres when the applicant proposes sinking a single-wheeled well and 100 acres when a double-wheeled well is to be constructed. In many instances the object of the applicant is to secure a piece of ground where he may construct a well, or bring an old one into use to water his cattle grazing in the *bár*. A piece of low-lying ground, where rain water will accumulate, with good grass in the neighbourhood, is generally selected. A little cultivation is also carried on, the extent depending on the character of the season. These wells, scattered all over the *bár*, form, as it were, little oases in the wilderness. There are many depressions in the *bár* where the drainage water of the surrounding high lands collects. Applications are received annually for permission to cultivate the land occupied by these depressions. The area brought under cultivation depends on the extent of the rains; and the lease given is only for one year. This cultivation is known as *kásht báráni*. Excepting the land thus occupied, the whole of the Government jungle is uncultivated. Many of the choicest and most favourably situated bits have been made into Forest Reserves, and are closed to grazing except on payment of forest fees. Grazing is permitted over the rest of the Government area with the exception of certain restrictions in the case of areas recently felled. Most of the villages of the district are assessed to *tirni* on account of the grazing thus afforded.

Rainfall, temperature and climate.

Except for the excessive temperature of summer there is nothing peculiar about the climate. From May to the middle of October, and more especially in June and July, the heat during the day is intense, but except on the frequent occasions on which heavy dust storms blow, the nights are comparatively cool. At the end of August in a favourable year the mornings begin to have some trace of freshness, and early in October a change in temperature after sunset may be noticed. Dust-storms in the hot weather are very common; while hail-storms are rare. The rains, such as they are should begin at the end of June or early in July. They generally cease in August. The winter rains seem, on the whole, more certain than those of summer. They should come early in January, but are not unfrequently delayed. During the four months, from November to February inclusive, the days are not hot, while the nights are cold with occasional frosts Statistics of temperature during the months of May, July and December are given in Table IV. These months are taken as they are adopted in all the volumes of the Gazetteer series.

Table No. III shows in tenths of an inch the total rainfall registered at each of the rain-gauge stations in the district for each year, from 1866-67 to 1896-97. The distribution of the rainfall throughout the year is shown in tables Nos. III A. and III B.

Disease.

The district is fairly healthy. Pneumonia is common in the cold weather, caused by the intense coldness and dryness of the atmosphere. Fevers are, of course, prevalent, as the mass of the population is located along the banks of the rivers and in the tracts irrigated by the inundation canals. January is usually the month of most mortality, and August that in which least deaths occur. The following table shows the death-rate per thousand for each month for seven years:—

Month.	1891	1892	1893	1894	1895	1896	1897
January	2·4	4·5	4·5	3·7	2·5	3·8	1·6
February	1·7	2·8	2·9	2·8	1·7	2·2	1·2
March	1·3	2·2	2·1	2·3	1·8	2·0	1·3
April	1·0	2·8	1·6	2·1	1·6	1·7	1·2
May	1·6	5·3	2·0	2·4	1·7	2·2	1·5
June	1·9	5·4	1·8	1·9	1·4	2·0	1·6
July	2·0	2·6	1·3	1·4	1·3	1·9	1·6
August	1·6	2·0	1·6	1·5	1·4	1·7	1·5
September	1·5	4·8	1·7	1·5	1·2	1·5	1·7
October	2·1	10·2	2·4	2·1	1·8	1·6	2·7
November	2·8	8·9	3·6	2·6	2·0	1·7	3·8
December	4·3	6·3	3·9	2·9	3·2	1·9	3·5

Chapter I, B.

Geology, Fauna and Flora.

Disease.

Tables Nos. XI, XIA, XIB, and XLIV give annual and monthly statistics of births and deaths for the district and for its towns during the last five years; while the birth and death-rates since 1887, so far as available, will be found in Chapter III, Section A, for the general population, and in Chapter VI under the heads of the several large towns of the district. Table No. XII shows the number of insane, blind, deaf, mutes and lepers as ascertained at the Census of 1891; while Table No. XXXVIII shows the working of the dispensaries since 1891.

SECTION B.—GEOLOGY, FAUNA AND FLORA.

Geology.

Our knowledge of Indian geology is as yet so general in its nature, and so little has been done in the Punjab in the way of detailed geological investigation, that it is impossible to discuss the local geology of separate districts. But a sketch of the geology of the province, as a whole, has been most kindly furnished by Mr. Medlicott, Superintendent of the Geological Survey of India, and is published *in extenso* in the Provincial volume of the Gazetteer series, and also as a separate pamphlet.

Kankar.

Saltpetre, *kallar.*

The mineral products of the district are few and unimportant. *Kankar* (*calcareous concrete*) is found principally on the right side of the Rávi, and in the shape of small nodules on the surface of the ground. These are swept up and used for making lime. Saltpetre (nitrate of potash), the vernacular name of which is *shora*, used to be made extensively in this district. The method of manufacture is described in "Punjab Products," page 79. Saltpetre is made from saline earth called *kallar*, found on the site of deserted villages and in the streets and the walls of old towns. This substance is used as a top-dressing by agriculturists. Some found at Dipálpur yielded about six per cent. of saline matter, which, on analysis, was found to consist of common salt mixed with a less quantity of sulphate of soda, and, in addition, very small quantities of lime and magnesian salt. This *kallar* must be carefully distinguished from *kallar shor*, the *reh* of Hindustán, which is most injurious to all cultivation. *Kallar shor* consists principally of sulphate of soda. When strongly developed, *kallar shor* seems to render all vegetation, except that of *phesak láni*, impossible. Soil impregnated with soda and other salts and known as *kallaráti* is common. It is found extensively in the Ganji Bár; in parts of the Sandal Bár bordering on the Rávi riverain; in the tract between the Rávi and the Deg; in the north-western part of the Pákpattan tahsil, and in a good many of the older estates in Dipálpur which have been long under canal-irrigation, and in the higher portions of several estates in the Sutlej riverain tract.

Mines, quarries.

There are no mines or quarries in the district excepting some beds of inferior *kankar*.

Vegetation.

From what has been said of the character of so much of the soil of the district and of the climate, it will be at once apparent that the natural vegetation cannot be of striking grandeur or beauty. Indeed, it might be called mean and monotonous.

Vegetation.

A closer examination shows, however, that though stunted, it is far from unvaried. The number of different kinds of grasses and other plants of low growth is considerable. But there are not more than half-a-dozen species of trees of spontaneous growth. With plenty of water the district might become very fairly wooded, and where irrigation has been extended, it is improving in this respect.

Trees.

Near the rivers there is a good deal of timber, and along the Khánwah canal, and in the villages adjoining it, more especially to the south, there is a fine belt of trees; while the abandoned station of Gugera presents specimens of most trees found in the plains of Upper India. The trees commonly met with are the *ukhán, kikar, bér, jand, wan,* and *karíl*. The *ukhán* (*Tamarix orientalis*), also known as *pharwán* and *farásh*, is the characteristic tree of the district. It is an evergreen, hardy and of rapid growth; it is the only tree that has a chance of thriving at Montgomery civil station. Wherever there is a hollow in the ground an *ukhán* springs up. The timber is of little use, except for fuel. It is sometimes, but rarely, used on the Rávi for the wood-work of wells. The galls of this tamarisk, called *máin,* are used for dyeing and tanning. There is another tamarisk with whitish leaves. It is apparently not found on the Sutlej, but it is abundant between Chicháwatni and Kamália on the Rávi. *Pilchí* or *jháu,* (*Tamarix Indica*) and *lei* (*Tamarix dioica*) are found on both rivers in flooded land. The difference between the two kinds is not very apparent. The twigs are used for making baskets and the cylinders of *kachcha* wells, also for fences to fields, and the sides of houses. The *kíkar* (*Acacia arabica*) is very rare in the *bár*. It is not uncommon along the canals and rivers. The timber is used for agricultural implements. The cog-wheels of the Persian-wheel are almost invariably made of it. The fuel is good and much liked. The seeds are eaten readily by goats. The bark is used in tanning and in the distillation of native spirits. A shrub, the *babúl,* bearing much the same relation to the *kíkar* that the *pilchi* does to the *ukhán,* is occasionally seen ; it never grows to such a size as would make its timber valuable. The *Kábuli kíkar* (*A. cupressiformis*) is rare. The timber is weak. The *bér* tree (*Zizyphus vulgaris ?*) is not uncommon in the cultivated parts of the district. The wood is of good quality, and is used in building. It yields a fine fuel, throwing out a clear heat. The fruit is not much esteemed except in the case of the *pewandi* or grafted *bér*. The *kokan bér* or *mala* is a small bushy tree. The fruit is much eaten. Good walking-sticks are got from this tree. The *jand* (*Prosopis spicigera*) is always a small tree, rough and gnarled. The wood is strong, and is made into agricultural implements and household furniture. It is much used as fuel, and charcoal is prepared from it. But the charcoal is said to emit too many sparks to be much liked. The seed vessels, called *sangri,* are used as an article of food. This tree is met everywhere in the district, where it has not been cleared away. The great demand for fuel on the North-Western

The *ukhán, jhau, lei.*

The *kíkar.*

Bábul.

Kabuli kikar, Bér.

Kokan bér. Jand.

Chapter I, B.

Geology, Fauna and Flora.

Jand.
Karil.

Railway is calculated to cause a decrease in the area of *jand* unless measures for reproduction are practised as they are at present A good growth of *jand* is a fairly certain sign of superior soil. The *karil* (*Capparis aphya*) sometimes but seldom becomes a tree. It generally remains a mere shrub. It is found throughout the district. The wood is hard; it is used for rafters and *laths* (*barga*) principally on account of its supposed immunity from the attacks of white-ants. As fuel, it has a high reputation. The unripe fruit is called *dela*, and is used as a pickle. When ripe, the fruit is called *pinju* and is eaten in its natural state. The fruit of this shrub is a great stand-by to the poor in seasons of scarcity.

The *wan*.

The *wan* will grow anywhere in the district. A somewhat saline soil seems to suit it best. In Montgomery it remains a shrub generally; it never becomes the fine tree it does in the Hindustáni parts of the province, where it is called *jál*. Camels are fond of its leaves, but no other animal touches them. The wood is used for roofing and fuel, but the fuel is very inferior. It burns badly, gives out a great deal of smoke, and leaves much ash. The fruit is eaten to a large extent. It ripens about May. It is called *pekri* when still unripe, *pílu* when ripe, and *kokan* when dried and preserved.* Certain trees are generally grown about each well.

Pípal.
Sohánjni.
The *chachhára*.

The most common are the *pípal* (*Ficus religiosa*) and the *sohánjni* (*Hyperanthera pterygosperma*) or horse-radish tree. The *chachhara* (*Butea frondosa*) is found on the Rávi, but not on the Sutlej. This is the Hindustáni *dhák*; but it never reaches the dimensions attained in the lower parts of the province. It is venerated by Hindus. The dye made from the flowers (*kesu*) and the gum exuded by the plant are well known. There are no other indigenous trees.

Plants other than trees; and grass.
Sarr.

There are very few plants, other than trees, and grasses deserving of much notice. The *sarr* and the *lána* are the most important. The *sarr* (*Saccharum munja*) is found generally in sandy soil. It is abundant along the rivers and the distributing channels of the canals. There are two kinds, the white-topped and the red-topped, or rather purple-topped. The ropes made from the latter are much inferior to those made from the former. Every portion of this reed is useful. It consists of three parts. The lowest is a stout reed, about half an inch in diameter. This is called *kána*, and is used for roofing houses, and forming the *bands* with which *kachcha* wells are lined, and *pallás* or circular store-houses for grain are made. Above the *kána* comes the *til* in a sheathing petiole called *munj*. The *til* is separated from the *kána* and pulled out of the *munj*. It is used for screens called *pakhi*, and for winnowing baskets. The *munj* is burned at one end, then beaten with a mallet, and finally twisted into a rope. The rope to which the earthen pots of a well are fastened is almost

---

* Mr. Purser, from whose Settlement Report the above paragraph is taken, writes:—"I had no opportunity of testing the correctness of the names *pekri* "and *kokan*. They are not given in 'Punjab Products.' The Punjábi name *vavr*, entered on page 597, is not used in the Bári Doáb. *Pílu* is certainly the name "of the fruit, and seems improperly applied to the tree itself; but it may be so "used locally."

Chapter I. B.

Geology, Fauna and Flora.

invariably made of *munj*. The price varies very much; twenty *sére* per rupee is about the average. This reed grows in tufts; and in land subject to inundation the limits of proprietary right are sometimes marked out by lines of *sarr* stools. The plant is usually burned down about the end of February. Fresh green shoots are then thrown out, which are fine fodder for cows and buffaloes, and increase the supply of milk. Many villages sell the produce of this plant for a round sum annually. A good deal of misapprehension seems to exist about the *lána* plant. There are three kinds of *lána—khangan khár* (*Caroxylon Griffithi*), *gora lána*, and *maitár lána* (*solsolas*). There is also a plant called *phesák láni* (*Sánœda molliflorqs*). *Sajji* (*barilla*, an impure carbonate of soda) is made from the first two. No *sajji* is made from the others. The best *sajji*, called *lota sajji*, is made from *khangan khár*; an inferior quality, known as *bhútni sajji*, from *gora lána*. There is no *khár* in the Dipálpur tahsíl; at least only stray specimens will be found; but it is plentiful in Pákpattan. *Khangan khár* and *gora lána* are smaller plants than *maitár lána*; the first is a thicker and juicier plant than the second; *maitár lána* is usually as ugly a plant as one could wish to see. It grows four or five feet high. It is found everywhere. Miles upon miles of the Pákpattan tahsíl are covered with it. *Phesák láni* is found in the Dhaya uplands in huge stretches. In the lowlands there are occasionally large patches of it. Wherever it is found, the soil is bad and full of *kallar shor*. It is of a blackish-purple colour, and of no use whatever. Camels and goats eat all kinds of *lána*. Charcoal made from *maitár lána* is used by blacksmiths; while that of *gora lána* is much used in *hukkás*. Both these plants are utilized for fuel. They flower about the end of October. Some bushes have red, and some white flowers. When in flower, the three *lánás* present a very pretty appearance. The manufacture of *sajji* is described in Chapter IV. The *ák* (*Calotropis procera*) is common, and found generally in poor sandy soil. Goats eat the leaves; and so will cattle if hard pushed, and if the leaves have been dried. The milky substance in the ducts is applied as an embrocation in some diseases of sheep and goats. The wood is used as fuel. The alleged anti-kallar properties of the plant are unknown in this district. No use is made of the floss in the seed-vessels. The *pitáka* is a fibrous plant abundant about Dipalpur, near the Serai. It has large indented cordate leaves, and bears an orange flower. It flowers about the beginning of September. The fibre is made into ropes in the same manner as that of *suni*, but the ropes are weak. The plant strongly resembles the jute plant (*Carchoras capsularis*), as described on page 242 of Dr. Royle's "The fibrous plants of India," a resemblance extending even to the name. Another fibrous plant commonly found in cotton-fields is the *jhújhan* (*Seshania aculeata*), also called *jaintar*, but this name applies properly to a different species. This plant grows five or six feet high, and may be seen about September in any canal village. The fibre has been used, but in this district the people consider the plant as almost useless. The stalk is occasionally employed in making thatches. This supposed

Khangan khár.
Gora lána.
Maitár lána.
Phesák láni.
Sajji.

Ák.

Pitáka.

Jhújhan.

Chapter I, B.

Geology, Fauna and Flora.

uselessness is the subject of a popular saying :—

Jhújhan dá ki seona,
*Jidhi dhúp na chháwn.**

Bhophalli. *Jawáhán.*

The *bhophalli* is also a fibrous plant, but except as fodder for goats it is not put to any use. The *jawáhán* or camel-thorn (*Alhaki Maurorum*) is common enough. Good *tattis* can be made from this plant.

Harmal. *Gilo.* *Dhámah.* *Poli.* *Aleti or galehti.* *Gharrar madhána.* *Búin.* *Reshan.* *Farid múli.* *Puthkanda.*

The *harmal* (*Peganum harmale*) grows in most places. It is abundant in the ground covered with broken pieces of brick about Pákpattan. The seeds yield a black and brown dye, but are not utilized here. The *gilo* or *garham* (*Tinospora cordifolia*) is a creeper. An extract is made from the root, and is considered a good remedy in cases of fever and ague. The *dhámah* (*Fagonia cretica*) is a small prickly shrub like the *jawáhán*. It is in flower about the end of August. The flowers are of a light pink colour. A medicine is prepared from it. The effects are very similar to, but not so certain as, those of the *gilo*. It is much used in cases of headaches, boils, &c. Native women in the villages often make use of it in a *ghútti* or medicine given to new-born children. A plant not unlike a thistle is the *poli*. It is plentiful in spring about Gugera. An oil is extracted by *telis* from the oblong seeds. This is used as an article of diet. *Aleti*, commonly called *galehti*, is a small low-growing plant, with little black seeds. In seasons of scarcity these are used by the poor people, made into bread. As the bread is intensely dry, it has to be eaten with butter-milk or milk. Sheep, goats and camels eat the plant. It belongs to the *dúdak* family, or that in which the plant contains milky juices. The flower is yellow. It appears in the beginning of August. *Gharrar madhána* is a plant growing about 18 inches high. The seeds are small and dark red : they ripen about the middle of August. The plant is considered good fattening fodder, especially for horses. The flower is supposed to resemble a churning staff (*madháni*) ; hence the name. This plant is hardly a grass. There are two kinds of *búin*, the white and the black *búin*. The former is the more common. It is usually found in light sandy soils, and is a guide in determining the quality of the soil. It is, however, far from being a certain guide. Camels eat the plant, and villagers apply it to boils and pimples. It is supposed to ease pain. Another plant, almost invariably found in poor light soils, is the *reshan*. But it is met with elsewhere. It grows about a foot high, and has a flower of the same shape and colour as that of a thistle. It abounds between the old Beás and Dipálpur. The *farid múli* or *farid búti*, also called *láthia* (*Farsetia Hamiltonii*), is very common. It is a small plant with pink flowers. The seeds are said to be poisonous, but were habitually used by Bába Farid Shakarganj, when he was hungry. The *puthkanda* (*Achyranthes aspera*) grows five or six

* "Why take any care of the *jhújhan*, which yields neither sun nor shade ?" *Vide* "Punjab Products," pages 342, 508.

feet high. It has but few leaves, and those near the ground. The long slender stems are covered with thorns which lie back close to the stem with their points directed downwards, hence the name *puth*, meaning the wrong way, and *kanda*, a thorn. The stem is used for cleaning the teeth; and the seed and leaves are employed medicinally. *Itsit* is a plant that grows along the ground. It is very like *chauldi* (*Amaranthus frumentaceus*). But the latter grows upwards. *Itsit* is of no use; but *chauldi* is used as a vegetable by poor people. Owners of dogs will soon become acquainted with the plant called *bhakra* (*Tribulus terrestris*). The spiked fruit of it constantly sticks in the feet of dogs, causing them to limp. The *háthi-súndi* is a plant which is not mentioned in any of the books under that name. The fruit is said to resemble the trunk of an elephant, and hence the name. Among other plants commonly found may be mentioned the *gawára, majehtra gandi búti, ratkán, bukhan, kháb* or *kala míra, babúna soi, pálak, pára, arári* and *chilitra*. The last three are generally met with in lowlands flooded by the rivers.

Puthkanda. *Itsit.* *Chauldi.* *Bhakra.* *Háthi-súndi.*

It remains now to briefly mention the more common grasses. The most common is *chhimbar*. It is a low-growing grass with round culms, and throws out runners. It is found in good sweet soil, and is readily eaten by cattle. The flower is called *phumni*; *chhimbar* is not unlike *khabbal* or *talla* (*H. dubh*), but the blade of the latter is much broader, and the whole leaf-branch larger and flatter than that of the *chhimbar*; and the stems thrown out at the joints of the *khabbal* are horizontal, while those of the *chhimbar* are vertical. The *khabbal* is an excellent grass and found only in good soil. *Talla* is not to be confounded with *talli*, which is something like a shamrock, with leaves of a bright rich green colour. It is found in inundated land where the soil is good. It is a fine food for buffaloes, cows and bullocks. *Dabh* is a coarse strong grass, which remains green most part of the year. The leaves are long, narrow, flat, and have a tendency to curl up. They are used for thatching and for covering the floors of mosques. The roots are coarse and long, and grow down to a point; in fact form a triangle with the apex at the bottom. It is not a strengthening grass. The long slender flower is pretty. *Lonak* is also a poor grass except when green; and then even it is of only middling value. Cattle do not care for it much. It is often found in somewhat saline soils. The culms are round and slender, and generally about 18 inches high. Sometimes it grows as high as 30 inches. On the other hand, *dháman* is a fine grass, and is said to increase the yield of milk of animals eating it, and the quantity of *ghi* obtained from the milk; but horses will not eat it, as it is bitter. The leaves are long and flat. The plant grows vertically. The head, which is not unlike that of *kangni*, is black when unripe, and white when it has come to maturity. The *palwáhan* is a tall grass, generally several feet high, with slender stems and flat narrow leaves. It is usually found in good soil. By some it is considered the best of all grasses. There are four flower-stalks at the end of each culm, bearded like

Grasses. *Chhimbar.* *Khabbal or talla.* *Talli.* *Dabh.* *Lonak.* *Dháman.* *Palwáhan.*

Chapter I, B.

Geology, Fauna and Flora.

Kheo. *Gharm.* *Dhiddan.* *Sawánk.* *Kúri.* *Kúra.* *Khawi.* *Panni.* *Dila.* *Murk.* *Murkan.* *Lamb.* *Chinikki.* *Lúki.* *Lúmbar.*

barley. The grass is of a purple colour. *Kheo* is a grass consisting of slender round stems growing straight up. *Gharm* or *gharb* is a tall, coarse grass with a woody stem. It is often found growing round a *karil* bush. Goats and camels are said not to eat it. It is an inferior grass. *Dhiddan* is not unlike *kheo*. It is common in the *biláras* of Pákpattan. It grows about two feet high. It is sometimes called *sarkuli*. It should not be confounded with a plant found in rice-fields of the same name. This is not unlike wild *sawánk*; but *sawánk* grows more horizontally than *dhiddan*. *Sawánk* is of two kinds—*bijwán*, or cultivated, and *saia* or wild. The wild *sawánk* is a good grass. It fattens and brings cattle into condition soon. The grain is small and eaten by Hindus on fast days. It is also used by poor people, made into paste called *bhát* or *phát*, and eaten with milk or butter-milk. It grows in firm soil. *Kúri* is a grass not unlike *chhimbar*. It is a different grass from *kúra* which is found in *kangni* fields generally. The latter has a thick stem, broad leaves, and grows a couple of feet high. *Khawi* grows about two feet high, in clumps; often in hard low-lying lands. But it is plentiful in the *bír*, along the Montgomery and Dipálpur road. The flowers are fluffy. When ripe, the plant is of a brownish red colour. It is a fragrant grass, and a scent is said to be made from it. The milk of cattle eating it is supposed to become perfumed. The people assert that the roots yield the *khus* with which *tattís* are made; and that *panni* is a different grass. But the two seem very like each other. *Panni* is used for thatching. *Dila* is a grass found in hard inundated lands. It is very common in the rice-fields about Dipálpur. There are two kinds, the big and the little. The former is yellow, the latter brown. Cattle eat both, but there is no nourishment in them. The root is like the grain of gram. Pigs root up the ground to get at it. It is called *mothra*, and is considered useful in brain diseases. Pigs are also said to have a fancy for the roots of *murk*, a small low-growing grass, with double compound stems, and a small red knob at the end of each branch of the stem. It is found in soft soil, and is abundant on the banks of the Deg. It is a fair grass for fodder. It differs from *muruk*, which is also a small low-growing grass. *Murkan* has very fine and slender round culms. It is a famous grass, having given its name to a famine. *Lamb* is not unlike *lonak*, but it is much smaller and more irregular. It is produced when there is heavy rain. It is eaten by cattle; and when green, increases the yield of milk and butter. *Chinikki* is a small grass, growing about one foot high. It is not unlike *lonak*; but the difference is easily seen. The flower of *chinikki* is broader, and not so long as that of *lonak*. It is eaten by all cattle; but is an ordinary grass, and has no great reputation. It is generally found in soft high land. *Lúki* is a grass about 7 or 8 inches high. It consists of a slender stem, with a number of whorls. The lower whorl consists at times of as many as ten arms; the upper ones generally of five. This grass may be at once known by the regularity with which the arms of the whorls spring from the same centre. *Lúmbar* is a small low grass, not unlike the tail of a fox. It is said to derive its name from this resemblance. *Kanh* is simply a rush found in inundated lands. The roots resemble those of *dabh*. *Maina* is a grass not unlike *talla*, and found also in lowlands. The flower is said to be different. Poor people boil the leaves and use them as a vegetable. *Salyára, itsit*, and *leli* are not grasses. The first is a large shrub, the second has been noticed before, and the third is a creeper found among wheat in spring. *Leha* is said to be a thorny plant.

Chapter I, B.

Geology, Fauna and Flora.

Kanh.

Maina.

Salyara.

Itsit.

Leli.

Fauna:

Domestic animals.

Wild beasts.

The fauna of the district is, if anything, more uninteresting than the flora. Camels are numerous ; the cattle of the Rávi are well known. Sheep are common. The domestic animals will be noticed in more detail in Chapter IV. Wild animals are rare ; tigers were occasionally found prowling about the Sutlej many years ago. The Rája of Kapúrthala and Mr. John Oliver are credited with their extermination. Wolves and wild cats (*bár-billi*) are the most dangerous beasts of prey. Jackals are common, as might be expected; wild pigs have been reduced in numbers by the extension of cultivation into the jungle tracts along the rivers. They do exist, however, but tame pigs are unknown. Ravine deer are fairly numerous ; but *nílgái* and black buck are confined to a small portion of the Gugera tahsil, about the Ravi, near the Lahore border. Bustard, florican, partridges, grey and black sand-grouse and quail are found ; and water-fowl of various kinds, from the goose to the snipe, frequent the *budhs* of the rivers. *Kúnj* visit the district in the cold weather ; and *tilyar* (*H. golia*), a small bird with black back and brown breast, is one of the worst enemies of the farmer. Crocodiles bask on the sand banks of the Sutlej, and now and then one appears in the Ravi. Fish of many kinds abound in the rivers. Snakes are by no means rare. The cobra is the snake usually met. The people talk of a white snake, the bite of which is, if possible, more fatal than that of the cobra. The banks of the Ravi are its chosen abode. Scorpions, centipedes, hornets, wasps, mosquitoes and flies may close the list of unpleasant denizens of the district. During the past five years rewards to the amount of Rs. 1,796 have been given for the destruction of 431 wolves and 8,597 snakes.

Game.

Kúnj, tilyar.

Alligators ; fish.

Snakes, reptiles, insects.

Honey is occasionally found in the *bár*, in nests attached to trees. The yield of a hive is said to amount to about three *sérs* at the outside. The honey, which is called *makhír*, is sold to druggists at the price of *ghi*. The honey is taken from the nest in Katik, during the day time. A saccharine substance, finer and sweeter than sugarcandy, and less than a *chittáck* in weight, is said to be found in wasps' nests. The gatherer finds it prudent to rob the wasp by night.

Honey.

Montgomery is not a good district for game now, and hardly any sportsmen come here for shooting. Pigs abound along the rivers in *kunds* or in forest reserves, and cause considerable damage to the crops. They are only shot or netted by Sikhs and Mahtams, and that rarely. Some of the leading zamíndárs possess guns and go in for shooting themselves, or keep *shikárís* to supply them with game. Hawking is also a favourite pastime

Sport.

Chapter I, B.

Geology, Fauna and Flora.

Sport.

with many, and partridges and quails are netted a great deal by the people of the district. There is not sufficient game to tempt bird-catchers from Lahore or Multan. Black partridge can be found all along the rivers and in the reserves. The grey partridge abounds all over. Sand-grouse are plentiful in the *bárs* in the cold weather and *obára* can also be found. Hares are also found in reserves, river *kunds* and wooded plots in the *bár*. Of other winged game, blue rock-pigeon is found in numbers almost everywhere; quails in spring and autumn in cultivated parts; geese of both kinds and *kunj* along the rivers (both these abound, and are very destructive to the young crops in spring). Ducks of several varieties are met with in the *budhs* and creeks of the Sutlej river, and in some places on the Ravi. Plovers are plentiful, and black ibis is also found in most places.

Snipe does not exist in this district, and bustard and flamingo are very rare. The ordinary spotted deer are found all over in the jungle, but black buck are only met with rarely between Satghara and Wán Rádhá Rám.

Fishing.

There are no fishing towns. Fishermen, who are called *jhabels*, do not depend exclusively on their earnings from fishing. They live scattered about in the villages bordering on the rivers. Fish are rarely caught from the beds of the rivers, as the fishermen have not the means of carrying on operations successfully in deep and rapid streams. A fish called *tirkanda* is, however, sometimes caught in the hot weather when the rivers are in flood. Most fish are caught in the *budhs* during the cold season. Fish go up these to spawn, and on the rivers falling, the fish in the *budhs* are shut up as in a lake. Fishermen make their own nets. Four kinds are in use. The meshes of the first three about one inch square; those of the fourth much smaller. The nets are called on the Sutlej—(1) *Hánd;* this is a long net made of several breadths joined together. A number of men drag this net, sweeping the whole width of a *budh* with it. (2) *Sátwán;* this is a round net, about 7 to 10 feet in diameter. The edge all round is weighted with iron rings through which a cord passes. The fisherman holds this cord in his hand, and flings the net into the water, so that it opens, and the weighted edge sinking to the bottom prevents anything under the net from escaping. By pulling the string going through the rings, the net is closed like a bag, and anything inside is caught. (3) *Kudalli;* this is a cone covered with netting. Its size is proportioned to the size and strength of the person using it. It is generally about four feet high, and the same in diameter at the bottom. The fisherman plunges this cone with the broad end downwards through the water to the bottom. If there are any fish inside, their motion in trying to escape tells him. If they are small, he inserts his hand under the net and seizes them; if large, he first spears them with an iron spit, about one foot long, called *súa.* (4) *Sambhi;* this consists of two sticks fastened together at an angle. The intermediate space is covered with fine netting. One man stands in the water holding the net below the surface, while an-

Chapter I, B.

Geology, Fauna and Flora.

Fishing.

other comes towards him beating the water. When he gets near, the man with the net lifts it out of the water, and the fish at that moment over the net are caught. This net is used only for catching very small fish. The principal kinds of fish found are the following—

Batti,	Gogu,	Dungna,	Tirkanda,
Dambra,	Bhúsan,	Jalli,	Patwi,
Singhári,	Machhána,	Paráhi,	Pránda,
Mori,	Petrate,	Lesi,	Makhni,
Saul,	Khagga,	Nái machhi,	Durra,
Malhi,	Telia,	Gurdi,	

besides the *gangal* or *jhinga* (shrimp), and the *goj* (eel). Fishermen do not sell by weight, but barter so many of their fish for so much grain; they are not usually paid in cash. Fish oil, obtained by boiling down fish and skimming off the fat that rises to the top, is not made to any extent here. It is called *vaho*, and is used in some cases of cattle-disease. It is possible that some of the names given above apply to the same fish at different stages of its growth, and do not all represent different species.

CHAPTER II.

HISTORY.

Chapter II.

History.

Early history.

Alexander's invasion.

The history of the district is chiefly that of certain wild pastoral tribes which appear to have occupied the Rachna Doáb from time immemorial, maintaining a sturdy independence of the successive rulers of northern India, and ever noted for their lawless turbulence. Some account of them is given in the next chapter. Their history goes back, probably, as far as the time of Alexander. From the historians of his expedition, we learn that the northern part of the district was at that time held by a race whom they called Kathæans,* and the southern part by another race, the Malli, whose capital town was Multán. Both these tribes in turn severely tested the valour of the Macedonian troops. The history of the Malli is discussed in the account of Multán,† and need not be repeated here. Their towns in this district were probably those of Kot Kamália and Harappa. ‡ Kot Kamália has been identified by General Cunningham with the first city taken by Alexander in his campaign against the Malli. He also supposes Harappa to have been the "another city of the Malli, into which a great body of the Indians had fled for safety," against which Perdiccas was sent with the cavalry. The similarity between the name Kathaioi, the people whose capital city, Sángla, was stormed by Alexander, and that of the present Rávi tribe, the Káthias, has often been noticed. Sángla, situated in the Rachna Doáb, is at no great distance from the country now occupied by the Káthiás; and it is not improbable that they are the descendants of the old Kathaioi, though they claim a very different origin. They say they came from Káthiáwár. But the Káthiáwár Rájás, on the other hand, trace their origin from the Punjab. The history of Alexander's campaign against the Kathaioi is given in the *Gazetteer* of the Jhang district.

Of pre-Muhammadan times there is nothing to add save that to this period are probably to be referred those remains of ancient towns and village sites already referred to on page ? which are frequent upon the banks of the rivers, and dot the central portions of the district, at present a waste, almost devoid of fixed abodes, and inhabited only by the nomad tribes already alluded to. The towns of Pákpattan, Dipálpur, Kot Kamália, and Harappa, are all places of great antiquity, and once were places of importance. An account of each is given in Chapter VI under their respective headings. The villages of Akbar and Satghara, both of them in the neighbourhood of Gugera, the former six miles to the south-

* Arrian, Lib. v., cap. 22, 23, 24.

† See *Gazetteer* of the Multán district.

‡ *Ib.* See also Chap VI, headings "Kot Kamália" and "Harappa."

Chapter II. History. Antiquities.

west, and the latter 13 miles to the east, are also old towns containing interesting remains. They have been examined and described by General Cunningham, who is unable, however, to suggest any clue to their former history.* All seems to point to a time when Montgomery was a populous country, with towns large and flourishing, and resources at least equal to those of the more northern portions of the province. The antiquities of the district are fully described in the Archæological Survey Reports, Vol. V, pages 103 to 111 ; Vol. XIV, pages 139 to 145 ; and at pages 208 to 219 and 244 to 248 of Cunningham's *Ancient Geography of India.* For nearly 1,600 years after the capture of Kamália and Harappa, there is a great blank in the history of the district, for the accounts about Rasálu, son of Salváhan, are vague and unreliable. He is said to have lived much about Dhaular, a very old town in the Pákpattan tahsíl, and there is still an old mound in the jungle called after him. In the reign of Firoz Shah Tughlak (1351-1388), Dipálpur was a favourite residence of the Emperor. He "erected a mosque outside the city and drew a canal from the Sutlej for the irrigation of its lands." (*Ancient Geography of India,* page 213.)

Rasálu, son of Salváhan.

Firoz Sháh Tughlak at Dipálpur.

In 1398, Tamerlane marched from Multán to Pákpattan. No resistance was made, and the place was spared out of respect for the memory of Bába Faríd Shakarganj, who had died and been buried there about 1264-65.† After the lapse of nearly a century and-a-quarter, another conqueror, a descendant of Tamerlane

Tamerlane takes Pakpattan.

* *Ancient Geography*, page 212.

† A legend of Pákpattan relates that Gházi Beg Tughlak was a poor village boy living in the neighbourhood of Baba Faríd. Thanks to the spiritual influence of the saint, this poor boy became governor of Multán and finally king of Dehli. He then visited Pákpattan, and, to show his gratitude, had the Bishárat *nala* dug by one of his officers, Bishárat Khán. It is an objection to this story that Ghází Beg did not come to the throne till 1321, or at least 56 years after the death of the saint. Bishárat Khán may have opened the mouth of the *nala*, but the channel is certainly not artificial. The legend continues that when the Bisháratwah was dug the stream ran so deep and strong that it was necessary to have a ferry over it, where there is now a bridge between the town and tahsíl. One evening, Bába Faríd came down to the ferry and saw the sun shining on the rippling waves, people in bright attire bathing and drawing water, while the boats glided backwards and forwards. Enraptured with the sight, he exclaimed : *Ai kya pák pattan ?* "Oh, what a beautiful ferry," and after that the old name of the town Ajudhan was given up, and Pakpattan adopted. The truth of the story is doubtful. The name may have been changed to Pákpattan on account of a ferry over the Bisháratwah, but the town was known as Ajudhan in Tamerlane's time. In the Aín-i-Akbari it is called simply *pattan* or "the ferry." *Pák* is probably an epithet applied to the town on account of its containing the tomb and having been the residence of such a famous saint, much the same way as Mecca is called *sharíf.* In fact, Pákpattan means simply the holy *pattan.* It is difficult to see how it could mean "the ferry of the pure one," as has been stated. The comparison of a spiritual teacher, who carries his disciples across the river of existence into paradise, with a ferry-man, has been made in respect of Pír Baka, another celebrated holy man of the district, who lived at Shergarh. Of him it is said—

Beri bahtí shah darya vich,
Pár asáde láwan nun ;
Pír Baka malláhi karda,
Bhar bhar pár langháída.

"A boat is floating in the mighty river to carry us over ; Pír Baka is acting as boatman. He ships a boat-load and carries it across."

Chapter II.

History.

Bábar takes Dipálpur.

entered the district. This time the invasion came from the north. Daulat Khán Lodhi was then governor of the Punjab under Ibrahím Khán Lodhi, the Afghan King of Delhi (1517-1526). He encouraged Bábar, the ruler of Kábul, to attempt the conquest of India. It is probable that at that time the south-west portion of the district was subject to the Langah chiefs of Multán; but the upper portion was held by the Viceroy of the Punjab. In 1524 Bábar, having taken Lahore, marched on Dipálpur and took it by storm. The country attached to Dipálpur was then made over to Sultán Ala-ud-dín Lodhi, who had been an unsuccessful competitor for the throne of Delhi. Bábar had to fall back on Kábul owing to the defection of Daulat Khán, who drove Ala-ud-dín out of the country. Next year Bábar incited Shah Hassan, the ruler of Sindh, and Arghun Tartar, to attack Multán. After a siege of 15 months the place was taken. In 1526 Bábar, having returned to India, defeated Ibrahím Khán Lodhi at the battle of Pánipat, and became king of Dehli. Shortly after, the Arghuns were expelled from Multán, and Shah Hasan made over the country to Bábar, who conferred it on his son Askari. Thus the whole of the district came into Bábar's hands. On his death Humáyún had to give it up to his brother Mirza Kámrán, who held it till the successful revolt of Sher Shah in 1540.

Sher Shah builds a fort of Shergarh.

Sher Shah spent some time at the commencement of his reign in the Punjab, and is said to have built a fort at the town of Shergarh to protect the Nakka country. But it is not known against whom the country was to be defended. On Humáyún's return, one of his lieutenants, Abu Moáli, defeated the Afgháns in 1555 at Dipálpur. On Akbar's accession the district passed into his hands. One naturally turns to the Aín-i-Akbari, compiled in his reign, to obtain information concerning the district. The result is most unsatisfactory. Almost all that can be made out is this. The *súba* of Multán seems to have included the whole of the present district. Of the three *sarkárs* into which the *súba* was divided, one was Dipálpur, containing 29 *maháls* or *parganás*. The names of only five of these can be identified, *viz.* :—

1. Pattan. | 3. Kabúla.
2. Dipálpur. | 4. Satghara.
5. Farídábád.

In *sarkár* Multán appear the *parganás*—

1. Chukandi. | 3. Haveli Shahr.
2. Shergarh. | 4. Deg Rávi.
5. Jalálábád.

1, 2, and 4 of which were in this district, and 3 and 5 may have been. Of course nothing is known about the limits of the *parganás*. Six *parganás* of *sarkár* Dipálpur lay on the left side of the Sutlej. The Deg Rávi is the country about Kot Kamália, and Jalálábád may be the town, the abandoned site of which is still to be seen on the old Beás to the south of the Dipálpur and Gugera road. But native report gives that *theh* a different origin. There is said to have been a fine village here more than 100 years ago, with a number of wells; it was abandoned on the water in the wells becoming brackish. It seems in the same *dastúr* as Shergarh, near which it is actually situated. It was during Akbar's reign that the Khán-i-Khánán is said to have restored the Khánwah canal. This was Mirza Abdul Rahím, son of Bairám Khán. He held Multán in *jágír* about A.D. 1590. He is also said to have re-built Dipálpur, which had not recovered from the effects of the attack by Bábar.

Chapter II.

History.

The Khán-i-Khánán.

In Alamgír's reign (1658-1707) the old term for a cluster of *parganás, karorí*, was changed to *chakla*. Dipálpur is said after that to have been called *chakla* Dipálpur. In the time of Alamgír the foundation of the Háns' power was laid. The Háns were simple *zamíndárs*, living a little to the north-west of Pákpattan. Among them was a learned man Shekh Kutb Háns, who appears to have been a teacher of some of the Dehi nobility. He obtained some influence in this way, and finally, in 1663, Alamgír conferred a *sanad* on him, granting him several villages in the *táluka* of Kutbábád. The deserted site of Kutbábád may still be seen on the bank of the old Soház, nearly south of Malka Háns, and close to the western boundary of Chak No. 33 of the Soház-Pára Colony. Owing to his ability and court influence, Shekh Kutb became a powerful man, and as the Pára, Soház and Dhaddar flowed through his lands he rapidly became rich. At the downfall of the Mughal empire, his descendant made himself independent, as will be noticed further on. *Tappa* Hánsán belonged to *pargana* Kabúla. But Alamgír founded a new *pargana* and named it Alamgírpur, to which the *tappa* Hánsán, with most of the Deg Rávi *pargana*, was attached. This connection with the Rávi may have been a main reason why the Háns ruler afterwards threatened the independence of the Kamália Kharrals—a proceeding which ended in his downfall. Alamgírpur is supposed to have been situated on the old Beás, a little north of Kabír, on the Harappa and Pákpattan road.

Chaklás: rise of the Háns.

Pargana Alamgírpur founded.

It was in the time of Alamgír that the Kot Kamália Kharrals rose to some importance. The fact of their chief still drawing considerable *talukdári* allowances and occupying a position of some dignity seems to show that they must have been powerful once. According to their own accounts, their leader was much superior to the princes of the royal family, though not quite as great a man as the emperor. But, from the facts incidentally ascertained, they appear to have had no power at all, and to have been at the mercy of all the neighbouring tribes. Saádat Yár Khán was the son of one of the Kharral chiefs, who held some post at the court of Dehli. He followed the vocation of all noble families in those days, and robbed every one he could. The emperor was pacified by Saádat Yár Khán's father, until some presents from the King of Persia to him were appropriated by the Kharral. Then Saádat Yár Khán was called to account, arrested and sent to Dehli. Here his witty excuses resulted in his obtaining honorary dresses, a *jágír* worth Rs. 1,09,000 per annum, and being sent with 12,000 men to punish some rebellious Afgháns at Pind Dádan Khán. This rebellion seems to have been

The Kamália Kharrals.

Chapter II.

History.

The Kamália Kharrals.

that which occurred in 1672, in which prince Sultán led the Imperial forces. He is probably the prince who insulted the Siáls by proposing that Ghází Khán, the eighth Siál chief, should betroth his daughter to Saádat Yár Khán.* The fact of this proposal being considered insulting, makes one suspect that

Saádat Yár Khan succeeds.

Saádat Yár Khán's *jágír* cannot have been so large as said. He succeeded his father Mahábat Khán, who was murdered at the instigation of a Multán Kureshí in 1706. He again went to Dehli, and was sent by Alamgír with prince Muiz-ud-dín to put down the Lughári Biloches, who had revolted under one Rugha.† Just then Alamgír died, Muiz-ud-dín went off post-haste to Lahore, leaving Saádat Yár Khán to bring up the baggage behind. On the return of the latter, coming down the Rávi in boats, he got involved in a quarrel with the Upera Kharrals, and a great battle was fought at Dánábád, in which the Uperás were totally defeated. It seems probable that there was a riot in the jungle, and that the Montgomery men came off victors.

Quarrels of the Rávi tribes.

After this the Kamália or Lekherá Kharrals with their allies the Káthiás, Beghelás, Wahniwáls, and other lower Rávi tribes, appear to have been engaged in constant quarrels with the Kharrals of the upper Rávi, and desperate battles took place at Waliwála, Pindi Kháí, and elsewhere. Sometimes one party succeeded in carrying off the stolen cattle, and sometimes the other succeeded in recovering them. In spite of his court influence, experience in war and valuable *jágír*, Saádat Yár Khán could not protect his country against Walidád Khán, the Siál chief

The Jhang Siáls occupy Kamalia.

of Jhang. The Siáls held the country till the death of Walidád Khán in 1747. This chief effected great improvements. With the usual exaggeration of native stories, he is said to have set 125,000 *pakka* wells at work in the tract called Jhangar, and to have taken one rupee and a blanket annually from each as revenue. There is no doubt he greatly extended cultivation, sunk wells, dug water-courses, and put down robberies vigorously. Saádat Yár Khán seems to have died before Walidád Khán. On the death of the latter, the Kamália Kharrals became their own masters again, till they were conquered by the Nakkai Sikhs.

Ahmad Shah's invasions; break up of the empire.

After the death of Alamgír in 1707, the Mughal power, already grievously shaken, hastened with accelerated pace to its overthrow. Internecine struggles for the throne indirectly favoured the rise of the ferocious and enthusiastic Sikhs at the same time that the Mahrattás and Afghána made themselves masters of the best provinces of the empire. In 1739 Nádir Shah took the emperor Muhammad Shah prisoner and sacked Dehli. In 1747 the first invasion of Ahmad Sháh took place. He is said to have come back seven times; the last invasion took place in 1767.

* The Punjab Chiefs, volume II, page 64.

† This is probably the expedition mentioned by Elphinstone (*History of India*, p. 588, Ed. 4). He considers the insurgents were Sikhs. But the Sikhs were not force about Multán so early as 1707. The rebels seem to have been Afgháns. The Kharral account is that given above.

Chapter II.

History.

Ahmad Shah's invasions, break up of the empire.

The complete manner in which the country was swept of everything valuable by the Afgháns is forcibly expressed in the couplet :—

Khádá pitá laheda,
Te rehndá Ahmad Shah eda.

Implying that what one eats and drinks is of profit to one and anything that remains goes to Ahmad Shah. In 1758 the Mahrattás overran the country and took Multán and Lahore. Next year Ahmad Shah drove them out again. The next invaders were the Bhangí Sikhs.

Independent States formed.

Till the incursions of the Duráni monarch commenced, the present Montgomery district was subject to the governor of Lahore. After that various men of influence made themselves independent, and exercised all the privileges of independent rulers, as regards fighting with their neighbours and robbing and murdering those weaker than they. The manner in which the country was parcelled out among these separate States is roughly shown in a map attached to Mr. Purser's Settlement Report of the district. The following paragraph contains a brief account of each :—

The Bahrwál Nakkais.

The Nakka country lies between the Rávi and Sutlej, in the south of the Lahore district. The word *nakka* means border edge. Híra Singh was a Sikh *zamíndár* living at Bahrwál in the Nakka. He took possession of the country, and founded a *misl* or confederacy, which was known as the Nakkai *misl*. He seems to have joined the Bhangís in their plundering expedition under Hari Singh about 1760 (?), when they were beaten back from Multán. He had always an inclination to extend his territory to the south ; and forming an alliance with the Háns, he attacked the Diwán of Pákpattan, who was supported by the Wattús. A battle was fought at a place called Bhúman Shah or Kutbwála on the old Sohág. The Sikhs and Háns, who were probably in small numbers, were beaten, and many of them drowned in the rivers. Hira Singh was killed. He was succeeded by his nephew, Nar Singh, who was killed in 1768 at Kot Kamália, fighting against the Kharrals. His son, Ran Singh, was the most important of the Nakkai chiefs. He extended the possessions of his *misl*, and held the *tálukas* of Bucheke, Farídábád, and Jethpur. He also got possession of Saiyadwála, which had before been held by Kamr Singh, of the Gugera Nakkai family On Ran Singh's death, Wazír Singh, brother of Kamr Singh recovered Saiyadwála from Bhagwán Singh, the son of Ran Singh. After the marriage of Bhagwán Singh's sister to Ranjit Singh, the Nakkais seem to have turned their attention to Pákpattan again, and finally conquered the country of the Háns. This they retained till Ranjit Singh seized all their possessions in 1801.

The Gugera Nakkais.

Kamr Singh of the Gugera Nakkais was a greater man in this part of the country even than Ran Singh. He occupied

Chapter II.

History.

The Gugera Nakkais.

both sides of the Rávi, from Faridábád to the Multán border. When the Háns threatened Kamália or, as one account says, actually took it, the Kharrals called on Kamr Singh for help. He drove off the Háns and kept Kamália for himself. He took away the *jágir* of the Kamália chief, and gave him a *tálukdári* allowance, locally known as *athog*, of five *páis* in the *kharwár* of *nijkári* crops, and Re. 1 per *kanál* of *zabti* crops. He rebuilt Satghara which had been sacked by the Sikhs about 1745, and abandoned by the inhabitants. He built a brick wall, still in good preservation, round the town. This was in 1775. He also constructed forts at Harappa and Kabír. He was an able ruler and kept the Rávi tribe in good order. The Kathiás, Kharrals and other robber clans settled down to comparatively quiet lives. A great increase in cultivation took place in his time. In this respect, considering the difficulties under which he laboured, his rule will compare not unfavourably even with that of Sáwan Mal. The country subject to him seemed to have been divided into two *parganás*, Satghara and Saiyadwála, and five *garhis*, Killiánwála, Dhaulri, Kamália, Chicháwatni and Harappa. He died about 1780 after having been engaged in constant warfare with the rival house of Bahrwál. It is said he was murdered by an Upera Kharral at Rabna Mohárán near Saiyadwála. He was succeeded by Wazír Singh, his brother, who more than held his own against Bhagwán Singh. In 1783 Jai Singh, Kanhaia, seized his country. After two years the Kanhaia *misl* was shattered at Batála. Wazír Singh assisted in its overthrow and recovered his country. In 1790 he was murdered by Dal Singh of Bahrwál, and was succeeded by his son, Mahar Singh. In 1798, when Shah Zamán invaded the Punjab, Muzaffar Khan, governor of Multán, attacked Kamália and expelled the Sikhs. In 1804 Ranjít Singh appropriated all the territory still held by Mahar Singh.*

The Háns.

The rise of the Háns has been already noticed at page 35 of this chapter. About 1764 Muhammad Azím was chief of the Háns clan. He seized as much of the country round about Malika Háns as he could. When Jhanda Singh and Ganda Singh, the Bhangi *sardárs*, invaded Multán in 1766, they seized upon the country of Muhammad Azim Háns. After they had come to terms with the Bahálwapur Khán they seem to have almost deserted the country, so that the Háns easily expelled the remaining troops. It must have been before or about this time that the battle in which Hira Singh Nakkai was killed, occurred, as Abdus-Subhán, the Diwán of Pákpattan, was murdered in 1767. About this time, too, Muhammad Azím, Háns, was treacherously taken prisoner by Kamr Singh, Nakkai, and died

* The accounts of these petty States are derived from oral tradition. They are of doubtful authenticity. The only check on them is Mr. Griffin's history of the Punjab Chiefs, which has been constantly referred to for the purpose. The history of the Punjab Chiefs says, on Kamr Singh's death Saiyadwála fell into the hands of Ran Singh (son of Nar Singh), head of the rival Nakkai house of Bahrwál. Tradition says Ran Singh was Wazír Singh's servant. Ran Singh's name does not occur in the pedigree table of the Bahrwál Nakkais given on page 118 of the Punjab Chiefs.

Chapter II. History.

The Háns.

in confinement. He was succeeded by his brother, Muhammad Haiyát, who quarrelled with Ghulám Rasúl, the successor of Abdus-Subhán. Getting the worst of the contest, he called in the Bahrwál Sikhs to assist him, promising them half his country. They came, took the land, and did not interfere with the Díwán, but they did interfere with cow-killing and the calling to prayers (*báng*). So Muhammad Haiyát was not pleased, and called on the Dogars, who were then numerous in the district and desperate characters, to help him. The Nakkaís were expelled, and the Háns ruled again. Before this the Pára, Sohág and Dhaddar had dried up, and with the water the source of wealth and power of the Háns had gone; so when the Sikhs returned, after the betrothal of Mái Nákkaian to Ranjít Singh, Muhammad Haiyát could not resist them, and sought refuge with the Díwán of Pákpattan, and the Nakkaís occupied the country till Ranjít Singh took it from them.*

The *kachhi* occupied by Baháwalpur.

About the same time that the Háns shook off their allegiance the ruler of Baháwalpur, Mubárik Khan, moved across the Sutlej and annexed the strip of land lying along the right bank of the river, from about Pír Ghani southwards, called the *kachhi*, a word meaning simply lowland lying between a river and highland. When the Bhangís invaded Multán in 1766, Mubárik Khán joined the Afghans and assisted in the indecisive battle that was fought on the Sutlej. Peace being made, he retained the *kachhi*. In 1772 the Bhangís defeated the Afgháns and Dáúdputrás, but the latter kept the land to the north of the Sutlej. In 1779 Diwán Singh, Bhangi, was driven out of Multán. In 1810 Sádik Khán, of Baháwalpur, was obliged to assist Ranjit Singh, against his old allies, the Afgháns, at the siege of Multán. Next year, after the repulse of the Sikhs, the Afgháns attacked Baháwalpur, but were defeated. About this time Ranjít Singh "demanded tribute for the Baháwalpur territory north of the Sutlej. Sádík Muhammad Khán sometimes refused payment altogether, and always resisted till he succeeded in gaining more favourable terms." The demand was successively raised till the Khán could no longer pay it. Ultimately, in 1831, General Ventura occupied the country on the part of the Lahore Government.

The Diwáns of Pákpattan.

The Diwán of Pákpattan is the successor of Bába Faríd Shakarganj. The respect inspired by the memory of this saint was shown as early as the invasion of Tamerlane, when it procured the safety of the town. The succeeding Diwáns had great influence over the wild clans of the country, and were much respected by the

* This account of the Háns is far from satisfactory. Considering that the Bhangi invasion of Jhanda Singh and Ganda Singh occurred in 1766, and that Abdus Subhán, fighting against whom Hira Singh was killed, died in 1767, it is impossible to reconcile the statement given above. It can only be supposed that Muhammad Azim lost his country during Hari Singh's invasion, and was captured before the Bhangís appeared for the second time, and that Muhammad Haiyát formed an alliance with the Nakkais against Abdus-Subhán as well as against Ghulám Rasúl. The Dogars afterwards emigrated, and went up through Chunián into Mamdot, where they retained their reputation for lawlessness.

Chapter II.
History.
The Diwáns of Pákpattan.

Imperial officials. They held a good deal of land on a sort of *jágír* tenure. They received the government share of all crops on which revenue was levied in kind. But indigo, cotton, tobacco, and sugarcane were *zabti* crops, and paid in cash. All revenue paid in cash was taken by the *kárdárs*. It was then the interest of the Diwán to induce the people to sow crops, of which the revenue was paid by divisions of the produce, and to neglect those paying in cash. As, moreover, cash rents were collected, whether the crops matured or not, he was able to make a show of seeking the benefit of the people when he exhorted them to sow only such crops as would pay nothing if there was no outturn. As might be supposed, the Diwán, being a man of influence and having a brick fort at Pákpattan, was determined to be independent if possible; and when the Háns and Dáúdputrás seized on all the land they could, he appropriated a small tract of country in the west and south-west of the present Pákpattan tahsíl, estimated to yield a revenue of Rs. 30,000. The Díwán then was Abdus Subhán. He is said to have made himself independent in 1757. He entered into an alliance with Mubárik Khán, and joined in an attack on the Bikáner Rája. This resulted in his getting some land on the other side of Sutlej. He then fought the Nakkaī Sikhs, and defeated them. His territory was then occupied by the Bhangís. In 1767 he was killed by an Afghán retainer by mistake. This Afghán had a grudge against one of the Hujra Saiyads. The Saiyad came on a visit to the Diwán, and the Afghán resolved to shoot him. He lay in ambush as the Saiyad and Diwán were riding past, and observed the Saiyad was first. When the cavalcade got close to him, he fired at the foremost man, who turned out to be the Diwán, as the Saiyad had fallen back. In this way Abdus Subhán came to his death. After the expulsion of the Bhangís his successors recovered their territory till Ranjít Singh appropriated it in 1810, but they had to pay tribute to the Sikhs who held the Háns' country.

Death of Abdus-Subhán.

The Wattús.
Lakha and Ahmad Yár.
The Bhangís.

The situation of the Wattús on the Sutlej is described in Chapter III. Not only do they occupy a large tract of country on the right bank of the river, they also extend for some distance on the left bank, principally in the Sirsa district. There was a famous Wattu *chaudhri* called Lakha, who used to pay in the revenue of a considerable part of the Wattu country on both sides of the river. About the middle of last century he became independent. He held the villages about Atári and Haveli, and some 40 more on the other side of the Sutlej. He built an enclosure or *haveli* near the latter village, hence the name Haveli, though the present village does not stand on the same site as Haveli Lakha Wattu. This chief seems to have had to fight for his territory, and to have been able to retain only the Wattu villages. It does not appear when he died, but he was succeeded by his grandson, Ahmad Yár Khán, who was present at the defeat of Hira Singh, Nakkai. His triumph was short-lived, for very soon Fateh Singh, Bhangi, attacked him, over-ran the country, and, after defeating him at Khadwáli, drove him across the Sutlej.

Chapter II.

History.

The Wattús.

Lakha and Ahmad Yár.

The Bhangís.

One account says the leader of the Bhangís was Sardár Budh Singh. He improved the country greatly, and the Wattús, who had been ill-used before, were well off and as contented as they could be under the Bhangís. An occasional attempt was made to oust the latter, but ineffectually. It would seem as if the Bhangis treated Jahán Khán, successor of Ahmad Yár, with consideration, and did not entirely despoil him of his property. The territory of the Bhangis extended from Márúf in the east to Bhangiánwála near Pákpattan in the west. The Sutlej bounded it on the south, and it ran up nearly to the old Beás on the north. Atari fell to the lot of some *sardár* about whom nothing is known. The famine of 1783 A.D. occurred in Budh Singh's time. He is said to have sold all his property, and to have fed the people with grain bought from the proceeds. In 1807 Ranjít Singh took the country from the Bhangís, and made it over to Káhn Singh, Nakkaí.

The Afgháns of Dipálpur.

There was an Afghán, belonging originally to Kasúr, called Dáúd Khán. He lived near Shergarh, and seems to have been a freebooter. About the time of the Mahratta invasion he settled at Jalálábád on the old Beás, about 10 miles north-west of Dipálpur. He built a mud fort, and collected a number of similar characters to himself, and plundered right and left. Thus he became a man of influence. At that time Dipálpur, which had brick wall and bastions, was held by one Hari Singh, apparently a *thánadár* of the Mahrattás. His position soon became difficult, for the people did not care to have him, and the Mahrattás were driven out by the Afgháns. He therefore entered into an agreement with Dáúd Khán to make over the town to him on payment of Rs. 4,000. Dáúd Khán paid Rs. 2,000, and was admitted into the town. Hari Singh was very anxious to get the balance due, and Dáúd Khán was equally anxious to get back what he had paid. In the end, Hari Singh found it advisable to get away as fast as he could. Dáúd Khán then became ruler and oppressed the people of the Dipálpur *iláka* most grievously. He died after 10 years, and was succeeded by his son, Jalál-ud-dín Khán, after whom the mud fort had been called. He was a greater tyrant than his father. As he found persons of property who were worth fining absconded, he made them give sureties not to leave without permission. Hence it became a saying that one should be careful to take one's sureties with one when going off—"*sane zámináin jána bhái, sane záminán jána!*" He appears, however, to have kept a hold on his territory till the last decade of the century. Then the Gugera and Bahrwál Sikhs seized all his villages to the north and west, while the Kanganpur *sardárs*, who occupied Márúf, took the remaining villages and built a fort under the very walls of Dipálpur, where the canal bridge now stands. Finally, peace was made on the basis of the *statu quo*, which left Jalál-ud-dín Khán simply Dipálpur, and when his cattle went out to graze, the neighbouring villages stole them. He appears to have died in 1804. His successor and son, Ghiás-ud-dín, was expelled in 1807 by Ranjít Singh, who

Chapter II.
History.
The Afgháns of Dipálpur.

made over the place to the Bahrwál *sardár*. Afterwards Ghiás-ud-dín took service with Ranjít Singh. His son Mohi-ud-dín owned two villages—Ghiás-ud-dín and Mahtáka Nauábád—in the Dipálpur tahsil. He was not a man of any importance.

The Saiyads of Hujra and Basírpur.

In the town of Hujra are the shrines of two saints, Miran Lál, Baháwal Sher, and his great-grandson Shah Mukím. The incumbent was always a man of influence, and held some villages in *jágir*. When the Mughal empire broke up, the incumbent was Saiyad Sadr-ud-dín. He made himself master of the *táluka* of Hujra, which he and his successors seem to have held till 1807 The country about Basírpur was inhabited chiefly by Muhammadans, Wattús and Aráins. When the Bhangís occupied this part of the Doáb, Basírpur seems to have been made over to Karm Singh, Cháhal. The Wattús preferred their old master, Lakha. Both they and the Aráins were discontented, because Karm Singh paid scant attention to their old customs. They resolved to get rid of the Sikhs. The Aráins wanted to call in the Saiyads of Hujra, the Wattús preferred their connections, the Afgháns of Dipálpur. They finally arranged to send for both, and that the place should be given to those who came first. Now there was a fort at Basírpur and a garrison in it, and it was necessary to get rid of the latter. The Afgháns and Saiyads were summoned one evening, and during the night a great noise of people crying for help was heard outside the fort at a little distance. The men in the fort went out to see what was the matter, when the zamindárs set on them in the dark, and killed many of them. The rest fled. In the morning the Saiyads came up, and the fort was made over to them. Next the Dipálpur forces came up; but they were too late. The Saiyads after that held Basírpur *táluka* till 1807. It does not appear when the Cháhals were ejected, but it was probably about 1780, when the Bhangi *misl* was growing weak. Sadr-ud-dín was succeeded by Saiyad Kutab Ali, and he by Sardár Ali Shah, a cruel tyrant. He appears at first to have been kept in some sort of order by the Gugera Nakkaís, but afterwards he gave loose rein to his bad disposition. After the conquest of Kasúr in 1807, Ranjít Singh made over the Hujra and Basírpur territory to Bedi Sáhib Singh in *jágir*. The end of Sardár Ali Shah was tragic. He went to Una, got involved in a quarrel with the Bedis, and was put to death by them. Sadr-ud-dín seems to have been a good ruler, and to have encouraged agriculture, to have laid out gardens, and sunk 150 wells.

The Saiyads of Shergarh.

The incumbent of the shrine of Dáúd Bandgi Shah at Shergarh had also some *jágir* villages during the Mughal empire. He set up as independent chief on the downfall of the empire, and held his three villages till Ranjít Singh took them away and made them over to Fateh Singh, Gandhi.

The *sardár* of Shamkot

Sardár Lál Singh resided at Shámkot, in the south of the Lahore district. When the Sikhs were seizing all the country round about, he made himself master of the *tálukás* of Kanganpur in Lahore (which also extended a little way into this district) and of Márúf. Subsequently

Chapter II.

History.

The sardár of Shamkot.

when the Dipálpur Afgháns grew weak, he seized on their villages to the south up to the gates of Dipálpur. In 1807 Ranjít Singh deprived him of his possessions, and made over the *táluka* of Márúf in *jágír* to Fateh-ud-din Khan, nephew of the chief of Kasúr, which had just been conquered.

The country under Ranjít Singh.

Thus between 1804 and 1810 Ranjít Singh had taken possession of all the country except a small strip on the Sutlej held by the Khán of Baháwalpur, who paid tribute for it. The old divisions were abolished, and the country parcelled out into *tálukás*. Over each a *kárdár* was appointed, who was very nearly independent. He exercised judicial and executive powers. He collected the revenue and settled disputes. The revenue collected in the shape of fines was not much less than the actual land revenue. Almost the whole of the Dipálpur tahsíl was held by influential *sardárs* in *jágír;* with the exception of Chendpur and a block of land south of Faridábád, the rest of the district was *khálsa.* Occasionally, a *táluka* would be given in *jágír* and almost immediately resumed. Thus Kanwar Khark Singh held Kamália from 1814 to 1816. The *tálukás* seem to have been farmed to the highest bidder. As might be expected from such a system, oppression flourished. There was little security either. The people had only two ways of protecting themselves,—the first was to go to Lahore and complain; the second to murder the *kárdár;* neither was very satisfactory, as the result was only to introduce a still more rapacious party on the scene. The ruins of old forts are still numerous in the district. Wells used to be provided with little towers to which the cultivators might fly on the approach of danger. A couple of matchlocks were kept in them, and beneath there was an enclosure for cattle. Thus cultivators carried on their work. Ranjít Singh had a *thána* at Kabúla, and there was another belonging to Baháwalpur at Tibbi, four miles off, yet the country was so unsettled that people scarcely dared to cross between the two if they had anything worth stealing with them. About 1830 Diwán Sáwan Mal, governor of Multán, obtained charge of a considerable portion of the district: all in fact, except the Dipálpur tahsíl and the cis-Rávi portion of Gugera. His rule was decidedly vigorous. At first villages in which serious crimes took place were burnt as examples. The track law was strictly enforced. He had canals dug, and by light rents and a just administration caused large areas to be brought under cultivation. The tribes of the Ravi were, however, not to be weaned from evil ways in a hurry, and in 1843 they were out, and plundered half the country. The Wattús on the Sutlej were very little better. In 1844 Sáwan Mal was killed. Next came the first Sikh war. The Kharrals and Siáls rose again, but were severely handled by Sádik Muhammad, the *kárdár* of Múlraj. The result of the war was the establishment of the English residency at Lahore. A summary settlement was made; but otherwise no startling changes occurred. The second Sikh war ended with the introduction of British rule in 1849. During the war Dhara Singh, the Gugera Nakkai, son of Mahar

The country under Diwán Sáwan Mal.

Chapter II.

History.

The country under Diwán Sáwan Mal.

Singh, endeavoured, at the instigation of the Kharral chief, Ahmad of Jhamra, to hold Satghara against the British. Ahmad, of whom we shall again hear later on, betrayed him and brought a force against him, which defeated him with considerable loss. Dhara Singh subsequently fought in the battles of Rámnagar and Gujrát.

Political divisions under the Sikh monarchy.

The state of things, towards the end of Ranjit Singh's reign is shown in a map appended to Mr. Purser's Settlement Report, in which the approximate limits of the country subject to Sáwan Mal are marked. After Dipálpur *táluka* had been taken from the Nakkais, about 1810, it was given in *jágir* to Kanwar Khark Singh, and in 1828 to Sardár Jawand Singh, Mokal. He held it till his death in 1840. Then his son, Bela Singh, succeeded. He was drowned in the Sutlej when the Sikhs were defeated at Sobráon. The *jágir* was then resumed. Hujra and Basirpur *tálukás* were held in *jágir* by Bedi Sáhib Singh. On his death, his son, Bishn Singh, succeeded. He was followed by his son, Atr Singh. Ranjit Singh and Bishn Singh died about the same time. A court intrigue ended in the resumption of Atr Singh's *jágirs*, while he himself was shortly after murdered by his uncle, Bikrama Singh. The *tálukás* were farmed to Sáwan Mal, and then to Fakír Chirágh-ud-dín. In Mahárája Dalip Singh's reign the sons of Atr Singh, Bábás Sampúran Singh and Khem Singh, recovered a considerable number of their villages in the Basirpur *táluka*. They then divided them, not being on good terms with each other. Sir Bába Khem Singh, K. C. I. E., is still alive while Bába Sampúran Singh died in 1882, and has been succeeded by his sons Bábás Deva Singh, Parduman Singh and Uttam Singh. *Táluka* Atári was held for some time by the Bahrwáliás. Then Dal Singh (Nabarna), Kaliánwála, and after him his son, Atr Singh, held it in *jágir*. It was resumed in 1851 on his death. It was for some time under Sáwan Mal. *Táluka* Jethpur, consisting of 40 villages, was another *jágir* of the Kaliánwála family. It was held by Chatar Singh, brother of Atr Singh. He was killed at Ferozeshah (Ferushahr), and the *jágir* was then resumed. A portion of the Dipálpur *tahsil* was at that time attached to the Chúnián *iláka*, which belonged to Kanwar Khark Singh. It was managed for him by Mangal Singh (Siránwáli), who appears afterwards to have enjoyed it himself. It was subsequently made over to Atr Singh (Nabarna), probably on the accession of Mahárája Sher Singh. *Táluka* Márúf had been given to Fateh-ud-din, Kasúria by Ranjit Singh. It was held by him till 1845, when he was killed at the battle of Ferozeshah. The Kanganpur *táluka* belonged to Lahore. It appears to have been held by the Bahrwál family, and then by Jawand Singh, Mokal. *Táluka* Shergarh belonged to Fateh Singh Gandhi, who is said to have been a follower of Sardár Gyán Singh, Nakkai. So was Sardár Sada Singh, who held the *táluka* of Shádiwála, consisting of only two villages. It does not appear when these two *tálukás* were resumed. Indeed, it seems hardly correct to give them such a grand title, as they were simply parts of *tálukás* Hujra and Jethpur till granted in *jágir*. Haveli was held in *jágir* till the death of Khark Singh, first by a member of the Kalál family, and then by Mahán Singh Datt. Chendpur (or Kot Táhir) was part of the *jágir* of Sardár Dal Singh.

Chapter II.

History.

Political divisions under the Sikh monarchy.

British Rule.

On the occupation of the country in 1849, a district was constituted with its head-quarters at Pákpattan. It included so much of the present district as lies between the Rávi and the Sutlej, the trans-Rávi portion belonging to the Jhang district. In 1852 this latter tract was attached to the district, and the head-quarters moved to Gugera, near the south bank of the Rávi, and upon the old military road from Lahore to Multán, 26 miles to the north-east of the present station of Montgomery. In 1855 twenty villages were transferred from the Lahore to the Gugera district. On the opening of the railway it was held to be indispensably necessary that the head-quarters of the district should be removed from the Rávi riverain to a point on the central water-shed traversed by the railway which was ultimately to come under irrigation from a permanent canal, presumably the Bári Doáb. A peculiarly barren and arid spot had been selected on the railway near the small cattle village of Sáhiwál for a half-way station between Lahore and Multán, and it was unhesitatingly held that it was advisable to locate the railway and civil establishments together; one of the grounds being that medical attendance and religious privileges would thus be more easily afforded to the fortunate residents. Sáhiwál was thus fixed upon as the future head-quarters of the district which were removed thither in 1865. The anticipated canal has up to date (1898) only reached the border of the Lahore district, 40 miles distant. By way of a doubtful compliment to Sir R. Montgomery, then Lieutenant-Governor, the new station was in the year of its foundation named Montgomery. About the same time the interior arrangement of the district was re-cast. It had previously been divided into five tahsíls having their head-quarters at Gugera, Saiyadwála, Hujra, Pákpattan and Harappa. Now, however, Saiyadwála and Harappa ceased to be tahsíl stations, and the district was divided into four quarters, the tahsil of Gugera in the north, of Hujra in the west, of Pákpattan in the south, and Montgomery in the east, the trans-Rávi or Saiyadwála *parganah* being included in the Gugera tahsíl. Subsequently, in 1871, the head-quarters of the Hujra tahsil were removed to Dipálpur.

The Mutiny of 1857.

The more turbulent tribes of the district had, during generations of anarchy, become too much accustomed to robbery and violence to settle down with pleasure to a quiet humdrum life, the invariable concomitant of British rule. When the mutiny broke out in 1857, they thought the time had come to resume their old habits, and the district was the scene of the only popular rising which took place north of the Sutlej. Emissaries from Dehli appeared before the end of May to have crossed the river from the direction of Sirsa and Hissár, which districts were already in open rebellion, and to have commenced an agitation. The

Chapter II.

History.

The Mutiny of 1857.

Kharrals are divided into many *góts* or sub-divisions. Among them are the Upera and Lakhera *góts*. The Upera Kharrals belong principally to Jhamra and Dánábád, in the Gugera tahsíl; the Lakhera Kharrals are found about Kamália, in the Montgomery tahsíl. There is little love lost between these kinsmen. The battle of Dánábád, in which the Lakherás beat the Uperás, has been mentioned. The Káthiás, who hold with the Lakherás, have always been engaged in quarrels with the Uperás. In 1857 Ahmad, a resident of Jhamra, was the leader of the Uperás, and Sarfaráz Khan, of Kamália, was the chief of the Lakherás. Ahmad was a man above the average—bold and crafty. In 1848 he had, as already related, induced Dhara Singh, of the Gugera Nakkai, to hold Satghara against the English, and then betrayed him. It was this man who roused the tribes. All the important Rávi tribes rose, but the Sutlej tribes, with the exception of the Joyás, kept generally quiet. News of the Meerut mutiny and massacre and of the disarmament of the native troops at Mián Mír reached Gugera *viâ* Lahore on the 13th May. The Deputy Commissioner, Captain Elphinstone, forthwith disarmed the detachment of the 49th N. I. stationed there as Treasury guard, and sent it back to Lahore; their place was taken by sepoys of Captain Tronson's Police battalion, for whom were substituted at the Jail the retainers of Bábás Khem Singh and Sampúran Singh who remained in active attendance on the authorities all through the disturbances. About the end of May news was received of the mutiny of the Hariána Light Infantry and the 14th Irregular Cavalry at Hánsi, Hissár and Sirsa, and the accompanying massacres of Europeans. In reply to an appeal for assistance from Mr. Oliver at Fázilka a force of 226 men was despatched across the Sutlej under Lieutenant Pearse, who subsequently took part in the operations of the Hariána Field Force. June passed away without any overt act of rebellion taking place. By way of precaution arms licenses were withdrawn, and extra police and *sowárs* recruited to replace those despatched to Fázilka. On the 8th July and subsequent days a slight disturbance occurred at Lakhoke in the Pákpattan tahsíl. The Joyás of that place assisted by their clansmen across the Sutlej in Baháwalpur refused to pay balances of land revenue, and assumed a threatening attitude, but quickly dispersed on the arrival of reinforcement from Gugera. The first real precursor of the storm that was brewing occurred on the night of July 26th in the shape of an outbreak in the Gugera Jail. This appears to have been in all probability the work of Ahmad Khan, as he had managed with the connivance of the *darogah* to pay an unauthorized visit to the jail during June, when he no doubt conferred with the more turbulent of its inmates. Shortly after his visit a large quantity of tobacco, sweetmeats and other prohibited articles were discovered under the prisoner's cots. The *émente* in the jail was promptly suppressed: 51 prisoners were killed and wounded. Apparently no satisfactory proof could be found against Ahmad Khan, who, however, had promptly fled from Gugera as soon as the jail outbreak occurred. He was brought back, and together with other chiefs of the predatory tribes on the Rávi and Sutlej required to

Chapter II.

History.

The Mutiny of 1857.

enter into heavy recognizances not to leave the Sadr without special permission. August passed without any important occurrence. A local military levy was raised, and 200 of its recruits had been despatched to Peshâwar on the 15th September. Two days subsequently the storm broke. At 11 P. M on the night of the 16th September Sarfaráz Khán informed Captain Elphinstone that all the chiefs of the Rávi tribes who had been called into Kamália had fled, evidently with the intention of rising in their villages. A force was at once despatched to protect Kámalia, and expresses were sent to inform the Commissioner at Multán and the tahsíl officials at Harappa. Both messengers were stopped by the Murdánás of Muhammadpur. Mr. Berkley, Extra Assistant Commissioner, was despatched on the 17th with 20 *sowárs* to capture Ahmad before he could cross the Rávi on his way to his village Jhamra. In this, however, he was unsuccessful, but an interview appears to have taken place at which Ahmad renounced his allegiance to the British, and gave himself out as a subject of the King of Delhi, from whom he had received orders to raise the whole country. Meanwhile the Government treasure and records were removed into the tahsíl at Gugera, and the jail was vacated, the prisoners being placed in a *serái* near the tahsíl. Captain Elphinstone on the same day, the 17th, then joined Mr. Berkely with reinforcements. The Rávi was crossed, and the rebels were put to flight on the first slight skirmish. Some 20 prisoners and 700 heads of cattle were taken, and Jhamra itself was burnt. This effectively quelled the Kharrals of that part of the country, and Ahmad had in future to rely upon the support of the neighbouring Wattú tribe to the west of Jhamra. On the 18th Mr. Berkley was sent towards Kaure Shah in order to re-open communications with Multán, and to give needful assistance to the tahsíl at Harappa. Meanwhile troops were moving down from Lahore. Lieutenant Chichester, with a detachment of the 1st Sikh Cavalry, reached Gugera on the 19th, and were sent across the Rávi on the 20th to scour the country westwards. On the same day in their rear Ahmad accompanied by a large body of Wattús crossed to the south bank of the Rávi with the intention of attacking the Sadr station. The re-inforcements from Lahore, under Colonel Paton, consisting of three horse artillery guns, one company of the 81st, one company of a Native regiment, and a party of mounted police accordingly hurried forward to Gugera, and messages were sent recalling Mr. Berkley and Lieutenant Chichester. Meanwhile the rebels had advanced close to the Sadr station; the troops were moved out to meet them, and after receiving a few rounds of grape and shrapnel they retreated slowly beyond Fattehpur into the jungles near the river. They do not appear to have been hotly pursued, and suffered but small loss. On the next day, the 21st, reliable information was received to the effect that Ahmad with a large body of Wattús had retreated into the jungle near Gashkori, some six miles south of Gugera. Captain Black was sent with a detachment of cavalry to destroy them. He was joined by Lieutenant Chichester. A sharp skirmish took place in which the cavalry had to retreat. They were, however, rallied,

Chapter II.

History.

The Mutiny of 1857.

and Ahmad together with Sárang, chief of the Begke Kharrals, was killed. Our losses were severe, nearly twenty of the *sowárs* being killed. Meanwhile Mr. Berkley was at Kaure Shah with the object of re-opening communication with Harappa which had been interrupted by the Murdánás of Muhammadpur under their headman, Walidád. On the 21st, with 60 horsemen, he dispersed near the above place a large gathering of Fattiána, Tarána and Murdána Siyáls, killing 14 of them On the next day he marched towards Muhammadpur, taking a circuitous route towards the Rávi in order to disperse any bodies of insurgents which might again have assembled. He was suddenly attacked in a river-side jungle near Kaure Shah by a considerable body of them. In the confusion Mr. Berkley was cut off, and, after making a gallant resistance single-handed, was killed. More that 50 of his detachment were also killed. The remainder rallied, and returned to Núr Shah. On the afternoon of the 23rd Captain Elphinstone, accompanied by Captain Black and Lieutenant Chichester, started for that place. On the way he learnt of the sack of the Harappa tahsil, and that the whole country down to Tulamba in Multán was in open insurrection. Next day he was joined by Captain Paton from Gugera with the whole of his infantry and the three guns. On the 25th Harappa was reached, and then information was received that Captain Chamberlain who had marched with a party of cavalry from Multán, was surrounded by the rebels in the *serái* at Chichbáwatni who were about to attack him. On the 26th Colonel Paton's force advanced from Harappa ; the insurgents were met with about two miles from that place. They were dispersed by artillery fire, and no very effective pursuit appears to have been made. The force then marched to Chichâwatni, where it halted several days. It was reinforced on the 28th by fresh detachments from Lahore under Captains Snow and MacAndrew. On the 30th Colonel Paton's force returned towards Gugera after leaving garrisons at Chichâwatni and Harappa. On the way an unsatisfactory skirmish with the rebels took place in which Captain Snow was wounded. At Gugera the force was joined by a party of the Lahore Light Horse. In the early part of October some ineffectual operations were carried out on the north side of the Rávi against the Fattiánás, Murdánás, &c., who had collected in the dense Jalli jungles after being joined by the Bhainiwáls and Baghelás, who had previously aided the Káthiás in thoroughly sacking Kamália. Meanwhile the Kharrals submitted and the Wattús returned to their villages, but the tribes assembled at Jalli and the Káthiás broke across the *bár* towards the Sutlej, and concentrated near Jamlera and Lakhoke, Joiya villages. There they were brought to action and defeated. By the 4th November the insurrection was over, and the force employed in its suppression broke up. The Joiyás, even now a turbulent tribe, had risen and murdered an English officer, Lieutenant Neville, who was travelling on the Sutlej. They also plundered Kabúla. Their leader, Lukmán, behaved in the most ludicrous manner, and looked heartily ashamed of himself when twitted by the people about his conduct.

Chapter II.

History.

The Mutiny of 1857.

Claims for compensation for property destroyed or plundered by the insurgents were admitted to the extent of Rs. 5,22,104 ; of this nearly three lakhs was on account of the sack of Kamália alone. Against this, plundered property to the value of Rs. 1,18,000 was recovered and restored to the owners. The result of the insurrection was not such as to encourage similar attempts. The leaders were executed or transported, and many persons sentenced to other punishments. Over four lakhs of rupees were realized from the insurgent tribes by fine or by confiscation and sale of property, much of which consisted of cattle. It is more pleasant to record the names of those who were conspicuous for their loyalty, and were rewarded accordingly ; they are—Bábás Khem Singh and Sampúran Singh ; Sarfaráz Khan, Kharral Chief of Kamália ; Kanhaya, Khatri ; Dhara Singh ; Jíva Khan, lambardár of Akbar, father of Hussain Bakhsh, at present Zaildár; Sirdár Shah ; Máchhi Singh, Arora, of Kaliána, father of the present Zaildár Hukam Singh ; Gulám Ali, Chishti of Tibbi, father of Aláyár at present a man of influence in those parts ; Jamiyat Singh, Khatri ; and Murád Shah. Immediately after the insurrection roads were made for military purposes, and additional police were entertained. Since then much jungle has broken up, and a taste for agriculture has to some extent developed. The present generation has grown up since the mutiny days, but it is more or less imbued with the memories of unsuccessful revolt and its evils. This combined with the quieting and steadying effect of a gradually more organized and generally more effective administration has turned the inclinations of even the more turbulent tribes towards peaceful pursuits. Some of them would probably not hesitate to create a disturbance were the firm hand of British authority removed, but the majority of the agricultural tribes are now loyal and well-disposed.

Character of seasons : Famines.

In 1874 Mr. Purser thus noticed famines and the nature of the seasons :—

"Mr. Saunders has stated that 'intelligent agriculturists admit that rain is more frequent than it was during the Sikh rule' in the Lahore district ; they certainly do not admit that here. They talk of the time when grass used to grow high enough to hide the cattle grazing. Now-a-days people are very glad to get grass high enough to hide a hare. But intelligent agriculturists are the last people in the world to be believed. It is, however, a notorious fact that for a long period, from 1861 to 1871, there was an unusual number of bad seasons. If the increase or decrease of vegetation has anything to say to the rainfall it is obvious that in this district, where cultivation has fallen off, and where the jungle was being cleared away by tens-of-thousands of acres, there is no reason to expect the rainfall to be larger than it was. From records in the district office and personal knowledge I have prepared a statement showing the character of the seasons from 1858-59 to 1872-73. The letters G. A. I. and B. stand for 'good,' 'average,' 'inferior,' and 'bad' :—

Chapter II.

History.

Character of seasons: Famines.

Year.		Character of seasons.
1858-59	I	Average rainfall. Crops injured by hail and rain in April.
1859-60	I	Rainfall below average. Harvest average. Vast numbers of cattle died.
1860-61	B	Rainfall below average. Pasturage scanty. Harvest middling. Famine year.
1861-62	A	Rain opportune. Harvest average, except in canal villages. Said to have failed there
1862-63	G	Rain abundant. Harvest good. Cotton injured, especially in Pákpattan. Attributed to curse of Bába Fard.
1863-64	I	Rain scanty. *Kharif* harvest poor. Cattle disease epidemic in autumn. Good average spring harvest owing to unusual inundations, especially on Rávi.
1864-65	B	Rain failed both harvests. Many cattle died of starvation. Wheat good. Gram destroyed by unseasonable inundations.
1865-66	G	Seasonable rains. Excellent spring harvest.
1866-67	I	Rain scanty. *Kharif* poor. *Rabi* average. Grass scanty.
1867-68	A	Rain apparently average. *Kharif* good. *Rabi* below average. Cattle better off than in previous year.
1868-69	B	Rain scanty. *Kharif* bad. Grass scarce. *Rabi* fair.
1869-70	G	Heavy rain. Winter showers scanty. On whole, good year.
1870-71	A	Fair for crops : bad for grass. On whole, not good.
1871-72	B	Bad for crops and grass. Good floods on rivers. Khánwah failed
1872-73	A	Heavy autumn rains. Winter rains failed. Heavy showers in May 1873 did some injury to crops. *Jowár* a general failure. Grass good.

"During these 15 years there have been four average, three good, four inferior, and four bad. The great famines do not appear to have spared this district. The principal were Tituniwála, Lukiwála, and Murkanwála famines during the Sikh times, and that of 1860-61, during British rule. The Tituniwála famine occurred in A. D. 1783 (*san chálís*), and was so called from a black beetle *titún* that was produced in abundance in the dung of cattle, and devoured by them in turn. The Lukiwála famine happened in A. D. 1813, and the Murkanwála in A. D. 1833. They derive their names from grasses that sprang up abundantly when rain did come at last. The famine of 1860-61 was severely felt. Many cattle died, and it is said to have permanently raised the price of stock."

The agricultural characteristics of each of the last 10 years 1888-89 to 1897-98 inclusive are very briefly summarizeed in the following table :—

Chapter II.

History.

Character of seasons : Famines.

Year.	Kharíf.	Rabi.	Remarks.
1888-89	Average ...	Average ...	Summer rains fair. Winter rains good. Sailáb abundant Some damage by hail and by rain in May.
1889-90	Average ..	Average ...	Summer rains good. Sailáb rather short. Winter rain deficient.
1890-91	Good	Good	Summer rain full, but ceased early. Winter rain commenced early.
1891-92	Below average	Inferior ...	Autumn and winter rains short.
1892-93	Good	Excellent ...	Autumn and winter rains good. Sailáb favourable.
1893-94	Average ...	Superior ...	Early summer rains good, deficient in August. Winter rains good. Sailáb good.
1894-95	Inferior ...	Below average ..	Summer rains fair. Winter rains poor. Sailáb good, but yield poor on the Rávi.
1895-96	Bad	Inferior ...	Summer rains scanty. Winter rains late, but fairly abundant. Sailáb failed.
1896-97	Bad	Below average...	Summer rains poor. Winter rains good on the whole. Sailáb failed, yield good.
1897-98	Above average	Average ...	Summer rains late, but abundant. Winter rains fair. Sailáb fairly good.

The three inferior years 1894-95 to 1896-97 coming in succession, to a considerable extent affected adversely the general agricultural prosperity of the district. This was to some extent remedied by the favourable character of 1897-98, but unfortunately the current year 1898-99 promises to be, in the Rávi tahsíl at any rate, not much better than 1896-97. In the latter year the adverse agricultural conditions which resulted in a famine in many parts of India, caused more or less pronounced distress in this district. The following amounts were expended on charitable relief :—

	Rs.
For purchase of bullocks	7,235
Ditto of seed	14,189
Miscellaneous to invalids	41
Total ...	21,465

Chapter II, History.

Character of seasons: Famines.

In addition to the above, the following sums were advanced as *takávi* loans :—

	Rs.
For construction of wells	1,710
For purchase of seed and bullocks	15,580

Changes of boundary.

Since the revision of tahsíls in 1865 several villages on each side of the Rávi have been transferred from the Gugera to the Montgomery tahsíl, 19 villages and a large area of waste land have been transferred from tahsíl Pákpattan to tahsíl Dipálpur, and other villages from the same tahsíl to Bahâwalpur by river action. Minor changes of this nature are of constant occurrence in the banks of the Sutlej. The changes of head-quarters and tahsíl divisions have already been noticed at pages 45 and 46.

District Officers.

The following table shows the officers who have held charge of the district since 1873. No similar information is forthcoming for the preceding years :—

From.	To.	Name of District Officer in charge.
	4th November 1873	Mr. T. W. Smyth.
5th November 1873 ..	3rd May 1875 ...	Lieutenant-Colonel F. M. Birch.
4th May 1875 ...	19th June 1875 ...	Mr. F. E. Moore.
20th June 1875 ...	25th February 1876	Lieutenant-Colonel F. M. Birch.
26th February 1876...	29th July 1876 ...	Mr. M. Macauliffe.
30th July 1876 ...	1st October 1876 ...	Mr. A. H. Benton.
2nd October 1876 ...	26th June 1877 ...	Mr. M. Macauliffe.
27th June 1877 ...	30th July 1877 ...	Mr. G. L. Smith.
31st July 1877 ...	16th May 1878 ...	Mr. M. Macauliffe.
17th May 1878 ...	23rd December 1878	Lieutenant-Colonel H. V. Riddell.
24th December 1878	24th January 1879 ...	M. A. R. Bulman.
25th January 1879 ...	3rd February 1879 ...	Lieutenant-Colonel H. V. Riddell.
4th February 1879 ..	29th March 1879 ...	Mr. A. R. Bulman.
30th March 1879 ...	27th March 1881 ...	Lieutenant-Colonel H. V. Riddell.
28th March 1881 ...	11th May 1881 ...	Mr. H. W. Steel.
12th May 1881 ...	14th March 1882 ...	Lieutenant-Colonel H. V. Riddell.
15th March 1882 ...	30th April 1882 ...	Major R. Bartholomew.
1st May 1882 ...	21st August 1882 ...	Major H. J. Lawrence.
22nd August 1882 ...	13th November 1882	Mr. G. L. Smith.
14th November 1882	16th March 1883 ...	Mr. G. Knox.
17th March 1883 ...	12th August 1883 ...	Major C. McNeile.
13th August 1883 ...	12th November 1883	Mr. J. G. Silcock.
13th November 1883	3rd March 1884 ...	Major C. McNeile.
4th March 1884 ...	6th August 1884 ...	Mr. T. O. Wilkinson.
7th August 1884 ...	25th June 1885 ...	Mr. C. E. Gladstone.
26th June 1885 ...	17th April 1886 ...	Mr. T. Troward.
18th April 1886 ...	29th April 1886 ...	Mr. J. G. M. Rennie.
30th April 1886 ...	19th April 1887 ...	Mr. T. Troward.
20th April 1887 ...	8th September 1887	Mr. A. H. Diack.
9th September 1887...	8th February 1888...	Mr. T. Troward.
9th February 1888 ...	31st January 1889 ...	Mr. T. J. Kennedy.
1st February 1889 ...	6th March 1889 ...	Colonel C. Beadon.
7th March 1889 ...	5th May 1890 ...	Mr. T. J. Kennedy.
6th May 1890 ...	10th October 1890 ...	Sardar Muhammad Afzal Khan.
11th October 1890 ...	30th March 1891 ...	Mr. T. J. Kennedy.
31st March 1891 ...	24th November 1891	Mr. H. Scott-Smith.

Chapter II.
History.
District Officers.

From.	To.	Name of District Officer in charge.
25th November 1891	23rd February 1892	Mr. J. M. Douie.
24th February 1892...	21st March 1892 ...	Mr. R. M. Dane.
22nd March 1892 ...	27th August 1892 ..	Mr. H. Scott-Smith.
28th August 1892 ...	9th November 1892	Mr. A. I. Harrison.
10th November 1892	13th April 1893 ...	Mr. T. J. Kennedy.
14th April 1893 ..	13th July 1893 ...	Mr. A. I. Harrison.
14th July 1893. ..	1st December 1893...	Mr. T. J. Kennedy.
2nd December 1893 ..	9th December 1893 ..	Captain C. P. Egerton.
10th December 1893	14th May 1894 ...	Mr. T. J. Kennedy.
15th May 1894 ...	21st October 1894 ..	Mr. P. J. Fagan.
22nd October 1894 ...	10th April 1895 ..	Mr. W. C. Renouf.
11th April 1895 ...	10th May 1895 ...	Mr. P. J. Fagan.
11th May 1895 ...	11th February 1897	Diwán Narendra Náth.
12th February 1897...	18th November 1898	Abdul Ghafúr Khan of Zaida.
19th November 1898		Mr. A. J. W. Kitchin.

General review of the past of the district.

From the above sketch of the history of the district it will be seen that there is no prosperous past on which to look back with pleasure. From the earliest time the district has been inhabited by robber tribes; for centuries it has been a prey to anarchy and savage warfare; it has been traversed by the most ferocious and sanguinary conquerors of whom we read in history. Nature itself has affected the district unfavourably. Tracts of country once irrigated from branches of the large rivers had to be abandoned when the water ceased to flow. Every inducement has in the past been given to the people to adopt a restless roving life. That they should have clung to their old habits is not surprising.

Development since annexation.

Some conception of the development of the district since it came into our hands may be gathered from Table No. II, which gives some of the leading statistics for five yearly periods, so far as they are available, while most of the other tables appended to this work give comparative figures for the last few years. In the case of Table No. II, it is probable that the figures are not always strictly comparable, their basis not being the same in all cases from one period to another. But the figures may be accepted as showing in general terms the nature and extent of the advance made.

The development has been on the whole steady, but, as can only be expected in a tract where agricultural conditions are so fluctuating, and so dependent on precarious river floods, and the comparatively small but at the same time indispensable assistance given by the scanty rainfall to well-irrigated cultivation, that development has not always gone on at an uniformly rapid rate. For really permanent agricultural development all depends on the extension of irrigation by canals; without this the district must always remain in a backward condition compared with other

Chapter II.

History.

Development since annexation.

neighbouring parts of the province. A sufficiency of grazing has hitherto been an element of prime importance in the economic prosperity of a district, a great part of the wealth of which has consisted in its cattle. But there can be little doubt that the people are learning more or less rapidly to prefer agriculture to a pastoral and nomadic life, and the number of cattle will in all probability more or less continuously decrease in future years.

CHAPTER III.

THE PEOPLE.

SECTION A.—STATISTICAL.

Chapter III, A.

Statistical.

Description of population.

Table No. V gives separate statistics for each tahsíl and for the whole district, of the distribution over towns and villages, over area, and among houses and families, while the number of houses in each town is shown in Table No. XLIII. The statistics for the district as a whole give the following figures. Further information will be found in Chapter II of the Census Report of 1891 :—

		1881	1891
Percentage of total population who live in villages	Persons...	94·47	96·2
	Males ...	94·39	96·0
	Females	94·62	96·4
Average rural population per village		250	258
Average total population per village and town		264	268
Number of villages per 100 square miles		29	30
Average distance from village to village, in miles		2·00	1·96
Density of population per square mile of — Total area	Total population	77	87
	Rural population	72	88
Cultivated area	Total population	764	735
	Rural population	738	677
Culturable area	Total population	545	129
	Rural population	527	106
Number of resident families per occupied house	Villages	1·14	1·27
	Towns	1·23	1·46
Number of persons per occupied house	Villages	5·70	6·47
	Towns	5·64	6·94
Number of persons per resident family	Villages	5·01	5·08
	Towns	4·58	4·75

It has already been explained that nearly three-fifths of the total area is practically uninhabited, being occupied only by nomad pastoral tribes, and deserted even by them during certain seasons of the year.

Migration and birth-place of population.

Table No. VI shows the principal districts and States with which the district has exchanged population, the number of migrants in each direction, and the distribution of immigrants by tahsíls. Further details will be found in Table No. XI and in abstracts Nos. 64, 65, 71, 72, 77-80, 83, of the Provincial Census Report for 1891, while the whole subject is discussed at length in Part I, Chapter X, of the same report. The total gain and loss to the district by migration as returned at the censuses of 1881 and 1891 are shown comparatively in the table on the margin. The total number of residents born

PROPORTION PER MILE OF TOTAL POPULATION.

	Gain: census of 1881.	*Gain: census of* 1891.	*Loss: census of* 1881.	*Loss: census of* 1891.
Persons ...	89	97	99	115
Males ...	91	98	101	118
Females ...	87	96	98	113

Chapter III, A.

Statistical.

Migration and birth-place of population.

out of the district by the census of 1891 was 48,359, of whom 26,311, or 54 per cent., were males, and 22,048 females. The corresponding percentage of males by the census of 1881 was 55. The number of people born in the district and living in other parts of the Punjab including Feudatory States is 57,447, of whom 31,509, or 55 per cent., are males and 25,938 females. The corresponding percentage of males by the census of 1881 was 50.

The migration according to the census returns of 1891 has been principally to and from the following districts of the Punjab and the Baháwalpur State :—

District.	Immigration from			Emigration to		
	Males.	Females.	Total.	Males.	Females.	Total.
Ferozepur	3,134	3,285	6,419	5,593	4,473	10,066
Multán	1,418	1,174	2,592	4,193	3,037	7,230
Jhang	2,573	1,993	4,566	1,418	1,027	2,445
Lahore	8,106	8,452	16,558	8,629	8,271	16,900
Amritsar	1,843	1,135	2,978	281	169	450
Baháwalpur	2,764	2,575	5,339	9,390	7,716	17,106

The figures below show the general distribution of the population by birth-place :—

Born in.	Proportion per mille of resident population.								
	Rural population.			*Urban population.*			*Total population.*		
	Males.	Females.	Persons.	Males.	Females.	Persons.	Males.	Females.	Persons.
The district ...	908	906	907	760	857	802	902	904	906
The province ..	996	998	997	971	986	978	995	997	993
India	1,000	1,000	1,000	996	1,000	998	1,000	1,000	1,000
Asia	1,000	1,000	1,000	1,000	1,000	1,000	1,000	1,000	1,000

Chapter III, A.

Statistical.

Migration and birth-place of population.

It will be seen that as regards both immigration to and emigration from the district the males have been slightly in excess among the migrants; thus pointing to the conclusion that these movements of population have been of a permanent character.

The following remarks on the migration to and from Montgomery are taken from the Census Report of 1881 :—

"Of late years canal irrigation in the Montgomery district has received an enormous impetus from the construction of new inundation cuts, and immigrants have been attracted from the surrounding districts, and more especially from Lahore. Yet the similar extension of irrigation in Lahore, Ferozepore, Multán and Baháwalpur has caused extensive emigration, which has on the whole exceeded the immigration; though if the large emigration to Baháwalpur which took place when the State came under English management were deducted, the movement would be markedly in the opposite direction. The moderate percentage of males among both emigrants and immigrants shows how largely permanent the migration has been, though a portion of it is doubtless due to the movement of herds to the river valleys in consequence of the drought which preceded the Census."

A good deal of the immigration from Ferozepore, Lahore, Amritsar and Baháwalpur shown in the returns of the last census (1891) is due to the formation of the Sohág-Pára Colony in the former extensive waste areas in the western portion of Dipálpur and in the central and eastern portions of Pákpattan.

Increase and decrease of population.

The figures in the statement below show the population of the district, as it stood at the four enumerations of 1855, 1868, 1881 and 1891 :—

	Census.	Persons.	Males.	Females.	Density per square mile.
Actuals.	1855	308,020	175,633	132,387	55
	1868	360,445	200,567	159,878	64
	1881	426,529	232,947	193,582	77
	1891	499,521	269,613	229,908	87
Percentages.	1868 on 1855 ...	117·0	114·2	120·8	117
	1881 on 1868 ...	118·3	116·1	121·1	120
	1891 on 1881 ...	117·1	115·7	118·8	113

The figures given above for 1855 refer to the district as it then stood. Between that year and 1868 A.D. a tract with a population of 1,826 persons was lost, and another with a population of 3,302 gained; so that the population with which the comparison should be made is really 309,496. The figures of 1868 have been corrected for transfers of territory. It will be seen that the annual increase per 10,000 of population between 1881 and 1891 was 157 for males, 188 for females and 171 for persons, at which rate the male population would be doubled in 45·6 years, the female in 37·2, and the total population in

Chapter III, A.

Statistical.

Increase and decrease of population.

40·6 years. Supposing the same rate of increase to hold good for the next ten years, the population for each year would be in hundreds.

Year.	Persons.	Males.	Females.
1891	4.995	2,696	2,299
1892	5,081	2,738	2,343
1893	5,169	2,781	2,388
1894	5,260	2.826	2,434
1895	5,348	2,868	2,480
1896	5,437	2,912	2,525
1897	5,534	2,959	2,575
1898	5.629	3.005	2,624
1899	5,723	3,052	2.674
1900	5,825	3.099	2,726
1901	5,923	3,149	2,777

It seems probable that the rate of increase will be sustained. Part of the increase is doubtless due to increased accuracy of enumeration at each successive enumerations, a good test of which is afforded by the percentage of males to persons, which was 57·02 in 1855, 55·62 in 1868, 54·61, in 1881 and 54 in 1891. But the loss by emigration which marked the period between 1868 and 1881 will probably not continue, while the district is an exceptionally healthy one.

The percentages of increase in total, rural and urban population, between 1881 and 1891, were as follows :—

	Total population	Rural.	Urban.
Persons	17·1	17·2	14·4
Males	15·7	15·9	12·7
Females	18·5	18·8	16·5

The proportionate increase in urban population has thus been smaller than in rural : and the same was the case for the period intervening between the census of 1868 and that of 1881. This is probably due to the attraction exercised upon the commercial classes of the towns by the great trading centres of Lahore and Multán, now that railways have made communication easy and local centres less necessary and important. The populations of individual towns at the respective enumerations are shown under their several headings in Chapter VI. Within the district the increase of population for the various tahsíls is shown in the following table :—

Tahsil.	Total population.				Percentage of population.		
	1855.	1868.	1881.	1891.	1868 on 1855.	1881 on 1868.	1891 on 1881.
Montgomery	72,940	76,316	94,127	98,64[illegible]	104·8	123	99
Gugera	81,067	95,410	99,200	113,447	117·7	104	114
Dipálpur	102,281	129,839	154,500	180,455	127·0	119	117
Pákpattan	53,208	57,735	78,612	111,971	208·5	136	142
Total District ...	309,496	359,80[illegible]	426,529	499,521	116·13	119	117

Chapter III, A.

Statistical.

Increase and decrease of population.

The table in the margin shows the distribution of the populations of 1868, 1881 and 1891 over the three main tracts into which the district may be divided:—A, that irrigated by canals; B, that inundated by rivers; C, that neither irrigated nor inundated. The increase that took place in the population of the district as a whole between 1855 and 1868 was confined entirely to the tracts styled, respectively, A and C. In tract B there was an actual decrease in each of the four tahsíls.

Tahsil.		Tract A.	Tract B.	Tract C.
Montgomery ...	1868 ...	...	63,078	13,330
	1881 ...	...	75,484	4,113
	1891 ...	...	76,104	5,890
Gugera ...	1868 ...	...	55,933	38,471
	1881 ...	...	58,2[illegible]7	15,689
	1891 ...	...	69,5[illegible]6	20,476
Dipálpur ...	1868 ...	65,654	28,081	36,913
	1881 ...	118,341	23,592	8,102
	1891 ...	135,11[illegible]	28,254	12,255
Pákpattan ...	1868 ...	2,840	17,451	87,441
	1881 ...	30,493	38,918	6,850
	1891 ...	42,286	41,459	13,555
Total ...	1868 ...	68,494	164,543	126,155
	1881 ...	148,834	196,291	34,704
	1891	177,399	215,513	52,176

Mr. Purser noted that the population remained stationary between 1855 and 1868 in the cis-Rávi *sailába* tracts of Montgomery and in the well-irrigated Shergarh circle in Dipálpur; otherwise there was a general falling off in the *sailába* tracts, and a considerable increase in the well-irrigated and canal circles. The increase in the parts of Dipálpur and Pákpattan irrigated by the canals was especially large. It was in these parts that most of the grants of waste lands were made. The increase which took place in population between 1881 and 1891 was confined almost entirely to the Dipálpur and Pákpattan tahsíls; the increase was both absolutely and relatively largest in the latter. Canal

* These figures do not agree with the published figures for the whole district. They are taken from the registers in the District office, and are the best figures now available. The difference is very slight.

Chapter III, A.

Statistical.

Increase and decrease of population.

irrigation has been developed and improved in both, but mainly in Pákpattan by the construction of the new Sohág-Pára Canal, and this has, of course, led to a marked increase in population. The number of new colonists in the Sohág-Péra Colony at the last census was 13,105.

In Montgomery a decrease of population took place, and in Gugera the increase was moderate. Montgomery had evidently not recovered from the crippling effects of the loss of river *sailáb*, which in Gugera had to some extent been counteracted by a development of canal irrigation.

Births and deaths.

Table No. XI shows the total number of births and deaths registered in the district for the eleven years from 1887 to 1897. The distribution of the total deaths and of the deaths from fever for these eleven years over the twelve months of the year is shown in Tables Nos. XIA and XIB. The annual birth-rates per mille, calculated on the population of 1891, have been as shown below :—

	1887.	1888.	1889.	1890.	1891.	1892.	1893.	1894.	1895.	1896.	1897.
Males	26	32	38	37	34	36	31	43	44	41	39
Females	27	33	39	37	36	37	32	45	47	45	42
Persons	26	33	39	37	35	36	31	44	46	43	40

The figures below show the annual death-rates per mille since 1887, calculated on the population of 1891 :—

	1887.	1888.	1889.	1890.	1891.	1892.	1893.	1894.	1895.	1896.	1897.
Males	18	21	28	29	24	57	30	27	21	24	21
Females	18	21	29	30	25	59	29	27	22	25	24
Persons	18	21	28	30	24	58	29	27	22	24	23

The monthly rates from 1891 to 1897 are shown at page 21.

The registration is still imperfect, though it is yearly improving ; but the figures always fall short of the facts, and the fluctuations probably correspond, allowing for a regular increase due to improved registration, fairly closely with the actual fluctuations in the births and deaths. Such further details as to birth and death-rates in individual towns as are available will be found in Table No. XLIV, and under the headings of the several towns in Chapter VI.

Chapter III, A.

Statistical.

Age.

The figures for age, sex and civil condition are given in great detail in various tables of the Census Report for 1891; while the numbers of the sexes for each religion will be found in Table No. VII appended to the present work. The age statistics must be taken subject to limitations, which will be found fully discussed in Chapter V of the Census Report. Their value rapidly diminishes as the numbers dealt with become smaller; and it is unnecessary here to give actual figures, or any statistics for tahsils. The following figures show the distribution by age of every 10,000 of the population according to the census figures:—

Chapter III, A.

Statistical.

Age.

	Under 1 year.	1 year.	2 years.	3 years.	4 years.	Total 0-4.	5-9.	10-14.	15-19.	20-24.
Persons	496	363	357	332	379	1,948	1,551	946	944	777
Males	464	354	330	379	363	1,852	1,525	975	946	777
Females	533	373	378	354	397	2,060	1,581	911	943	778
	25-29	30-34	35-39	40-44	45-49	50-54	55-59	60 and over	...	...
Persons	874	593	647	318	468	183	371	380	...	...
Males	842	606	633	328	488	201	410	410	...	...
Females	912	577	664	307	444	161	322	341	...	...

Chapter III, A.

Statistical.

Sex.

Population.		Villages.	Towns.	Total.
All religions	1855 ...	...	...	5,702
	1868 ...	...	...	5,565
	1881 ...	5,450	5,585	5,461
	1891 ...	5,388	5,630	5,397
Hindús	...1881 ...	5,405	5,509	5,417
Sikhs ...	.. 1881 ...	5,924	...	5,958
Musalmáns	.. 1881 ...	5,449	5,593	5,455
Hindús	...1891 ...	5,374	5,456	5,380
Sikhs ...	...1891 ..	5,784	6,702	5,773
Musalmans	...1891 ...	5,377	5,693	5,387

The number of males among every 10,000 of both sexes is shown in the margin. The decrease at each successive enumeration is almost certainly due to greater accuracy of enumeration.

In the Census of 1891 the number of females per 1,000 males in the earlier years of life was found to be as shown in the margin. Infanticide is not now practised directly, but among some of the Rávi tribes who undoubtedly practised it in the past there is probably no very great solicitude for infant female life.

Years of life.	All religions.	Hindús.	Musalmáns.
Under 1 year	980	1.011	968
1 year	898	920	901
2 years	950	954	954
3 "	975	943	989
4 "	938	915	942

Civil condition.

The figures for civil condition are given in Table No. X, which shows the actual number of single, married, and widowed for each sex in each religion, and also the distribution by civil condition of the total number of each sex in each age-period. The Deputy Commissioner wrote in 1881 as follows in his Census Report for the district :—" Early marriages are not the custom in this district. Girls are married between the ages of 15 and 20 ; but it is not at all uncommon for a woman, whether Hindu or Muhammadan, to be still unmarried at the age of 25. Perhaps the lateness of marriage accounts for the prevalence of the crime of running away with another man's wife that is so common in Montgomery." A comparison of the figures for age-periods given by the last census as compared with those of 1881 tends to show that the average age of marriage both for males and females, is somewhat lower than it was formerly.

Table No. XII shows the number of insane, blind, deaf-mutes and lepers in the district. The proportions per 10,000 of either sex for each of these infirmities are shown in the margin. Tables XII, XIII, XIV and XV of the Census Report of 1891 give further details of the castes of the infirm. The climate and health of the district have been already noticed

Infirmity.	Males.	Females.
Insane ...	6	4
Blind ...	34	32
Deaf and dumb.	12	7
Leprous ...	1	...

Chapter III, B.

Social and Religious Life.

Infirmities. Sanitation.

at page 21. As regards sanitation this district does not differ in any marked way from others ; but the general dryness of the climate probably renders the prevailing insanitary habits more innocuous than in moister climates. Villages are dirty as elsewhere ; manure is stored close under the walls, and the usual excavation pits are common. The greatest amount of sickness, mostly fever, occurs near the canals, and where there has been much river inundation. Small-pox and pneumonia are fairly common in the cold weather.

The people are, with comparatively few exceptions, an excessively hardy set and abstemious, except in the use of tobacco ; they are also fond of opium.

European and Eurasian population.

The figures given below show the composition of the Christian population, and the respective numbers who returned their birth-place and their language as European. They are taken from Supplementary Table A, Part II, and Tables Nos. X and XI of the Census Report for 1891 :—

	Details.	Males.	Females.	Persons.
Races of Christian population.	Europeans and Americans ...	37	24	61
	Eurasians ...	7	4	11
	Native Christians ...	6	7	13
	Total Christians ...	50	35	85
Language.	English ...	41	28	69
	Other European languages ...	1	...	1
	Total European languages ...	42	28	70
Birth-place.	British Isles ...	13	2	15
	Other European countries ..	1		1
	Total European countries ...	14	2	16

The figures for the races of Christians are discussed in Chapter XI of the Census Report. The distribution of European and Eurasian Christians by tahsíls is shown in Table No VII.

SECTION B.—SOCIAL AND RELIGIOUS LIFE.

Types of villages.

There are three types of villages—the Kamboh type, the Jat type, and the Aráin type. To one or other of these most of the villages in the district may be referred. In the Kamboh type of

Chapter III, B.

Social and Religious Life:

Types of villages.

village the houses are solidly built of mud, and have flat roofs. There is a small yard in front of the house with mud walls. The houses are close together. The whole village has a compact look. In the Jat type of village the houses sometimes are built of mud, sometimes they are made of plaited switches. Sometimes they have a mud roof, but generally they are thatched. If not built in a square, the houses are scattered all over the village site. There are no walled yards, but there are huge enclosures for keeping cattle about each house. These enclosures are very simple, as a rule. A few forked branches with the forks sticking up are planted in the ground, and horizontal branches are placed on these, their ends resting in the forks. The Aráin type of village partakes of the characters of the other two, modified to some extent. Sometimes the Kamboh characteristics predominate, sometimes the Jat features are more marked. There are no walls round the villages nor ditches, as in Hindustán, nor thorn hedges. But the houses are built with their fronts facing inwards; and their backs form as it were an outer wall. There are generally some trees about the village; and occasionally the fields are fenced along the roads leading out of the *abádi*. So altogether stealing cattle out of a village is not so simple as might be thought. Human habitations are of five kinds—(1) *pakhi*: this means primarily a screen of *til*:* and a shed made of such screens is also so called. It is commonly used by wandering tribes, and by people grazing cattle in the *bár*; (2) *chhán*: this is a shed with thatched roof and thatched sides: (3) *jhuga*: a shed with thatched roof and sides made of plaited *kána** or switches; (4) *khudi*: a house with mud walls and thatched roof; (5) *kotha*: this is a house with walls and a flat mud roof. The walls are usually built of large cubes of sun-dried mud called *dhimán*. These are made by watering a piece of ground and ploughing it. It is then watered again and ploughed, and levelled while under water. The cubes are cut with a sickle, and when dry are dug out with a *kahi*. Walls built of these blocks are plastered with mud.

Houses.

Description of a village.

On coming to a village the traveller will sometimes see in the outskirts a number of little children amusing themselves with a *chachíngal*, which is a horizontal bar, moving round a vertical post about two feet high. Here the infant villager practises walking. More common is a piece of wood, a portion of the trunk of a tree, about two feet long and eighteen inches in diameter, with a bit hollowed out on one side, so as to form a handle by which the block may be grasped. This is the *budgar* or dumb-bell, with which the athletes of the hamlet amuse themselves in the evening. Further on, at the first houses, he is stopped by a rude-gate (*phalha*) made of thorns fastened to a couple of cross-bars: while this is being removed, we may observe a cord passing across the road with a square piece of wood not unlike a prisoner's ticket, covered with hieroglyphics, suspended in the middle. This is a

* Part of the *sarr* plant (see page 24).

Chapter III, B.

Social and Religious Life.

Description of a village

charm (*tawiz*) to keep off cattle-disease. A holy *fakir* gets some small sum annually in bullion for providing these charms. They are the Hindustáni *túna*, and are in great request in times of murrain. If the village is of a good size, there will probably be a flour mill (*kharás*) worked by one bullock, or if there is much custom, by a pair. Near the wall of each house is a small earthen oven, on the top of which a pot of milk preparatory to churning will be simmering. The pot and the oven are called *dúdh-kárhni*. Several other earthen pots are hung upon a stick with branches called *nihni*. Several earthen cylinders or oblong receptacles for grain (*bharola*), five or six feet high, will be ranged in the front yard. A baby will be sprawling in a cradle (*pingha*) swung to a bar under a shed; and the women of the family will be spinning thread close by. In the lane may be seen a raised platform (*munna*), on which the master of the house takes his ease on hot nights, if his roof is thatched, or he too lazy to go to the top if it is flat. A little further on, a fire is crackling in the public oven of the village (*máchhi*), and a crowd of women with dishes containing dough stand round chattering till their turn comes to get their cakes baked. A couple of huge cylinders, 12 or 15 feet high, in shape like a conical shot, are seen near the house of the village money-lender (*kurár* or sahukar). These are made of thick bands of *kána*, fastened together by pegs and plastered with mud. These are called *palla*, and contain the grain given to the money-lender in repayment, with compound interest, of cash advanced, or more commonly in partial settlement of the *zamindár's* perennial account. The autocrat himself will be sitting on the ground, working a cotton-gin (*belna*) with the utmost vigour, while near him several bedsteads (*chárpáis*) are standing in the sun covered with cotton drying. Going out of the village, a plain mud building with three pinnacles on the roof, a platform in front strewed with grass and surrounded by a mud enclosure, is seen. Several water-pots stand on the edge of the platform. Often there is an oven for heating water. This is the *masít* or mosque. If the proprietors of the village belong to a pious tribe, half-a-dozen little boys will, in the forenoon, be seen sitting on the platform in company with their preceptor, the village *mullah*, swinging themselves backwards and forwards and repeating the Koran at the top of their voices. The book itself lies before them on a stand. If we go all through the village we probably come across a few weavers at work; a carpenter is making the cog-wheels of a well; there are no carts; but several nags of sorts, by the vigorous use of their lungs, insist on being noticed. At certain seasons of the year there will be a pen of young lambs at the *máchhi's* house. At other times the roofs will be red with pepper pods drying in the sun. The stacks of dried dung cakes used for fuel must not be forgotten; nor the village dogs. There is not much else to see in an ordinary village, and some of the things mentioned here will not be found in most. There are no tanks and no large trees such as are found on the other side of the Sutlej. But, in return, there are no pigs and no peacocks.

Chapter III, B.

Social and Religious Life.

Nomad encampments.

Besides regular villages, the district contains *rahnás* or permanent encamping-grounds which deserve a few remarks. The encamping-grounds are scattered all over the vast space which intervenes between the cultivation on the banks of the Rávi and that on the Sutlej. They generally consist of a large circle of sheds which form the habitation of the cattle herds of the pastoral tribes during a large portion of the year. The centre is occupied at nights by the herds, and generally contains a narrow and deep well from which water can only be obtained with much labour, and apparently in very insufficient quantities. The immense herds of cattle which roam about the centre of the Bári Doáb and used to do so in the Rechna Doáb until the colonization, which is still in progress was commenced, remain in the vicinity of these *rahnás* from the commencement of the rains till the end of February. On the approach of the hot season the scanty herbage of these tracts becomes generally insufficient for their support, and they are driven down to the banks of the rivers, where the vegetation, which covers lands thrown up by the floods of the previous year, affords them ample pasturage till the commencement of the next rainy season. The word *rahna* is applied to permanent encamping-grounds, to which the herdsmen regularly resort every season, and which are known by the names of the tribes to whom they have belonged for generations. Temporary stations for a single season are called *bhainis*, and, when the herd is chiefly composed of camels, the encampment is known by the name of *jhok*.

Household furniture.

A list of the furniture and household utensils, with their prices, found in families of average means, is given at page 55 of Mr. Purser's Settlement Report. The total cost as given by him was Rs. 41-6-0 ; it is much the same now, if anything a little higher. No doubt many families manage to get on with less. There are also a number of earthen plates, pots, &c., made by the village potter as part of his contract duties.

Clothing of men.

The clothes worn by natives in this district seem few and simple ; but the more one inquires into the matter, the more hopeless one becomes of ever understanding it. Men invariably wear a turban of white cloth called *pag*, and costing from Rs. 2 to 8 annas; the cloth is often of European manufacture ; they wear shoes costing from Rs. 2 to Re. 1 ; also boys' shoes cost 8 annas a pair. Besides, they have two sheets : one they wear round the upper part of the body, the other is wrapped round the waist, and is either tucked in at the back after being passed between the legs, in which case it is called *dhoti*, or else it is allowed to hang down round the lower part of the body like a tight petticoat, when it is called *majhla*. This is the Hindustani *tahmad*. A *dhoti* is, however, usually of only one breadth and 10 *háths* long ; while a *majhla* is only 6 to 7 *háths* in length, but has two breadths of cloth in it. *Dhotis* are worn by Hindu men ; *majhlás* by Hindús and Muhammadans, men and women. Occasionally a tunic, called *kurta* when worn by men, and *jhagga* when worn by women and children, is seen. But among men of the agricultural tribes its use

Chapter III. B.
Social and Religious Life.
Clothing of men.

may be said to be unknown. The dress worn by Muhammadan and Hindu boys and adults in the cold weather and hot weather, with the prices of the garments, is shown in great detail at page 57 of Mr. Purser's Report. *Múka* is simply the checkered upper sheet worn by boys; it is adout 2 feet by 2¾ feet. It is said to be called also *dola* when worn by Hindus, and *rounta* when worn by Muhammadans. *Khaddar, adhotar, dres,* and *khása* are kinds of cloth. *Lungi* is a sheet woven in checks, generally white and dark blue. The lower *lungi* has a border at one end called *kanni*: the upper *lúngi* has a border at both ends. *Khes* is a cloth woven in a peculiar way. It may be plain or variegated (*dabba*). It has in the latter case usually blue and white checks, and is much worn by Kambohs and Muhammadans.*

Clothing of women.

Women's shoes cost from Re. 1 to 8 annas; girls' shoes the same as boys. Women wear trousers called *suthan* made of *súsí*, a cloth with stripes lengthwise. The ground is usually blue and the stripes red or white, or else they wear a petticoat called *lahinga* or *ghagra*. The former name is more in use by towns-people, the latter by villagers. The *lahinga*, too, is usually made of finer stuff than the *ghagra*. They are both generally dyed red or blue. Sometimes, at the time of dyeing, some parts of the cloth are tied, and so remain uncoloured. On the upper part of the body a boddice is worn, either with or without a *kurti* or *jhagga*. The *kurti* is a shirt with sleeves reaching only half way to the elbows. It may be of any cloth or colour. When worn without the *kurtí*, the boddice is called *choli*. It covers the breasts, and has a slip running further down in front. It has short sleeves, and is tied behind. This is usually worn by Hindus. The *angi* is a boddice worn with the *kurti*, and differs from the *choli* only in having no front slip. Muhammadan women mostly wear this kind of boddice under the *kurti*. Over their heads women wear a shawl. There are several kinds. The most common are as follows: the *phulkári*. The cloth of this is dyed, and then designs are worked on it with silk of different colours with the needle. *Chuni* much the same as *phulkári*, but smaller, and worn by girls. *Salári*: this shawl has two colours, woven in lengthways. *Chakla* is the same as *salári* with broader stripes. *Bhochan* or *dopatta*, if coloured; the colours are printed and not woven in. *Sálu* and *lassa* are dyed a rusty red, called *thandápáni*, and differ chiefly in the kind of cloth of which they are made. Lastly, *shál q. d.* shawl, printed in gaudy colours, and mostly worn by women of the *kamín* class. A statement showing the clothes worn by women and girls, similar to that given for men and boys, will be found at page 59 of Mr. Purser's report. *Chop* is a *phulkári* with flowers on the border only. It is dyed red. *Bágh* is the same as *phulkári*, but the designs are closer together and more numerous. It is not to be suppposed that the *phulkári, chop, bágh* and *bhochan* are all worn at one and the same time by the same person.

* Handbook of Manufactures and Arts of the Punjab (p. 1 *et seq.*) concerning the different kinds of cloth.

Chapter III. B.
Social and Religious Life.
Ornaments.

A woman ought to have the following ornaments. It is a point of family honour to provide them, if possible. Other ornaments are luxuries, these necessaries :—

Silver bracelets (*hathkarián*), costing Rs. 10 to Rs. 30 the pair.

Armlets of silver (*bhawatta* before marriage, *tád* after marriage), costing Rs. 10 to Rs. 12 the pair.

Silver ear-rings (*wálián*), costing Rs. 4 to 5 the set.

Silver ear-drops (*patar*) " " 12 the pair.

Gold nose-ring (*nath*) " " 3 to 20 each.

Bedding.

Bedding consists of a *lef (liháf)* of printed *khaddar*, stuffed with cotton. It has a cover or *ulara*. This is worn over the body; a similar quilt called *tulái* is placed beneath. Another covering is the *dohar*, a coarse cotton sheet with blue border and black stripes lengthwise. Fine blankets (*loi*) are also used; but coarse blankets (*bhura*) are left to farm labourers and other poor people.

Food.

As a rule, the people have their food cooked at home during the cold weather, and at the public oven of the *máchhi* during the hot season. The *máchháni* gets a portion of whatever she bakes, for the cook is generally a female. This wage is called *bhára*. The staple food consists of wheaten cakes. In the cold weather, *jowár*, *chína* or *kangni* generally takes the place of wheat, but if a *zamindár* has wheat, he eats it. *Bájra* and maize are also eaten to a small extent. *Chína* is boiled and used like rice; *kangni* is made into large thick cakes which are palatable enough when hot, but very dry when cold. *Jowár* is also used in the shape of cakes. With these cakes *dál* (the split grain) of gram, *másh*, or *mung*, or vegetables, are eaten. In the hot weather especially, vegetables, chiefly pumpkins of sorts, are used. In the cold weather, turnips, carrots and *ság* (greens) take the place of pumpkins. Besides, all *zamindárs* drink large quantities of milk or butter-milk, generally the latter. Meals are taken twice a day, about 10 A. M. and after sunset. The food is almost always cold. If any food remains over from the evening meal it is eaten in the morning with some butter-milk. Parched gram is occasionally eaten in the afternoon, between the two meals. Butter or *ghi* (clarified butter) is commonly used with the cakes; salt, spices, and *gur* (molasses) are also articles of diet in common use. It is not easy to ascertain the quantity of food which a man consumes per diem. But it is approximately from $\frac{3}{8}$ to $\frac{3}{4}$ of a *sér* of flour, 2 *chitáks* or $\frac{1}{8}$ of a *sér* of *dál*, $\frac{1}{2}$ *chiták* of *ghi*, and from $\frac{1}{2}$ to 1 *sér* of butter-milk or milk, with 8 *máshás* of salt, or 6 pounds per annum. The allowance of salt is rather under the average consumption in the Punjab. The following form will show roughly the amount of food used by a man during the year and its cost :—

Chapter III, B.

Social and Religious Life.

Food.

Articles of food.	Daily allowance.	Total amount used in a year, say	Cost in *sérs* per rupee, say	Total cost, say Rs.	A.	P.
Flour (of various sorts)...	¾ *sér.*	6 mds. 3¼ *sérs.*	20 *sérs.*	13	11	0
Dál ...	⅛ ,,	1 ,, 6 ,,	16 ,,	2	14	0
Milk or butter-milk ...	¾ ,,	6 ,, 3¼ ,,	20 ,,	13	11	0
Butter ...	½ *chiták.*	11⅜ ,,	8 ,,	3	11	0
Salt ...	8 *máshás.*	3 ,,	9 ,,	0	5	4
Red pepper ...	...	½ pound.		0	8	0
Vegetables ...	...	5 *marlás.*	2 annas per *marla.*	0	10	0
Gur, spices, parched gram, &c. ...	...	...		3	9	8
			Total ...	39	0	0

This is a fair estimate for a *zamindár* in average circumstances. People well off will spend more, and the poor fare worse; women and children of course consume less food. The *zamindár* has to buy next to nothing on account of food. No allowance has been made for fuel, because as much as is wanted can be got in the jungle for nothing.

The following estimate of the annual consumption of food by a family of five persons, including two children, was furnished for the Famine Report, of 1869 :—

For an agriculturist's family.			*For a family of a non-agriculturist.*		
Description of grain.	Maund.	Sérs.	Description of grain.	Maund.	Sérs.
Wheat	20	0	Wheat	20	0
Rice	1	30	Rice	3	0
Jowár (great-millet) ...	4	0	*Jowár* (great-millet) ...	1	3¼
Kangni and *chína* ...	2	7½	*Makki*	1	0
Makki (Indian-corn) ...	2	0			
Jau (barley)	2	0	Total ...	25	3¼
Total ...	31	37½	*Dál* as above	1	8
Gram *dál*	1	8			
Moth (*Phaseolus radiatus*)	1	32			
Masur (*Ervum lens*)	0	15			
	3	15			

Use of tobacco and opium.

Every man smokes, and so does every urchin as soon as he is big enough to carry the *hukka* : women do not smoke. The use of opium is very common. Almost every man has a bit wrapped up in the end of his turban. Religious mendicants are especially addicted to the use of this drug.

Amusements.

The amusements of the people, to an ordinary observer, seem few and dull. Little boys may be seen beating a ball about with

Chapter III, B.

Social and Religious Life.

a stick, and their elders pitch the *budgar* or dumb-bell about. On occasions of extraordinary festivity, such as fairs, they are completely satisfied with incessant tom-toming, riding about two on a horse or three on a camel, and a swing in a merry-go-round, now and then.

Daily occupations.

The male portion of the agricultural population is more or less employed in some one or other of the operations of husbandry all the year round, and this is especially the case in the tracts where crops are artificially irrigated; but the men of the pastoral tribes lead a comparatively lazy life, the demands on their labour being limited to drawing water for the cattle and milking the cows. Women, on the other hand, are everywhere hard worked, the drudgery of their domestic occupations leaving them scarcely any leisure for rest or amusement. They must be up before it is light, to churn the milk of the night before, and then sweep the house, throw away the rubbish, and make cakes of the cow-dung. Water has then to be fetched. When this is over, it is time to commence cooking the morning meal, which, when ready, has to be taken to the men working in the fields. If after this their services are not required to watch the crops and frighten away the birds, they are expected to spin cotton or wool to be made into clothing for the family,—indeed the two occupations are often combined. Again, early in the afternoon preparations have to be made for the evening meal, the vegetables or *dál* are placed on the fire, and a second trip made to the village well for water. By the time they return, it is time to knead the flour, make it into cakes, and cook it for their husbands, sons, and brothers; these lords of creation will assist in tying up and milking the cows. This done, the milk is put over a slow fire to warm, and the family sits down to dinner; and so the days pass with little variation from year to year.

Divisions of time.

The following is the list of the recognized divisions of time:—

Recognized division of time with		Corresponding English time.
Muhammadans.	Hindus.	
Namáz wela ...	Parbhát wela ...	A little before sunrise.
Wada wela ...	Wada wela ...	Till one hour-and-a-half after sunrise.
Roti wela ...	Roti wela ...	From wadi wela till a watch and a half after sunrise.
Kulahar ...	Kulahar ...	One watch and a half after sunrise.
Dopahar ...	Dopahar ...	Noon.
Peshi wela ...	Laudha wela ...	3 P. M.
Dígar wela ...	None	An hour before sunset.
Nimashan wela or Shám wela ...	Sandhia wela, Tarkalan wela ...	Sunset.
Sota wela ...	Sota wela ...	From sunset till one watch of the night has passed.
Adhi rát ...	Adhi rát ...	Midnight.
Pahar rát báqí ...	Pahar rat báqí ...	When one watch of the night remains.

Chapter III, B.

Social and Religious Life.

Marriages.

Sindh is a song sung between 3 P. M. and sunset, so *sandhia wela* probably embraces that period of time.

The ceremonies connected with births, marriages, and deaths are much the same as in other districts, and need not be described; but a few words may be said concerning negotiations preliminary to marriage and marriage expenses. Muhammadans generally marry after the harvest in Jeth and Hár (middle of May to middle of July); Hindús do not marry in Chetar (middle of March to middle of April) or Kátik (middle of October to middle of November). Among the former, the *mirási* conducts the negotiations for betrothal, coming from the boy's father: among Hindús, the Brahman does, coming on the part of the girl's father. Among persons closely connected, it is considered disgraceful to make marriage a money matter; but not so if the families are of different clans, or even different sub-divisions of the same clan. As a rule, the girl is always bought, the price ranging from Rs. 50 to Rs. 500. "Over-assessment" not seldom means that a fancy price has been given for a daughter-in-law. According to the universal opinion of the people, the mercenary nature of marriage has been developed only since the introduction of English rule. This may be perhaps explained by the fact that former rulers took good care their subjects should not squander the money, by appropriating it for their own use. If the go-between is successful, the father of the boy goes to the girl's father and arranges matters. For the girl's father to move in the matter first would be disgraceful. The betrothed pair may be mere children, in which case the marriage takes place when they have grown up. Marriage is attended with few expenses except the dowry. Few people attend; the food provided is of a cheap kind; and the cost of bringing the guests (who are expected to make the bridegroom a present) to and fro is *nil*. After marriage, the married pair live in a house prepared for them near that of the husband's father, with whose family they have their meals.

General statistics and distribution of religions.

Table No. VII shows the numbers in each tahsil and in the whole district who follow each religion, as ascertained in the Census of 1891, and Table No. XLIII gives similar figures for towns. Tables Nos. V to IX of the report of that Census give further details on the subject. The distribution of every 10,000 of the population by religions is shown in the margin according to the returns of the last two censuses. The limitations subject to which these figures must be taken, and especially the rule followed in the classification of

Religion.	Rural population.		Urban population.		Total population.	
	1881	1891	1881	1891	1881	1891
Hindu	1,851	2,362	3,862	4,174	1,969	2,432
Sikh	282	320	251	345	280	321
Musalmán ...	7,865	7,318	5,869	5,439	7,748	7,245
Christian ...	1	...	18	42	2	2

Chapter III, B.

Social and Religious Life.

General statistics and distribution of religions.

Hindus, are fully discussed in Chapter IV of the Census Report. The Musalmáns of the district almost entirely belong to the Sunni persuasion; the proportion of Shiáhs per 1,000 of the total Musalmán population has been 5·9 and 8·1 at the last two censuses, respectively. The increase in the numbers of the various religions has been very unequal according to the Census figures. It has been as follows;

Religions.	*Increase per cent., 1881 on 1891.*
Hindus	44·0
Sikhs	48·0
Musalmáns	9·3
Total all religions	17·1

Taking the figures for Hindus for what they are worth, it would appear that the Hindu population of the district is in point of numbers somewhat rapidly overhauling the Musalmáns. The sects of the Christian population are given in supplementary Table A, Part I of the Census Report. Table No. IX shows the religion of the major castes and tribes of the district, and therefore the distribution by caste of the great majority of the followers of each religion. A description of the great religions of the Punjab and of their principal sects will be found in Chapters III and IV, respectively, of the Census Report. The religious practice and belief of the district present no special peculiarities; and it would be out of place to enter here into any disquisition on the general question. The general distribution of religions by tahsíls can be gathered from the figures of Table No. VII; and regarding the population as a whole, no more detailed information as to locality is available. The great majority of the land-owning classes and of the village menials are Musalmáns; but there are also many Hindu Arorás and Khatrís, whose proprietary connection with the land dates from Sikh times; they are found in considerable numbers in the Dipálpur and Pákpattan tahsíls. Hindu Kambohs are also an important element in the land-owning community in Dipálpur. The commercial classes are mainly Hindú Arorás, and to a less extent Khatrís. These two castes combine land-owning with trade.

Superstitions.

The people are very superstitious, but probably less so than formerly. The charms against cattle-disease have been mentioned elsewhere. There are lucky and unlucky days for commencing agricultural operations, and extraordinary care has to be taken to prevent demons carrying off grain that has been threshed, but not stored. When a boat is about to sail, or when the rivers are abnormally low, or set against a man's land and commence to wash it away, vows are made and sacrifices offered to the rivers. Vows are called *asísa:* Muhammadans make them in the name of Khizr. Their sacrifice is wheat *daliya* mixed with *gur*. Hindus prepare a dish called *chúrma*. Part of both is thrown into the river. The Hindus eat what remains of the *chúrma* themselves, sharing it

Chapter III, B.

Social and Religious Life.

Superstitions.

with those present; the Muhmmadans give what remains of the *daliya* to the poor. The agricultural Hindu has cast off many prejudices still clung to elsewhere. He will carry cooked food about with him and eat it anywhere. He cares nothing for the *chauka*. He will drink water from the hand of any other Hindu or Sikh, and from the leather water-bag of a Muhammadan.

Fairs.

Intimately connected with the subject of the last paragraph are the fairs of the district. These are all semi-religious meetings. Fairs for the mere purchase and sale of goods are unknown; nor are there any weekly *bazárs* or market-days. The gatherings that do take place are often the occasion of a little trafficking. All the principal fairs are held in the two Sutlej tahsíls. Below is a list of them:—

Place where fair is held.	Person in whose memory it is held.	Date on which fair is held.	Numbers of visitors.
Pakpattan ...	Bába Faríd ...	5th and 6th of Muharram ...	50,000
Sheikh Fazil ..	Sheikh Muhd. Fazil	Jamádi-ul-awwal	4,500
Bahlolpur ...	Bhuman Shah ...	Hár ...	3,000
Jhang Abdulla Shah	Abdulla Shah ...	Hár ...	1,000
Kadirábád ..	Bhai Sewa Singh ...	Baisákh (1st) ...	4,000
Bhuman Shah ..	Bhuman Shah ..	Ditto „ ...	3,000
Shergarh ...	Dáúd Bandagi ...	Chait ..	7,000
Dipálpur ...	Lálujas Ráj ...	Mágh, each Sunday	2,000
Chak Lachhma Dás...	Bhai Lachhman Dás	Baisákh (1st) ...	1,500
Faridabád ...	Game Shah ...	10th Phágan ...	2,000
Shekhu ...	Saiad Muhammad ...	21st Chait ...	1,500
Shiráza ...	Nathu Shah ...	15th January ...	1,500
Mir Shaink ...	Háfiz Dáim ...	June ...	2,000
Tibba Dak Sala ...	Mián Kádir Bakhsh	5th Jeth ...	3,000

Language.

Table No. VIII shows the numbers who speak each of the principal languages current in the district separately for each tahsil and for the whole district. More detailed information will be found in Table No. X of the Census Report for 1891, while in Chapter IX of the same report the several languages are briefly discussed. The figures in the margin give the distribution of every 10,000 of the population by language omitting small figures. The prevailing, in fact practically the only, language or dialect of the district was returned as Punjabi at the last census. In point

Language.	Proportion per 10,000 of population, 1881.	1891.
Hindústani ...	24	28
Bagri ...	10	8
Kashmíri ...	1	...
Punjabi ...	9,952	9,958
Jatki ...	3	3
Pashtu ...	7	3
All Indian languages	9,998	9,999
Non-Indian languages	2	1

Chapter III, B.
Social and Religious Life.
Language.

of fact it differs materially from the true Punjabi of the Mánjha, and contains a considerable admixture of *jatki*; the prevailing dialect of Multán and the south-western portions of the province. It may be regarded as occupying a medium position between those two almost distinct forms of speech. The *jatki* element is most noticeable in the western portions of the district. A glossary of many of the agricultural terms used in the district, which was compiled by Mr. Purser, late Settlement Officer of Montgomery, is given as an appendix to his report.

Education.

Table No. XIII gives statistics of education as ascertained at the Census of 1891 for each religion and for the total population of each tahsíl. The figures for female education are probably very imperfect indeed. The figures in the margin show the number educated among every 10,000 of each sex according to the census returns. Statistics regarding the attendance at Government and aided schools will be found in Table No. XXXVII. The distribution of the scholars at these schools by religion and the occupations of their fathers, as it stood in 1896-97, is shown in the margin. Besides Government and aided schools, there are 77 indigenous Muhammadan schools or *maktabs* and 54 *patshálás* or Hindu schools. Mr. Purser noted that the people had no taste for instruction. Comparing the figures of the last census with those of that of the previous one the increase in the proportions of literate to total males stands at 25 per cent. in the case of total, and at 35 per cent. in the case of rural population. The proportion itself compares favourably with that returned for other districts; but of the literate males and those under instruction as returned at the last census, 59 and 74 per cent, respectively, were Hindus, while the corresponding percentages for Musalmáns were 33 and 16 per cent, respectively. There is no doubt that as indicated by the above results the population of the district, including the landowning classes, are waking up to the advantages of education. The

	Education.	Rural population, 1881.	1891.	Total population, 1881.	1891.
Males.	Under instruction	113	105	141	131
	Can read and write	408	553	487	608
Females.	Under instruction	2·1	4·2	3·2	6
	Can read and write	1·5	9·5	2·4	11

Details.	Boys.	Girls.
Europeans and Eurasians	...	.
Native Christians ...	4	...
Hindús	1,135	45
Musalmans	581	.
Sikhs	230	9
Others	...	...
Children of agriculturists ...	601	...
„ of non-agriculturists	1,349	54

Chapter III, B.

Social and Religious Life.

Hindus are no doubt much ahead of the Musalmáns in this respect at present, but the more intelligent of the latter are certainly beginning to abandon the attitude of careless indifference and prejudice.

Character and disposition of the people.

The character and disposition of the people was thus described by Mr. Purser :—

> " The people of this district are a bold, sturdy set; they are unsophisticated, and can laugh. But they avoid speaking the truth upon principle, and withal lie in such an artless and reckless way that a Hindustání would blush with shame at their silliness They completely fail to grasp the idea of rights in property, when the property appears in the shape of their neighbour's cattle or wife. They are only moderately industrious. Some say they are lazy, but they are not. They are extravagant, ignorant, and superstitious. To travellers they extend a tolerable hospitality; but Hátim Tái need not look to his laurels on account of their rivalry. In fact they seem made up of bad qualities and half-hearted virtues; yet there must be something good about them, for one gets to like them; but why, it would be hard to say."

The above description coming as it does from an officer who had an intimate knowledge of, and great sympathy with, the people cannot with fairness be regarded as erring in the direction of harshness or severity. It is still fairly applicable, at least to the generality of the Musalmán tribes, but the general progress of civilization, in which the district has had some share, has tended to some extent to remove the elements of pristine coarseness and uncouthness in the character of the people. Cattle theft is still very common, and the disposition to appropriate other people's wives continues to be prominent. Sexual immorality prevails extensively. The more violent forms of crime are rare, and murders are in a large number of cases traceable to irregular sexual relations. House-breaking is not common and rick-burning almost unknown. There is only one punitive police post in the district and only one village under the Criminal Tribes Act. The population is generally moderate in the consumption of liquors and narcotic drugs, and drunkenness is very rare.

Table Nos. XL, XLI and XLII give statistics of crime while Table No. XXXV shows the consumption of liquors and narcotic stimulants. The large number of convicts shown in Table XLII is due to the existence of the Montgomery Central Jail, in which convicts are received from all districts in the province.

Poverty or wealth of the people.

It is difficult to form any satisfactory estimate of the wealth of the commercial and industrial classes. Table No. XXXIV gives statistics of the working of the income-tax for each year from 1886-87 to 1896-97 inclusive. According to the income-tax returns of 1871-72 there were then only ten bankers and money-lenders in the district who enjoyed an income of over Rs. 750 per annum, while in 1869-70 there were only 23 shown as having incomes of over Rs. 500. In 1896-97 there were in all 1,117 assessees, with annual incomes of Rs. 500 or more; and of these 62 enjoyed incomes of Rs. 2,000 or over.

Poverty or wealth of the people.

The business of the commercial classes consists mainly of money-lending and the purchase and export of the agricultural produce of the district and the import of commodities required for the consumption of the district. A certain amount of capital has of late years been sunk in cotton-ginning factories. There are no traders of very extensive wealth, and no large commercial houses having branches in other parts of the country. Export business is carried on largely through the agents and brokers of firms situated in the large trade centres of other districts. Many of the village shopkeepers are the minor partners or the agents of more substantial traders living in the larger towns, such as Pákpattan or Kamália. The commerical classes are, on the whole, thriving and prosperous. Many of the artisans in the few towns of the district are, as is commonly the case, in greater or less poverty; while their fellows, the village menials, are generally better off, and in some cases seem to be more prosperous than the land-owners and tenants. Living among a somewhat thriftless and indolent population, they are, as a rule, paid fairly well, and combining, as they generally do, a certain amount of agriculture with the pursuit of handicrafts they generally manage to lead a fairly comfortable existence.

The mass of the purely agricultural population of the district, including landowners and cultivating tenants, are moderately prosperous. In the absence of permanent and reliable means of irrigation, so much depends on the precarious and constantly fluctuating conditions of rainfall and river flood that it is impossible for them to attain to any generally very high standard of prosperity; and this state of things combined with the thriftless and somewhat indolent disposition of many of the agricultural tribes occasionally results in more or less pronounced and wide-spread distress, mainly in the parts not benefited by the inundation canals, in the not unfrequently recurring years in which rain and river floods fail or are unusually scanty.

SECTION C.—TRIBES, CASTES AND LEADING FAMILIES.

Statistics, tribes and castes.

Table No. IX gives the figures for the principal castes and tribes of the district, with details of sex and religion; while Table No. IXA shows the number of the less important castes. It would be out of place to attempt a description of each. Many of them are found all over the Punjab, and most of them in many other districts; and their representatives in Montgomery are distinguished by no local peculiarities. Some of the leading tribes, and especially those who are important as land-owners, or by position and influence, are briefly noticed in the following sections; and each caste will be found described in Chapter XI of the Census Report for 1891. Details of the main agricultural tribes by tahsíls are given below :—

Chapter III, C.

Tribes, Castes and Leading Families.

Statistics, tribes, and castes.

Name.	Montgomery.	Gugera.	Dipálpur.	Pákpattan.	Total.
Aráin ...	1,536	4,374	16,955	5,059	27,924
Awán ...	108	1,293	530	4	1,935
Biloch ...	4,797	4,846	3,166	3,432	16,241
Jat .	9,767	8,301	15,384	12,152	45,604
Kamboh ..	29	4	9,326	7,615	16,974
Kharral ...	2,694	13,014	4,451	1,814	21,973
Khokhar ...	2,069	2,418	2,014	2,076	8,577
Rájpút ...	18,112	14,436	20,649	13,728	66,925
Sheikh ...	925	946	1,417	1,953	5,241

The general distribution of the more important land-owning tribes, which is shown on maps attached to Mr. Purser's Settlement Report and to the assessment reports of the Dipálpur and Pákpattan tahsíls prepared during the recent Settlement is broadly described below. A good deal of information regarding the origin, traditions, and early history of many of the tribes has already been given in Chapter II.

Caste superseded by tribe.

In Montgomery, as in all the western districts, where the influence and example of the frontier races is strong, caste is, for the great mass of the population, little more than a tradition of origin; and the social unit is the tribe. Thus many of the local tribes have returned themselves indifferently as Jats or as Rájpúts, and appear partly under one heading and partly under the other; while many claim Arab or Mughul descent, and have returned themselves as Sheikh or Mughul. The following account of the principal tribes and castes is taken for the most part from the Settlement Report by Mr. Purser, who had intimate and extensive local knowledge. In some cases the conclusions he arrives at do not exactly agree with those stated in the Census Reports of 1881 and 1891, where the field reviewed was broader; but so little is known of the people that the difference is only one of opinion; and as regards this particular district, Mr. Purser's opinion is probably the more correct.

Jats and Rájpúts.

The term Jat is, for the reasons stated in the last paragraph, of the most indefinite significance, and is commonly used to include all those miscellaneous pastoral and agricultural tribes who, being Musalmáns of Indian origin, do not distinctly lay claim to Rájpút rank. In common parlance it is often used as almost equivalent to peasant or country fellow. Thus it becomes almost a matter of opinion whether each tribe should be classed as Jat

Chapter III, C.

Tribes, Castes and Leading Families.

Jats and Rájputs.

or as Rájpút, and, as already stated, the same tribe often appears under both headings. The following figures show the headings under which Jats and Rájpúts were classed in the Census returns of 1891. No further details of the Jats tribes or clans are available :—

Sub-divisions of Jats and Rájpúts.

JAT.

Name.	*Number.*
Uthwál	541
Sindhu	1,079
Silpra	851
Miscellaneous	38,436

RAJPUT.

Name.	*Number.*
Bhatti	18,462
Chauhán	2,642
Dhudhi	1,345
Joiya	5,177
Khichi	3,375
Punwár	2,802
Satti	610
Siyál	9,040
Wattu	12,382
Miscellaneous	8,654

Pastoral and agricultural tribes.

A far more essential distinction than that between present Jat and Rájpút status is afforded by the political position of the respective tribes, and the corresponding difference in their favourite pursuits. Captain Elphinstone in his report on the Regular Settlement writes as follows :—

"The population is distinctly divided into marked sections—the purely agricultural inhabitants and the pastoral tribes. The former consist of the castes, both Muhammadan and Hindu, which are generally met with throughout the Eastern Punjab, *viz.*, Aráins, Kambohs, Hindu Jats, &c. But the latter are almost entirely confined to the region which extends from the southern extremity of Multán district to within thirty miles of Lahore. They are all Muhammadans, and their favourite occupation is breeding and grazing of cattle. They are locally known by the name of Jats, in contradistinction to the more settled inhabitants, who call themselves ryots or subjects. The most important tribes are the Kharrals, Fattiánás, Murdánás, Káthiás, Wahniwáls, Baghelás, Wattús and Joiyás. The two latter are chiefly confined to the Sutlej, but the others only possess land on the Rávi, and graze their herds in the two Doábs adjoining that river.

Great and Little Ravi tribes.

"The Rávi tribes just enumerated call themselves the 'Great Rávi,' and include all the purely agricultural class residing within their own limits under the name of 'Small Rávi' or 'Nikki Rávi,' a term of reproach with reference to the more settled pursuits of these people, their comparatively peaceful habits, and probably the state of subjection in which they were placed when the 'Great Rávi' had uncontrolled authority in this region. Besides the 'Small Rávi' there is another class in this tract, who unhesitatingly recognize the 'Great Rávi' men as their superiors. It is composed of refugees and emigrants from other parts of the Punjab, and of the Mhatams, a peculiar Hindu tribe, who delight in the most swampy parts of the alluvial lands, and rarely appear as proprietors of the soil they cultivate. These are included under name of Wásiwáns, and are not unsimilar in origin to the class of that name among the Afghán tribes."

The "Great Rávi" Jats are a handsome, sturdy race. Their appearance has been remarked upon by several writers. The Greeks (supposing the identification of the Káthiás with Arrian's Kathæoi to be correct) speak of them as being tall and handsome in person. According to Curtius and Diodorus, Sophites (to whom General Cunningham attributes a close connection with the Kathæans) far exceeded all his subjects in beauty, and was upwards of six English feet in stature.

Chapter III, C.

Tribes, Castes and Leading Families.

Great and Little Rávi tribes.

Burnes speaks of the Káthiás as "a tall and handsome race," and the author of the History of the Sikhs calls them "tall and comely."* Captain Elphinstone speaks of the Kharrals as "generally above the average height; their features very marked, and their activity and endurance remarkable." Most of the Great Rávi tribes lay claim to a Rájpút origin, and they one and all look down with some contempt upon men who handle the plough. They possess land, but its cultivation is left to inferior castes. The most characteristic perhaps of the customs attributed to these clans is their aversion to early marriages. None of them allow their children of either sex to marry until after they have attained the age of puberty. It is probably owing to this fact that their physical superiority is maintained to this day unimpaired. Their language is the local type of Punjabi, and their Hindu origin is attested by the fact that they still keep up Hindu *parohits*, who take a prominent part in their marriage festivals.

Origin of the chief tribes.

There is a good deal of similarity among the traditions of the different tribes regarding their origin. The ancestor of each tribe was, as a rule, Rájpút, a Rája of the Solar or Lunar race, and resided at Hastinapur or Dáránagar. He scornfully rejected the proposals of the Dehli Emperor for a matrimonial alliance between the two families, and had then to fly to Sirsa or Bhatner, or some other place in that neighbourhood. Next he came to the Rávi, and was converted to Islám by Makhdúm Baháwal Hakk or Bába Faríd. Then, being a stout-hearted man, he joined the Kharrals in their marauding expeditions, and so his descendants became Jats. In Kamr Singh's time they took to agriculture and abandoned robbery a little, and now in the *Sarkári Ráj*, they have quite given up their evil ways, and are honest and well disposed.

Location of the principal tribes.

On the Rávi to the north, the first considerable clan is that of the Mánes, who are succeeded by the Kharrals, occupying both banks of the river; next come the Wattús on the border lands of the Montgomery and Gugerá tahsíls, and after them the Khaggás. They are followed by the Siyáls. Then come the Káthiás and Kamália Kharrals. The succession of tribes on the Sutlej bears some resemblance to that of the Rávi clans. Thus the Gugerá Mánes are represented by the Dipálpur Arars on the Lahore border; the Wattús take the place of the Kharrals, and extend the whole length of the Sutlej to nearly due south of Pákpattan. As there is a Wattu colony on the Rávi, so there is a Kharral colony on the Sutlej, nearly on the border of the Pákpattan and Dipálpur tahsíls. The Khaggás are represented by the very similar Chishtís, while the Háns, though as regards numbers and influence now far inferior to the Siyáls, may, from, their past importance, pair off with them. Finally, the Joiyás in the extreme south-west of the Pákpattan tahsíls represent the Káthiás. Arorás are numerous about Pákpattan and Kamália,

* Cunningham's Arch. Rep. ii., p. 35—6. General Cunningham adds the testimony of Abul Fazl in the *Ain-i-Akbari* (ii, p. 70); but the passage quoted refers to the people of Káthiáwár in Gujerat, and it is by no means certain that these are of the same race as the Káthia Jats of this district.

Chapter III, C.

Tribes, Castes and Leading Families.

while their place is taken in the northern portion of the district by their kinsmen, the Khatrís. Kambohs occupy a good deal of land on the Khánwah canal, between Hujra and Dipálpur, and are to be found also to the north and west of the town of Pákpattan.

The Kharrals.

The Kharrals are the most northerly of the great Rávi tribes, occupying a great portion of the land between Gugera and the Lahore district on both sides of the river, and extending some distance into the Gujránwala district. The Kharrals were Ráj-púts. Their ancestor was Rája Karn of Hastinapur. His descendant Bhúpa left that place and came to Uch, where he and his son Kharral were converted by Makhdúm Jahania Shah. From Uch the Kharrals spread over the country about the Rávi. They appear to have settled first in the Sandal Bár, no doubt with a view to having plenty of pasture for their cattle. Ranjít Singh is said to have induced or compelled them to move to villages nearer the river, possibly with a view to exercising more effective control over them. Their principal *muhins* or clans are the—

Lakhera with head-quarters at	Kamalia
Upera .. „ „	Jhamra and Dánábád.
Rabera .. „	Fatahpur.
Gogairah ..	Gugera
Ransinh .. .. „	Pindi Cheri and Pír Ali.

The Kharrals never got on with each other. The feuds of the Lakherás and upper Rávi Kharrals have been noticed. The tragic adventure of Mirza and Sahibán is said to have been the cause of desperate quarrels. Mirza was a Kharral of the Sahi *muhin*, and resided at Dánábád. He went as a boy to Khewa in Jhang, where he fell in love with his cousin Sahibán, the daughter of the chief man of the place. Her parents betrothed her to a youth of the Chadhar tribe; but before the marriage could take place, Mirza ran away with her. He was pursued and slain. Her relations strangled Sahibán. The Dánábád Kharrals then attacked the Chadhars and Mahnike, to which clan Sahibán belonged, and recovered the corpses of the lovers, and buried them at Dánábád, where the graves may be seen to this day. These murders were the cause of such bloody feuds between the clans that it at length was thought inauspicious to have daughters, and as soon as they were born they were strangled as Sahibán had been. This custom of female infanticide was common among the Kharrals till Colonel Hamilton, Commissioner of Multán, persuaded them to discontinue it. It does not appear whether Sahibán's father was a Siyál or a Kharral. But enmity to the Siyáls was the bond of union among the Kharrals. Of the latter, Captain Elphinstone remarks :—"In stature the Kharrals are generally above the average height; their features are very marked, and their activity and endurance are remarkable. In turbulence and courage they have been always considered to excel all the others except the Káthiás." They are wasteful in marriage expenditure, hospitable to travellers, thievish, and have very little taste for agriculture; the cultivation in

Chapter III, C.

Tribes, Castes and Leading Families.

their villages being largely left to the inferior castes, and the Kharrals contenting themselves with realising their share of the produce. They possess land only in tracts inundated by the rivers, mere well cultivation being too laborious a task even for their dependants. They still follow many Hindu customs, especially on the occasion of marriage.

The Wattús.

The Wattús, who occupy both banks of the Sutlej for about 60 miles, and the tract about Gugera, claim descent from Rája Salvahan of Siálkot. They have probably a close racial connection with Hindu Bhattis, Mussalman Bhattis, Joiyás, and with Sidhu and Barar Sikh Jats (*vide* pages 124 and 127—129 of the Hissár Gazetteer). One of Salvahan's sons settled in Bhatner. Adham, the 12th in descent, came to the Sutlej near Ferozepore. There he found the Rajáda Kharrals, the Dogars, and the Joyás. They picked a quarrel with him, but he beat them. On account of venting his displeasure on them he was called Wattu, *wat* meaning displeasure. The next great man was Khewa, who was converted by Bába Faríd. He expelled the Kharrals, Joiyás, and Dogars. After him there was no famous chief till Lakha appeared. His achievements have been recorded. It does not appear when the Wattús of the Rávi settled there; but they came from the Sutlej, and were hospitably received by the Kharrals. There is very little to choose between the two tribes on the Rávi. There the Wattús rose in 1857, and are still addicted to cattle-thieving. The Sutlej Wattús, however, behaved generally well during the rebellion. The tract owned by them possesses little jungle; that part of the clan therefore has taken of late years to agricultural pursuits. Some of their estates are well cultivated; their herds have diminished, and many of them cannot now be distinguished in appearance from peaceful Aráins or Khokhars. The change in their habits is remarkable, as they still speak of the *kárdárs* they used to kill during the Sikh rule, and of the years in which they paid no revenue because the Sikhs were unable or afraid to collect it. The Wattús pride themselves on their politeness and hospitality. They are of only moderate industry, profuse in expenditure on special occasions, indifferent to education and exceedingly fond of cattle.

The Káthiás.

The Káthiás have been identified with the *Kathaioi* of Alexander's time. The subject is discussed at length at pages 33 to 37, Vol. II of the Archæological Survey Reports. It is probable that the name, as used by the Greeks, had a wider application than to one clan only. Whether the Káthiás at that time enjoyed a supremacy over the great Rávi tribes, and their name on this account was applied by the Greeks to the race collectively, or whether the mistake arose from the fact that Sángala, the capital town of the Kathæans, was brought most prominently into notice by its stubborn resistance of the Macedonian army, it is impossible to decide with any confidence. The coincidences, however, which point to the identity of the race of two thousand years ago with that of the present day are too strong to be accidental. According to their own account the Káthiás are descended from Rája Karan, Súrajbansí. Originally they resided in Bikáner, whence they emigrated and founded the State of Káthiawár.

Chapter III, C.

Tribes, Castes and Leading Families.

The Káthiás.

From there they went to Sirsa, and then to Baháwalpur. Next they crossed over to Kabúla and went on to Dera Dínpanah. Here they quarrelled with the Bilúches and had to leave. They then settled at Mirah Siyál in Jhang. They stole the cattle of Alawal Khan of Kamália, who was killed pursuing them. Saádat Yár Khan obtained the release of their leaders (who were imprisoned on account of this affair), on condition of their settling on the Rávi. Thus the Káthiás obtained a footing in this district. They always held by the Kamália Kharrals, but plundered the others whenever they could get a chance. The character given to the Kharrals applies equally to them. "They are a handsome and sturdy race. Their chief and favourite article of food is butter milk; the consumption of wheat among them is very inconsiderable." They, of course, took part in the rebellion of 1857. Their leaders were Jalla and Muhammad Khan. The Káthiás claim to be and not improbably are Punwár Rájpúts. There are two main divisions, the Káthiás proper and the Baghelás; the latter are confined to the neighbourhood of Kamália, and appear to have been originally merely retainers or dependants of the more powerful Káthiás.

The Baghelás.

The Siyáls, Fattiánás and Tahránás.

The Siyáls of this district are divided into two principal branches—the Fattiánás and the Tahránás. They were Punwár Rájpúts of Dháránagar. Rái Siyál or Siu, from whom the name of the clan comes (Siyál Srúwál), was the son of Rái Shankar who settled in Jámpur. Quarrels arose at Jámpur, and Siyál left for the Punjab in Ala-ud-din Ghori's reign. About 1258 he was converted to Muhammadanism by Bába Faríd of Pákpattan. He settled at Sáhíwál and married the daughter of the chief of that place. The Siyáls increased, and ultimately ousted the Nauls from the lowland of the Chenáb, and founded Jhang Siyál. They afterwards became very powerful, and, as we have seen, over-ran and held Kamália and the neighbouring country, under Walidád Khan. It was about this time that the Siyáls settled on the Rávi. They took part in the outbreak in 1857 under Baháwal, Fattiána, and Jhalla and Murad, Tahránás. Jhalla was killed in action, and the others transported. They are large in stature, of a rough disposition, fond of cattle, and care little for agriculture. They observe Hindu ceremonies like the Kharrals and Káthiás, and do not keep their women in *parda*. They object to clothes of a brown (*úda*) colour, and the use of brass vessels. Their history is fully given in the Settlement Report of the Jhang district.

The Wahniwáls.

The Wahniwáls or Bahniwáls appear to have come from the Hissár direction. They call themselves Bhatti Rájpúts. There is a Hindu Jat tribe of the same name in Hissár, and the adjacent parts of Bikáner who appear originally to have been Chauhán Rájpúts of Sambhar in Bikáner, whence they spread northwards. In number they are weak; but in audacity and love of robbery they yield to none of the tribes. They were chiefly concerned in the village of Kamália in 1857, as well as in the nearly total destruction of that city in 1808. In appearance and habits they do not differ from other Jat tribes. Their leaders in 1857 were Sarang, Nathu and Mokha. The adven-

Chapter III, C.

Tribes, Castes and Leading Families.

tures of the last, till his surrender several years later, are well known. The name is said to have its origin in the fact of one of their ancestors having been born in a depression in the ground (*wáhan*). They with the Baghelás hold the country immediately round Kamália on the right bank of the Rávi.

The Biloches.

The Biloches of this district are found chiefly in the Montgomery and Gugera tahsíls, but there are not a few in Dipálpur and Pákpattan. They claim to be descended from Amír Hamza, the uncle of the prophet. Their ancestor emigrated from Mecca to Baghdád, and thence, owing to the persecutions of the Abbasides, to Kech Mekran. They appear to have come to this country during the Langa monarchy of Multán, or a little earlier, about the first quarter of the 15th century. One Khan Kamál of this tribe held a large tract of country between the Rávi and the central ridge from Shergarh to Waliwála. The *theh* of his capital exists near Núr Sháh. This seems to have been about the beginning of the 16th century. The Montgomery Biloches belong chiefly to the sub-divisions Hot and Rind. Those of Gugera are mostly Lisharis; and those of Pákpattan, Rinds and Lisharis. The Rávi Biloches are not much better than the surrounding clans. They joined in the rebellion of 1857; and as they owned some large villages on the Multán and Lahore road, they gave a good deal of trouble by interrupting communications. They pay little attention to agriculture, and occupy themselves mostly with breeding camels and letting them out for hire. Though always Muhammadans, they practise some Hindu ceremonies; but attach more importance to learning the *Korán* than their neighbours do. One of their principal clans, the Murdána, possess much land on the main road from Multán to Lahore, between Gugera and Harappa.

The Joiyás.

The Joiyás* are the last of the essentially robber tribes. They are an extensive tribe on the lower Sutlej, occupying both banks of the river from nearly opposite Pákpattan to Kahror in the Multán district. A few of them have migrated and settled near the Rávi. Two of their principal clans, the Admerás and Salerás, are almost confined to Baháwalpur territory. According to the accounts given by the tribe in this district they are descended from Benjamin, the son of Jacob. One of his descendants settled as a *fakír* in Bikáner, where he married the Rájá's daughter. Their son was Joiya Before his birth his father abandoned his family, and wandered into the world as a religious mendicant, Consequently Joiya had to endure many gibes about his having no known father. The Joiyás of Hissár and Bikaner claim descent through the female line from Bhatti, the eponymous ancestor of the Hindu Bhattís and Musalman Bhattís. They probably have a more or less distant racial connection with the Wattús, Bhattís,

---

* The Joiyás are discussed by General Cunningham at pages 244 to 248 of his Ancient Geography of India, and at pages 139 to 145, Vol. XIV of his Archæological Survey Report.

Chapter III, C.

Tribes, Castes and Leading Families.

The Joiyás.

&c. (see above). The word *joi* means a "wife," and it would seem as if the tribe got the name on account of no one knowing who their male ancestor was. They appear to have been Rájpúts, residing about Bhatner in Bikáner, who left that country about the middle of the 14th century and settled in Bahawalpur, and became allies of the Langa dynasty of Multán. They subsequently took to quarrelling with each other, and one party called in the Dáúdpotrás to help it. The usual result followed. The Daúdpotrás took the country from the Joiyás, who then came across the river in considerable numbers. This was about the time of Nádir Shah, or early in the last century. In 1857 they revolted. They were fined heavily, and have not recovered from the effects of their punishment yet, and subsequently lost a good deal of land from riverain action. The principal *muhins* are the Akhoke and Lakhwera. The Admerás and Salerás do not possess any village in this district, though some Salerás do reside here. They are notorious thieves. They care little for agriculture, and occupy themselves with cattle-breeding. The islands in the Sutlej afford excellent pasturage for their buffaloes. They are prodigal in expenditure. "They are of smaller stature than the great tribes of the Rávi, and are considered inferior in regard to the qualities on which the latter especially pride themselves, namely, bravery and skill in cattle-stealing."* The Mahárs are almost exclusively found along the Sutlej, just opposite Fázilka. They claim relationship with the Joiyás, as Mahár, their ancestor, was the brother of Joiyá, and, like them, they came from Bahawalpur too. They own 13 villages, generally in poor condition. The Mahárs are said to be quarrelsome, silly, thievish, fond of cattle, and to care little for agricultural pursuits. Contrary to the usual Jat customs, they generally inherit *per stirpes, chúndawand*, and not *per capita, pagwand*.

The Mahárs.

Agricultural tribes—The Mánes.

The tribes already noticed are all more or less addicted to cattle stealing. The following—Mánes, Khichi, Awán, Sagla, Arar, Háns, Rath, and Dhudhi—are fair cultivators and respectable members of society. The Mánes are found chiefly along the Deg stream. Some are Sikhs, some Hindus, and some Muhammadans; the last predominate in this district. They claim to be Rájpúts, and to be descendants of Mánes, the grandson of Salvahan, Rája of Siálkot. They appear, however, to be racially connected somewhat closely with the Wattús and Bhattís, &c. As their story involves a war between Salvahan (A.D. 90) and the Muhammadans of Mecca, it cannot be accepted with confidence. Most of the rice grown in the Gugera tahsíl is raised by them. The Khichís are another tribe met with almost exclusively in the northern part of the Gugera tahsíl. They claim to have been Chauhán Rájpúts residing near Delhi,

The Khichís.

* Mr. Purser quotes this sentence from Lieutenant Elphinstone's report, and notes on it thus :—"I doubt the great superiority of the Rávi men over those of the Sutlej. We know the latter conquered the former (as the history of the Háns and Bahrwál Nakkaís shows) ; but we never hear of the tables being turned. The mistake of supposing the Joiyás extinct, made by Tod (Ed. II, I?, p. 164) and repeated in the History of the Punjab Chiefs, p. 602, has been pointed out by Cunningham—History of the Sikhs, p. 7."

Chapter III, C.

Tribes, Castes and Leading Families.

who emigrated to Multán, where they were converted by Babáwal Hakk. They wandered up the Rávi, and gave up agriculture for cattle-breeding, and were hand-in-glove with the Kharrals in all their robberies. In Kamr Singh's time they resumed their agricultural habits, and are now an industrious and persevering set of men. A third Gugera tribe is that of the Awáns. They are also found in the upper part of the tahsíl between the Rávi and the Deg. They claim descent from Ali, the son-in-law of Muhammad, and say they are called Awán because they were helpers (*áwán*) of Husain in his struggle with Yazid. The tribe is an interesting one, and has been the subject of much disquisition (Punjab Chiefs, Volume I, page 344, Races of N.-W. P., Edition 1869, Volume 1, page 113, and Punjab Census Report, 1881, para. 465). The Awáns in this district were patronized by the Kharrals, and they helped their patrons in robbing as far as they could. They are now quiet and tolerably industrious cultivators.

The Awáns.

The Saglás.

The Saglás are a Muhammadan tribe in the Montgomery tahsíl. Their villages are situated on the right bank of the Rávi near Idalwála. They were originally Rájpúts, and claim descent from the Rája of Dhárángar. It does not appear when they became Muhammadans. They say they came into this part of the country in Akbar's time, but their principal villages were founded during the rule of Muhammad Shah and Kamr Singh.

The Arars.

The Arars are a Musalmán tribe settled on the Lahore border along the upper course of the Kháuwah canal. They are fairly industrious and tolerably good cultivators. They say they are Mughals, and originally came from Arabia (?). About 500 years ago their ancestor left Delhi, where he was in service, for some reason unexplained, and settled in the tract where the tribe is now found. Having contracted matrimonial alliances with the Jats, his descendants were also considered Jats.

The Hindu Jats.

A few villages of Hindu Jats are situated near those of the Arars. The Hindu Jats are also fair cultivators, and in this respect superior to the ordinary run of Muhammadan Jats. They are mostly Sikhs by religion and of the Sidhu clan.

The Raths and Dhudhís.

In the Pákpattan tahsíl the Raths and their kinsmen, the Dhudhís, are considered fair agriculturists. They are met with about 15 miles to the south-west of the town of Pákpattan. They claim to be Punwár Rájpúts. Their ancestors settled in the Mailsi *iláka* of Multán, where they became Muhammadans. One of the tribe, Háji Sher Muhammad, was a very holy man. His shrine still exists in the village Chaoli Mashaikh in Multán. They are mentioned in historical records as early as the first-half of the 14th century. When the Delhi empire was breaking up, some of them left Multán and settled about Kabúla, and subsequently founded the villages they now occupy.

The Háns.

The Háns tribe has been noticed in Chapter II. They are one of the clans who do not assert a Rájpút origin, but say they are Kureshís, who came from Arabia, settled in Afghánistán, and afterwards came to this country and fixed their residence where Pakka Sidhár now stands. At present the Háns do not own one entire village, and have preserved none of their former influence.

Chapter III, C.

Tribes, Castes and Leading Families.

Three industrious tribes.

There are three hardworking tribes in this district—the Mahtams, Aráins and Kambohs. The last two are first-rate cultivators; and if there is anything to choose between them, the Kambohs are the best. Mahtams are chiefly found in Dipálpur on the Lahore border, and about the junction of the Dipálpur and Pákpattan tahsíls. A considerable number of them have of late years come into the district as settlers in the Sohág-Pára colony. There are a few of them in the Rávi villages. They are a low Hindu caste, and are looked down on by their neighbours. Their story is that they were Rájpúts; and one of their ancestors was a *kánúngo.* Akbar was then on the throne. *Kánúngos* were called *mahta,* and thus they got their name. The first *mahta* was dismissed, and then settled at Mahtpur in Jullundur. His descendants emigrated, and settled along the banks of the rivers as they found quantities of *sarr* in such situations, and working in *sarr* was their chief occupation. It was not till the Nakkai chiefs held sway that they settled down permanently in this district. They adopted the custom of marriage with widows according to the form of *chaddar dálna,* and so became Sudrás. They are also called *bahropiás,* which name is a corruption of *bho-rup-ias,* and means people of many modes of life, because they turned their hands to any business they could find (yet cf. *Races of* N.-W. P., Volume I, pages 17 and 54). Cunningham (*History of the Sikhs,* page 17) says "the hardworking Hindu Mahtams are still moving family by family and village by village eastward away from the Rávi and Chenáb." This would seem to give the Mahtams a western instead of eastern origin as claimed by them. They own a good many villages, most of which are in fair condition. When they are not proprietors of the whole village, they reside in a separate group of huts at some distance from the main *ábádi.* They are great hands at catching wild pigs, but it is in cutting down the jungle on inundated land that they excel. Though industrious, they do not care much for working wells, and prefer cultivating land flooded by the rivers. They are quarrelsome and addicted to petty thieving. They are of medium stature and stoutly made.

The Mahtams.

The Aráins.

The Aráins of this distrct are all Musalmáns, and cannot give any very definite account of their origin. They claim to be Surajbansi Rájpúts, and to have come up to this district from the Delhi part of the country. They are usually supposed to be simply Muhammadan Kambohs, and this is borne out by the fact that the names of several of the Aráin and Kamboh clans (*góts*) are identical. The Kambohs undoubtedly came from the west; so it is likely the Aráins did too. This is rendered more probable by the fact that the Aráins (Ráins) of Sahéranpur are said to have come from Afghánistán about 1650 A. D. (Select Glossary, Volume I, page 294), while the Aráins of the Sirsa tahsíl state that they were expelled from Uch near Multán. Their villages are situated exclusively in the Dipálpur and Gugera tahsíls. They do not appear to have got much below the Lahore border. Their chief sub-divisions are—Gablan, Chandúr, Chháchar, Sindhi, and Barar. In this district they are far removed from ordinary

Chapter III, C.

Tribes, Castes and Leading Families.

The Kambohs.

market gardeners, and are among the best general agriculturists which it contains. The Kambohs claim to be descended from Rája Karan. But one of the ancestors had to fly to Kashmír, and married the daughter of a gardener to save his life. The Rája reproached him with contracting such a low alliance, and said "*Tumko kuchh bú Khándáni ki nahín hai; tum kam bú wála ho,*" meaning, there was no trace of high family in him: hence the name. There are other derivations (*Select Glossary*, Vol. I., page 294). It is evident the Kambohs came from across the Indus. They are found on the Sutlej side of the centre-ridge, in the Dipálpur and Pákpattan tahsíls. There are no Kambohs on the Rávi. Those in this district divide themselves into two main branches, according to the country from which they came. These are the Lammawála Kambohs and the Tappawála Kambohs; *lamma* means west, and is said to be the country about Multán; *tappa*, they say, is the region between the Beás and the Sutlej. The majority of the Kambohs settled in the district during Sikh rule. They are almost without exception Hindus; but people do talk of Muhammadan Kambohs. They are generally considered to be superior in social rank to Aráins. As tenants the Kambohs are greatly sought after, as they are most industrious and skilful cultivators. They are, as a rule, well off. Their women are said to do a good deal of business in the money-lending line.*

The holy clans.

There are several Muhammadan clans claiming peculiar sanctity in this district. The principal are the Khaggás in Montgomery; the Chishtis in Pákpattan, and the Saiyads in Dipálpur. To these may be added the Bodlás and Táhirs. The Khaggás came to the district after the conquest of Multán by Ranjít Singh. They claim to be Kureshís; and name as the first Khagga Jalál-ud-dín, disciple of Muhammad Irak. *Khagga* is said to mean a peculiar kind of fish; and the name was given to Jalál-ud-din by his spiritual teacher on the occasion of his rescuing a boat overtaken by a storm. The Chishtís belong to the family of Bába Faríd Shakarganj, and have settled in the district more than 600 years. They claim to be descended from the Caliph Umar. They are Farrukhi Kureshís. The first of their ancestors to take the name of Chishti was Abu Izhák, who lived at Chisht in Syria. Chisht is said to have been a ward of Damascus. The most illustrious descendant of Abu Izhák was Bába Farid Shakarganj, the saint of Pákpattan. All local Chishtís claim descent from him, but the caste appears to have been extended by the inclusion from time to time of the followers (*muríds*) of Bába Faríd and of his ancestors. The Saiyads are met with chiefly about the shrines of Daúd Bandagi at Shergarh; and of Mirán Lál, Bahawal Shah and Shah Mukím at Hujra. They settled in this country early in the 16th century. Some of the Saiyad families, however, did not come till the Sikh time. The Pákpattan

The Khaggás.

The Chishtís.

The Saiyads.

* According to Blochmann (*Aín-i-Akbari*, I., p. 399), it was a distinction to belong to this tribe in the reigns of Akbar and Jahángír. The Kambohs, he mentions, were Muhammadans.

Chapter III, C.

Tribes, Castes and Leading Families.

The Bodlás.

Saiyads are located mostly in the old Háns country, about Pakka Sidhár; and settled there during the Háns supremacy. The Bodlás seem to have come from Multán through Baháwalpur. They are found between Dipálpur and Pákpattan, and came during the Sikh times. The tribe is supposed to have miraculous powers as regards the cure of bites by mad dogs. These semi-saintly tribes are generally somewhat lazy, and affect to live in the odour of sanctity. *Odási fakirs* own several fine villages in the west of the Dipálpur tahsíl. Among them is Bhuman Sháh at which there is a shrine of the saint of that name. The *bhái* of Bhuman Shah contrasts favourably with some of his Muhammadan compeers. There is a *langar*, or place at which food is distributed gratuitously, at Bhuman Shah. This is supported partly by the proceeds of the *jágír* enjoyed by the incumbent of the shrine, and partly by the contributions of the Kambohs, who look upon Bhuman Shah as their patron saint. He is said to have lived from 1687 to 1756. He was a Kamboh who entered the *udási* order.

Odasi Fakirs—Bhuman Shah.

The trading tribes.

The two great trading and money-lending tribes, the Khatrís and Arorás, deserve a passing notice. The latter are generally spoken of by the people as *Kirárs*. It has already been pointed out that the Khatrís predominate in the Gugera and Dipálpur tahsíls, and the Arorás in the Montgomery and Pakpattan; also that Dipálpur is the capital city of the Khatrís in the Punjab. The Khatrís claim to be the second of the four great Hindu castes. There is no record of when they settled here, but it is only since the time of the Nakkai Sikhs that they have become of much importance. They are divided into three main classes—(1) the Charjátís, consisting of the Seths, Mahrotrás, Khannás and Kapúrs; (2) the Bárajátís, or the twelve clans; and (3) the Báwanjátís, or the 52 clans. Among the last are the Sodhís and Bedís, celebrated among the Sikhs, as Gurus Rám Dás and Govínd belonged to the Sodhi family, and Guru Nának to that of the Bedís. Some of the Khatrís are Sikhs, but most continue Hindus. They are active and enterprising, often well-to-do, and have a very good opinion of themselves. They do not confine themselves to agriculture or trade, but take service readily. The Arorás have more than one legend explaining the origin of the name Arora. One story is that they were originally Khatrís; at the time of the persecution of the latter by Pars Rám some of them found safety in disclaiming Khatri rank by saying "*main aur hun;*" by a not too obvious process of corruption the name Arora adhered to the survivors. There is another but less generally credited version which need not be repeated here. Their tribal connection with the Khatrís seems not improbable. Their main divisions are Utradhi, Dakhana and Dahra. Each of them again is subdivided into numerous clans (*zát*). The three main divisions are endogamous, while the clans are exogamous. They were settled about Uch and Shikárpur. When the Nakkai *sardárs* were establishing some sort of order in this country and refounding the deserted villages, many Arorás came and settled here.

The Khatrís.

The Arorás.

Chapter III, C.

Tribes, Castes and Leading Families.

The Arorás.

Like the Khatrís, some are Sikhs, some are Hindus. They are active and enterprising. They are the money-lenders of the district; and have more taste for shop-keeping and trading than for agriculture; but they are far from objecting to lay their clutches on a lightly-assessed village; almost all the *dharwaís* (village weighmen) are Arorás. A good many of them acquired some proprietary connection with the land during Sikh times. As a rule, neither the Khatrís nor Arorás cultivate their lands with their own hands. They employ tenants to do this, but the Arora when he does turn his hand to agriculture generally makes a very fair cultivator.

Other tribes.

Other tribes of the district are the following:—Moghal, Afghán, Bhatti, Khokhar, Langah, Dogar, Jamn, Hindal, Phularwan, Nonari, Paracha, Harl, Wirk, Naul, Baori, Kalera, Dahir, Seho, Kes, Nohil and Chhatta. These are Muhammadan tribes; most of them are Jats, and some are mere sub-divisions of more important clans. The menial classes, such as *mochís*, *hajáms*, &c., belong to a different category. The Sarás are both Hindus and Muhammadans. Other Hindu tribes are the Sandrana, Gopirai, Bopirai, Aulak, Hinjra, Brahmin and Rathor.

Intermarriage among tribes.

Among the Muhammadans, Chishtís, Khaggás, Kharrals Kathiás, Wattás and Patháns ordinarily marry their daughters in their respective tribes only, but they will all give their daughter in marriage to a Saiyad. A Saiyad will not marry his daughter to other but a Saiyad. Though none of the above will marry their own females to lower caste Muhammadans, they not unfrequently take a bride from among the daughters of these people. Hindus in this district observe the same customs as elsewhere, save that they marry at a later age. With them marriage is always inside the caste and outside the *gôt*. Among Aroras and Khatrís marriage is also avoided inside the *gôt* of a man's mother and of both grandmothers. Among Sikh Jats apparently marriage is permitted within the three latter, provided that the bride is not nearly connected. The rules as to social intercourse in the matter of food and drink are much as elsewhere, though possibly somewhat more lax in the case of Hindus except Khatrís.

Leading families.

A large portion of this district was formerly held in *jágír* by various servants and favourites of the Sikh Government. Some of these were resumed at annexation; others lapsed by the death of the holders, so that, in 1854, the proportion between *jágír* and *khálsa* estates had fallen from 60 per cent. to 12 per cent. The largest estates of this class are held by Bedí Bába Khem Singh, K.C.I.E., who is looked upon as the lineal descendant and representative of Bába Nanak, and therefore held in much veneration among a large class of Sikhs, and by his nephews Babás Deva Singh, Parduman Singh and Uttam Singh, the sons of Bába Sanpuran Singh. He also possesses *jágírs* in the Jullundur district, and is a man of considerable influence and resources. His *jágír* villages are situated near Basírpur in the Dipálpur tahsíl. He also owns

Chapter III, D.

Village Communities and Tenures.

Leading families.

eight estates in the Pákpattan tahsíl, of which four are included in the Sohág-Pára Colony; three others were purchased by him in 1893 free of land revenue. A Pathán family, of whom Muhammad Amín Khan, Zaildár, and Shahbáz Khan, both Honorary Magistrates, are the chief members, hold five estates in *jágír* in the Dipálpur tahsíl. With these exceptions there are no considerable estates of this class, and the holders are men of no importance or influence. There is only one *tálukdár* of any importance in this district, Saadat Ali Khan, Kharral, of Kamália, the representative of a family which at one period appears to have exercised a kind of feudal authority on the lower Rávi. The family of the Kamália Kharral has already been noticed on page 35 (see also *Punjab Chiefs*, Volume II, page 63). In recognition of services performed to the Sikh Government, they were allowed to retain a right to collect one-eighth of the gross produce of *táluka* Kamália; the administration, however, being vested in *kárdárs*, to whom they were obliged to render every assistance their influential position enabled them to give. This right to one-eighth of the produce, here called *athokh*, was reduced by Díwán Sáwan Mal to one-twentieth, a *nazrána*, however, of Rs. 1,600, and the obligation of repairing the wood-work of wells formerly incumbent on them, being remitted at the same time. The *táluka* consists of 43 estates, from the sub-proprietors of which the *tálukdár* receives two *páís* in the *kharwár*, or one-twentieth of the grain produce: and four annas per *kanál* on *zabti* crops. Attempts were made in 1854 to convert the demand into a rate in cash on the Government *jama*, but the objections of both the *tálukdár* and the *zamíndárs* to this system were so decided that it had to be relinquished. In all other cases where there were two classes of proprietors, the Settlement was made with the sub-proprietors.

Tálukdárs.

SECTION D.—VILLAGE COMMUNITIES AND TENURES.

Village tenures.

Table No. XV shows the number of villages held in the various forms of tenure. But the accuracy of the figures is more than doubtful. It is in many cases simply impossible to class a village satisfactorily under any of the ordinarily recognised tenures; the primary division of rights between the main sub-divisions of the village following one form, while the interior distribution among the several proprietors of each of these sub-division follow another form which itself often varies from one sub-division to another. Mr. Elphinstone wrote as follows in 1856 regarding the village tenures of the district :—

"That people accustomed to a semi-independent nomadic life should accommodate themselves to all the intricacies of tenure which prevail among more civilized communities in India, could hardly be expected; my observations on this head will therefore be brief. The *zamindári* tenure, which involves obedience to the elders of a village, observance of local customs, and a generally pacific

Chapter III, D.

Village Communities and Tenures.

Village tenures.

disposition, is by no means in favour with the Jat tribes, except in its most simple form, that of a village belonging to a single proprietor. It prevails however, among the Aráins on the Khánwah Canal, the Kambohs and Khatrís, of Pákpattan and Gugera, and to some extent among the small tribes, who have been before explained as being included among the Wasiwáns. In form it does not appear to differ from the *zamindári* tenures of the North-Western Provinces. It includes all estates belonging to a single proprietor, as well as those where possession of land has not been separately defined among the different shareholders, and the Government revenue is paid by an allotment on shares according to the custom of the village. I may remark that the term *biswa* denoting the amount of each proprietor's share in the produce of the estate, and his liability with regard to the Government *jama*, was unknown before our rule. It was introduced by the Hindustáni officials, but the people themselves now fully understand it, and have adopted it. Their own mode of explaining the amount of a proprietor's share was more simple. They merely designated him as a shareholder of one-third of the whole, or one-fifth, as the case might be. "The *bhayachara* form of tenure is very common, and in great favour with the Jats. Each member of the brotherhood is in separate possession of his part of the estate. He only pays that portion of the revenue assessed on the land in his possession, and enjoys the whole surplus profits accruing from his property. The joint responsibility of members of a village community, so prevalent in some parts of India, and now also introduced in this part of the Punjab, appears to have had no existence under the Sikh rule—at least as regards this district. The Government took its prescribed share of the actual produce; proprietors, therefore, who had allowed their lands to fall out of cultivation, did not contribute towards the revenue of the estate. The existence of separate village communities, composed of members connected with each other by ties of race or blood, appears not to have been owing to any interest the Government felt in the matter, but solely to the habits of the people themselves. So long as the marketable value of the land shall remain low, and the monied classes find no advantage in investing their capital in land, there is very little fear of the *bhayachára* communities in this district being broken up by any but natural causes, as the deterioration of the soil, or the destruction of the estate by inroads of the river. The rule of pre-emption enforced by our Government will also, of course, have a most important effect in preventing strangers from entering village communities. Cases in which questions of pre-emption were involved could only have been of very rare occurrence under the Sikh rule, as the distinctions between the several classes of the community were then more marked, and the Hindu, for instance, would hardly have ventured to buy land in a village belonging to half-civilized Jats. I have therefore not been able to trace any precedent of similar rules having obtained at that period. In some towns, however, it has been at least customary for the *kárdárs* and authorities not to sanction the sale of houses to strangers without the concurrence of the villagers. *Pattidári* estates are not numerous: their origin may be traced almost in every instance to the founders of a village having been of different castes or tribes, and their descendants thus not having been able to amalgamate into a single community. Since annexation a few sales of land have also tended to introduce this tenure into some estates. I may observe, however, that perfect *pattidári* villages are not known. The *banjar*, and often a portion of the inundated land, is held in common throughout the district, whether the tenure of the cultivated portion be *bhayachára* or *pattidári*."

Statistics of village tenures.

According to the Settlement Report of 1874 the villages of the district were distributed in the different *parganahs* as regards their form of tenure according to the accompanying statement:—

Name of tahsil.	*Zamindári.*	*Pattidári.*	*Bhayachára.*	Total.
Gugera	295	151	108	554
Montgomery	320	44	128	492
Dipálpur	455	140	15	610
Pákpattan	411	35	66	512
Total ...	1,481	370	317	2,168

Chapter III, D.

Village Communities and Tenures.

Statistics of village tenures.

Comparing the above figures with those given in Table XV a large decrease in the number of villages will appear to have occurred. This is due to the fact that a large number of small plots and scattered wells, which were originally held on lease or other forms of grant from Government, and which used to be treated as separate estates for the purposes of the revenue records and agricultural statistics, have in recent years for these purposes been amalgamated with larger units, and the latter dealt with as estates. Such amalgamated estates are generally classed as *bhayachára,* although, of course, their resemblance to the true *bhayachára* type of estate prevalent in upper India is of the smallest, more especially as regards their origin. The individual plots or wells are held either jointly or with separate possession regulated by ancestral or other shares The ordinary classification into *zamindári, pattidari* and *bhayachára* tenures, as distinguished in the stereotyped official nomenclature, is in point of fact not very applicable to the kinds of estates found in this district. Among the nomadic and pastoral tribes, the majority of the population, joint tenure of a village or villages by the family or clan was in all probability the original form of proprietary right so far as the germs of this existed under native rule. In some cases the separate possession, which has been subsequently developed, has been defined by ancestral or other recognized shares ; in others it has depended on the number of wells sunk by the respective shareholders individually or in groups, together with the amount of area attached to such wells. Well-sinking has in fact been, there is every reason to believe, at once the motive for the separation of joint interests and the measure of the extent of such interests. The shareholders or group of shareholders who sank a well in the village waste soon, if not at once, obtained a recognized right to its exclusive possession, and to that of a reasonable area round it which it could irrigate; and such right subsequently developed into proprietorship under our rule. Among the more strictly agricultural tribes, such as Kambohs and Aráins, it is probable that in the case of many estates there was no initial stage of joint tenure of the whole village area, but that from the first separate possession by families or groups obtained, consequent on separate well-sinking. The construction of a well seems in short to have been the chief form of original separate appropriation of portions of the village area. In Sikh times the local officials would, with a view to further development, frequently allow outsiders to appropriate portions of the waste area of villages and to sink wells. It is common to find the same individual proprietors included in varying combination or with varying shares in several joint holdings in one and the same estate. One reason for this, no doubt, is that the original settlers, where they formed a body of agriculturists, or the descendants of the original single pastoral owner or group of owners, combined in different groups and in different shares to construct the several wells in the village area. The complication in some cases goes even further, and the proprietors who own the actual

Chapter III, D.

Village Communities and Tenures.

Statistics of village tenures.

well cylinder form a group differing more or less from those who own the land attached to and irrigated by the well. Where separation has progressed far the areas attached to individual wells are themselves owned in separate holdings. The process of the separation of interests by means of well construction may in some cases be seen in operation even now, where an estate or sub-division of an estate recorded as held jointly by several shareholders has been in reality divided among them by the appropriation of separate portions of the joint area and the construction of wells therein. On a formal partition taking place the wells would in most cases be allotted to the sharers who had sunk them so far as this was consistent with recorded shares. The holy clans, Chishtís and Saiyads, have in the past acquired a good deal of land in some parts of the district by a process known as *háth rakhai* (protection). In the former days of perpetual turbulence their religious position seems to have secured them a good deal of immunity from the attacks of robber tribes; the weaker clans taking advantage of this in a good many cases transferred a share of a village to them, and thus shielded themselves under their superior sanctity. The Chishtís of Pákpattan appear to have acquired a good deal of land in this way.

Riverain law.

On the Rávi the custom which regulates the limits of ownership in riverain villages varies considerably. In the Montgomery tahsíl as between whole estates on opposite sides of the river the *kishtibána* or deep stream rule modified for cases of so called avulsion is universal. The main channel of the river in the cold weather as determined by the course which boats take is the common boundary of ownership except in cases where the main stream has otherwise than by gradual erosion bodily changed its course and left land (*chákar* or *gatti*) so far in *statu quo* between its old and present course as to be recognizable. In the latter case the proprietary right, both as between whole estates and as between individual owners, is left unaffected. In these cases of so called avulsion due to a bodily shifting of the river's course the dry bed is, as a rule, divided equally between the two estates which it separates.

As between estates on the same side of the river, land not shown in the field map of the previous settlement and gained by accretion due to the gradual retreat of the main channel is divided in proportion to the *maház* or frontage of each estate on the river; but where an estate has lost land shown in the last settlement map fresh land subsequently thrown up on its site belongs to such estate. The custom regarding the distribution of accreted land between individual proprietors varies a good deal. The general custom is that land shown in the settlement field map and subsequently washed away, but which has again emerged (*burd shuda barámad*) belongs to its former owners, while land thrown up in excess of that included in the settlement field map (*nau-barámad*) is the common property of the estate or sub-division of an estate (*shamilát deh* or *patti* or *taraf*) opposite which it emerges. Here again the *maház* rule

Chapter III, D.
Village Communities and Tenures.
Riverain law.

comes into play. In some estates, however, all land which accretes by alluvion is considered *shámilát* whether it be *nau-barámad* or *burd shuda barámad,* and in others again *nau-báramad* is divided by the *maház* rule between individual proprietors.

In the Gugera tahsîl out of 94 riverain villages in not less than 73 the boundaries, whether in the stream of the river or on either side of it, are fixed, and changes whether by gradual shifting of the river's course or by avulsion do not involve any change in ownership. The custom is known as *wár-pár.* In 5 out of the remaining 21 villages, *viz*., Chendpur, Chak Chendpur, Kot Táhir, Sandrana and Sheikh Baláwal, the deep stream rule pure and simple without any modification for cases of avulsion prevails. In the remaining villages, 16 in number, the rule is the more common one of the modified deep stream which prevails in the Montgomery tahsîl, and as the dry beds in cases of avulsion are divided equally between the opposite villages, the general custom regarding the division of accreted land as between estates on the same bank of the river and as between individual proprietors of the same estate is, with one or two exceptions, the same in both tahsîls.

On the Sutlej throughout its whole course in this district the rule regulating the limits of the proprietary right is the deep stream modified for cases of avulsion. In the villages fronting the Ferozepore district in cases of avulsion the dry bed is divided equally between the estates on either side of it; in the case of those opposite Bahâwalpur the dry bed goes to the estate which has not suffered the avulsion. The general custom regulating the distribution of accreted land as between estates on this side of the river and as between individual proprietors in the same estate is, as on the Rávi, *i.e.*, *burd shuda barámad* belongs to its former estate or individual proprietor, but *nau-barámad* is divided between adjacent estates by the *maház* or frontage rule, while within any given estate it is *shámilát.* There are exceptions to this custom in a few cases, *e.g.*, in Dona Tája *nau-barámad* land goes by the *maház* rule to the proprietors against whose holdings it is thrown up; while in Laluki Mohar all land gained by alluvion, whether *burd shuda barámad* or *nau-barámad,* becomes the common property of the whole estate (shámilát-deh).

The question of the jurisdiction boundary arises on the Sutlej. As between this district and Ferozepore, it is regulated by Punjab Government Notification No. 121, dated 25th February 1891, under which the common boundaries of ownership of certain riverain estates in each of these two districts were declared to be the common boundaries of the two districts.

Formerly the boundary of jurisdiction between this district and Bahâwalpur was the deep stream of the Sutlej, but since 1874, when the ruling given by the Government of India in 1860 in the

Chapter III, D.

Village Communities and Tenures.

Riverain law.

Kachi Chauhán case was made applicable to all cases of river changes between British territory and Baháwalpur, this rule has been modified in the usual way for cases of avulsion. The boundaries of jurisdiction as between Baháwalpur and British territory thus coincide with the boundaries of ownership as between villages in Baháwalpur and in this district.

For the few estates on the Rávi in the Gugera tahsíl which face the Lahore district and follow the deep stream rule in regard to ownership, no definite rule for determining the boundaries of jurisdiction has ever been laid down: in practice they coincide with those of ownership.

Proprietary tenures.

Table No. XV shows the number of proprietors or shareholders and the gross area held in property under each of the main forms of tenure, and also gives details for large estates and for Government grants and similar tenures. Here again the accuracy of the figures is exceedingly doubtful; indeed, land tenures assume so many and such complex forms in the Punjab that it is impossible to classify them successfully under a few general headings: but they serve to show that the area per proprietor and lessee is sufficient over the whole district, and in the Sutlej tahsíls, Dipálpur and Pákpattan, ample. In the Rávi tahsíls the area per proprietor would come out larger were it not that in many cases the same proprietor has been counted more than once because he owns land in several estates. There is in point of fact no congestion of landowners in any part of the district except in the case of a limited number of estates belonging to Arafns in Gugera and to Kambohs in Dipalpur. It must, however, be borne in mind that as expensive well-irrigation is an essential adjunct to the agriculture of the district, the capital expenditure falling on the proprietor is heavy, and this renders it necessary that the area owned per proprietor should generally be larger than in tracts where the initial expenses of cultivation are lower owing to the less need for artificial irrigation.

Tenants and rent.

Table No. XVI shows the number of tenancy holdings and the gross area held under each of the main forms of tenancy as they stood in 1896-97; while Table No. XXI gives the current rent-rates of various kinds of land as returned in 1896-97. But the accuracy of the latter set of figures is probably doubtful; indeed, it is impossible to state general rent-rates which shall even approximately represent the letting value of land throughout a whole district. Table XV shows clearly how important a position the tenant-at-will occupies in the agricultural economy of the district. Of the total area cultivated in 1896-97 the percentages in the hands of occupancy tenants and tenants-at-will paying rent were as follows :—

Chapter III, D.

Village Communities and Tenures.

Tenants and rent.

	Montgomery.	Gugera.	Dipálpur.	Pákpattan.	Total District.
Occupancy tenants...	5·34	3·45	3·36	·22	2·65
Tenants-at-will ...	56·0	60·0	69·0	73·0	68·0
Total	61·34	63·45	72·36	73·22	70·65

The area in the hands of occupancy tenants is very small comparatively in all tahsíls. The figures for tenants-at-will include land cultivated by persons who are co-proprietors in such land and who pay rent for it to the joint proprietary body; but even allowing for this it is clear that by far the greater part of the cultivation, more especially in the Sutlej tahsíls, is carried on by tenants-at-will. The proportion would be greater than appears from the figures for the Rávi tahsíls were it not that in 1896-97, the famine year, and in the two preceding years many tenants threw up their wells and went to the Chenáb Canal. The fact is that in a tract like that comprised in this district, where laborious well-irrigation is an indispensable adjunct to agriculture and population is comparatively sparse, a self-cultivating proprietor can by himself cultivate only a comparatively small area, the profits of which would scarcely suffice to recoup his somewhat heavy initial and recurring annual capital expenditure; he is forced therefore to supplement his income by the rent derived from the cultivation of tenants. Mr. Purser estimated the cost of starting a well with six pairs of bullocks and irrigating 25 acres at Rs. 640; and the annual cost of keeping it in work at Rs. 80. It is certainly not less now than it was in his time.

Tenants. Rights of occupancy.

While stating that the distinction between hereditary and non-hereditary tenants was unknown under native rule in this part of the Punjab, Captain Elphinstone says:—

"It is remarkable, therefore, that the cultivators should in some portions of the district, notwithstanding their uncertain tenure, have had the right to sell the *kásht* or cultivation of land; instances of such a right being acknowledged frequently came under the cognizance of the Settlement Courts. This claim to sell the right of cultivation was always founded on the fact of the claimant having been the first plougher of the soil. It was therefore of importance when determining the position cultivators were to occupy, to ascertain to whom the claim of *butáh már*, or first ploughing of the land, belonged. In accordance with instructions issued on this subject by superior authority, all cultivators who could make out their claim to the *butáh már* were recognized as hereditary

Chapter III, D.

Village Communities and Tenures.

Tenants. Rights of occupancy.

cultivators—a privilege also conferred on those who had cultivated for eight years, if residents in the village, and twelve years, if non-residents. The privilege, however, owing to the abundance of land, was by no means sought after at the Settlement of 1856; facility of removal, on the contrary, being the chief object aimed at. An idea was prevalent that by becoming *maurúsi* (hereditary) they would eventually become responsible for the land revenue to Government. Thus, a spectacled unusual in the Punjab, was often seen at the time of Settlement, of cultivators strenuously refusing to be recorded as hereditary, to the despair of the proprietor, who in the desire of the cultivator to be recorded as non-hereditary, recognised a sure indication of his readiness to leave the village, whenever superior temptations should be held out by his neighbours."

Butáh már.

It must always be remembered that under native rule no such thing as absolute proprietary right was recognized. The missing class was not the hereditary tenant, but the proprietor. When the British Government made a present of the land to certain individuals, all the hereditary cultivators did not share in this boon, yet they undoubtedly had rights of occupancy which the Sikhs would have respected, and it is for this reason that we find Captain Elphinstone giving *butáh már* as a ground for superior tenant right, while Major Marsden says :—"The principal title to proprietary right in this district seems to be clearing the jungle and bringing the land under cultivation. It generally extends to each member of a fraternity or association engaged in this original task, and does not reach beyond the land actually cultivated. Thus *butáh már* here conferred proprietary right, and proprietary right was simply the right to hold the land as long as the tenant cultivated it, or arranged for its cultivation." No doubt he might dispose of it with the approval of the *kárdár*, as Captain Elphinstone's *butah már* tenants could do. In the Atári *iláka* it was a regular custom for hereditary tenants to sublet their lands. The system of raising non-hereditary cultivators to the position of hereditary tenants after they had cultivated the same land for a certain number of years, was continued after completion of the Settlement of 1856, till it attracted notice and was stopped. In his report on the subject, the Deputy Commissioner stated that no cases had been known of proprietors seeking to oust their tenants, but that they had occasionally tried to make them stay by an appeal to the law courts.

Migratory character of tenant population.

From the earliest days of our rule, the migratory character of the tenant population of this district has been a subject of anxiety to the revenue officers. In 1853 Major Marsden, then Deputy Commissioner, wrote on the occasion of the failure of the Khánwah Canal :—"There is a strong probability that extensive desertions of *asámis* will take place, and the villages proportionally suffer. It is unfortunate that the present unusual *sailáb* on the Sutlej should occur in a year when the Khánwah has so signally failed, as it holds out inducements to cultivators to abandon their villages and reap a more profitable harvest with less labour." And again, writing of villages with low *jamás*, he says :—"The extent of *sailába* land, which could be cultivated at small expense, enables the *zamindárs* enjoying these easy *jamás* to offer such advantageous terms to cultivators as might induce them to abandon their present holdings, and thus embarrass the more laborious and less favoured farmers." These lucky villages were

Village Communities and Tenures.

Migratory character of tenant population.

subsequently ruined by the failure of *sailáb*. In 1855 Mr. Vans Agnew recanted his opinion that it was the "laziness of the cultivators which caused them to abandon their villages and lands on the slightest pressure." In paragraphs 50 and 51 of his Settlement Report, Lieutenant Elphinstone speaks in no uncertain tone of the supremacy of the tenant. He describes the tenant as declining to be recorded hereditary, "facility of removal being the chief object aimed at;" and the despair of the proprietor at his tenants insisting on being entered as non-hereditary. He points out the evils of the competition for tenants caused by the taste for cultivation that was springing up. "Several instances have come to my knowledge where *zamindárs* have been obliged to agree to receive only one-eighth of the produce from their cultivators, in order to prevent their leaving, although the usual rate had formerly never exceeded one-third or one-fourth of the produce. Mr. Cust says of the cultivators :—"The least pressure, either of season or demand, would cause them to abscond." In 1864, Mr. Ford, Commissioner of Multán, wrote *apropos* of new grants of Government waste lands :—"Cultivation has spread during the past year, but with our scanty population * * * I think that we are giving with one hand and taking with the other * * * We are now weakening our villages and forcing them to become impoverished. Mr. Blyth mentions this fact very forcibly." The manner in which the grant of Government waste lands has encouraged this tendency will be noticed under the land revenue history of the district.

Economic position of the tenant.

It will be seen from what has been said above that the economic position of the tenant-at-will, or, as he is locally termed, the *rahak*, is a strong one. It is no exaggeration to say that he is the mainstay of cultivation. The demand, except in a limited number of estates, is for tenants to cultivate the land, and not for land to be cultivated by tenants. The prosperity of individual estates and proprietors depends on their ability and success in attracting and keeping tenants. For this purpose advances more or less liberal have to be made to the tenant for seed, for food and for personal expenditure either in cash or in kind, or in the case of the poorer proprietors by giving collateral security for the tenant to the money-lender. Tenants insist on being allowed to cut *jowár* and wheat freely as fodder for their agricultural cattle, and also to some extent for those which are kept for domestic purposes, and, as a rule, for such cuttings no rent is paid. In bad seasons or even at other times tenants have little hesitation in migrating to more favoured estates or tracts, very often without repaying the advances which they have received. Outstanding advances due from an incoming tenant to his former landlord are, on the other hand, often paid by his new landlord. The tenant is, broadly speaking, master of the situation, and the expenses incurred in connection with him are generally a considerable tax on the landlord's agricultural profits. There are, of course, more or less marked variations in the tenant-attracting power of different estates ; tenants going far more readily to those

Chapter III, D.

Village Communities and Tenures.

which get plentiful canal-irrigation or *sailáb* than to those more dependent on well-irrigation.

Rent.

Rent is almost universally taken in the form of *batái* or actual division of the produce; *kankút* is rarely practised and *zabti* crops are generally divided. *Zabti* cash rents are in a few cases taken on pepper and cotton, and range from 9 to 12 annas per *kanál*, or Rs. 4-8-0 to Rs. 6 per acre. The share of produce paid by the tenant varies in different parts of the district. In the Montgomery tahsíl the common rate for well-irrigated crops in riverain estates is given in the assessment reports as one-third, and in the *bár* estates as one-fourth, but in some estates where well lands get abundant *sailáb* the well-irrigated rate is one-half. In Gugera the usual rate is one-fourth, while one-fifth is common in the Ganji Bár. In Dipálpur one-fifth is generally taken for well-irrigated crops if they do not receive canal water as well, and one-fourth if they do; in Pákpattan the latter is the prevailing rate for all well-irrigated crops. For crops receiving canal-irrigation alone two-fifths and one-third are the common rates in the Gugera tahsíl; while in Dipálpur it is nearly always one-fourth; the latter is also the usual rate in Pákpattan, but there one-third is not unfrequently taken. For crops grown on river *sailáb* one-half is the most usual rate in Montgomery, but two-fifths is also taken; in Gugera, the latter rate is not uncommon, but one-third is more often taken; in Dipálpur one-fourth is the prevailing rate; in Pákpattan one-fourth and one-third rates are equally common. For pure *báráni* crops the usual rates are one-third in Montgomery, one-fourth in Gugera and Dipálpur, and one-third and one-fourth in Pákpattan. Tenants supply their own seed and well cattle; although in order to enable them to do so they very often receive *takávi* advances from the landlord either in cash or by the latter giving security for such advances from the money-lender. In some estates tenants who receive *takávi* advances pay in consideration thereof a higher rate of *batái* than those who do not. On the Rávi and also in the Pákpattan tahsíl the landlord supplies at his own expense all the woodwork of the wells, while in Dipálpur its cost is generally shared between landlord and tenant by the payment of 6 maunds of grain per annum per well wheel from the *túla* or common heap mentioned below to the owner of the wheel. In the latter two tahsíls the landlord nearly always bears the cost of the annual silt clearances of the canal water-courses.

Green fodder and straw.

Besides his share of the ripe produce, the owner is entitled to a certain amount of green fodder each harvest. This varies from 10 *marlás* to one *kanál* per well each season, and is calculated to be worth Rs. 5 per *kanál* for wheat, and Rs. 2-8-0 per *kanál* for *jowár*. On the other hand, the tenant is allowed to grow turnips and to cut green *jowár* and wheat for fodder; and such fodder is exempt from *batái* or other rent charge. In theory there are certain limits to the area which may be devoted as above to fodder, but in practice the tenant expects and generally succeeds in obtaining as much of the turnips, *jowár* and well-irrigated wheat as he

Chapter III, D.

Village Communities and Tenures.

Green fodder and straw.

needs for his agricultural cattle, and to some extent also for those kept for domestic purposes. From three-fourths to the whole of the turnips grown are generally used for fodder; in the case of purely well-irrigated wheat the limits are one-fourth and one-seventh in different parts of the district; while in the case of that receiving both well and canal water they are one-twelfth and one-fourteenth. In the cases of purely canal-irrigated, *sailáb* and *báráni* cultivation the only crop cut for fodder is *jowár;* the proportion of this crop so consumed varies from three-fourths to the whole for all kinds of cultivation. In addition to the above the tenant takes the whole of the straw of harvested crops which receive well-irrigation. In the case of those ripened by canal-irrigation alone the landlord in Gugera generally takes the same share of straw as of grain; in Dipálpur and Pákpattan he does so in respect of a small proportion of such crops. The same share of straw as of grain is generally taken on *sailáb* and *báráni* crops (except where *batái* is one-half, when one-third share is taken). The main straw crops are *jowár, másh* and wheat. If the tenant leaves his well before all the dry fodder is used up, or if he sells it he has to give the owner the same share of it as of the grain produce.

Manner of dividing the crops.

Division of the crop is carried out by the *dharwái,* or village accountant. When the grain heap is ready he commences to divide it at the appropriate rate of *batái;* the division is carried on until the amount of grain left, called *tála* or *talwera,* is considered approximately sufficient to cover the payments which have to be made to the village menials and others, and the landlord's *málikána,* also called *malba* or *kharch,* which he takes over and above his *batái* share. The above amounts are taken from the *tála;* if there is any deficiency it is made up rateably out of the amounts previously distributed to the landlord and tenant, and any small surplus that there may be in the *tála* is given to the *chúhra* or *mochi,* or sometimes to the tenant. Cotton, the chief rabi crop, is picked at intervals from the middle of September to the middle of December. The pickings are made by the women of the village under the superintendence of the *muhásil,* or landlord's care-taker; after picking the cotton is at once divided between tenant and landlord, the payment in kind to the pickers being first deducted.

Málikána.

Málikána, or the landlord's extra proprietary due, comes out of the *tála.* In the Rávi tahsíls and also in Dipálpur it is, as a rule, calculated at a definite rate on the landlord's share of the produce which is known as *leá.* For well-irrigated crops the common rate is one *topa* per *man,* which is equivalent to one-sixteenth; but it is often higher in estates where canal-irrigation is obtainable, and also on *sailáb* and *báráni* crops. Where one-half *batái* is taken on *sailáb* crops in the Rávi riverain *málikána* is not charged in addition. In Pákpattan the *málikána* is generally calculated on the whole produce divided between the landlord and tenant. On well-irrigated crops one *pái* per *máni,* equal to one-forty-eighth of the produce, is the most common rate: on *nahri*

Chapter III, D.

Village Communities and Tenures.

Málikána.

sailáb and *báráni* cultivation the rates are often higher, sometimes as much as 3 *páis* per *máni*, or one-sixteenth of the divisible produce. For the district, as a whole, the *málikána* averages from 2 to 3 per cent of the divisible grain produce after deducting the payments made to *kamíns*. In the case of *zabti* crops, cotton, pepper, tobacco, and maize the rate is commonly one sér per standard maund of 40 sérs calculated generally on the divisible produce. At the regular settlement *málikána* was often recorded as *malba*.

Canal rates.

It is the almost universal custom on the Inundation Canals in the Sutlej tahsíls for the tenants to pay the fluctuating canal water-rates charged for irrigation, except where one-half *batái* is taken on purely canal-irrigated crops when the water-rates are paid by the landlord. These rates have been recently converted formally into occupier's rates payable by the tenant, supplemented by a fluctuating canal-advantage land-revenue rate payable by the landlord.

Payments to village menials and others.

The principal village menials, who are paid in kind for services rendered out of the produce of cultivated land, are the *kumhár* (potter), and *tarkhán* (carpenter), who are known as superior (*vade*) *kamíns*, and the *lohár* (blacksmith), *mochi* (leather-worker) and *nái* (barber) who are inferior (*laude*) *kamins*. The first four are all more or less directly concerned with the provision of agricultural implements; the *nái* is not directly concerned with agriculture, but as the village barber, messenger and general factotum, he renders a very considerable amount of indirect assistance in agricultural operations. These *kamíns* are called *sepi*, from the *sep* or customary services which they render. A considerable number of payments other than the above are made out of the grain produce; such as those to the *mullah* (village priest), *mirási* (bard), *dharwai* (weighman and accountant), *muhásil* or *thápi* (guardian of threshing floor), *chuhra* (sweeper) and others. The payments to the first two are, of course, not agricultural expenses, nor those to beggars. In many cases no *thápi* is employed. The *dharwai* generally pays a lump sum to the proprietors in consideration of the grain dues which he takes for weighments. It forms a kind of tax on his business; he also generally takes the contract for the *dharat* dues levied on sales and purchases in some villages which will be noticed below. The *chuhra* is paid both for winnowing grain crops and for domestic services. He is considered a *sepi*. The above payments are made as a general rule out of the common heap or *tála*, and thus fall partly on the landlord and partly on the tenant. In some cases, however, the tenant defrays the payments to the five agricultural *kamins* and to the *chuhra* out of his own share; while in others the two superior *kamíns* are paid out of the *tála* and the tenant settles with the remainder. In addition to grain the *kamíns* generally receive some head loads or bundles of the unthreshed crop, and are also allowed the last day's cotton picking (*oú*). On lands attached to wells the grain payments to *kamíns* are generally made at so many maunds per well; in the case of others at so much per plough or at a certain proportion of the produce. In the *kharíf* they are made

Chapter III, D.

Village Communities and Tenures.

Payments to village menials and others.

from rice, maize, *jowar*, *másh*, *chíná* and *kangni*; when there is a deficiency in these it is made up from cotton at a lower rate. In the *rabi* the dues are paid from wheat, barley and gram. The rates at which the payments dealt with above are made vary considerably; they will be found recorded in full detail in the settlement records. On lands attached to wells the *tarkhán* and *kumhár* generally receive more than the *lohár*, *mochi* and *nái*; three to four local maunds of 16 *topás* each per well of six yokes per harvest is a common rate for each of the first two, and two to three maunds for each of the other three. Not unfrequently less is given in the *kharif* than in the *rabi* harvest. Each of the above also generally gets one or more loads (*bhari*, *púli* or *gadda*) of unthreshed crop of varying size per cultivating holding (*banna*) attached to the well. On *sailáb* land the practice is very various. In a good many cases only the *tarkhán*, *lohár* and *nái* receive dues on this class of cultivation, but the *mochi* is sometimes paid; 4 *topás* per plough for the first two and two *topás* for the *nái*, and for the *mochi* when paid are common rates, or two *topás* per *máni* of 12 local maunds for the *tarkhán* and *lohár* each, and one *topa* for the *nái*. As in the case of well lands, each of the above receives one load or bundle of unthreshed crop per cultivator's holding. The sweeper generally receives four *topás* per *máni* of the grain which he winnows (*udái*) in addition to further grain payments for domestic services. A further payment of four *topás* per *máni* is also made to the *kumhár* for carrying grain from the threshing floor (*dhuai*). The *dharwai's* weighment fee varies from one to two *topás* per *máni* on the whole produce, and is taken from the *tála*. The *muhásil* or guardian of the grain heap receives generally one *topa* per *máni* of 12 maunds, or per *khalwár* of 10 maunds. He is also called *thápi*, a name derived from the wooden stamp or *thappa* with which he stamps bits of mud placed here and there on the grain heap to prevent its being tampered with prior to division. The five agricultural *kamíns*, *tarkhán*, *kumhár*, *lohár*, *nái* and *mochi*, get a fee of one or two *topás* per plough from the cultivator at seed-time; this is known as *biyái*. The *tarkhán* also gets one *topa* of grain for fixing the pole (*hal*) of the plough in the boot, and the *lohár* the same for putting on the staple into which the share fits. These fees are known as *dhurái* and *kundái*, whence the saying: Katik *biyái*, Sáwan *dhurái*. The *chuhra* generally gets the dead cattle, including the hides. Other village servants and retainers who have to be paid at harvest time from the *tála* are the village bard (*mirási sepi*) and the wandering bard (*mirási jakh*). They receive a small amount of grain, generally one *topa* per heap or per cultivator's holding. The former also gets a share of *thánapatti* where levied; this is a charge made on the occasion of the marriage of the daughter of a non-proprietor, and paid by the conductor of the marriage procession. The *mullah* writes charms to keep off goblins and cattle diseases. His fee is called *rasúlwáhi*, and amounts to about the same as that of the *mirási*; so also does that of the *brahman*. *Faqírs* and attendants at *dharmsálás* receive small gratuities. The herdsman (*vági* or *chheru*) is generally paid in grain out of the *tála* at the rate of four *topás* per well, and one

Chapter III, D.

Village Communities and Tenures.

bundle per cultivator's holding. The *khoji* tracks stolen cattle and has plenty to do. *Mullahs, brahmans* and *faqirs* do not reside in every village; they have villages as their constituents, but reside where they see fit.

Dharat.

The *dharat* is a tax levied on sales in the village; it generally amounts to 3 pies, or one pice in the rupee *ad valorem*, and is paid by the buyer. It was a legacy of the Sikh rule. The *dharwai* takes the farm generally. He pays the proprietors a lump sum annually, part of which is the price paid for the right to collect the *dharat* and part is in consideration of the weighment fees which he levies at harvest time for dividing the produce.

Malba.

The proceeds are used as *malba* for common village expenses, such as feeding destitute travellers, travelling expenses of *lambardárs* attending court, &c. *Dharat* is now levied in only a few villages. *Malba* used to be levied as such, either by a money *báchh* or by a fixed charge on the produce. The latter was the more popular method. The accounts were kept by the *dharwai*, and were subject to annual scrutiny in the former case, and half-yearly examination in the latter. The *lambardárs* had full control in this matter.

What crops tenants to grow?

Rent for wood-work of wells.

There is no rule prescribing what crops a tenant is to grow. The customs regarding the supply of the wood-work of wells and the clearance of canal water-courses have already been noticed in connection with rent rates. When the owner of the well-cylinder is a person other than the owner or cultivator of the land irrigated by it, he generally receives one-eighth share of the divisible produce after deduction of *kámiána*, &c. This is called *athok*.

Agricultural labourers.

Day labourers (*mazdúrs*) are rarely employed except at harvest time. In the canal villages they may be entertained to clear the silt from the water-courses, but this is more frequently done on contract. The *lava* or reaper is paid in one of two methods. He receives 45 to 50 handfuls (*káins*) of unthreshed crops *per diem*, or otherwise a smaller amount per day sufficient for subsistence while engaged in reaping, *plus* an amount of grain after the crop has been threshed, calculated either at 4 *topás per diem* or at the equivalent of a daily cash wage which is generally 4 annas. The amount is kept by the *muhásil* or the *dharwai*. The grain payment is generally made from the *túla* or common heap. The reaper cuts on the average two *kanáls* per day. Cotton picking is generally done by the women of the village. They are generally paid by a share of the amount picked, the share varies; in the earlier pickings when the yield is less, they get $\frac{1}{10}$th or more; in the later pickings when it is more plentiful their share is $\frac{1}{25}$th. The wages of labour are shown in Table No. XXVII; but the figures refer to the labour market of towns rather than to that of villages.

Chapter III, D.

Village Communities and Tenures.

Farm servants—*Kámás* and *ádhjogias.*

Farm servants, not daily labourers, but who are kept on for a period of time, are called *káma* or *ádhjogia.* The wages of the former vary in different localities; but he generally gets eight annas a month in cash and two pairs of shoes and a blanket in the year. In addition, he gets two meals a day, or 12 maunds of 36 sérs each of grain, with two suits of clothes, consisting each of a turban and two sheets. The *ádhjogia* gets no pay, but he shares in the produce. When the crops have been cut and dressed, and the preliminary deductions (which have been dealt with above) have been made, the master and his man divide what remains. First the master deducts his *málikána,* the seed-grain, and the value of the *máhls* of the well used up during the season. The remainder is then divided, so that the *ádhjogia* gets half the share he would have got had he been the owner of the yoke of bullocks he minded. The master pays for the seed of *jowár* eaten by the bullocks. Sometimes the *ádhjogia* gets an advance from his master, for which he pays no interest, and which is recovered as may be arranged. The *ádhjogia,* or half-yokeman, is the more commonly found farm-servant. For each yoke one man is usually considered necessary. But five men are enough for six yokes. One man is required to drive the cattle at the well, and another to open and close the water channels leading into the beds. When these men have done their turn of work, they have to be relieved by two others. A fifth man is required to look after the bullocks not at work. The persons employed in turning on the water must be stout fellows; but the cattle-drivers may be boys or old men. The herd will usually be a well grown lad.

Village officers.

The figures in the margin exhibit the existing number of these in the tahsíls of this district. The village headmen succeed to their office by hereditary right, subject to the approval of Deputy Commissioner, each village having generally one, some large villages and a few small ones, have each three or four *lambardárs.* They all represent their clients in dealing with the Government, and are responsible for the performance of their duties, such as the collection of the revenue, carrying out the orders of Government, and reporting all deaths, and abscondings, &c., of *máfidárs,* and are bound to assist in the prevention and detection of crime. The numerous small scattered well plots in the district have generally a separate *lambardár* for each, sometimes even more than one. Such plots, as a rule, originated

Tahsíl.	Zaildárs.	Village head-men.
Montgomery ...	7	543
Gugera	10	669
Dipálpur	11	814
Pákpattan	10	635
Total ...	38	2,661

Chapter III, D.

Village Communities and Tenures.

Village officers.

in separate grants from Government, and at the time of the grant each grantee was either tacitly or specially recognized as *lambardár*. Proposals are being worked out for the reduction of many of these petty *lambardáris*. The office of chief headman or *ala lambardár* has recently been abolished throughout the district. *Zaildárs* are appointed under the ordinary rules. The *lambardár* is remunerated by a five per cent. cess on the fixed and fluctuating land-revenue of his villages, which is known as *pachotra*.

Proposals have been submitted for a reconstruction of *zails*. The head-quarters of those proposed with the prevailing tribes in each are as follows :—

Tahsíl.	Zail.	No. of villages.	Annual fixed land revenue.	Prevailing tribe.
			Rs.	
Montgomery.	Kamália ...	44	4,806	Kharral, Arora, Sayad, Káthia, Jakhar, Chishti.
	Chicháwatni ...	40	3,611	Káthia, Arora Sanpal.
	Harappa ...	22	1,880	Káthia, Fatiána, Háns, Baghela, Sáhu.
	Dhaulri ...	27	2,002	Káthia, Sayad, Baghela, Wehniwál, Dadra, Khagga, Dullu.
	Montgomery ...	33	2,750	Murdána, Fatiána, Sayad, Sagla, Káthia, Tarána, Bodla.
	Núr Shah ...	39	3,095	Arora, Khagga, Sayad, Fatiána, Biloch, Wattu.
	Garh ...	27	3,598	Fatiána, Sayad, Purbána, Khagga, Wash, Kureshi.
Gugera.	Chendpur ..	30	4,643	Manes, Kharral, Khatri, Báth, Chadhar.
	Bucheke ...	32	6,203	Kharral, Awán, Manes, Khatri.
	Faridabád ...	29	4,338	Kharral, Awán, Máhtam.
	Danabád	40	6,984	Kharral, Arora, Khatri, Sayad.
	Jhámra ...	38	5,411	Kharral, Wattu
	Gugera ...	32	5,100	Wattu, Kharral, Sayad.
	Akbar ...	18	2,320	Sindhu Jat, Kharral, Aráin, Mughal.
	Jandráka ...	30	5,494	Kharral, Khatri, Khichi, Sayad.
	Mapálke ..	36	5,571	Kharral, Chakarke, Biloch, Jat Sikh, Bhati, Rájpút, Aráin.
	Mirak ...	21	4,585	Kharral, Mujiána, Khatri.

Tahsíl.	Zail.	No. of villages.	Annual fixed land revenue.	Prevailing tribe.
			Rs.	
DIPALPUR.	Shergarh ...	39	6,615	Sayad, Arora, Sheikh, Aráin, Kamboh.
	Dipálpur ...	41	9,265	Khatri, Aráin, Kamboh, Arora, Khokhar, Wattu.
	Mancharián ...	38	9,330	Kamboh, Arora, Sarai, Sayad, Aráin.
	Wendla ...	31	10,745	Khatri, Kamboh, Pathán, Wattu.
	Haveli ...	50	6,200	Rájpút, Gil, Jat Sikh, Arora, Wattu, Khatri, Chishti, Kharral, Mahtam.
	Dharanga ...	47	6,572	Mahar, Wattu, Kharral, Mahtam, Arora.
	Basirpur ...	63	16,015	Pathán, Arora, Wattu, Khatri, Aráin, Chishti.
	Atári ...	57	9,437	Pathán, Wattu, Mahtam.
	Dograi ...	37	11,805	Phularwan, Khatri, Wattu, Mahtam, Jat Sikh.
	Shahpur ...	52	11,905	Kamboh, Aráin, Sayad, Arora.
	Dhuliána ...	37	9,675	Kamboh, Arar, Jat, Rájpút, Chishti, Arora, Mahtam.
PAKPATTAN.	Bunga Hayát ...	34	6,025	Pathán, Wattu, Khatri, Arora.
	Malka Hans ...	28	3,510	Arora, Bodla, Khatri, Sayad.
	Sheikhupur ...	43	2,955	Chishti, Joiya, Arora, Sayad.
	Tibbi ...	59	6,442	Rájpút, Arora, Chishti, Sayad, Kamboh, Rath, Joiya.
	Hota ...	43	4,398	Arora, Chishti, Sayad, Dhudhi, Hotiána, Rath.
	Kalyána ...	31	4,555	Arora, Sayad, Jat, Dogar.
	Chánwat ...	35	5,725	Jat, Rájpút, Kamboh, Jat Sikh, Dogar, Khatri, Wattu.
	Pákpattan ...	41	5,442	Arora, Chishti, Jat Sikh, Khatri, Biloch, Wattu.
	Malleke Taruke ...	38	3,547	Wattu, Mahtam, Bodla, Arora, Pathán.
	Ghumáriwála ...	32	6,485	Wattu, Mahtam, Khatri, Arora, Jat Sikh, Kamboh.

Zaildárs.

At the Settlement of 1874 *zaildárs* were appointed over clusters of villages. These office-holders are meant to serve as a link between the Government officers and the *lambardárs.*

Chapter III, D.

Village Communities and Tenures.

Zaildárs.

They were selected with reference to their personal fitness and the influence they possess among their clansmen. As far as could be managed, villages of the same clan were included in the same *zail;* but, of course, this principle could not be carried out in its integrity. The *zaildár* is *lambardár* of one or more villages, and as such receives his remuneration as *lambardár*. As *zaildár* he is at present paid a deduction of one per cent. from the fixed and fluctuating land revenue of his *zail;* but it is proposed to arrange *zaildárs* in grades, and give them fixed grade pay out of a fund formed by deduction from the land revenue of the district. The grades proposed are as follows :—

Tahsíl.	1st grade. Rs. 150.	2nd grade, Rs. 125.	3rd grade. Rs. 100.
Gugera	2	6	2
Montgomery	1	4	2
Dipálpur	3	5	3
Pákpattan	3	5	2
Total ...	9	20	9

In the Dipálpur and Pákpattan tahsíls small portions of waste land were at last settlement exempted from revenue by Government and made over to the *zaildárs.* Similar grants were made in some cases in Gugera and Montgomery, but as they were not made in a strictly correct manner, the *zaildárs* have occasionally not been able to get possession. It has now been proposed to abolish these grants. The average number of estates in each *zail* is 38. Of the *zaildárs* six are Kharrals and six Wattus, and five are Arorás ; the Khatrís, Káthia, Fatiánas, Joizás, Jat Sikhs and Kambohs have each two representatives ; and the Khaggás, Maránás, Sandránás, Mughals, Phularwáns, Patháns, Arars, Háns and Chishtis one each.

Inámdárs.

In addition to the *zaildárs* it has been proposed to appoint 38 *sufaidposh inámdárs* on Rs. 40 per annum, one to each *zail.* The post of *ála lambardár* has been abolished. The number of *lambardárs* in the disrict is 2,661, which gives about 7 *lambardárs* to every four estates ; many men are *lambardárs* in more than one estate.

Patwáris.

According to proposals which have been submitted, the strength and pay of the *patwári* staff will be as follows :—

Chapter III, D.

Village Communities and Tenures.

Patwaris.

Tahsíl.	Number of Patwaris.					Averages per Circle.	
	1st grade on Rs. 14 per mensem.	2nd grade on Rs. 12 per mensem.	3rd grade on Rs. 10 per mensem.	Náíb Patwáris on Rs. 8 per mensem.	Total.	Estates.	Total area.
							Acres.
Montgomery	15	16	7	3	41	6	5,637
Gugera	18	18	10	3	49	7	5,401
Dipálpur	31	32	15	4	82	6	6,583
Pákpattan	19	20	10	3	52	7	7,373
Total ...	83	85	42	13	224	7	6,474

There are no *Hindi-khwán patwáris.* The pay of *patwári* is all fixed.

The Dharwai.

The *patwári,* we are told, is the village servant. In this district he never was, and never will be, a village servant. He is, as Captain Elphinstone says, "a new creation of our Government." The *dharwai,* who still flourishes, was the village accountant; the modern *patwári* corresponds rather to the Sikh *mutsaddi.* The *dharwai* still keeps the village accounts and weighs the grain as he did of yore. He keeps a shop, and generally takes the contract for the collection of the *dherat.* His papers are drawn up in *Lande,* not *Gurmukhi.* In former days he used to accompany the *mutsaddi,* and make a copy of the papers prepared on the field; and he assisted the *lambardár* in collecting the revenue from the tenants, and waited on travellers. In 1863 it was proposed to employ the *dharwais* as a subordinate *patwári* agency. It appeared then that in some villages there was no *dharwai,* in some there were two. Some *dharwais* actually collected the revenue and paid it in. The *patwáris* got all their information from the *dharwais.* So books with columns were prescribed for the use of *dharwais.* But the *dharwais* did not use them, and the whole thing came to nothing. The *dharwai* is the village servant. The *patwári* is a Government servant. Village watchmen are paid at the rate of Rs. 3 *per mensem.* Their beat includes often more than one village. The amount due is *báchhed* every six months.

Village watchmen

Mortgages.

Mortgages are of two kinds in this district. In one form, known as *lekhá mukhi,* the mortgagor manages the cultivation. The mortgagee pays the revenue and takes the produce. Accounts are made up annually, and interest is charged. If the produce is in excess of the expenses, the surplus is credited to the mortgagor; and if less, he is debited with the deficiency. Sometimes the mortgagee takes possession and manages the estate. In the second form of mortgage, called *viáj panára,* no accounts

Chapter III, D.

Village Communities and Tenures.

Mortgages.

are kept. No interest is charged. The mortgagee holds the land till the mortgage-money is paid up. He is responsible for all loss, and takes all the profit that may accrue on the land. It is an ordinary usufructuary mortgage. Both forms are common on the Sutlej; on the Rávi the *lekha mukhi* form is the more frequent. A stipulation for conditional sale after a fixed period (*bai-bil-wafa*) is often inserted in the deed in both forms of mortgage.

Poverty or wealth of the proprietors.

Table No. XXXII gives statistics of sales and mortgages of land; Tables Nos. XXXIII and XXXIIIA show the operations of the Registration Department; and Table No. XXXIX the extent of civil litigation. The old agriculturists mentioned in Table No. XXXII include many Arorás and Khatrís who, although they are now money-lenders, were proprietors at the settlement of 1871-72, and are therefore shown in the returns as old agriculturists. Mr. Purser wrote as follows on the subject of the indebtedness of the agricultural classes:—

"The revenue and the seed are usually borrowed; and there are very few villages that are not seriously in debt. This is a matter of little importance so long as the *karár* does not try to oust the proprietors and get the land into his own hands. But such a course is very rare in this district, because, except in the canal villages, a *karár* makes a great deal more as creditor of the owner of the land than he would as owner himself. But the people are very bitter about the exactions of the *karárs*, and make unpleasant comparisons between now and the good old Sikh times. Then, if a man owed a *karár* money, and they could not arrange matters, the case went before the *kárdár*. The *kárdár* had the *karár's* books examined, and on being told how much principal and how much interest was due, he would say 'strike off so much interest!' Then he would inquire how many cattle the debtor had. He would be told, so many. 'And what are they worth?' 'Ten rupees each head.' 'Good! the *karár* must take the cattle at Rs. 12 each in payment of his debt;' and everybody went off satisfied. Now the debtor offers cattle; but the creditor prefers *chehra shâhi* rupees. A suit is the consequence, and the debtor has to pay the costs in addition to the claim. The creditor who before the suit had no desire to have the cattle, suddenly discovers that they are not without merit. He executes his decree, attaches the cattle worth Rs. 10 each, and buys them himself for Rs. 5. There is a great deal of truth in this account of matters; but the fact seems to be totally forgotten that the *karárs* did not rob the people then so much as they do now, simply because the Sikh *kárdár* took very good care that the people should have nothing whereof to be robbed."

With the exorbitant interest generally charged and the mortgagees' opportunities for juggling with the prices at which produce is credited the *lekhá mukhi* form of mortgage generally precludes any possibility of redemption. In addition to the indebtedness secured by mortgage there is, of course, a very large amount of floating debt on book account or secured by bonds. The latter class of liability it is which is more directly harmful to the *zamindár* than the actual alienation of land; indeed the former is generally the cause and precursor of the latter; the result is due to the extortionate interest charged on floating accounts; very commonly the rate is 4 pies (*pakka paisa*) per rupee per mensem which is equivalent to 25 per cent. per annum.

The following figures show the percentages of total area under mortgage with possession in 1896-97:—

Chapter III, D.
Village Communities and Tenures.
Poverty or wealth of the proprietors.

Tahsíl.	Total mortgaged.	To old agriculturists.	To new agriculturists.
Montgomery	16	8	8
Gugera	10	5	5
Dipálpur	8	4	4
Pákpattan	5	3	2
Total District	9	5	4

The proportion is not alarming in any tahsíl, but it is quite sufficiently high in the first two. Under the action of processes now at work it will, no doubt, increase. As regards causes of agricultural indebtedness the assessment reports prepared during the recent settlement should be consulted. They may be summarized as follows :—

(*i*) The thriftless and extravagant disposition of many of the agricultural tribes.

(*ii*) The heavy capital expenditure involved in the construction and maintenance of wells and in a minor degree of canal water-courses, both of which, but more especially the former, are essential to successful agriculture. Under this head may also be included unrecouped advances to tenants.

(*iii*) The precarious nature of agricultural incomes in this district, depending as they do on precarious river flood and rainfall.

(*iv*) The rise of an enterprising and energetic class of traders and money-lenders, fostered as it is by our educational and legal system, and hankering as it does for land both as a source of income and a door to social consideration.

(*v*) Our alien law of contract and the consequent tendency to regard the *zamindár* as a free agent capable of properly judging of his own interests ; a tendency which is exaggerated when the administration of the law is left in the hands of native Judicial officers of the money-lending and trading classes.

(*vi*) The fact that the *zamindár* incurs debt in cash and has to discharge it by delivery of grain which may be and is credited at a depreciated rate.

CHAPTER IV.

PRODUCTION AND DISTRIBUTION.

SECTION A.—AGRICULTURE AND ARBORICULTURE.

Chapter IV, A.

Agriculture and Arboriculture.

General statistics of agriculture.

Table No. XIV gives general figures for cultivation and irrigation, and for Government waste land; while the rainfall is shown in Tables Nos. III and IIIA and B. Table No. XVII shows statistics of Government estates. Table No. XX gives the areas under the principal staples, and Table No. XXI the average yield of each. Statistics of live-stock will be found in Table No. XXII. Further statistics are given under their various headings in the subsequent paragraphs of this chapter. Land tenures, tenants, and rent, and the employment of field labour, have already been noticed in Chapter III, Section C.

Agricultural calendar. The weather.

The months of the year are known by the following names :—

Chetr,	middle of March	to	middle of	April.
Visákh	,,	April	,,	May.
Jeth	,,	May	,,	June.
Hár	,,	June	,,	July.
Sánwan	,,	July	,,	August.
Bhadron	,,	August	,,	September.
Assu	,,	September	,,	October.
Kátik	,,	October	,,	November
Maghar	,,	November	,,	December.
Poh	,,	December	,,	January.
Mágh	,,	January	,,	February.
Phágan	,,	February	,,	March.

The agricultural year commences on the day of the first full moon in Chetr. That day and the eight following days (*naurâta*) are lucky days.

Chetr.—*Rain.*—Two or three moderate showers are good, as the *rabi* outturn is then better and the grain large, and there is less danger of the diseases *kunghi* and *tela*. *Wasse Phagan te Chetr, an na mewe ghar, na mewe khetar.* "If it rains in Phagan and Chetr, neither the house nor the field will contain the grain." *Wind.*—The wind should always be moderate. If strong, the grain is light and the ground dries up, and if the crop has been watered, the plants shake about, and the roots become exposed. The wind should be from the east to bring up rain. After rain, from the west to ripen the crops. *Sunshine* and *heat* should be moderate.

Visakh.—*Rain* is most injurious. It injures the grain and rots the straw. *Wind* should be hot and of average strength coming from the west. This dries the grain and straw, and facilitates threshing and winnowing; *sunshine* and *heat* should be strong. In this month the spring harvest ripens, and is cut.

Chapter IV, A.

Agriculture and Arboriculture.

Agricultural calendar. The weather.

JETH.—In this month the harvest operations are completed and the crops housed. Weather should be as in Visákh. The hotter the *wind* and *sun* the better.

HAR.—Up to the middle of Hár the weather should be as in Jeth, for some crops may still be in the fields. After the middle there should be heavy and repeated *showers.* These are favourable for preparing the land for next harvest, and for the production of grass. The rains should commence in this month. The *wind* should be from the east, the rainy quarter. Strong *sunshine* and *heat* are bad, as crops artificially irrigated are injured by the water getting heated.

SANWAN.—Weather should be as in the latter half of Hár.

BHADRON.—In this month the crops commence to flower; *rain* is much wanted. The *wind* should be sometimes from the east, to bring on rain, and sometimes from the west to assist the maturing of the crops. The *sunshine* and *heat* ought to be moderate.

ASSU.—Heavy *rain* is injurious to the flowering crops ; but a few light showers at the beginning of the month are of benefit to the *rabi* harvest, and injure the *kharíf* crops little. *Wind* as before up to the middle of the month, then west. *Sunshine* and *heat* should be moderate. The month is thus described :—

Assu máh niràle ;
Dihán dhúpán ; rátin pále.

"Assu peculiar month, sunshine by day, chills at night."

KATIK.—There should be no *rain,* as rain stops the *rabi* sowing, and spoils the ripe autumn crops. However, it never does rain in Kátik. The *wind* should be from the west, and not strong, as otherwise irrigated lands of the *rabi* harvest dry up. *Heat* and *sunshine* should be moderate.

MAGHAR.—The weather should be as in Kátik. Frosts at night retard the growth of the crops.

POH.—It should *rain* in Poh, according to the saying—

Wase Pohín máhín,
Kaun ákhe meri jami náhín?

"If it rains in Poh and Mágh, who will say my (crop) has not come up ?" The less *wind* the better, as the weather is cold, and cattle suffer from the wind, especially from the north and west winds.

MAGH.—There should be *rain* in this month. Gentle westerly *breezes* are good for the crops, as they bring them on and keep off *kunghi* and *tela.* The north wind is injurious, as it is cold and dries up the crops. The east wind, too, is hurtful, according to some, but not so according to others.

Chapter IV, A.

Agriculture and Arboriculture.

Agricultural calendar. The weather.

PHAGAN.—The weather in this month should be of the same kind as in Chetr. This is the end of the cold weather.

Pála gayá singálián charhde Phagan Máh,
Turián bhi jhulián sattián charhde Phagan Máh :

"The cold weather went for horned cattle at the commencement of Phagan; horses, too, cast off their coverings at the commencement of Phagan."

The winds and their effects.

The winds are the north-wind or *pahár;* the east-wind or *pura;* the south-wind or *dakkhan;* and the west-wind, called *dháwi* by the people, because it keeps off rain, and so floors or knocks down (*dhaona*), the farmer. But *mahájans* call it *soni* or the golden, according to village etymology, but the word may come from *suna* empty, or *sona* to sleep. The effect of the winds is thus expressed :—

Dakkhan mele, pura wasáwe;
Dháwi wasdeán nun wanjáwe.

"The south-wind collects (the clouds), the east-wind causes them to rain, the west wind disperses them when raining." One may have too much of the east-wind though; for "if the east-wind always were to blow, that were also exceedingly bad:" "*Nit ghule pura, oh bhi bure se bura.**"

Winter and summer rains compared.

The winter rains are so important that one is tempted to put them on an equality with the ordinary summer rains. When the winter rains are good, the *rabi* crops flourish, and the maximum outturn is obtained with a minimum of labour spent in irrigation. But the summer rains besides greatly aiding the preparation of the land for the *rabi* sowings, produce abundant grass, and on this account should be held the more important of the two. Tables Nos. III, IIIA, IIIB, show the rainfall of the district.

Monthly statement of agricultural works.

A statement of the operations of ploughing, sowing, and reaping for each month of the year is given below for convenience of reference. When ploughing immediately precedes sowing, no special mention is made of it :—

Month.	Crops for which ploughing takes place.	Crops sown.	Crops cut.
Chetr (middle of March to middle of April).	...	...	*Zira*, barley, gram, *chural*, *masar*, *sarhon*, poppy and *saunf* during the latter half. Vegetables, turnips (for seed), and *methra*.

* One more distich, partly bearing on the weather, may be quoted. It runs thus :—

Titar kambhi badli, rând malâi khâe :
Oh wasse, oh ghar kare, bachan na khâli jâe.

"If the cloud is like partridge feathers and if a widow eat cream, the former will rain, the latter will marry; this saying will not prove empty." There are several versions of this proverb.

Chapter IV, A.

Agriculture and Arboriculture.

Monthly statement of agricultural works.

Month.	Crops for which ploughing takes place.	Crops sown.	Crops cut.
Visakh (middle of April to middle of May).	...	*Charri*, cotton, *sankukra*, melons, *rawán* and rice (in beds).	*Zira*, wheat, *rawan*, gourds, gram (at beginning, if late).
Jeth (middle of May to middle of June).	.	Cotton, *sankukra*, rice (broad-cast), *rawán*. In latter half *sanni*.	Gourds and *rawan*. In second half *china* and tobacco.
Hár (middle of June to middle of July).	...	Rice broadcast, *sanni*, *jowar*, *bájra*, *makki*, *kangni*; pepper is transplanted at the beginning of the month.	*Rawán*, tobacco and *china*. In first-half, *charri* and gourds.
Sáwan (middle of July to middle of August).	Wheat, barley, and *sarhon*.	Rice broadcast and transplanted, *jowár*, *bájra*, *til*, *moth*, *makki*. In second-half *mung*.	...
Bhadron (middle of August to middle of September).	As in Sáwan	In first-half, *makki*, *máh*, and *china*. In second-half, gram, turnips, *sarhon* and vegetables.	*Rawán*; in second-half *kangni*.
Assu (middle of September to middle of October).	...	Vegetables, gram, *charal*, *masar*, turnips, *sarhon*. In second-half poppy and barley.	In first-half *kangni*, cotton, *makki*, *rawán* and *sankukra*; rice in second-half.
Kátik (middle of October to middle of November).	Tobacco	Poppy and *methra* in first-half. Also tobacco in beds. Wheat, barley, *masar* *charal*, *zira*, and vegetables.	Rice in first-half; cotton, *bájra*, *makki*, pepper, *sankukra*, and *sanni*. In second-half *jowár*, *moth*, *mah*, *mung*, *til*, and sugarcane.
Maghar (middle of November to middle of December).	Tobacco	Barley in first-half. Wheat and *zira*.	In first-half *jowar*, *moth*, *mah*, *mung*, and *til*. Cotton, sugarcane, pepper and *sanni* during whole month; *china* and tops of turnips in half.

Chapter IV, A.

Agriculture and Arboriculture.

Monthly statement of agricultural works.

Month.	Crops for which ploughing takes place.	Crops sown.	Crops cut.
Poh (middle of December to middle of January).	Tobacco, cotton, vegetables and sugarcane if it rains.	*Zira.*	In first-half cotton and *china*. Sugarcane, pepper and tops of turnips the whole month
Magh (middle of January to middle of February).	As in Poh	...	Turnips (roots).
Phagan (middle of February to middle of March).	..	Sugarcane, pepper in beds, melons, vegetables, *china*, *rawan*, and transplant tobacco.	Turnips in first-half.

Soils.

The soils of the district are, as usual in the plains, of three kinds: clay, loam, and sand. By loam is meant a mixture of clay and sand. The common name for clay soil is *sikand* or *pakki* in the trans-Rávi portion of the Gugera tahsíl, and *mal* in the south-western part of Pákpattan. A sandy soil is known as *retli*, and a loamy soil as *gasra*. In the purest *sikand*, however, there is always some slight admixture of sand, and no *retli* is cultivated that does not contain some little clay. The quantity of pure clay or sand, respectively, is so small though that it need hardly be considered. *Sikand* is the Hindustáni *dákar*. *Gasra* is *rausli*, and *retli* is *bhur*. If well cultivated, *sikand* is the best soil, and will give the largest outturn; but with the system of cultivation now in vogue among the people, *gasra* must be held to rank first. *Sikand* is the only soil in which rice is grown, chiefly it would seem because it is the only soil which, when thoroughly saturated, will support the bullocks ploughing it up. Seed does not germinate in it as well as in *gasra*, and so a larger quantity of seed-grain, about 25 per cent. more, is required. Owing to its greater capillarity it is considerably less absorbent than *gasra*, and water consequently lies longer on its surface before percolating down. The irrigation beds or *kiárís* on *sikand* soil can thus be more quickly filled up with water than on *gasra*, and the *zamíndár* therefore considers that *sikand* can be more quickly irrigated than *gasra*. *Sikand*, however, dries more quickly. There is usually a sandy substratum to both kinds of soil; but it is not unfrequently much nearer the surface when *sikand* is the upper crust than when *gasra* is. This substratum is said to act as a sponge, and absorb the water poured on the land, and its being nearer the surface in *sikand* soils is one cause why more water is required. Another cause is the greater evaporation that

Sikand.

takes place owing to the non-absorbent qualities of *sikand* which are due to its great capillarity. Two waterings of *sikand* are stated to be required where one watering of *gasra* would be sufficient. *Sikand* is of a blackish colour, it splits into fissures when drying after irrigation, and is very hard, as a walk across a rice-field will prove. The test of *sikand*, if one is in any doubt, is to throw a lump into the air. If on reaching the ground it splits into little pieces, the soil is *sikand;* if it pulverizes completely it is *gasra*. This latter soil is soft, and of a soft brown colour when irrigated. It is excellent soil for all crops, except rice; and is much liked by the people on account of the little labour and irrigation it requires to produce a good outturn. If it has not been sufficiently ploughed, or if there is any admixture of *kallar*, it will crack too after irrigation, but not to the same extent as *sikand*. *Sikand* is common in the tract lying near the Deg *nála* in the Gugera tahsil; in estates irrigated from the Kháuwah Canal in Dipálpur and in parts of the canal-irrigated tract in the Pákpattan tahsíl and generally in lowlying areas which receive local drainage. In the rest of the district *gasra* or loam of varying consistency is the prevailing soil; when the admixture of sand is marked it is sometimes known as *retli* or *hauli:* but the latter term simply means light. Sandy soil is of poor quality and *khip, buru*, and *resham* flourish on it; though found in light *gasra* too. The soil of the Rávi riverain is generally of more uniform and better quality than that of the corresponding portions of the Sutlej tahsíls. Soils impregnated with soda and other salts and known as *kallar* or *kallaráthi* is common. It is often hard and clayey. It is found extensively in the Ganji Bár; in part of the Sandal Bár bordering on the Rávi riverain; in the tract between the Rávi and the Deg *nála;* in the north-western part of the Pákpattan tahsíl; in a good many of the older estates in the Dipálpur tahsil which have been long under canal-irrigation, and in several riverain estates in that tahsíl. When the *kallar* is not bad, wheat can be grown with fair success. Other crops do not do so well. The seed is sown in such soils with a drill and not broadcast, as is usual in good land. Soil impregnated with *kallar* is highly non-absorbent. Up to the present the canals have done very little damage, as regards producing it.

Chapter IV, A.

Agriculture and Arboriculture.

Soils.

Gasra.

Kallarathi.

Kalar-shore.

As a rule, the soil of the district is of good quality and the people rarely complain of it. It is not unlikely that it has grown somewhat old and exhausted in the older canal-irrigated tracts, but there is no reason to think that any serious deterioration has taken place. The vicissitudes of seasonal conditions ensure a certain amount of rest and fallow.

Means of cultivation.

With a scanty and precarious rainfall anything like systematic *báráni* cultivation in this district is impossible. Agriculture depends almost entirely either on artificial irrigation from wells or inundation canals, or on river floods (*sailáb*) or river water lifted by *jhallárs* (*ábi*). Even wells if unassisted by canals

Chapter IV, A.

Agriculture and Arboriculture.

Means of cultivation.

or river floods are except in seasons of unusually good rainfall a precarious and unreliable means of cultivation. In tracts entirely dependent on them, cultivation is generally confined to scattered plots which are favourably situated for collecting local rain drainage such as it is, and if the district had to depend on its wells alone, it would soon become an uninhabited desert. With the exception of a comparatively few scattered estates varying in size from 50 acre well-plots to fairly sized villages, cultivation is confined to tracts which have in more or less recent times received river floods or floods from the Deg, or which are irrigated by the Sutlej Inundation Canals.

The inundation canals have been noticed in Chapter I. The dates at which they commence and cease flowing are uncertain, depending partly on the rise and fall of the rivers, and partly on the direction in which the main stream runs. From the middle of May to the middle of September may be taken as the normal time for the canals to flow. Under ordinary circumstances they thus supply full irrigation for the sowing and ripening of the *kharif* crops, though not seldom wells have to be worked to afford moisture for sowing when they begin to flow late or to ripen crops when the flow ceases too soon. For the *rabi* crops the canals can give only the preliminary flushing, and wells have to be worked to ripen wheat; although in many places wheat sown on canal water can with fair winter rainfall be matured in areas of suitable quality and situation. The system on which the Government canals are administered, and the arrangements for their clearance, are described in Chapter V.

Value of the inundation canals.

The inundation canals are doubtless uncertain. Sometimes they fail just in time to ruin the harvest; but for all that they are most essential to the prosperity of the country irrigated by them. They have considerably raised the water-level in the wells, among other benefits. Without them the Dipálpur tahsil would be as dreary a waste as the western portion of Pákpattan. Canal-water is, according to popular report, better than well-water for all crops except onions, melons, and tobacco, but it is held to be good for cotton and other plants that flower conspicuously, to water them with well-water just before they flower, as canal-water is too with

Canal and well-water compared.

Wells, general. Area irrigable from a well in a year.

The greater portion of the cultivated land of the district is watered from wells, of which there were 10,884 in the district in 1896-97; of these 9,588 were in use. The use of the *lao* and *charsa* is not known. Water is raised by the Persian-wheel. Wells are lined with brick-work, in which case they are called *pakka*; or they have no such lining, and are known as *kacha*. The depth of the well to the water varies from a few feet in the *kunds* and *donas* along the rivers to about 60 feet or more in the Ganji Bar and the Sandal Bar. The cost of a well and the area it can irrigate annually depend very much on the depth to the water. The area a well can water depends so much on the nature of the soil, the character of the season, the quality of the cattle employed, and the industry of the cultivators, that it is

Chapter IV, A.

Agriculture and Arboriculture.

Wells, general. Area irrigable from a well in a year.

not possible to say the area irrigated is so much, neither more nor less. Mr. Purser found the average area irrigated in the spring was just $3\frac{1}{8}$ acres per yoke, in fair average soil, with water 25 feet from the surface. This would give about 25 acres as the area irrigated from a well per annum. The area, however, varies in different parts of the district; fair averages would be 25 acres in Dipálpur, 20 acres in Pákpattan and Gugera and 15 acres in Montgomery. Including *cháhi-nahri* and *cháhi-sailába* land, no doubt more than 30 acres might be irrigated from a well. The cost of constructing a single-wheeled *pakka* well varies from Rs. 250 to Rs. 550. The depth of water, the cost of a well, and the area irrigable by it, are shown for different parts of the district in maps attached to Mr. Purser's Settlement Report. In sinking a well, a hole rather larger than the proposed brick cylinder is dug down to the sand. This is called *pár*. Then a circular frame is laid down in the *pár*, and the cylinder of brick and mud, or in rare cases of brick and lime, is built on it. When this has got a few feet above the surface, the sand and earth inside and under the *chak* are dug out, and hoisted up and thrown aside. As the cylinder sinks, it is built up at the top. The excavation, after laying down the *chak* till the water is reached, is called *tor*. It is made by a class of men called *tobás* or *thobas*. The *toba* is armed with a broad heavy pick-shovel like an exaggerated *kahi* or *kassi*. This he strikes into the sand or earth, and when it has got a good grip it is pulled up with its load by those above. When the water is reached the excavation is called *tobái*. On the water becoming deep the *toba* has to dive. The work is very hard, and he is fed in the most sumptuous way. As soon as the cylinder has been sunk deep enough, the parapet is completed, and the wood-work put in its place. There is no fixed depth to which a cylinder should be sunk below the water level. If the *chak* rests on firm soil, a smaller depth will suffice than when the foundation is shaky. In a single-wheeled well the diameter of the interior of the cylinder will be ten to twelve feet, and the thickness of the brick-work from eighteen inches to two feet. Sometimes in sinking a well, hard sticky clay occasionally mixed with *kankar*, called *jillhán*, is met with. If there is much of this, it is found impossible to sink the large cylinder or *kothi*, and a smaller one has to be sunk inside it. Similar smaller cylinders are sunk, when the water-level in well has fallen, or the bottom has given way. They are known as *bachcha*.

Construction of wells.

The cost of sinking a well which was 40 feet deep and one mile from the brick-kiln is given in great detail by Mr. Purser at page 91 of his Report. It amounted to Rs. 300-7-6. The account begins with an item of Re. 1-4 for *gur*, for good luck, and ends with Rs. 2 given in charity. A *toba* will be fed in this way: flour, one *ser* four *chittáks*; *dál*, two *chittáks*; *ghi*, two *chittáks*; sugar, three *chittáks*; and tobacco, two *chittáks*. The labourers get some parched gram in the afternoon to encourage them.

Cost of sinking a well.

Double-wheeled wells or *wáns*.

Wells are built sometimes large enough to allow of two Persian-wheels

Chapter IV, A.

Agriculture and Arboriculture.

Double-wheeled wells or *wáns.*

working at the same time. Such a well is called *wán.* Its cylinder has an interior diameter of about 15 feet. It costs about one-quarter, or as much as one-third more than a single well of the same depth. When water is near the surface, and the supply is good, such double wells are common. But where the water-level is deep tenants dislike working at *wáns*; for the men working one wheel may be put to much inconvenience by those at the second wheel driving on their bullocks at an extraordinary pace, and so reducing the water-level below the limit reached by the buckets of the first wheel.

Water-supply in wells.

In this district wells have no springs. They are filled by percolation. In some wells the water level is never much reduced—the water is then said to be *pakka-páni.* In some the water-level is reduced by ordinary working of the well; the water in this case is called *ubkás.*

Cleaning of wells.

If a well is not subject to much influx of sand, it is cleaned out once in 10 or 12 years, but otherwise in five or six. The cost is small. As long as the water is shallow, the cultivator does the clearance himself; when it becomes deep, *tobás* are employed.

Kacha wells.

Kacha wells are not common. They are found only near the rivers. Sometimes they last very well—four or five years; but two years would be a high average. They are very uncertain, and may tumble in at any moment; and sometimes do, just when they are wanted to mature the crops. From the bottom to a few feet above the water they are lined with a cylinder made of wood, or branches of *pilchi* or *kána.* They cost about Rs. 20, of which a little more than half is the cost of excavation. Such wells are the only ones found in tracts subject to serious inundation, as it matters little whether they are knocked in or not. The irrigating capacity of a *kacha* well is but little inferior to that of a *pakka* well.

The *harat* or Persian-wheel.

The wood-work of a well is called *harat.* This is the ordinary Persian-wheel. It consists of many parts, the names of which are given in great detail by Mr. Purser. The size of the wheel depends upon the depth of the well. The larger it is, the easier work for the bullocks. The *jora* or horizontal and vertical wheels are made of *kíkar*, but on the Rávi *ukhán* is sometimes used. A *jora* of *ukhán* costs Rs. 20; of *kíkar*, about Rs. 30. The *máhal* or rope frame to which the buckets are fastened is made of *munj.* Ropes made of *dab* grass are sometimes used, but they last only a month. On an average five *máhals* are required in a year, and cost about Rs. 2 each. In *kacha* wells the *máhal* is subjected to rougher treatment than in a *pakka* well; and so seven or eight *máhals* are used up in a year. The size of the water-pots depends on the depth of the well—the deeper the well the smaller the pots. Where wells are deep, there will be 11 or 12 to the *háth* of depth; where shallow, 9 to 10. The usual number is 10 or 11.

Jhallárs.

A *jhallár* is merely the Persian-wheel of a common well transferred to the bank of a canal, the margin of a *jhíl*, or the high bank of a river or creek. A small pool is excavated immediately below the *jhallár* to collect the water, and afford the wheels a sufficient surface to work upon. As almost the

Chapter IV, A.

Agriculture and Arboriculture.

Jhallars.

whole expense consists in the wood-work, *jhallárs* are constructed in great numbers, and abandoned again without materially affecting the prosperity of the zamíndárs. On the banks of the Deg river, which are high and narrow, they are in universal use. They are also frequently met with in favourable situations on the Rávi and Sutlej, but the cultivation depending on them in these situations is very precarious. On canals they can only be used for *kharíf* crops, as they contain no water from October to April. In the case of an ordinary *jhallár* the water is much nearer the surface than in an average well, and so the *jhallár* will irrigate much more than the well; at least half as much more.

Wáris-method of working a well.

A *kámil*, or thoroughly found well, has six yokes of two bullocks each. In some cases there are as many as eight yokes, but the average is under six. If the well is fully yoked, there are, as a rule, more than one set of cultivators. In this case they take turns at irrigating. These turns are called *wárís* or *bárís*. The length of each *bári* depends on the number of yokes and the aridity of the soil. The more yokes the longer each *bári*, the drier the soil the shorter each turn. The length of the *bári* is generally six hours in Montgomery, 12 hours in Pákpattan and Gugera, and 24 hours in Dipálpur. If there are eight yokes at a well, each will work one *pahar* or three hours; if there are six, three will work during the day, the others during the night. If there are four yokes, each works one *pahar* and a quarter; and when the fourth yoke has done its work, the first begins again. Four yokes can keep the well going day and night. Less than four cannot. A well with six yokes will irrigate about 5 *kanáls*, or $\frac{5}{8}$ths of an acre of fair *gasra* land in 24 hours, when the water is 25 feet from the surface, but very much depends on the seasonal conditions; if there has been good rainfall 6 or 7 *kanáls* can be watered. The deeper the water and the more sandy the soil, the less the area irrigable. About one acre of *sikand* could be irrigated by the same well in the same time, but less thoroughly owing to the slower rate of percolation downwards in *sikand* as compared with *gasra*. During the hot months irrigation is carried on only during the night. In the cold weather each homestead well is a small village in itself. The cultivators with their families, cattle and goats, reside at it. Sheds are put up for the cattle, and feeding troughs prepared; fodder is collected in circular stacks made of cotton-stalks (called *palla*); the oratory or *tharha* is put in order and strewed with straw; and every one settles down to five months' hard work. And standing out in a slushy field in one's bare legs, a couple of hours before sunrise on a January morning, with the thermometer marking 10 degrees of frost, opening and closing the water-courses leading into the little beds into which the fields are divided, is not the work those people would choose for themselves who are fond of calling the natives lazy.

Area irrigated in 24 hours.

Well cultivation.

The area attached to a well, some, but by no means the whole, of which is actually irrigated in any one year from the

Chapter IV, A.

Agriculture and Arboriculture.

Well cultivation.

well varies considerably; 40 to 50 acres is probably a fair average for a single-wheeled well. In villages where wells are numerous the area is often a good deal smaller; while where well cultivation is strong and canal-irrigation to aid the well plentiful they are larger. In sinking a well it is always an object to include as much low-lying land as possible. Where canal-irrigation is available in plenty the outer portions of the area attached to the well often cannot be reached by well water, or only with difficulty. The well cylinder is placed as high as possible above the surrounding land. In a well estate which gets little or no aid from canal irrigation or river *sailáb* the *kharíf* crops have to be placed as near the well as possible, in order to economise labour and water in the summer months. The small area immediately round the well, locally known as *káda*, naturally gets more manure than the land at a great distance. The cropping here is largely *dofasli*. On well lands which receive a fair supply of canal-irrigation, those portions of the well area which are at a distance from the well will generally be devoted to purely canal-irrigated kharíf crops. The area nearer the well and the *káda* will be devoted to rabi crops. In a tract where scanty rainfall and excessive heat render well-irrigation especially arduous in the summer months rabi crops naturally occupy far the larger portion of the well-irrigated cultivation. In many parts of the district, more especially in the Rávi, well-irrigation and river water obtained either by direct spill or by artificial water-courses or lifted by *jhallárs* intermingle largely; and in such circumstances every effort is made to supplement and, as far as possible, to supersede the former by the latter. In fact in some parts of the Rávi riverain a well is regarded not so much as an indispensable means of cultivation, but rather as one for eking out the supply of river water when it is deficient in quantity or fails.

Canal irrigated cultivation.

The combination of canal and well-irrigation has been dealt with above. Canal-irrigated cultivation unaided by wells is found chiefly in the Sutlej tahsils. It is carried on in suitable and comparatively low-lying areas which receive sufficient water for the sowing and ripening of *kharíf* crops, or after a flushing (*rauni*) from the canal retain sufficient moisture for the sowing and germination of the *rabi* crops, wheat and gram, which are subsequently ripened by the winter rainfall.

Sailáb.

The overflow of the rivers is called *sailáb*. The flooded land is *sailába* land. The area flooded varies greatly. Between the Regular Settlement of 1857 and the Revised Settlement of 1872-73, a great and permanent decrease took place in the area inundated from 156,585 to 82,412 acres. The cause of this decrease is not clear. There may have been less water in the river than formerly, and there certainly had been a series of dry years. The Sutlej set towards the west, covering what was once cultivated land with sand; but this occurred in very few places. Something was due to the silting up of *nallas* like the Bakhílwah and Ding. Changes in the course of the rivers were

Chapter IV, A.

Agriculture and Arboriculture.

probably as much the cause as anything. In 1852, the Rávi changed its course, going to the west; and a serious decrease in the *sailáb* took place in consequence in Gugera. In 1853 the Sutlej carried away a projection of stiff clay soil on the Baháwalpur side of the stream which had acted as a sort of dam, and the result was an immediate diminution in the *sailába* lands of Pákpattan: and other similar changes may have occurred. Whatever the cause may be, the result was most disastrous. In many instances the abandonment of the greater portion of the well lands in the *sailába* regions followed on the failure of the *sailáb*. This is a very usual sequence of events in the Rávi riverain tracts. If there is one thing a Jat likes nearly as much as his buffaloes, it is a fine fat piece of *sailába* cultivation. The flood saturates the land and leaves a deposit of rich mud. When the river goes down and the sowing season comes, he ploughs up the land and puts in the seed, and then can rest himself till the crop is ripe. If the saturation has not been through and the winter rains are not good, the outturn will be poor, and it may be needful to work the well (if one happens to be near by) to bring the crop to maturity. River flood water becomes available for agriculture broadly in one of three ways—(*i*) by passing down creeks and old river beds (*budhs*) over the shelving banks of which it spills, flooding the adjacent low-lying alluvial land; (*ii*) by being headed up against the apex of a sudden sharp bend of the river; if the bank is at this point not too high, and the set of the stream and the levels of the adjacent land suitable, the flood water will overtop the bank and spill over the country for many miles from the main stream of the river; such spill is locally called a *dhák*; (*iii*) by *chhárs* or artificial channels, which generally have their heads on creeks or old river beds. The flood water thus made available is, when needful, raised to the required level by *jhallárs* The latter are generally, however, used on the high bank of the main river or of the *budhs*. The principal *sailába* crop is wheat. Very few *kharíf* crops are, from the nature of things, grown on *sailába* land. Sometimes the land remains under water so long that it cannot be cultivated in time for the next spring harvest. This occurs only in very low-lying spots. The floods of the Rávi are more beneficial than those of the Sutlej, and the silt deposited is generally much superior. In some instances land is found along the rivers sufficiently moistened by absorption, though not flooded, "to produce crops without any further watering." This absorption or percolation is called *ugáj*. It is *ugáj* which is one of the causes of *kallar*. Cultivation by *jhallárs* has already been incidentally dealt with. In addition to being used near rivers they are extensively employed on the Deg *nala* for the cultivation of rice, and also to some extent on local depressions (*toás*) filled by rain water in the desert tract in the western part of Pákpattan.

Result of the failure of *sailába*.

Sailába cultivation.

Ugáj.

Abi (*jhallari*) cultivation.

There is, properly speaking, no *báráni* or rain cultivation. In a few villages on the Lahore border there may be a little in good seasons. But there are numerous depressions in the

Cultivation.

Chapter IV, A.

Agriculture and Arboriculture.

ground into which the drainage water of the neighbouring highlands pours, and in these depressions crops are grown without further irrigation. The area thus cultivated, and the quality of the produce, vary with the season. In autumn *til* and *moth* are usually sown; in spring, wheat and gram. The total rain cultivation of the district within village limits is only about 4 per cent. of the total average annual area of cultivation. About three-fifths of it takes place in the *kharíf*. But though the rain cultivation may be scanty and of no great value, it is an entire mistake to say that "drought, which, in regions that depend much on rain, form the chief cause of distress, is not likely to affect materially the resources of this district." There are few districts in which drought is more mischievous. Cattle die of starvation; the survivors give scarcely any milk, or are unable to do any hard work. *Dhagge turde náhín*—the bullocks cannot get along—is the complaint of every cultivator. The result is that the cultivated area is about half what it is in a good year. Then the white-ants commit serious ravage when there is no rain; and the yield of the crops is poor. Besides, the unfortunate agriculturist, instead of growing food for himself, has to grow an extra quantity of fodder for his cattle, and support himself and family on what he can borrow or steal. Again, cultivation is so expensive and requires such large means that, if once beaten down, the cultivating classes find it much harder to recover themselves than in purely *báráni* districts.

Drought.

Agricultural implements and appliances.

Table No. XXII shows the number of cattle, carts, and plough in each tahsíl of the district. The agricultural implements in use in the district are very fully described, and their prices stated at pages 95 to 98 of Mr. Purser's Settlement Report. They present few peculiarities; and it does not seem necessary to describe them here. The names of the principal implements which are constantly used in the following pages will be found in the glossary given as an Appendix to the Settlement Report.

Agricultural operations.—Ploughing.

If possible in ploughing, several ploughs are brought together in the same field, as bullocks work better in company. The furrows are straight. It is quite an unknown thing to plough in curves. The ploughman should make his furrows as long as possible, according to the saying—

Lamí usrí háliyán, chhoti láwí hár.

"Long tacks for ploughmen, short for reapers." A plough will break up 4 *kanáls* of *sikand* or 5 *kanáls* of *gasra* in a day. On the 5th, 7th, 9th, 10th, 21st, and 24th of each month the ground is supposed to be sleeping, and it is not considered lucky to commence any agricultural operations on these days; but, once begun on another day, there is no objection to going on, whether the ground is asleep or not. Sunday, Monday, and Thursday are the best days on which to commence sowing. Most crops are sown at once in the field in which they are to

Sowing.

Chapter IV, A.

Agriculture and Arboriculture.

Sowing.

grow. They are sown either broadcast or with the drill. In unirrigated lands, such as *sailába* and *báráni* lands, generally in canal-irrigated lands, and where there is much *kallar*, the drill *náli* is used. In *kallar* soil, the object is to get the seed below the mass of the *kallar*, which is found usually at the surface; in *nahri-sailáb* and *báráni* lands the object is to get the seed into a stratum that will not soon dry up, and to shield it from the influence of the weather, which would often prove fatal to it in unharrowed and unrolled fields. On lands which receive well water (*rauni*) before sowing the seed is generally scattered. Some crops are, however, always sown broadcast. When the seed is very small, like that of poppy and *til*, it is mixed with earth before being sown, as otherwise it would be difficult to distribute it equally. Cotton seeds are smeared with cow-dung to keep them from sticking together. Some crops are grown from seedlings (*paníri*) raised in nurseries: such are tobacco and pepper, and rice on the Deg. Sugarcane is grown from cuttings. In broadcast sowing the seed is held in one end of a sheet coming over the left shoulder; the other end, after passing under the right shoulder, is tucked in under the end on the left shoulder. Seed is not changed, and is said not to deteriorate. A drill will sow nearly one acre in the day. The crop of course grows much thicker when the seed is scattered than when it is sown with the drill, whence the saying—

Náli nalá muthí darya.

Seed-grain generally borrowed.

Except in the canal villages, seed grain is almost invariably borrowed from the *karárs*. They give the grain at the market rate of the day, or a little under it, and when the harvest is completed, they are repaid with interest in kind, at the market rate of the day, or somewhat over it. A *karár* gives, say, 8 *topás* of grain and debits the cultivator with one rupee. He charges 4 pies interest per mensem on this amount, a rate equal to 25 per cent. per annum; when Hár comes round, the *karár* makes up his account and finds, say, Re. 1-2-8 due to him. The market price is then 12 *topás*; so he takes 14 *topás* from the borrower in repayment of 8 *topás* he lent him eight months before.

Harrowing—clod-crushing.

After ploughing, fields that are to be artificially irrigated are harrowed. The clods are broken and pulverized and the surface smoothed down at the same time that the seed is covered by means of the *soháqa* or clod-crusher. This is drawn backwards and forwards by a couple or four pairs of bullocks, and answers its purpose very well. The man guiding the bullocks stands on the *soháqa* to increase the weight brought to bear on the clods. Weeding is admitted to be a good thing, but is very rarely practised. Anything more disgraceful than some cotton fields can hardly be imagined; here and there a melancholy bush in a jungle of weeds. Weeding is done either with the mattock or the trowel. In the former case the ground is dug up as well as weeded. When the trowel is used, it is not uncommon to manure the roots of the plants at the same time.

Weeding, hoeing.

Chapter IV, A.

Agriculture and Arboriculture.

Fencing.

The former operation, which may be called hoeing, is known as *godi karna*, the later as *choki karna*. Fields are not usually fenced near the village; and along roads where cattle are constantly passing, fences are made of branches of *kikar, káríl* bushes, thorns,—in fact, of anything that comes handy. In river villages fences of *pilchi* are not rare, where wild pigs are about. They are made by sticking stout *pilchi* branches into the ground and weaving smaller branches in among them. When young, some crops have to be protected against deer and other animals.

Watching—scare-crows.

For this purpose scare-crows, called *daráwa*, are put up. Bones, heaps of stones, strings fastened to sticks, are the usual scare-crows. But rustic art occasionally shows itself in the form of a straw man with one leg, and arms stretched out at right-angles to it; gram, poppy, melons, *charri*, and wheat have thus to be protected.

Watchmen.

When the crop is ripening, birds have to be kept away from it. In the case of *jowár, makki*, and *bájra*, a platform called *manna* is raised on stakes or fixed on the top of a tree, about 10 or 12 feet from the ground, or a mud pillar (*burji*) is raised to that height, and on it a watchman stands, armed with a *khabáni* with which he slings mud pellets made by himself at the birds. Each time the sling is discharged it causes a crack, and the watchman yells. One person can watch about two acres this way. Poppy is watched with the *khabáni*, but the watcher does not use any platform. Wheat, gram, barley, and *moth* are also watched, but not with the *khabáni*, nor is the *manna* in use. The watchman is provided with a long hempen rope, called *titála*, with which he goes wandering about the field. Every now and then he whirls it round his head and brings it down with a crack. One man can watch about 10 acres this way. The fields are watched only at night in Assu and Kátik, Phágan and Chetr. The watchmen are mostly Machhís and Menhs. They are paid 3 *mans* (*topa*), or about 2 *pakka mans* for each harvest.

Reaping.

Reapers are called *láwa*. They belong chiefly to the class of village servants. But they do not confine themselves to their own village. They go wherever they can get work. The method in which they are paid has been already noticed in the last chapter. Reaping is carried on during moonlight nights in the last few hours before day if the straw is very dry, as the moisture of the night air is supposed to strengthen the stalk and prevent the ears falling off. If clouds gather, great efforts are made to get in the crops, as hail is much feared at this season; but hail is very uncommon in this district. Sunday and Wednesday are lucky days to commence reaping. As soon as the grain is cut it is stacked. The reaper gets his share when the crop has been threshed and is divided. He is paid from the *dheri shámilát* or common heap. There are several ways of

Threshing.

threshing. The most common is to yoke a number of bullocks together, fasten the one at the left hand of the line to a post, round which the straw to be threshed is piled, and drive them round and round from right to left. This is known as *khurgah nál gáhna*, to thresh by the trampling of hoofs. Wheat and barley are first threshed with the *phalha* or threshing-frame. A pair

Chapter IV, A.

Agriculture and Arboriculture.

Threshing.

of bullocks are yoked to the *phalha* and driven round the stake about which the straw is heaped; there may be several *phalhas* at work one after the other, but there are never more than four. One man is required with each, and a couple more with forks to throw the scattered straw back into the heap. One pair of bullocks with the *phalha* will thresh the produce of a quarter of an acre in a day. They will work 8 hours at a stretch, from 8 A.M. to 4 P.M. in the sun. Buffaloes are never used for threshing. When the wheat or barley has been threshed with the *phalha*, the straw is shaken up with the pitchfork, and is blown on one side, while the grain falls to the bottom. Many unthreshed ears are found, and these and the grain are called *send*. They are again threshed *khurgah nál* without the *phalha*. Generally there are four bullocks in a row, and two rows may work at the same time. Each row is called *merh*. Only wheat and barley are threshed with the *phalha*. Rice, *jowar, china, kangni masar charal* and *zira* are threshed by bullocks. The straw is then shaken and the grain winnowed. *Moth, múng, máh*, and *rawán* are treated at first as wheat is after the preliminary threshing, and, after being well shaken, are threshed by bullocks; gram is treated as wheat, but both threshings are by bullocks. *Til* is not threshed at all; the pods open and the grain is shaken out; *makki, saunf* and *dhania* are threshed with sticks. *China* is often threshed in this way. A hole about 5 feet wide and 2½ deep is carefully plastered. The thresher takes a bundle of *china* straw by the side where the roots were, and beats the ears against the side of the hole. Or else a piece of ground is swept and a log of wood put on it, against which the ears are beaten. One man is required with each *merh*, and there should be one man with a pitchfork for each heap. Eight bullocks will thresh two acres of gram, *jowár, charál* or *masar*, or one acre of rice, *china*, or *kangni* in one day. *Khurgah nál* threshing and winnowing should be carried on, if possible, when there is a hot wind blowing and a fiery sun blazing over-head, as the thorough breaking up of the straw and separation of the grain are facilitated by these circumstances. There should properly be three persons winnowing. One fills the *chhajj* and gives it to another, who shakes out the contents to the wind; the third sweeps down from the heap forming below all the bits of stick, earth, straw and unthreshed ears, which are found in the heap after threshing. From the time the grain is cut till it is finally weighed, the agriculturist has to be on his guard against *bhúts*, or demons and goblins. Fortunately they are of but middling intelligence, and their principal habits are well known, and so a goblin can be done with a little care. Till winnowing, all that need be done is to get the *mulwána* of the village to write a charm on a piece of paper, which is then stuck in a cleft piece of *kána*, and put on the heap of grain and straw. This is paid for by a fixed fee called *rasúlwahi*. Hindus are said to neglect this precaution, unless there is a *mulwána* in their village. Greater care has to be taken when winnowing commences. Friday is the regular weekly holiday of the

Winnowing.

Goblins.

Chapter IV, A.

Agriculture and Arboriculture.

Goblins.

goblins, and if any cultivator commences to winnow on that day he may expect to have his grain vanish. When a fit time has come to winnow the grain, the cultivators and a couple of *chúhras* proceed in silence to the heap, and a couple of other men stay at a little distance to prevent any living thing approaching. Then winnowing is carried on vigorously, but no one speaks. In the evening, if the operation is not complete, the charm remains on one heap and the other is carefully pressed down with the *chhajj*. Goblins are always asleep at night, but any somnambulist is unable to do harm if this plan is adopted. When all the grain has been winnowed and the time comes to divide the produce, the same precautions are adopted. As the goblins are always asleep, or engaged on household duties, at noon and in the evening, one of these hours should be selected for weighing the grain; this is done with the *topa;* or if there is any hurry, the amount of a *chhajj*-full is ascertained, and the number of *chhajjes* in the heap is found. The weighman is provided with pieces of straw, one of which he puts down for each *topa* or *chhajj*. He must carefully avoid counting the number aloud. As soon as the quantity of grain has been ascertained, the goblins are powerless. It is not clear how far the people really believe in these matters, or how far they act up to their belief. But there are very few who do not believe most thoroughly in goblins being abroad, though they sometimes seem shy about admitting it.

Manure.

Manured land is commonly called *gorha*. But the proper name is said to be *máín*. Some crops are always manured, such as tobacco and most vegetables; some are never manured, and some only occasionally. The total manured area at the Settlement of 1874 was only 16,458 acres, or 4·4 per cent. of the total cultivated land. Most of the manured area was under wheat. Manure is supposed to force the straw at the expense of the ear; and as plough-cattle have to be fed on green wheat, it is an advantage to have a thick crop of stalks. Manure consists of the excrement of cattle, horses, sheep, goats and human beings, and all sorts of refuse thrown on the village or well dung-heap; or of ashes, or of *kallar* obtained by scraping up the earth on the sites of old villages or brick-kiln, or where saline matter appears in streets and lanes. Buffalo's dung is considered the best of all manures, especially for tobacco, as it increases the size of the leaves. Droppings of sheep and goats are usually put in tobacco trenches. The tobacco acquires an acrid and pungent taste from this manure. The quantity of stable manure used depends much on a man's means. About 10 tons an acre is probably a fair average. From one to two *borás*, weighing about one maund and a half each, are applied to each *marla;* that gives from 240 to 480 maunds per acre. The dung-heap is removed twice a year; the cold weather heap in Phágan and Chetr, for tobacco, cotton, &c.; and the hot weather heap in Asu and Kátik, for wheat. Such manure is called *áhal*. A fire of cow-dung is always burning at each well. The ashes are used as a top-dressing for poppy, *zíra*, *methra*,

Chapter IV, A.

Agriculture and Arboriculture.

and *ság*. Four *borás* go to the *kanál*. A *bora* of ashes is reckoned at a quarter of a maund less than that of *áhal*. So nearly a ton and a half of ashes go to the acre. Ashes are called *suha*. *Kallar* is applied to tobacco, pepper and cotton; and to wheat, barley and onions. It is put to the roots of the first three, and scattered over the others; as regards wheat and barley, when they are about 18 inches high, about 24 hours before they are irrigated, generally in Mágh. Seven or eight *borás* are put on one *kanál*. The people collect the *kallar* themselves, and do not buy it. No attention is paid to the difference in soils in choosing what manure to apply. No manure is used, but those kinds mentioned above. Fallowing is a matter which is by no means universally attended to. In the wells with small areas, such as are found in villages where wells are more or less crowded together, it is largely dispensed with, more especially when canal water is available; the principle then is to make the most of the water by sowing every acre possible. In the case, however, of canal-irrigated wells with big areas attached, and in the case of many of the *bár* wells fallows are more or less systematically given. Among the better cultivators, such as the Kambohs, the area attached to the well is divided into four portions (*phiránas*), each consisting of disconnected plots or fields; of these two of a larger area are kept for *rabi* and the other two smaller ones for *kharíf* crops. A *kharíf* and a *rabi* plot are cultivated each year, and the other two lie fallow. In some cases only two *phiránas* are made up; one lies fallow during the year and the *kharíf* and *rabi* crops are sown in the other. As regards rotation of crops: on well lands which get no canal-irrigation the small *kada* area close to the well is to a considerable extent double cropped; the area beyond this generally gives one crop in the year; *i. e.*, a *rabí* crop one year followed by *kharíf* in the next. A succession of *rabi* crops can, however, be taken on the same plot for two or three years, but this cannot be done with the *kharíf* except in the case of maize and perhaps *jowár*, as *kharíf* cropping appears to exhaust the soil more than *rabi*. *Kharíf*, however, does well in succession to *rabi* on the same plot as it gets some advantage from the superior tillage given to the latter. The most distant lands commanded by the well are cropped with *rabi* each year as far as possible, but short rainfall, of course, largely contracts this kind of cultivation; while, if rainfall is good, a certain amount of *báráni* kharíf crops, mainly *jowár*, will be raised on the outer parts of the well estate.

Fallows—Rotation of crops.

If the well lands receive plentiful canal-irrigation the low-lying area at a distance from the well is cropped regularly in the *kharíf* and that nearer the well in the *rabi*. On purely canal-irrigated lands a rotation of crops occurs in the case of rice and gram. In rice cultivation the ground gets very little air, in gram cultivation a great deal: so gram succeeds rice, and rice gram, and the soil is benefitted. The leaves and roots of gram are said to be good for rice; and then, as the rice lands are moist, they can be ploughed up for gram without any fur-

Chapter IV, A.

Agriculture and Arboriculture.

Fallows—Rotation of crops.

ther trouble as regards irrigation. Manured lands may be cropped harvest after harvest till the effect of the manure is exhausted, but most land is cropped only once in the year; after some time the land gets an extra fallow. Forced fallows, owing to want of cultivators to till the land, or adverse seasonal conditions, are in most places only too common. Owing to some crops not being off the ground when the time for sowing others arrives, the latter cannot immediately follow the former. For this reason, excepting cotton, *kangni*, rice, *sawánk* and *makki*, none of the *kharif* crops are followed by *rabi* crops; and the same remark applies, *mutatis mutandis*, to *china*, as a *kharif* crop. Cotton may be followed by *methra* and *sinji*; rice and *sawánk* by gram, *charál*, *masar* and coriander; and *makki* by all the *rabi* crops. *Kangni* is held to exhaust the soil, so no rabi crop follows it. As regards the spring crops, *sarhon*, poppy, tobacco onions, melons, *methra* and *sinji* may be followed by any autumn crop; wheat and barley by cotton, *jowár*, *moth* and *til*; gram and coriander by rice, *sawánk* and *máh*; *zíra* by *moth*; *charál* by *sawánk*, *máh*, and *múng*; and *masar* by almost all the autumn crops.

Manner of laying out land at a well.

At a well, fully yoked, irrigating about 25 acres in the year, the land will be laid out somewhat in the following fashion. Three-quarters of an acre of early *chína* or *charri* will be sown to bring the cattle over the end of the hot weather and commencement of the rains. Half a *kanál* will be put down under vegetables of sorts. The regular autumn crops will be an acre; or an acre and a half of cotton; the same of *charri*; one acre of *chína* or *kangni*; half a *kanál* of pepper and 2½ to 3½ acres of *jowár*, most of which will be cut for fodder. The regular spring crops will be 2½ acres of turnips or *sarhon*; 15 acres of wheat; and one *kanál* of tobacco. This scheme gives 6½ *kanáls* of intermediate crops; 6 *ghomáos* (or acres), 4½ *kanáls* of autumn crops; and 17 *ghomáos*, 5 *kanáls* of spring crops. Often no *china* or *kangni* is sown in the autumn, and sometimes a couple of acres of barley may be put down in place of as much wheat. The crops invariably cultivated are cotton and *jowár* in the autumn, and turnips and wheat in the spring. On canal-irrigated lands there is no custom as to what crops should be sown, or as to the proportion of each to the others; and cultivation on *sailába* lands depends on the character of the inundation.

Principal staples.

Table No. XX shows the areas under the principal agricultural staples.

List of principal crops.

In the following list the names in English and vernacular of the crops principally grown are given. The botanical names usually employed are added :—

Chapter IV, A.

Agriculture and Arboriculture.

List of principal crops.

English name.	Vernacular name.	Botanical name.
	Autumn Crops.	
Rice ...	*Dhan* or *munji* ...	*Oryza sativa.*
Great millet ...	*Jowár* ...	*Sorghum vulgare.*
Spiked millet ...	*Bájra* ...	*Penicillaria spicata.*
Italian millet ...	*Kangni* ...	*Penisetum Italicum.*
Maize ...	*Makki* ...	*Zea mays.*
Sesamum ...	*Til* ...	*Sesamum orientale.*
... ...	*Moth* ...	*Phaseolus acontifolius.*
... ...	*Máng* ...	*Phaseolus mungo* and *Ph. max.*
... ...	*Máh* ...	*Phaseolus Roxburghii.*
Cotton ...	*Kapah* ...	*Gossypium herbaceum.*
Hemp ...	*Sann* or *sanni* ...	*Crotalaria juncea.*
" ...	*Sankukra* or *sinjubara* ...	*Hibiscus cannabinus.*
Red pepper ...	*Lál Mirich* ...	*Capsicum fastigratum.*
Sugarcane ...	*Paunda (kamád)* ...	*Saccharum officinarum.*
Melons, &c. ...	*Kharbuza &c.* ...	*Cucumis melso, &c.*
	Autumn and Spring Crops.	
... ...	*China* ...	*Panicum miliaceum.*
Beans ...	*Rawán* ...	*Dolichos sinensis.*
	Spring Crops.	
Wheat ...	*Kanak* ...	*Triticum vulgare, T. durum.*
Barley ...	*Jau* ...	*Hordeum hexastichum.*
Gram ...	*Chhola* ...	*Cicer arietinum.*
... ...	*Charal* ...	*Lathyrus sativus.*
Lentils ...	*Masar* ...	*Lens esculenta.*
? ...	*Methra* ...	...
Turnips ...	*Gonglu* ...	*Brassica rapa.*
Rape ...	*Sarhon* ...	*Sinapis juncea.*
Tobacco ...	*Tambáku* ...	*Nicotiana tabacum &c.*
Poppy ...	*Post* ...	*Papaver somniferum.*
... ...	*Saunf* ...	*Fœniculum vulgare.*
Cummin ...	*Zira* ...	*Cuminum officinale.*
Vegetables ...	*Tarkári* ...	..

In autumn, *guár* (*Cyamopsis psoraloides*), *mándwa* (*Eleusyne caracona*), and *sawánk* (*Oplismenum frumentaceum*), all three pulses; and hemp—*i.e.*, *bhang* (*Cannabis sativa*),—and senna, are grown, but very rarely. In spring *tárámíra* (*Brassica erucal*), *sinji* or trefoil (*medicago* ?), *dhaniún* or coriander (*Coriandrum sativum*), and *ajwáin* (*Ptychotis ajwáin*) are occasionally grown.

Time of sowing and cutting crops.

In the following list the time of sowing and cutting the principal crops are noted :—

Crops.	Time of sowing.	Time of cutting.
	Autumn Crops.	
Rice ...	Middle of April to middle of May in beds. Transplant second-half of July ... Broad-cast from middle of May to end of July.	October.

Chapter IV, A.

Agriculture and Arboriculture.

Time of sowing and cutting crops.

Crops.	Time of sowing.	Time of cutting.
Jowár ...	Middle of June to middle of August ...	November.
Bájra ..	Do. do ..	Middle of October to middle of November.
Kangni ...	Middle of June to middle of July ...	September.
Maize ...	Middle of June to end of August ...	Middle of September to middle of November.
Til ...	Middle of July to middle of August ...	November.
Moth ...	Do. do. ...	Do.
Múng ...	First half of August ...	Do.
Máh ...	Second half of August ...	Do.
Cotton ...	Middle of April to middle of June ...	Middle of September to end of December.
Sann or *Sunni* ...	End of May to middle of July ...	Middle of October to middle of December.
Sankukra ...	Middle of February to middle of March, and middle of April to middle of June.	Middle of September to middle of November.
Red pepper ...	In beds middle of February to middle of March. Transplant about middle of June.	Middle of October to middle of January.
Sugarcane ...	Middle of February to middle of March ..	November to middle of January.
Melons, &c. ...	Middle of February to middle of March..	Middle of April to middle of September.
	Middle of April to middle of May, if sown with cotton.	Middle of July to middle of August if sown with cotton.
	Autumn and Spring Crops	
China (1) ...	Middle of February to middle of March.	June.
(2) ...	Middle of August to middle of September.	December.
Rawán ...	Middle of February to middle of March	Middle of April to middle of June.
	Middle of April to middle of June ...	Middle of August to middle of October.
	Spring Crops.	
Wheat ...	Middle of October to middle of December	Middle of April to middle of May.
Barley ...	October and November ...	First half of April.
Gram ...	September and first-half of October ..	Do.
Charál ...	Middle of September to middle of November.	Do.
Masúr ...	Do. do. ...	Do.
Methra ...	Middle of September to end of October	Middle of March to middle of April.
Turnips ...	Beginning of September to middle of October.	January, February and March.
Sarhon ...	Do. do. ...	First-half of April.
Tobacco ...	Second half of October in beds. Transplant from middle of February to middle of March.	June.
Poppy ..	October ..	First-half of April.
Saunf ..	Middle of September to middle of October	Do.
Zíra ..	Middle of October to middle of January.	Middle of March to middle of May.
Vegetables ...	September, October, and first-half of November	Middle of December to middle of April.

The spring vegetables are turnips, carrots, onions, radishes, *methi* and *pálak*.

Chapter IV, A.

Agriculture and Arboriculture.

Manner of cultivating the various staples.

In the following statement is shown whether the crops are grown on canal, well, *sailába* or *báráni* land, whether they are manured or not, and the manner of propagation adopted, whether by seed sown broadcast or by drill, or by transplanting seedlings or by cuttings. An asterisk in any column implies that that column refers in the affirmative to the crops opposite which the asterisk is placed. Thus an asterisk opposite rice in the column "canal-irrigated land" means that rice is grown in such land. For *rabi* crops in the canal tracts the canals can generally give only a preliminary watering (*rauní*) to provide moisture for sowing; but only such as can be brought to maturity by canal-irrigation are shown as grown on canal land. "R" stands for "rarely."

Autumn Crops.

Crops.	Class of land.				Manured or not.			How sown or propagated			
	Canal irrigated.	Well irrigated.	*Sailába.*	*Báráni.*	Always.	Sometimes.	Never.	Broadcast.	Drill	Transplanted.	Cutting.
Rice	*	...	*	...	...	...	*	*	*	*	...
Jowár	*	*	...	...	...	...	*	*	...	...	...
Bájra	*	*	*	*	...	...	*	*	...	...	...
Kangni	*	*	...	...	...	*	...	*	...	...	...
Maize	*	*	...	...	*	...	...	*	...	...	...
Til	*	...	...	*	...	...	*	*	...	...	...
Moth	*	...	...	*	...	...	*	*	...	...	...
Múng	*	...	*	*	...	...	*	*	...	...	...
Máh	R	...	*	...	...	...	*	*	...	...	...
Cotton	*	*	...	...	...	*	...	*	...	...	...
Saun	*	*	?	...	...	...	*	*	...	...	...
Sankukra	*	*	?	...	...	...	*	*	...	...	...
Redpepper	*	*	...	...	*	...	...	...	...	*	...
Sugarcane	...	*	...	...	*	...	...	...	...	...	*
Melons, &c.	*	*	*	...	...	...	*	R	*	...	...

Autumn and Spring Crops.

Crops.	Canal irrigated.	Well irrigated.	*Sailába.*	*Báráni.*	Always.	Sometimes.	Never.	Broadcast.	Drill	Transplanted.	Cutting.
Chiná	*	*	...	...	...	*	...	*	...	...	...
Rawán	R	...	*	...	...	...	*	R	*	...	...

Spring Crops.

Crops.	Canal irrigated.	Well irrigated.	*Sailába.*	*Báráni.*	Always.	Sometimes.	Never.	Broadcast.	Drill	Transplanted.	Cutting.
Wheat	...	*	*	R	...	*	...	*	*	...	...
Barley	...	*	*	R	...	*	...	*	*	...	...
Gram	*	...	*	...	...	...	*	*	...	...	...
Charal	*	...	*	...	...	...	*	*	...	...	...
Masar	*	...	*	...	...	...	*	*	...	...	...
Methra	...	R	*	...	...	...	*	*	...	...	...
Turnips	...	*	*	...	...	*	...	*	...	...	...
Sarhon	...	*	*	...	...	*	...	*	...	...	...
Tobacco	...	*	...	...	*	...	...	...	...	*	...
Poppy	...	*	...	...	*	...	...	*	...	...	...
Saunf	...	*	...	...	*	...	...	...	...	...	...
Zíra	...	*	...	...	...	...	*	*	...	...	...
Vegetables	*	*	*	...	*	...	...	*	*	...	...

Chapter IV, A.
Agriculture and Arboriculture.
Manner of cultivating the various staples.

Rice grown on the Deg is generally transplanted. *Charri*, which is *jowár* grown for fodder, is often manured. *Bájra* is scarcely known here. *Saunf* and *zíra* too are rare. *Kangni* is grown in the spring also occasionally. The seed of *til, sarhon*, poppy, and often of turnips, is mixed with earth before being sown. Cotton should be manured if possible; so should turnips be if grown with well-irrigation. Wheat and barley are sown by drill on *sailába* and *báráni* land.

Diseases of crops.

Some account of the diseases to which crops are liable will now be given. *Kunghi* is rust. It attacks wheat, and, according to some, *churál* and *masar*. All agree that barley is not attacked by it. This disease may occur at any time from the end of the year till the corn is cut. It is supposed to be caused by a continuance of cloudy weather, without wind, sun, or rain. It occurs chiefly to wheat sown late. Sunshine is the best remedy; and as the west wind disperses the clouds, it is useful, but in itself it possesses no virtues. If the disease attacks the crops before the grain has set, the ears are empty. If after, the grain is small.

Kadur.—An orange-coloured rust settles on the leaves and stalk, which comes off on the plant being brushed against. The grain is not discoloured. The leaves are attacked first.

Khudru.—This is another disease of wheat. Only a plant here and there is injured; the grain becomes small, round, and black. The disease commences in Chetr, when the ears are first appearing. The cause is not known.

Valái and *kundi* are names for the same disease of wheat. The stalk grows spirally like a corkscrew. If the ear has formed, it is also twisted in coils. No grain is formed. Only a few plants are attacked. *Valái* is used in respect of the stalk and *kundi* as regards the ear. *Valái* occurs in Máh and Phagan, and *kundi* in Phagan and Chetr.

Dhanak and *jabdar* or *gandel* are said to be wheat that has deteriorated owing to some disease. *Dhanak* seems to be a sort of wild oats, and *jabdar* or *gandel* simply a weed which produces a small brownish-yellow grain, not unlike that of *china* in size and shape.

Tela is said to attack all crops, especially tobacco and melons in Jeth; wheat and *ság* (greens) in Poh and Mágh; *jowár, til, china*, cotton, *múng* and *máh* in Asu and Kátik. Wheat is not, however, injured by it; but generally the plant attacked dries up, and an oily liquid is found on it. This is caused by a small yellow-winged insect. The only remedy is rain, which is supposed to wash off the oil. A full account of the disease is given on page 487 of the "Hand-book of the Economic Products of the Punjab." This disease is also called *saresa* from *sarés*, glue; as *tela* is from *tel*, oil.

Hadda is a disease to which melons, gourds, and that class of plants are liable. It occurs in Jeth and Visákh, and is supposed to be caused by excessive heat and dryness. The plant withers

Chapter IV, A.
Agriculture and Arboriculture.
Diseases of crops.

away. The remedy is to burn bones of camels to windward of the field, so as to get the smoke to pass over the plants. The name of the disease is derived from this remedy.

Bhakri attacks *jowár* in Bhadron and the beginning of Asu. It is attributed to excessive dryness; and some say a sort of spider does the mischief; a web like that of a spider forms across the top of the plant and prevents the ear forming. Rain is beneficial.

Tukmár or *tuklamár* occurs to *jowár* at the end of Asu and beginning of Kátik. It is attributed to excessive rain and the east wind. An insect eats the stalk at the place where the ear is joind on to it; the ear is thus destroyed. Cattle eat the stalks. The stalk just below the ear is called *takka* or *tukla* or *túla;* the name of the disease is derived from the name of the stalk and *márna*. *Tukka* is said by the dictionary to be a corn-cob. In *túla,* which attacks *jowár* at the same time as *tukmár,* the ear does not form, but in its place a number of shoots are thrown out. The cause is not known. Only a few plants are attacked; the stalk is unusually sweet, and is used as fodder.

Káni or *kangiári* attacks barley, and, according to some though others deny it, wheat, in Phagan and Chetr, and cotton and *jowar* in Asu and Kátik. The grain of wheat, barley, and *jowár* turns black and is just like soot. *Jowár* grains become long and pointed. In cotton the balls do not open at all; if they do, there is nothing inside but a little yellow lint. The seed is affected like that of cereals. This disease seems caused by excessive rain. This disease seems smut, and smut undoubtedly attacks wheat. The names of the diseases are derived by the people from *kána,* one-eyed, because some grains are sound and some diseased; and from *kál,* famine, and *angiári,* a small coal.

Báhmni or *chittri* occurs to *moth, máh* and *múng* and some say to melons. It occasionally attacks *sann.* It appears in October. White spots *(chitti)* appear on the leaves. No grain forms. Only plants here and there are affected. The spots in the case of *báhmni* seem larger than in *chittri,* but otherwise there is no difference. The name *báhmni* comes from the custom of Brahmins to adorn themselves with white spots of *sandal.* The cause of the disease is unknown.

Batur attacks *moth, máh, múng* and *til;* the first three in Asu and Kátik, and the last also in Bhádron. It generally occurs when there has been much rain. The plant shrivels up, and the pods do not fill. The whole field is not attacked, but only scattered plants.

Mechanical injuries to crops, and agents of such.

Most of the above affections may be called diseases. The following are more mechanical agents in causing injury than diseases. *Wá*: wheat and barley are damaged in Chetr by heavy wind, *hawa* or *wá*. *Khewan* or *lishk* is lightning. All conspicuously flowering plants are affected by violent lightning when in flower, due possibly to the generation of ozone by the

Chapter IV, A.

Agriculture and Arboriculture.

Mechanical injuries to crops, and agents of such.

electrical disturbance. The flowers drop off and no pods form, or the grain gets black, as in the case of *zíra* and *saunf*, if it has set. One side of a field may be injured and another escape. The *sohánjná* or horse-radish tree is similarly affected. *Kummi* occurs to *jowár, chína*, and *kangni*, and some say to rice and melons. *Jowár* and *chína* are attacked in Asu and Kátik, and *kangni* in Bhádron. A small-winged reddish insect, about the size of a grain of *jowár*, appears and regales itself on the pollen *(búra)*,or, according to some, on the ear and stalk, just below the ear (*tukka*). Of course the ear does not mature. This insect does not come in swarms. Very little damage is done. *Kumma* means a tortoise. The insect is round-backed like a tortoise ; hence the name. It seems a sort of lady-bird. *Múla* or *ukhera* is an insect that attacks the roots (hence the name) of tobacco in Visákh and Jeth, of cotton and pepper in Asu and Kátik and of gram in Phagan and Chetr. It is said to be a kind of ant with a white body and red or black head. It is not the same as *síonk*, or the white ant, which eats up everything it comes across ; for *múla* occurs on flooded lands, and white ants are destroyed by irrigation. White ants do much mischief in dry years. *Sundi* is a green caterpillar that attacks gram and *charal* in Phagan and Chetr. It gets inside the pod and eats up the grain. *Toka* appears to be a grasshopper of a greyish-brown colour, which eats up the young shoots of all plants. *Jackals* have a great partiality for melons and other gourds. They also get *makki* and *jowár* stalks between their legs and walk down them when they feast on the cobs. *Rats* are not strong enough for that ; they nibble at the bottom of wheat and barley stalks when the grain is forming. Down come the stalks, and the rats eat the young ears. They also injure sugarcane and rice, if there is no water about it. *Parrots* are fond of pepper pods, poppy-heads *jowár* ears, and *sarhon*. *Crows* devote themselves to *jowár, makki* and germinating wheat. *Deer* (*hiran*), *porcupines* (*seh*), and *hares* (*saiyar*), eat all green crops. *Pigs* on the rivers destroy everything they can. *Wild cats* (*bár-billa*) are particularly fond of maize cobs. But they and porcupines are rare. Not so *tilyar*. *Tilyars* are the birds called *goliya* in Hindustáni. They are very common and fly in flocks. Their breast and neck are brown, otherwise their colour is black. According to popular report, they appear in Asu and Kátik, by which is probably meant that they then first attract notice ; and in Chetr and Visákh their colour changes to black with brown spots. They eat most fruits and seeds, such as those of the *karíl, wan, ber* and *pipal*, and of *jowár* and *bájra*. But in return they devour grasshoppers (*toka*) and locusts. It may be mentioned here that fogs (*kuhír*) are considered rather good for crops ; and if rain comes on while the fog is on the ground, the result is as if land had been manured.

Remarks concerning individual crops —Rice.

The method of cultivating the principal crops, with some remarks concerning them. will now be stated. Rice is usually called *dhán* on the Sutlej and *munji* on the Deg. In Dipálpur,

Chapter IV, A.

Agriculture and Arboriculture.

Remarks concerning individual crops —Rice.

the seed is soaked in water till it germinates, and is then sown broadcast; twenty-four *sérs* of seed go to the acre. The ground is watered and ploughed three or four times and harrowed. It is then watered again and ploughed up twice, and harrowed while under water. By this process, called *rafad karna*, the water gets thick with mud; the seed is then flung on it. The particles of earth held in suspension attach themselves to the seed and sink to the bottom with it. On the Deg a bed is prepared, and about two *sérs* of seed to the *marla* scattered over it. This is covered with manure and irrigated for about a month till the plants are a cubit high, when they are picked out and transplanted. The rice field is thus prepared. Water, plough twice, and harrow. Water again, plough and harrow twice while field is under water. Then plant the seedlings. The land should after planting be kept always under water. By the Deg plant 16 *sérs* of seed go to the acre, as one *marla* of seedlings suffices for one *kanál* of the rice-field. Seven kinds of rice are cultivated—*safeda, shakarchíni, ratúa, sohanpatar, nagoi, khasru*, and *mushkí*. *Safeda*, a beardless variety, with white ear and stalk of medium thickness, is the only kind commonly grown. The others are very rarely met with. If rice is watered just before cutting, the weight of the grain is supposed to increase; but the grain breaks in husking. So people water the fields of which they intend to sell the produce, and not those they intend for their own use. Rice is reaped when the ground is dry, bound in sheaves and stacked. It is threshed by bullocks without the *phalha*. After separating the straw and grain, the latter is husked in a mortar by Changars, a wandering tribe stated by Cunningham ("History of the Sikhs," page 9) to be the same as the Kanjars of Dehli; and probably the same as the Gypsies of Europe. They are paid two pies for every *sér* of cleaned rice, or 6 annas and 8 pies per *man*. Two men can clean from one *man* to one *man* and a quarter in the day. Rice husks are not specially applied to rice fields as manure. They are eaten by the Changars' donkeys, burnt or thrown away as refuse; nearly one-third of threshed rice is husk, so three *sérs* of threshed rice yield only two *sérs* of cleaned rice. The straw of rice is called *prál* or *práli*. It is considered warm and good litter, but inferior fodder, being devoid of strengthening properties. It is given to cattle mixed with green fodder. Rice does not seem to suffer from any disease. A plant called *dhiddan* is found in rice fields. The grain is red. The plant is not altogether unlike wild *sawánk*. It is picked out and given to bullocks as fodder. Some imagine this to be rice which has deteriorated owing to disease.

Jowár; Charri.

Great millet is sown either for the grain, in which case it is called *jowár*, or for fodder, when it is known as *charri*. As already noticed, a great part of the crop is cut for fodder. The best soil for both is good *gasra*. The ground is first watered either by well or canal, then ploughed twice and harrowed. Next the seed is sown broadcast; the ground is ploughed again twice and harrowed once. Beds are formed, and the plants

Chapter IV, A.

Agriculture and Arboriculture.

Jowár; Charri.

which come up in about six days are watered every three weeks. Good cultivators will harrow after each ploughing. Twelve *sérs* of seed are sown for *jowár* and 40 for *charri*, in each acre. *Charri* is used as green fodder; it is not dried and stored. It is sown either at the same time as *jowár* or in Visákh. In the latter case it is cut from the middle of Jeth and given to the cattle mixed with *túri*. About six weeks' supply is grown. *Jowár* plants are tied together like sugarcane to keep them from being blown down. They are cut down and placed in stocks with the ears pointing upwards. Then the heads are cut off and threshed by bullocks without the *phalha*. *Jowár* stalks are known, whether green or dry, as *tánda;* when green they are sometimes eaten as sugarcane. They are the best fodder obtainable, and are worth from Rs. 15 to Rs. 20 per acre. A bullock will eat about twice as much *jowár* stalks when dry by weight as it will of broken wheat straw (*túri*); say 30 *sers* per diem. *Jowár* husks are eaten by bullocks. All *jowár* stalks are *turon* or *kángar;* names derived from *tar*, moist, and *kána*, the stalk of *sarr*, which is useless for fodder. *Turon* stalks are juicy and good fodder; *kángar* stalks are dry and useless. The rib of a leaf of a *turon* is green; of a leaf of *kángar* white. The seed of a *kángar* plant is said to produce *kángar* plants. Nine kinds of *jowár* are commonly known, but only four are generally grown. The four are *chichka*, *rattar*, *bagar* and *gummi*. The other five are *jhandi*, *chúhri*, *haji*, *kubi*, *makhan* and *ramák*. They are mostly grown for the purpose of being roasted in ashes and eaten. The stalk of *chichka* is coarse and liable to become *kángar;* so this variety is not usually sown for *charri*. The ear of *chúhri* is black; of *rattar*, blue; of *makhan*, red and white; and of the other varieties, white. The ear of *gummi* is more compact and contains more grain than that of the others. Its stalk is *turon*. *Kángar* stalks are, no doubt, caused by some disease. *Jowár* is attacked also by *tela*, *bhakri*, *tukmár*, *túla* and *kangiári*.

Bájra.

Bájra is very little grown, but it seems to be making some way in popular favour. It is cultivated as *jowár*: water, plough twice and harrow, then sow broadcast, and plough and harrow as before. Make beds and irrigate about every three weeks. The field should be weeded in Asu. The crop is very inferior to *jowár*, as the stalks are worth very little. They are almost useless as fodder. This is the reason it is so little grown, and not, as the people say, because the birds won't leave them any share of the grain.

Kangni.

Kangni is extensively grown. The proper mode of cultivation seems to be to plough up the land in the cold weather. When the seed time comes, it should be ploughed up three or four times, and harrowed each time but the last. The seed is then sown broadcast, and the field smoothed down. Some plough once after sowing. The crop is irrigated five or six times. About 14 *sers* of seed go to the acre. It is a good thing to manure the ground for this crop, which is considered

Kangni.

an exhausting one. Good *gasra* is the best soil for it. *Kangni* is threshed with a stick, or trampled out by bullocks without the *phalha*. Two varieties of this crop are recognised—*kangan* and *kangni;* but they differ only in size, as *kangan* is larger and coarser than *kangni*. *Kangan* is rare. The straw of *kangni* is called *prál* or *práli*. It is not broken up like *túri*. It is considered good, strengthening food. The grain of *kangni* is used as an article of diet. The grain of dried *kangni* is to the straw, by weight, nearly as 27 to 73. Plants of *tándla*, wild *sawánk*, and *kúra* are very common in *kangni* fields; and the green seeds of the first two and the black seeds of the last are generally found mixed up with *kangni* grain. *Kangni* is subject to the disease *tela*, and is attacked by *kummi*. It is very rarely sown in the spring, in Phagan. It ripens then in four months.

Maize.

For maize or *makki*, the ground should, if possible, be ploughed in the cold weather and manured. It is then watered and ploughed and harrowed three or four times. The seed is sown broadcast, at the rate of 12 to 18 *sers* to the acre. The ground is next ploughed up twice and harrowed once and laid out in beds. One month after sowing the field is hoed and weeded, and again if the weeds become thick. As a matter of fact maize often does not get all this attention. At sowing time the ground is watered either by well or canal, the seed scattered by hand and ploughed in three times and the ground harrowed. Not more than one weeding is given. The maize irrigated by wells generally gets manure, but this is much more rare in the case of canal-irrigated crops. It is necessary to keep the ground moist; and so it is said to be irrigated every fifth day, but the number of waterings is almost always exaggerated in the accounts given by the people. A watering is said to be essential as soon as the cobs appear. The stalk of maize is called *túnda*, and is good fodder when green, especially when given with the cobs, but bitter and useless when dry, except mixed with green food. Maize suffers from *tela* and some say, *bhakri* and *láhmni*. But jackals and crows are its most dangerous enemies. Two varieties are known—the *doában* and *desi*. The former grows as tall as *jowár;* produces two, sometimes three, cobs on one stalk; the stalk is coarse and of a brown colour above the roots; the leaves are broad, and the grain coarse, and of a yellow colour. The grain of the *desi* is small and white; the plant is from 4 to 4½ feet high, and of a straw colour just above the roots. It rarely produces more than one cob on each stalk. The yield of the *doában* is more than that of the *desi;* but it takes three months for the former to ripen, and only 2½ for the latter.

Til.

Til is often sown with *moth* and *múng*, or *moth* alone; sometimes with *jowár*. *Til* is extensively grown on canal-irrigation and to some extent on rain. It never receives well water. After rain, plough, sow broadcast, mixing seed with earth if not sown with some other crops, and plough again. Sometimes the seed is simply thrown on the fallow ground and

Chapter IV, A.

Agriculture and Arboriculture.

Til.

ploughed in. On canal-irrigated land a watering is given and one or two ploughings. The seed is then scattered and ploughed in; the preliminary ploughings are often dispensed with. Two *sers* of seed go to the acre. *Til* plants should not be close together, according to the verse:—

Jau wirle, til sanghne, mahín jái kat;
Núhán ḍhiyán jaián; cháron chaur chopat.

"When barley grows scattered, and *til* close together, and the buffalo brings forth a male calf, and sons' wives give birth to daughters—all four are utterly bad." Only one kind of *til*, the black, is known. The plant is affected by *tela* and lightning. When the crop is cut, the stalks are placed in a circle with their tops pointing inwards, and are left there for a fortnight with a weight upon them. This heatens and softens the pods. Then the stalks are placed on the ground with their tops pointing upwards, leaning against each other, or a straw-rope. The action of the sun causes the pods to open, when the grain is shaken out on a cloth. Fifteen *sers* of *til* seed produce 6 *sers* of sweet oil. *Til* stalks, when dry, are used for fuel. They give forth a fierce flame.

Moth.

The cultivation of *moth* is very simple. The seed is thrown on the fallow ground and ploughed in. Occasionally the ground is ploughed up before sowing. *Moth* is often sown with *til* and *múng*; 8 to 16 *sers* of seed are sown on the acre. On *báráni* lands the smaller quanity would be used, and on canal lands the larger. There are three kinds of *moth*: *bagga, jhijru,* and *garára.* The first grows up straight; the leaves are not indented; it throws out no runners; and the grain is white. The other two kinds throw out runners; the leaves of *jhijru* are indented; those of *garára* are not. The grain of *jhijru* is white with black spots; of *garára* black with white spots. The three kinds are found growing together or alone. The plant is left to dry after being cut; then collected and beaten and shaken with the tringal, and the stalks and leaves thrown aside; the rest of the plant is then threshed by bullocks. The stalks and leaves are excellent fodder for cattle. It is broken up like *túri.* *Moth* suffers from *tela, báhmni* and *batúr.*

Múng—Múngi.

Múng is sown very much like *moth.* It is thrown broadcast on the field and ploughed in; some plough before sowing and give two ploughings after sowing. The amount of seed is from 8 to 16 *sers* per acre. This crop is very commonly grown on canal-irrigated lands. There are two varieties of *múng, viz.,* the black *múng,* called also *bharung,* on the Rávi towards Lahore; and the green *múngi,* which is that found on the Sutlej. *Múngi* again is divided, according to the colour of the grain, into green and yellow. It is often sown with *jowár* or *til,* and sometimes with *máh.* It is threshed like *moth,* and the stalks and leaves broken up are used as fodder. It is attacked by the same diseases as *moth.*

Máh.

Máh is cultivated in the same way as *mung;* the usual quantity of seed to the acre seems to be 16 *sers*. Two kinds are known, the black or *bharung*, and the green or *kachúa*. The former grows as a creeper along the ground, the latter upright. The pods of *bharung* are blackish-purple, long and thin, those of *kachúa* greenish-yellow, short and thick. The grain of the one is green, of the other black. The *dál* of *kachúa* is larger, has a better taste, and requires less time in cooking than that of *bharung;* hence it sells at 3 or 4 *sers* the rupee dearer. *Máh* and *rawán* are sometimes grown together. It is usually grown on *sailába* land. It is not eaten raw by human beings, and in that respect differs from *múng*. It is threshed as *múng;* and is a good fodder for all cattle, and especially so for camels.

Cotton.

The ground intended for cotton should receive two or three ploughings on the winter rainfall; but this is not often done except among the better class of cultivators. On well-irrigated lands before sowing in *Visákh* or *Jeth* manure is put down and a preliminary watering given. The soil is then ploughed and harrowed two or three times; the seed mixed with dung is then scattered and ploughed in, and the ground levelled and beds are formed. After one month the crops should be watered, and afterwards once every fortnight or three weeks, till the plants flower, when water should be given every week. When the plants are a span high, the field ought to be weeded, and again when the weeds grow high after the rains have begun. *Kallar* is often applied to the roots on this occasion. If needed a third weeding takes place. The weeding may be either with *ramba* or *kahi*. Less trouble is taken with the cultivation of cotton on canal irrigated lands. Manure is seldom used. If the canal supply is available sufficiently early in the season, the land is ploughed once or twice after receiving the preliminary watering and the seed is then scattered; the ground is then ploughed once or twice and harrowed. When the canals are late in commencing to flow, the ploughings between the preliminary watering and the sowing are dispensed with; the seed being merely thrown down on the moistened ground and ploughed in, and the soil being subsequently harrowed. The flowers form early in September, and the balls after the middle of that month. Cotton is picked chiefly by women, who are paid in kind, getting a smaller or larger share of what is picked, according to the smallness or largeness of the picking. This share ranges from $\frac{1}{4}$ to $\frac{1}{24}$, and averages $\frac{1}{8}$ to $\frac{1}{10}$. It is determined on the principle that each picker should get as wages one *ser* of raw cotton per diem. Most cotton is, however, not manured; and generally people plough only when about to sow; and many cotton fields look as if they were never weeded at all. Sometimes cotton is cut down in the cold weather and the roots are left in the ground for another year when the plant grows again and yields a second crop; but the outturn is inferior. A plant thus cut down is called *mudhi*. It is well to sow cotton early so as to escape the frosts of next cold weather

Chapter IV, A.

Agriculture and Arboriculture.

Cotton.

In some parts of the canal-irrigated tracts where levels are too high to be reached by the canals in the early part of the flow season, cotton sowing has to be done on well-irrigation, the plants being subsequently watered from the canal; on the other hand, where the canal supply fails prematurely, wells are used to save such of the canal-irrigated cotton as is sufficiently near. Three kinds of cotton are locally known: *hazára* or *nerma,* also called *ratti, kurmi* or *kapáh,* the ordinary kind, and *tillar.* The flower of *hazára* is red, and the leaves have a reddish tinge. A field of it looks as if withered. The lint is finer and longer than that of *kapáh.* The latter has white or yellow flowers. *Hazára* produces less than *kapáh,* and on this account is not commonly sown by itself. It is said to have been introduced by Major Marsden The fibre of *tillar* is somewhat fine and delicate. It gives the best yield. Faridkote near Dipálpur is noted for producing it. Uncleaned cotton contains about 29 parts by weight of seed and 11 parts of fibre. The cultivator retains what cotton he wants, and sells the rest after having had it cleaned. He keeps the seed for his cattle. Cotton is mostly cleaned by *karárs.* They are paid one anna for each *sér* of clean cotton they turn out, and can earn four annas a day at this rate.

Sann or sanni: sankukra or sinjúbára.

Sankukra or *sinjúbára* is not grown by itself, but around fields of cotton, and the ground is not specially prepared for it. The object of sowing a single row of *sankukra* round cotton fields is not clear. The people say it is to prevent passers-by helping themselves to cotton. The pods, leaf and flower of *sankukra* are not unlike those of cotton. The fibre is inferior to that of *sanni. Sann* or *sanni* is rarely grown in larger patches than a *kanál.* The land is ploughed and harrowed. Then the seed is sown broadcast. The plot is ploughed twice and harrowed after the second ploughing. Fifty-six *sérs* of seed go to the acre; the object of such wholesale expenditure of seed being to make the plants grow close together, and so oblige them to shoot up. *Sanni* has to be watered about every 15 days. When the crop is cut, it is tied in bundles and soaked in water for 10 or 12 days. It is then dried, and the skin is peeled off and twisted into ropes. The wood is used for fuel. *Sanni* is attacked by *báhmni* or *chittri,* but the harm done is trifling. *Sanni* with its tall and slender shape, yellow flowers, and narrow tapering leaves, is a pretty plant.

Red pepper.

Red pepper is planted first in manured seedling beds. When the plants are 8 to 9 inches high, they are transplanted. They are not removed all at the same time; but when each plant has reached the proper size, it is transplanted. The pepper field is ploughed twice and harrowed after each ploughing. Then beds are made and irrigated. The seedlings are next transplanted, holes being made with the hand to receive them. After transplanting the crop has to be irrigated every seventh or eight day. About one month after transplanting, the field should be weeded, and some manure put about the roots of each plant, and this treatment is repeated after another

Chapter IV, A.

Agriculture and Arboriculture.

Red pepper.

month has elapsed. After the third month the crop is weeded. When the pods ripen, they are picked every fourth or fifth and sometimes sixth or seventh day, till the frost comes, when all the remaining pods, red or green, are gathered. The pods are dried in the sun to keep them from rotting. The wood of pepper is of no use, not even for fuel. Pepper is another *mudhi* crop. It is cut down at the end of Maghar. At the beginning of Phagan the ground about the roots is dug up, and manure applied to them. Water is given every 15 days. The pods can be picked from the middle of Jeth to the end of Asu. Weeding should take place at the first watering in Phagan, and again a month after. Pepper does not suffer from any disease, but *múla*, white-ants, and parrots prey on it.

Sugarcane.

Sugarcane is very little cultivated, principally on account of the difficulty of getting a continuous supply of water. The Sikh settlers in the Sohág Pára colony cultivate it to some extent. Sugar (*gur*) is seldom made from that grown. It is used simply as a pleasant article of food in its raw state. The soil may be either *sikand* or *gasra*, but it must be manured. The ground is watered and ploughed up twice and harrowed once (in Phagan), and then manured. It is again watered, ploughed and harrowed in Chet. Both these waterings have to be given from wells, as the canals do not begin to flow by this time. Then shallow trenches are made, and pieces of cane, each containing a joint, are laid in the plane of the ground with the length of the piece at right angles to the length of the trench in holes made in the trenches, at intervals of about one foot. The holes are then filled up, and the trenches watered. Every fifth or sixth day water has to be supplied. After one month hoeing and weeding should take place, and should be repeated afterwards four or five times, whenever grass grows high. About three months after the young shoots appear, the earth is banked up, about the roots, and when the stalks get long and are in danger of being broken by the wind, several are tied together, so as to support each other. The above method of preparing the ground is slovenly. Good cultivators plough twice and harrow once in Poh and again in Máh. In Phagan they water, manure, plough twice, and harrow once, and again water, plough twice and harrow. Sugarcane is called *ponda* or *paunda*. There are two kinds, the *sahárni* or Sahâranpuri, and the *desi* or Jullunduri. The former is the coarser and larger of the two. The *desi* is sweeter, softer, and more juicy. Cultivators sell a certain area under cane to *karárs* who cut the canes and retail them in the *bazár*. A single good cane will fetch one anna or five pices. White-ants seem the most dangerous enemy of sugarcane.

Melons, &c.

Under melons, &c., are included *khíra*, *wanga* and *tar*, eaten raw before the seeds ripen ; *kharbúza* and *hadwána*, eaten raw after the seeds ripen, and *tori*, *karela*, *tinda*, *kadu*, *petha*, and all eaten cooked. *Kharbúza* and *hadwána* are grown on unmanured sandy soils, the others on manured land, good *gasra* if possible. On well-lands the ground is ploughed up several times during

Chapter IV, A.

Agriculture and Arboriculture.

Melons, &c.

the cold weather, and harrowed each time. When seed time comes the ground is watered, and the seed sown broadcast. Two ploughings and one harrowing are then given; beds are made, and irrigation afforded about once a week. One weeding, about a month after sowing, is enough. On *sailába* lands the ground is ploughed twice and harrowed once. The seed is then sown by drill. No weeding or watering takes place. Melons are often sown among cotton. In this case they are treated just as cotton is. From 4 to 8 *sérs* of seed are sown in an acre. *Badda* is the characteristic disease of melons. They are also attacked by *chittri*, and jackals are very fond of them.

China.

Chína is extensively cultivated both in spring and autumn. It is not generally grown on manured land, but if the soil is poor it should be manured. Some also scatter manure over the field after sowing. The best mode of cultivation is to plough up the ground twice, and let it lie for some time. Then plough twice again and sow broadcast. Plough again twice. After every second ploughing harrow. Some only plough four times and harrow twice, and some simply plough three times, harrowing after each ploughing but the last. Then they sow and harrow. From 12 to 16 *sérs* of seed go to the acre. This crop requires constant watering. Fifteen waterings are said to be necessary; but ten are certainly required. The people have a marvellous legend about a Rája declaring *chína* should pay no revenue on account of the quantity of water it takes. It is a precarious crop, especially in the spring, as high winds shake out the ripening grain, hence the saying—

Chína wá wahína
Je ghar áwe tá jápe,

"*Chína*, a thing knocked down by the wind, if it gets to the house, then perhaps (*i.e.*, perhaps the cultivator may get something)." There are two varieties of this crop—*chína*, which is white, and *chíni*, which is red. The former is larger and yields a larger return, but requires more water than *chíni*. It is more commonly sown. If there is great deal of *chína*, it is threshed by bullocks, otherwise by knocking it against the side of a pit or a block of wood. It is commonly grown as green fodder. The dry straw, called *prál* or *práli*, is eaten by cattle, but is not considered good food as it is heating. *Chína* is sometimes grown with *charri*. As less irrigation is required in autumn than in spring, and there is then less wind, *chína* is more commonly cultivated in the former season. *Tela* and *kummi* attack it. The straw is to the grain, by weight, very nearly as 3 to 1.

Rawán.

Rawán is grown in the spring, only for fodder. It is given to cattle while green mixed with *túri*. The land is ploughed up twice and harrowed once or twice; and then the seed is sown with the drill. Cattle are sometimes turned out into *rawán* fields to graze. The plants are usually pulled up, not

Chapter IV, A.

Agriculture and Arboriculture.

Rawán.

cut. When sown for the grain, which very rarely happens, the plants after being cut or pulled up are dried Then the leaves and pods are shaken off the stalks, and separated by the *chhajj,* and the pods are threshed by bullocks. The leaves are delicate, and would be destroyed if trampled on. When dry, they are used as food for cattle. They are fair fodder, but not good for horses. About 12 *sérs* of seed are sown in an acre. *Tela* is the chief disease of *rawán.* Only one variety of this crop is known.

Wheat.

Wheat is the staple crop of this district. For purely well irrigated wheat the ground should be ploughed two or three times after rain in August; this, however, as often as not is omitted partly owing to short rains and partly to the indolence of the cultivator. *Cháhi* wheat frequently gets manure; nearly always so when it is sown *dofasli* on a *kharíf* crop. At sowing time the ground is watered from the well, and ploughed and harrowed once or oftener, generally twice or thrice. The seed is then scattered, and the ground again ploughed and harrowed. In years of short rainfall in August the ground is in many cases not ploughed after the preliminary watering, and the seed is simply thrown on to the moistened ground and ploughed in, the soil being subsequently harrowed. This, of course, has a marked effect on the yield. For *cháhi-nahri* wheat one or two preliminary waterings are given from the canal in August; the land is then ploughed two or three times and harrowed and levelled in order that the moisture may be retained till sowing time. If the moisture left is sufficient the seed is scattered by the hand and ploughed in, if less of the moisture remains it is sown with the drill. The crop is subsequently irrigated by wells. Pure *nahri* wheat is cultivated in the same way, except that it gets no well irrigation, and is generally sown with drill. For *sailáb* wheat the land when it is sufficiently dry receives two or three ploughings and the seed is sown with the drill at the end of October somewhat before well wheat. Not unfrequently, however, the seed is simply thrown down the unploughed land and ploughed in. *Bár·ání* wheat is grown in much the same way. A couple of ploughings and harrowings take place in Sáwan, Bhádron and Asu. In Kátik the seed is sown with the drill, and the field harrowed. Purely well-irrigated wheat is watered four or more times according to the soil, character of the season, &c. Wheat sown after the ground has been flushed by the canal needs far less watering from the well. A top dressing of manure is sometimes given. Wheat is not weeded. About one maund of seed per acre is, as a rule, used, but the amount is somewhat greater in the case of late sowings. The way in which wheat is threshed has already been described. It is considered a point of good husbandry to commence to reap on the 1st of Visákh, whether the crop is ripe or not; but reaping need not continue. But all the wheat should be cut before the end of the month; for—*kanakán te kúnján, mahna je Visákh rahin.* "It is a fault (reproach) if wheat and *kúnj* are not off

Chapter IV, A.

Agriculture and Arboriculture.

Wheat.

in Visákh." The average height of wheat is $3\frac{1}{2}$ feet. Four kinds of wheat are grown: *Pamman* and *ratti* or *nikki*, both red wheats; and *dáúdi* and *ghoni*, white wheats. *Ratti* and *ghoni* are beardless; the others are bearded. The beards and ears of the red wheats turn black when they ripen; those of *dáúdi* remain white. So does the ear of *ghoni*. The ear of *ratti* is squarish, and does not taper; that of *pamman* is rectangular, and it does taper; so do those of *dáúdi* and *ghoni*, which are roundish. *Pamman* is the largest kind; next comes *ratti*, and then the white varieties. *Pamman* requires more cultivation than the others. It appears to be the same as the *vadának* of other districts. The grain of it is considered more strengthening than that of the other three, and will sell dearer; but well-to-do people prefer the white wheat. It is the regular custom to cut down green wheat, and give it as fodder to cattle. Each pair of bullocks will eat up about one-third of an acre of wheat, on an average, before the crop is cut. Green wheat is often more valuable than ripe wheat. But the demand is very limited being chiefly for fodder for milch-cattle of non-agriculturists in large towns and at fairs. On an average, the weight of the grain is to the straw as 1 to 3. In some *dáúdi* wheat Mr. Purser found $4\frac{1}{2}$ *sérs* of grain to $6\frac{1}{4}$ straw; but in the 5 feet, 11 inches *pamman* there were only 6 *sérs*, 11 *chitták*s of grain to 35 *sérs*, 5 *chitták*s of straw The average number of grains to the *tola* is 355. Wheat is very often mixed with barley, not intentionally, but owing to carelessness in selecting seed. It is said that if the seed of wheat grown on the Deg *sailába* lands is used there twice running, the crop deteriorates; that is to say, if the grain of one harvest is used as seed for the next, the produce of the grain of the second harvest will be deficient in quality and quantity. Wheat is sown mixed with barley intentionally. This crop is called *goji*. It is also sown mixed with gram. This crop is known as *berára*.

Barley.

Barley is treated as wheat, but is considered an inferior crop, and gets less attention from industrious cultivators. It cannot get any from the idle. Barley is considered only fit for horses: *jau kachche, pakke, daddare, jo joban turiyán*. "Unripe, ripe, half ripe barley, whatever excellence (it possess) is only for horses." The usual amount of seed grain to the acre is about one maund. Dry broken up barley straw is considered good fodder. *Káni* is the chief disease of this crop. The yield of barley in this district is to that of wheat on the same area as 5 to 4. Only one kind of barley is grown.

Gram.

Gram is the earliest of the *rabi* crops to be sown. It is cultivated in the most simple way. For canal-irrigated (*nahri*) gram two or three preliminary flushings are given from the canal in August; as soon as the soil is dry enough to plough, the seed is scattered and ploughed in twice. If the preliminary flushing has been deficient the seed is sown with the drill. *Nahri* gram is often sown *dofasli* on rice without any further flushing. On *sailáb* land the seed is simply scattered and

Gram.

ploughed in twice, the harrow not being used; if, however, the land is full of weeds or grass it is ploughed twice and the seed sown with the drill. Irrigation after sowing is considered injurious. About 30 *sérs* of seed are sown on the acre. Dry stalks and leaves of gram are used as fodder. They are considered injurious to milch-cattle, and little better than poison for horses, as they cause constipation. Three kinds of gram are known—the red, black, and white. The last is very rare. It is called *Kábuli chhola*. It is softer, parches better, and yields a better *dál* than the others. Confectioners use it to some extent, as the grains need not be peeled before use, as the red and black grains have to be. These last two are always grown together. Gram is not subject to any disease, but it is injured by lightning, and numerous insects and caterpillars.

Churál.

Churál is a kind of field pea. It is sown on inferior land, and invariably on *sailába* land. Hard ground recently thrown up is often planted with *churál*, as its roots are supposed to have the property of breaking it up and softening it. The ground is ploughed up; the seed is then sown broadcast, at the rate of 16 to 20 *sérs* to the acre, and ploughed in twice. This crop is grown chiefly for green fodder. The plants are pulled up or cut. The dry stalk and leaves are considered good fodder for cattle; but not for horses, as their effect is the same as that of gram stalks and leaves. The crop is more frequently grazed green. Only one variety is known. *Churál* is attacked by *sundi*.

Masar.

Masar is cultivated in the same way as *churál*. It is often sown on soft lands, newly thrown up, free from grass and weeds. About 16 *sérs* of seed are sown on an acre. *Masar* is not unlike gram when young; but the leaves of the latter are serrate, those of *masar* are not. The dry stalks and leaves of *masar* are used as fodder. Some consider them heating, and therefore bad for milch-cattle; others think them good food for all cattle, as being sweet. It is generally grazed green. *Masar* suffers from *tela* and lightning. *Múla* also attacks it. A plant called *arári*, with pink flowers like those of a pea, and growing about one foot high, is common in *masar* fields. It is said to twine itself round *masar* plants and choke them. Only one variety of *masar* is known.

Methra.

Methra is used exclusively as green fodder. It is usually grown on *sailába* lands, but often as a *dofasli* crop in cotton fields. The seed is sown broadcast, at about 16 *sérs* to the acre, and ploughed in once. On well-lands, after ploughing the ground is harrowed, and beds are made. The crop is watered about every 15 days. After three months it can be cut; it should then be watered, and may be cut three or four times more, at intervals of 15 days, being watered after each cutting. *Methra* has a white flower like that of a pea; compound ternate leaves, serrate, not unlike *sinji* leaves, but the side of the leaf furthest from the leaf stalk is flattened, and not pointed as in *sinji*.

Chapter IV, A.

Agriculture and Arboriculture.

Turnips.

Turnips should be grown on good *gasra* land. In the hard *sikand* they do not grow to any large size. It is a good thing to fold cattle on land destined for turnips. The ground should be ploughed up, if possible, a couple of times in the cold weather, or early in the rains. In Bhádron it should be manured, but seldom is. It is then watered, and ploughed, and harrowed twice. The seed is sown broadcast. Two *sérs* of seed mixed with the same quantity of earth go to the acre. The field is next ploughed and harrowed, and made into beds. The plants appear in a week. After three weeks they are watered, and after that once every 10 days From the middle of November the crop is used as fodder. The leaves are cut off, and any large turnips are pulled up. The leaves should not be cut as long as there is any dew on them. By the middle of January all the roots are fit for use. According to some, turnip roots given to cattle in Maghar (November-December) make them sick. Turnips grow to a great size sometimes; and generally are chopped up. They are considered poor food,—what rice is to man. They are much inferior to *charri* as fodder. However, they are filling, and are extensively cultivated. Turnips are sliced, dried, and stored for human food. Only one variety, the red, is common, though the white is occasionally grown. *Tela* is the principal disease. Some say *chittri* attacks turnips. Others assert that, if turnips are sown in Bhádron, mosquitoes destroy them. It is possible. On *sailába* lands two ploughings are given. The seed is sown broadcast mixed with earth, and the ground is then harrowed. Turnips if allowed to grow up produce flowers, and the crop then resembles *sarhon*. If the seeds produced are sown subsequently, the bulbs of the resulting crop will be smaller than those of its predecessor, and if the process is repeated the crop ultimately produced will be *sarhon*. To obtain turnip seed the turnip tops and the lower portions of the bulbs are cut off; they are then called *dhak* and are transplanted. The seed obtained from such plants will when sown produce turnips.

Sarhon.

Sarhon is grown either as fodder for cattle or for its seed, of which bitter oil is made. Sixteen *sérs* of seed yield 4 *sérs* of oil. The refuse or oil-cake (*khal*) is given to cattle. This crop is often sown with wheat and gram, when it is treated, as regards cultivation, as they are. When grown by itself the ground is ploughed twice and harrowed. The seed, 2 *sérs* to the acre, mixed with the same quantity of earth, is sown broadcast. The ground is then ploughed and harrowed, and beds are formed. A watering is at once given, and afterwards repeated at intervals of from 10 to 15 days. When used as fodder as is generally the case *sarhon* is treated much as turnips. It should be cut down before or very early in Mágh, or it will not yield a second crop. If well-irrigated and manured, a second crop can be obtained from plants so cut down. *Sarhon* suffers from the *tela* in Poh and Mágh. When the grain sets parrots eat it. Only one variety is known.

Chapter IV, A.

Agriculture and Arboriculture.

Tobacco.

Tobacco is a crop on which a great deal of labour has to be spent. Towards the end of October the seed-bed is prepared. It is manured and dug up with the *kahi*, and the earth is finely pulverized. Two *chittáks* of seed are mixed with as much earth, and gently scattered over a seed-bed, one *marla* in extent. This will supply plants for two *kanals*, when planted out. The seed is then rubbed in with the hand or thorn-bushes. Manure is scattered over the bed and water is given; or the manure may be scattered on the water. The seedlings are watered every 15 days. When the nights get cold, they are covered with screens or leafy branches of trees. The north side of the bed is screened completely, and the west side partially. In Kátik the preparation of the tobacco field commences. Manure is put on the ground to the height of about 4 inches. Water is turned on, and the field ploughed twice and harrowed. The ploughing and harrowing are repeated in Maghar, Poh, and Mágh. In Phagan, trenches about 15 inches deep and broad, with ridges of the same breadth, are made with the *jandra* and dressed with the *kahi*. They are filled with water; and the seedlings taken from the nursery are planted at intervals of 18 inches, about 6 inches from the top, on the sides of the ridges. The trenches are filled with water about once a week. One month after transplanting the ground is weeded, and a little *kallar* put at the roots of each plant. This treatment is repeated at intervals of 20 days to four weeks. At the last weeding, some hoe with the *kahi* and put goat's dung in the trenches. The flower is nipped off all plants, except those reserved for seed. This makes the leaves spread, and prevents the plant growing tall. When no more leaves form, the plants are cut down with the *dátri*, and left on the ground three days, during which they are constantly turned. Then a hole, big enough to hold the crop, is dug in the earth; the leaves are put in, covered with grass and earth, and left for 10 or 15 days. Next they are taken out, the stalks and hard ribs are removed, and the leaves dried in the shade, and then made into twists, called *subbs*. Stripping tobacco is called *chhilái*, and the person (generally a *kamín*) who does the stripping and twisting, is paid usually five *subbs* for each hundred he prepares, or two or three *subbs* for working till noon; sometimes he gets 4 *sérs* per *man* of tobacco prepared. It is very necessary to water tobacco just before cutting it, as otherwise it loses seriously in weight. It is not usual to mix tobacco with *gur*, nor are the stalks burned, and the ashes added to the mixture. Only one kind of tobacco, the *desi* or indigenous, is known. The disease from which tobacco suffers is *tela*. Its roots too are eaten by *wála*.

Poppy.

Poppy is not grown to any great extent, in fact not sufficiently to supply the local demand for opium. Its cultivation is prohibited except in the Gugera tahsíl. It requires a good *gasra* soil, well manured. The proper mode of cultivation is as follows: manure the land, water, plough seven or eight times, harrowing after each ploughing. Take 4 *chittáks* of seed for

Chapter IV, A.

Agriculture and Arboriculture.

Poppy.

each *kanal*, and mix with two *sérs* of earth, and sow broadcast. Before sowing beds are formed; and the seed is either covered by dragging thorns over the beds or by rubbing the surface of the ground with the hand. The ground is watered every 8th or 10th day till the plants are a foot or so high, after that every 15 days. At that time the field is weeded with the hand or the point of the *dátri*, and ashes are scattered over the plants. It is sometimes necessary to weed again after a month; and a third weeding may take place after the same interval. As soon as the heads form, the field has to be watched all day to preserve it from parrots. The heads are fit to be cut about the middle of March. Irrigation should then cease, as it is injurious. The poppy-heads are cut in the afternoon with a three-bladed instrument called *nistar*, not unlike a pen for ruling music lines. Two cuts of three incisions each are made from the bottom to the top of the head. These are repeated three times at intervals of four or five days. The crude opium is scraped off with a knife next morning. When required for use, the crude opium is dissolved in water; the impurities contained in it settle. The water is strained off and evaporated in an iron vessel. The opium is then removed from the pan. Poor crops are used for making *post*. The seeds afford an oil with which people anoint themselves, and Hindús on fast days make little cakes of them included in the *phlahár* or food lawful on such occasions. The poppy head is made up exactly of equal parts of seed and shell. The former sells at Rs. 10 and the latter at Rs. 40 per maund. Two kinds of poppy are grown, the white and red or *hazára*. The seed and flower of the former is white; the flower of the latter is red, and the seed black. The opium of the *hazára* is more intoxicating than that obtained from the white variety. Its seeds are slightly bitter; those of the white poppy are sweet, and are the more generally used. After the heads have been cut off, the poppy stalks are left to rot on the ground. Poppy does not appear to suffer from any disease except *tela;* but deer and hares eat the young plants, and parrots are very fond of the heads. Two or three *kanals* are the outside area sown by any one cultivator with poppy.

Zira, saunf, vegetables.

Zira is cultivated in only a few villages, such as in Manchárian, Dharmewála, and Daula Pukhta near Dipálpur, and *saunf* is still rarer. It is needless to describe the way in which they are grown. The same remark applies to the cultivation of vegetables, which are found only in very small patches, and belong more to the domain of the kitchen-garden than of agriculture.

Average yield.

Table No. XXI shows the estimated average yield in *sérs* per acre of each of the principal staples. Mr. Purser, who carried out the settlement of 1872-73, devoted much attention to this subject. After pointing out the difficulty of obtaining any trustworthy data he continues :—

Chapter IV, A.

Agriculture and Arboriculture.

Average yield.

"Concerning a few crops I have been able to form an opinion, partly from actual experiment and partly from enquiry; and I will state what I think the outturn on an acre of average soil, when the crop has been fairly cultivated, and has not suffered from, or benefited by, an unusual season. Irrigated wheat produces 16 maunds, or about 1,300 lbs. per acre. Barley, by all accounts, produces one-quarter more than wheat; so it ought to yield 20 maunds, but it does not get as good treatment, and may not produce so much. Rice gives 17 or 18 maunds, of cleaned grain. *Kangni* produces 14 maunds per acre; but the outturn varies very much. I would put the yield of *china* at 12 maunds. Cotton produces 6 maunds or, roughly speaking, 120 lbs. of cleaned fibre. Lieutenant Elphinstone puts the yield at 12 maunds or 240 lbs. of cleaned fibre. I believe that new land on the Rávi will produce that much, and 10 maunds on the Sutlej; but in a couple of years the outturn falls off by at least one-half. Poppy produces 6 *sérs* of opium, or 3 maunds of *post* and 3 maunds of seed. Tobacco produces 25 maunds of green plants, which will dry down to about 6 maunds. An acre of turnips sells for Rs. 24. Lieutenant Elphinstone says they sold at 1,600 to 3,200 lbs per rupee. Assuming the highest price now, the yield, would be nearly 17 tons, about one-half less than the English average including tops in both cases. But I doubt if 3 maunds are produced in the *maria*. As regards other crops I can give no opinion that would be of much value."

The subject of the average yield of the main agricultural staples was fully dealt with in the assessment reports prepared during the late settlement, and was also noticed in the Final Report. Reference may be made to these. The appended statement shows the average yields assumed for assessment purposes in the different tahsíls in standard *sérs* per acre.

Crop.	Class of cultivation.	Montgomery.	Gugera.	Dipálpur.	Pákpattan.
Rice ...	Cháhi and cháhi-nahri ...	...	560	480 to 560	440 to 560
	Nahri	...	560	520 to 640	520 to 640
Maize ...	Cháhi and cháhi-nahri ...	..	480	240 to 400	240 to 400
	Nahri	...	480	200 to 320	200 to 360
	Sailáb	...	...	160	160
Jowár	Cháhi and cháhi-nahri ...	280	280	220 to 280	220 to 320
	Nahri	.	200	160	160 to 200
	Sailáb	200	200	120 to 160	160
	Báráni	...	160	100	100
Kangni ...	Cháhi and cháhi-nahri ...	...	...	240	240
	Nahri	..	...	200	200
	Sailáb	...	...	120	120
	Báráni	...	...	100	100
China ..	Cháhi and cháhi-nahri ...	...	..	260 to 340	280 to 320
	Nahri	...	..	200	200
	Sailab	...	.	120	120
	Báráni	...	..	100	100
Moth ...	Nahri	...	..	160	160
	Sailáb	.	...	180	...
	Báráni	...	..	80	80
Múng ...	Nahri	...	...	100 to 120	120
	Sailáb	..	..	140	140
	Báráni	...	...	80	80

Chapter IV, A.

Agriculture and Arboriculture.

Average yield.

Crop.	Class of cultivation.	Montgomery.	Gugera.	Dipálpur.	Pákpattan.
Másh	Nahri	...	...	160	140
	Sailáb	...	..	160 to 180	140
	Báráni	...	...	80	80
Til	Nahri	...	..	80 to 120	100 to 120
	Sailáb	80	80	80	80
	Báráni	80	60	60	60
Cotton	Cháhi and cháhi-nahri	180	200	180 to 240	180 to 240
	Nahri	...	120	140 to 180	140 to 200
	Sailáb	100	120	80	80
Wheat	Cháhi and cháhi-nahri	360	400 to 480	320 to 400	320 to 420
	Nahri	...	320	240 to 300	240 to 300
	Sailáb	280	320	220 to 260	300
	Báráni	280	200	160 to 200	160 to 180
Barley	Cháhi and cháhi-nahri	400	400 to 480	400 to 480	400 to 520
	Nahri	...	320	260 to 320	260 to 320
	Sailáb	280	320	240 to 280	320
	Báráni	280	200	180 to 220	180 to 200
Gram	Nahri	...	480	280 to 300	260 to 340
	Sailáb	240	240	220 to 260	240
	Báráni	240	240	200 to 240	200 to 220

In the case of tahsíls Dipálpur and Pákpattan irrigated turnips were valued at Rs. 20, sugarcane at Rs. 160, tobacco at Rs. 25, and other miscellaneous crops at Rs. 16 per acre. In Montgomery and Gugera turnips were valued at Rs. 24 per acre, and all crops other than those dealt with above at Rs. 16 per acre in Montgomery and Rs. 20 in Gugera.

Production and consumption of food-grains.

The average consumption of food per head has already been noticed at page 69. The total consumption of food-grains by the population of the district as estimated in 1878 for the purposes of the Famine Report, is shown in maunds in the margin. The figures are based upon an estimated population of 359,437 souls. On the other hand, the average consumption per head is believed to have been over-estimated. A rough estimate of the total production, exports and imports of food-grains was also framed at the same time; and it was stated (page 152, Famine Report) that there was on an average an annual surplus of 1,295,000 maunds of *wheat alone* available for exportation to Multán and Lahore for transport to Sindh, Calcutta, and Bombay. Part of the

Grain.	Agriculturists.	Non-agriculturists.	Total.
Wheat ...	599,289	828,652	1,427,941
Inferior grains	363,854	213,082	576,936
Pulses ...	107,016	142,054	249,070
Total ...	1,070,159	1,183,788	2,253,947

Chapter IV, A.

Agriculture and Arboriculture.

Production and consumption of food-grains.

export was also said to go to Shahpur. As regards grains other than wheat, no estimate was framed. But in 1874 Mr. Purser thus discussed the surplus produce of the district, after the food and clothing of the people, the renewal of agricultural stock and machinery, and other necessary expenses had been provided for:—

"What is the surplus produce of the district, it is hard to say; but probably very little. There are, roughly speaking, 360,000 people in the district; and the cultivated area is nearly 365,000 acres. Deducting 40,000 acres on account of land devoted to green fodder, at the rate of ⅙th of an acre per yoke, there remain 325,000 acres. Of these nearly 32,000 are under cotton. There remain then 293,000 acres to feed 360,000 people. At ¾th of a *sér* per diem for each person some 2,466,000 *mans* annually would be required to feed the people, which consumption requires an average produce of nearly 8¼ *mans* per acre. Adding seed-grain, the amount comes to nearly 9¼ *mans* per acre. This is a large average outturn, especially when it is remembered that *til*, sugarcane, poppy, tobacco, &c., are included in the 293,000 acres. Thirty-two thousand acres of cotton, at 1½ *man* of cleaned cotton per acre, yield 48,000 *mans*, of which 18,000 *mans*, at 4 lbs. per head of population—(*vide Statistical Reporter*, page 80, December 1870)—for it is a cold district in winter—are required for local consumption. The remaining 30,000 *mans* are worth Rs. 4,36,000 at 2 *sérs* 12 *chittaks* the rupee: less than Rs. 1,36,000 cannot be allowed for salt. So the whole surplus is Rs. 3,00,000. This very rough calculation will, I think, show that the surplus production of the district cannot be very great. Profits from cattle are not included in this estimate."

The above calculation may be revised as follows with reference to the latest available statistics. The population of the district by the last census was approximately 500,000, and it is probably not less now. Taking ¾th *sér* per diem as the average consumption of food-grains for each person, we get a total annual consumption for the district of 3,375,000 *mans*. The average annual mature crop area of the district, including casual cultivation in Government waste, is very nearly 463,000 acres. The areas of *jowár* and wheat which are cut for fodder may be estimated at 55,000 acres annually. The average area under cotton is 38,000 acres. Deducting the fodder and cotton areas, there is left a balance of 370,000 acres of crop the yield of which must average 9 *mans* per acre to produce the annual grain consumption estimated above. Making an addition for seed the yield comes to nearly 10 *mans* per acre. This is high; the crop area, moreover, includes *til*, sugarcane, tobacco, *massar*, *charál*, &c. Taking only cereals and pulses and excluding *charál* and *massar*, the total average annual crop area is 348,000. Deducting 55,000 acres for fodder, the balance is 293,000 acres. For the latter area to produce the estimated annual consumption a yield of 11 5 maunds per acre is needed. The annual consumption is probably rather over-estimated, but even so the above calculation shows that the surplus grain production of the district as a whole is certainly not extensive. At 2 *sérs* of cleaned cotton per annum per head the total annual consumption of the district would be 25,000 *mans*. Taking 1¼ *man* per acre as the yield of cleaned cotton, the produce of 38,000 acres, the average annual cotton area would be 47,500 *mans*, which gives a large surplus for export. Cotton and oilseeds are in fact the main agricultural staples of export of the district.

Chapter IV, A.

Agriculture and Arboriculture.

Arboriculture and forests.

Table No. XVII shows the area of waste land which is under the management of the Forest Department. Of this, the Montgomery forests, with an area of 87·16 miles, are reserved; while the scattered *rakhs*, whose area amounts to 759·96 square miles, are unreserved. The following note on the forest lands of the district has been kindly supplied by Mr. Fazal-ud-dín, Extra Assistant Conservator of Forests, Montgomery Division, the District Forest Officer:—

"The forest lands under the Forest Department in the Montgomery district form one Division called the Montgomery Forest Division with head-quarters at Montgomery. This Division is subdivided into three forest ranges, called, respectively, Montgomery range, Chíchâwatni range and Gugera range.

There are twenty reserved forests, with an aggregate area of 87·16 square miles, which have been reserved under the Forest Act (Act VII of 1878).

The following note describes briefly the main facts regarding each reserve.

RANJIT SINGH.

Area 5,377 *acres.*—This reserve is situated about 15 miles north of the Railway Station of Chíchâwatni on the Lahore-Multán Section of the North-Western Railway, and three miles west of the town of Kamália. Formed out of *rakhs* No. 56 and 57, has been under the Forest Department since 1869; reserved under the Forest Act (VII of 1878) since September 1881. Formerly this area was one of Maharája Ranjít Singh's grass reserves, being in his time oftener flooded by the overflow of the Rávi, and thus being capable of producing large quantities of fodder. The ground is of almost one level, with the exception of depressions here and there. Occasionally the south portion becomes flooded if the river is very high. It is demarcated by 20 feet wide cleared lines and numbered wooden posts at corners. The tree growth consists chiefly of *jand* (*Prosopis spicigera*), *farásh* and *lei* (*Tamarix articulata* and *gallica*), *karír* (*Capparis aphulla*) and *wan* (*Salvadora oleoides*), with a limited quantity of saccharum grass here and there. No rights beyond a few rights of way. Closed to all animals except for some weeks after the rainy season, when cattle grazing is allowed on payment. The grazing is more often leased, preference being shown to the cattle-owners of the neighbourhood. But a portion, 1,300 acres, is kept closed to grazing throughout the year with the view of supplying grass for troops marching through the district. This forest was felled in 1883-84, 1888-89, to 1893-94, and the total outturn amounted to 2,671,104 cubic feet stacked, which were supplied as locomotive fuel to the North-Western Railway.

DARSANA.

Area 1,663 *acres.*—About 10 miles north of the Chíchâwatni Railway Station between the villages of Jhakkar and Bhusi on the east and west, respectively. Under control of the Forest Department since 1869, and declared a reserved forest in 1881. It was formed out of *rakh* No. 57. Demarcated by 50 feet cleared lines and numbered wooden posts like Ranjít Singh. Tree growth very similar to that in Ranjít Singh, except that the saccharum grass is much more abundant owing to the ground being flooded much oftener. No village rights except those noted in case of Ranjít Singh. Closed to grazing throughout the year except for some weeks after the rainy season when cattle are admitted on payment of dues either by permits or by contract. Was felled in 1887-88 to 1899-90, and the total outturn amounted to 861,785 cubic feet, stacked, which were supplied as locomotive fuel to the North-Western Railway.

KALERA.

Area 4,561 *acres.*—Formed out of *rakh* No. 58, and situated also across the Rávi about 6 miles from Chíchâwatni Station on the North-Western Railway. Bounded on the west by the mail cart road from Chichawatni Station to Jhang for 3¼ miles, and by the Rávi on the south for 2 miles, the other sides being demarcated with 50 feet cleared lines and wooden posts in the usual manner. Most of the area is liable to be inundated when the Rávi is in flood. Tree growth consists chiefly of *jand*, but a few *Tamarix* and *Salvadora* trees are also met with, but *karír* bushes are remarkably few. Saccharum growth is very dense, and affords facilities for spread of fires which have several times occurred here. No rights except those of way as in other reserves. The grazing arrangements are also similar to those of Ranjít Singh and Darsána. Part of this

Chapter IV, A.

Agriculture and Arboriculture.

Arboriculture and forests.

forest was felled in 1883-84, 1887-88, 1888-89, and 1897-98, the yield amounting to 820,335 cubic feet, which was supplied to the North-Western Railway. Saccharum grass is much sought after, realising about Rs. 300 annually on an average. It yields the well-known *munj* used in string making, grass for thatching and stalks (*tíl*) for *jaffari* work.

HARAPPA.

Area 1,945 *acres*.—Formed out of *rakh* No. 18. Situated cis-Rávi equi-distant from the Railway Station of Harappa and Chíchâwatni on North-Western Railway, each of which is about 8 miles distant, the former being on the south-east and the latter on the south-west. Under the Forest Department since 1869, and declared a reserved forest, under the Forest Act, in 1881. Demarcated by 20 feet wide cleared lines, and numbered wooden posts at corners. Lower parts sometimes become water-logged in consequence of the excessive flow from the adjoining *nála* which fills from the Rávi when in high flood. The higher parts of the forest have, however, poor soil. Tree growth chiefly *jand*, the *farásh* being in fair quantity, while other species are scarce. Free of rights except those of way only; closed to grazing of all animals for the greater part of the year, but thrown open to cattle grazing for some weeks in autumn like other reserves, the grazing being managed departmentally, or being leased out to cattle-owners for a fixed sum. A portion of this forest was felled in 1896-97 to supply wood fuel to the North Western-Railway when the outturn amounted to 207,205 cubic feet. The balance is now being felled (1898-99).

DAD FATIANA.

Area 1,072 *acres* —Situated 4 miles west of the formerly flourishing town of Harappa, and 1½ miles north of the Harappa Reserve. Formed out of *rakh* No. 27, nearly the whole of which it includes. Demarcated by 50 and 20 feet wide cleared lines except in north-east, where it is bounded by the Harrappa-Kamália road. The boundary lines are now being widened, as in parts the growth of saccharum is very abundant, and there is fear of the occurrence of fires; very similar to Harrappa as regards tree growth, grazing rights, &c.; was felled in 1893-94 and 1894-95 to supply fuel to North-Western Railway, the yield amounting to 526,202 cubic feet, stacked.

MIRDAD.

Area 3,405 *acres*.—Formed out of *rakh* No. 15, almost the whole of which it includes; under the Forest Department since 1869 and reserved in 1881. Consists of a long narrow strip irregular in shape, being 5½ miles by ½ to 1 mile. Situated near the main road from Lahore to Multan between the encamping grounds of Muhammadpur on the east and Harappa on the west, 3½ miles from Harappa and 6 miles from the Railway Station of Montgomery. Demarcated by 20 feet cleared lines and numbered wooden posts. Intersected by the old bed of the Rávi. In these depressions the growth consists principally of *jand* and *farásh*, and is very fair, while the higher parts are sparsely covered with *Salvadora* and *Capparis*. A small quantity of saccharum is also found in depressions. There is one small plot of private land within the forest limits. The usual rights of way only. A portion of the old road from Lahore to Multán which is now abandoned passes through the area, and is kept cleared as a compartment line. The grazing arrangements are the same as in Ranjít Singh and other reserves mentioned above. Felled in 1880-81, 1883-84, 1885-86, 1887-88 to 1889-90 to supply fuel to the North-Western Railway, when the total yield amounted to 1,555,464 cubic feet.

MUHAMMADPUR.

Area 1,748 *acres*.—Situated about 6 miles north-west of the Civil and Railway Station of Montgomery. Adjoins the new Lahore-Multán road, and is 2 miles distant from the Muhammadpur encamping ground. Western part of the forest is intersected by the old bed of the Rávi, locally called Sukhráwa. Under the Forest Department since 1869, and reserved in September 1881, together with other reserves. The forest growth is very open throughout even in dry *nálas; Tamarix* and *Prosopis* are the chief species. There is some saccharum grass met with in places which is in demand for *munj*, realising every year about Rs. 4. Cultural operations were carried out on the eastern portion many years ago, when the Rávi used to be flooded almost annually, but the work was abandoned, as the results obtained did not justify the expenditure. No rights except those of way. Grazing arrangements the same as in Ranjít Singh. Was felled in 1880-81, 1882-83, 1883-84, 1887-88 to 1889-90 to supply fuel to the North-Western Railway, the total yield being 461,338 cubic feet, stacked.

Chapter IV, A.

Agriculture and Arboriculture.

Arboriculture and forests.

MONTGOMERY.

Area 4,290 *acres.*—Three miles from the Civil and Railway Station of Montgomery. Formed out of *rakhs* Nos. 9 and 12. Under the control of the Department since 1869; declared a reserved forest in 1881. Demarcated by 20 feet wide cleared lines and numbered wooden posts. In the northern portion the tree growth is fairly dense in depressions and the Sukhráwa Nála, *Prosopis* predominating, while on higher ground the growing stock consists chiefly of *Tamarix*, *karil* and *Salvadora*. No rights except those of way. Kept as a grass preserve for the Civil Station of Montgomery. Was felled in 1882-83 to 1889-90, 1891-92 and 1892-93, when the outturn amounted to 1,403,371 cubic feet stacked, which was supplied as fuel to the North-Western Railway.

ALIWAL.

Area 1,228 *acres.*—Situated about 1½ miles to north of the Railway Station of Yusafwála and 6½ miles to east of the Civil Station of Montgomery. Formed out of *rakhs* Nos. 3 and 7. Under the Forest Department since 1869; and declared a reserved forest in September 1881. Occupies a plot of low ground on the *bár*, and consequently receives water from the surrounding country in the rainy season. Demarcated by 20 feet wide cleared lines and numbered wooden posts and 1 foot trenching in bare places. Species chiefly *Prosopis*, with a fair amount of *Tamarix* and *Capparis*, but *Salvadora* scarce. Small zizyphus bushes thick in low ground. A few rights of way only. Closed to all animals throughout the year except for a few weeks in autumn when cattle grazing is allowed on payment. Is now (1898-99) being felled to supply fuel to North-Western Railway.

NURSHAH.

Area 3,445 *acres.*—Formed out of *rakhs* Nos. 3 and 6 and situated near the town of Kaureshah and Nurshah; about 10 miles north-east of the Civil Station of Montgomery; 6 miles in a direct line from the North-Western Railway, and a short distance to south of the Lahore-Multán road. Under the Forest Department since 1869, and reserved under the Forest Act in September 1881. Demarcated by 20 feet wide cleared lines and numbered wooden posts. Intersected by the Sukhráwa *nala*. Tree growth consists of the usual species mentioned above, the growth being fair in depressions, but poor on higher ground. Closed to grazing, but grass cutting allowed on payment of fees. Was felled in 1885-86 to 1889-90 to supply fuel to North-Western Railway when the yield amounted to 823,055 cubic feet, stacked.

BURJ-JIWE KHAN.

Area 4,554 *acres.*—Formed out of *rakhs* Nos. 2 and 3 situated to south of Lahore-Multán road about equi-distant from the encamping grounds of Akbar and Kaureshah, and about 7 miles from the Gambar Station on the Lahore-Multán section of North-Western Railway. Under the control of the Forest Department since 1869, and declared a reserved forest in September 1881. Bounded by 20 feet wide cleared lines and numbered wooden posts. Only a few rights of way. Is much intersected by the Sukhráwa Nála. Growth consists of the usual species mentioned above, and is fairly good in the depressions formed by the bed of the Sukhrawa, but poor elsewhere. Closed to all animals, but cattle grazing allowed for some weeks in autumn on payment of fees. Was felled in 1885-86 to 1889-90 when the yield amounted to 1,723,675 cubic feet, stacked, which were supplied as fuel to the North-Western Railway.

GASHKAURI.

Area 4,024 *acres.*—Formed out of *rakh* No. 15 situated on the Lahore-Multán road, about 4 miles south-east of the encamping ground of Akbar, and about 8 miles north-west of the Okára Railway Station (N.-W. R.). Under the Forest Department since 1869, and reserved under the Forest Act in September 1881. Demarcated by 20 feet wide cleared lines and numbered wooden posts. Much intersected by the Sukhráwa Nála. Tree growth consists of the usual species already mentioned, but *Prosopis* and *Tamarix* prevail, growth fair in depressions, but poor on high ground; a small quantity of saccharum here and there. A few rights of way only. Only cattle grazing allowed for some time in autumn on payment of fees. Was felled in 1891-92 and 1892-93, when the outturn amounted to 256,438 cubic feet, and was supplied as fuel to North-Western Railway.

Chapter IV, A.

Agriculture and Arboriculture.

Arboriculture and forests.

OKARA.

Area 4,097 acres.—Formed out of *rakhs* Nos. 14 and 15. Under the Forest Department since 1869, and declared a reserved forest in September 1881. Three to six miles north of the Okara Railway Station (N.-W. R.) Bounded on the east by the Dipálpur-Gugera road, on other sides by 20 feet cleared lines and numbered wooden posts. Contains a large area of low-lying ground where water collects from the surrounding country after the rains. Tree growth consists of the usual species already mentioned in case of other reserves, but *Prosopis* and *Tamarix* prevail. Only a few rights of way; closed to all animals except for some weeks in autumn when cattle grazing is allowed on payment of fees. Was felled in 1881-82, 1885-86 to 1891-92 and the outturn (1,972,256 cubic feet, stacked) was supplied to the North-Western Railway.

One plot of private land of 103 acres situated inside the reserve.

BAGIANA.

Area 1,470 acres.—Formed out of *rakh* No. 13. Under the control of the Forest Department since 1869 and reserved in 1881. Six miles north of the Okara Station (N.-W. R.). Bounded by 20 feet wide cleared lines and numbered wooden posts. Tree growth consists chiefly of *Prosopis*, thick on low-lying grounds, but sparse elsewhere. Felled in 1880-81 and 1881-82 yielding 666,360 cubic feet, stacked, or 453 cubic feet, stacked, per acre. The whole of the outturn was supplied to the Railway. No rights except of those of way. Closed to grazing except for a part of the year in autumn when cattle are admitted on payment of fees.

BIBIPUR.

Area 864 acres.—Formed out of *rakh* No. 13. Under the Forest Department since 1869, and declared a reserved forest in 1881. Seven miles north-east of the Okara Railway Station and 2 miles south-west of the ancient town of Satghara. Bounded by 20 feet cleared lines and numbered wooden posts at corners. Growing stock—a remarkably good growth of pure *Prosopis* in lower parts; *Tamarix* (*farásh*) pevails on higher grounds, but is dying out. No rights except those of way. Was felled in 1880-81, 1881-82 and 1883-84 when the yield amounted to 386,844 cubic feet, stacked, or 448 cubic feet, stacked, per acre. The whole of the outturn was supplied to the Railway. Closed to all animals, except for a part of the year in autumn when cattle grazing and grass cutting is allowed on payment of fees.

SATGHARA.

Area 2,077 acres.—Formed out of *rakh* No. 3. Under the control of the forest. Department since 1869, and reserved under Act VII of 1878 in 1881. Seven miles from the Satghara Railway Station (N.-W. R.) and 1½ miles north-west of the town of Satghara east of the Dipálpur-Gugera road. Tree growth consists of *Prosopis*, *Tamarix* (farásh) and *karil* with a few bushes of zizyphus (*malla*). Of these species the *Prosopis* prevails. Growth much better on low-lying ground where rain water collects than in other parts. Only a few rights of way. A good grass-producing forest. Closed to all animals throughout the year, but cattle grazing or grass cutting is permitted for some time in autumn on payment of fees. Was felled in 1880-81, 1886-87 to 1889-90 when the outturn amounted to 522,501 cubic feet, stacked, which was supplied as fuel to the North-Western Railway.

CHAUKIAN.

Area 1,566 acres—Formed out of *rakh* No. 3. Under the Forest Department since 1869, and reserved in 1881. Four miles north-east of the town of Satghara and 1½ miles east of the Satghara reserve. The nearest Railway Station in the Satghara Station (N.-W R.) 8 miles distant. Demarcated by 20 feet cleared lines and numbered wooden posts. Tree growth similar to that in the above reserve, but there are four large blanks. Open to cattle grazing only for a part of the year in autumn. Was felled in 1887-88 and 1888-89 to supply fuel to the Railway. The outturn amounted to 432,584 cubic feet, stacked.

KOHLA.

Area 1,190 acres.—Formed out of *rakh* No. 3. Under the control of the Forest Department since 1869 and reserved in 1881. Touches the Lahore-Multán road on the south. Ten miles from the Satghara Railway Station.

Chapter IV, A.

Agriculture and Arboriculture.

Arboriculture and forests.

Demarcated by 20 feet wide cleared lines and numbered wooden posts; except where the boundary follows the Lahore-Multán road. The present growing stock consists of *Prosopis*, *Tamarix* (*farásh*) and *Capparis*; the area fairly well stocked except those parts where the soil is impregnated with *kallar*, and which are consequently only sparsely covered with stunted bushes of *Tamarix*. Only a few rights of way. Open to cattle grazing only for part of the year in autumn on payment of fees. Was felled in 1880-81, 1888-89 and 1889-90 to supply fuel to the Railway, and yielded 335,996 cubic feet, stacked.

KAMMAN.

Area 2,264 *acres*.—Formed out of *rakh* No. 3. Under the control of the Forest Department since, 1869 and declared a reserved forest in 1881. Six miles north-west of the Wán Radha Rám Railway Station on the road from Wán Radha Rám to Chúchak, and 4 miles from the Chúchak encamping ground on the Lahore-Multán road. Demarcated by 20 feet wide cleared lines and numbered wooden posts. In low-lying places the tree growth consists of almost pure *Prosopis*, and is fairly good. But the higher parts are very sparsely dotted with a few stunted *Tamarix Capparis* and *Salvadora*. No rights except those of way, a good grazing ground; open to cattle grazing only for part of the year in autumn on payment of fees. Was felled in 1882-83 to supply fuel to the North-Western Railway, the total yield amounting to 114,750 cubic feet, stacked.

SYEDWALA.

Area 4,958 *acres*.—Formed out of *rakh* No. 25. Under the Forest Department since 1869, and reserved in September 1881. Situated trans-Rávi 8 miles north-east of the town of Syewdála and 24 miles from the Railway line, the nearest Station being Wán Radha Rám. Demarcated by 20 feet cleared lines and numbered wooden posts, except on the north, where it borders on the Deg Nála. The north portion of the forest is liable to be flooded by the overflow of the Deg Nála. Forest growth consists of *Prosopis* and *Tamarix* mixed with some *Salvadora* and *Capparis*. The *Prosopis* prevails all over the area except the higher parts in the southern portion of the forest. Growth very good, in parts flooded by the Deg Nála. A few rights of way only. A very good grass-producing area; *panin* and *dabh* grasses, however, predominate on the low-lying areas. Open to cattle grazing for part of the year in autumn on payment of fees. A portion of the forest (1,262 acres) was felled in 1891-92 to 1894-95 to supply fuel to the Railway, and yield amounted to 218,434 cubic feet stacked.

In addition to the reserved forests mentioned above, aggregating 87·16 square miles, the Forest Department has the control of 759·96 square miles of waste land comprised in 51 *rakhs* now called unclassed forests. Out of these, 48 unclassed forests, comprising 550·99 square miles, are situated between the Railway line and the Rávi, while three forests with an aggregate area of 208·97 square miles are trans-Rávi.

Since the year 1889-90 the Forest Department has entered into an agreement with the North-Western Railway to supply annually to that Railway 20 lakhs cubic feet, stacked, of firewood at Rs 5-10-8 per cent. of cubic feet; and in order to obtain a sustained yield of firewood every year 164·21 square miles have been selected from the unclassed forests (122·63 square miles from the forest under the Forest Department and 41·58 square miles from those under the control of the Deputy Commissioner). These areas together with the reserves are now being worked systematically, the unclassed areas being closed to browsers (camels and goats) for a period of five years after the cutting. The areas selected from the unclassed forests are being demarcated with interrupted trenches, and will soon be surveyed and mapped. A working plan is in course of preparation for these areas as well as the reserves. They will be worked on a rotation of 20—25 years.

In addition to supplying fuel to the railway the requirements of the local population for the different kinds of forest produce are met from the forests on payment of fees The grazing of all the waste lands in the district is managed by the Deputy Commissioner, who credits a portion of the revenue to the forest Department on account of the areas under its control.

The following statement shows the quantity of wood supplied to the railway from the forests and total revenue and expenditure for the last ten years :—

Year.	Fuel supplied to N.-W. Railway.	Revenue.		Expenditure.
		From fuel, &c.	From grazing.	
	Cubic feet.	Rs.	Rs.	Rs.
1888-89	2,863,684	87,051	31,705	11,987
1889-90	1,770,868	77,489	32,497	59,654
1890-91	3,054,941	1,79,138	31,873	58,443
1891-92	2,284,043	1,39,306	34,253	71,681
1892-93	2,092,344	1,34,988	33,241	64,408
1893-94	2,606,526	1,49,219	28,217	58,525
1894-95	1,921,467	1,21,759	35,590	56,750
1895-96	2,471,675	1,89,253	38,695	1,34,425
1896-97	1,857,059	1,10,888	37,473	89,057
1897-98	1,689,658	1,26,388	32,779	89,415

SECTION B.—DOMESTIC ANIMALS.

Number of live-stock.

The live-stock of the district, as returned at various times in the Administration Report, are shown in Table No. XXII. The figures are probably very unreliable as anything like a really accurate enumeration of cattle in this district is impossible. There has probably been no very marked increase of late years, in the Rávi tahsíls at least; and the colonization of the Sandal Bár will probably cause a decrease before long.

Government breeding operations.

A cattle fair has lately been started at Gugera. It is held in April. There are three donkey and five horse stallions in the district; one of the latter is under the care of the Military Officer at the Probynabad stud farm, and the rest are in charge of the Tahsíldárs; they are distributed thus:—Gugera one donkey stallion (Imperial) and one horse stallion (District Board); Dipálpur one donkey and one horse stallion (both Imperial); Pákpattan two horse stallions (one Imperial and one District Board), one donkey stallion (Imperial). The donkeys are all of Italian breed; of the horses the one at Dípálpur is English bred; the one at Gugera and the District Board one at Pákpattan are Arabs and the Imperial one at the latter place is a Norfolk trotter. The number of branded mares in the district is as follows:—

Tahsíl Montgomery	44
" Gugera	41
" Dipálpur	155
" Pákpattan	109
" Probynabod stud farm	58
Total ...	407

Chapter IV, B.

Domestic Animals.

Government breeding operations.

No fees are charged for covering mares; only branded mares are covered by Imperial horse stallions. Mares not branded are covered by donkey stallions and by District Board horse stallions. A *zilladár*, on Rs. 25 a month, keeps up statistics and furnishes reports, &c., to the Assistant Superintendent, Horse-Breeding Operations, who visits the district during his annual tour, brands mares, and makes all suggestions necessary for furthering horse-breeding operations. The *zamíndárs* of the Sutlej tahsíls are beginning to appreciate the system of horse-breeding operations, and the taste for horse-breeding is increasing; mares are brought up to be branded, and young stock are gelt more extensively than used to be the case. Government Hissár bulls are not appreciated in this district. There is at present one in the Pákpattan tahsíl.

Horses.

The horses of this district never enjoyed any great celebrity, but the horses bred along the Lahore border, in the Nakka country, were held in good repute in olden times. A good mare, it is said, would fetch Rs. 800, and a horse from Rs. 200 to Rs. 500. These horses were country-bred, large, strong, and long-winded, and were much fancied by the Sikhs. There were some uncommonly fine mares or stallions, the produce of which was chiefly found among certain tribes or with certain individuals; such were Anmol and Kajal in the Manes tribe; Morni, among the Karrals and Wattús; Phabban, with the Kharrals; and Nili, with the Bahrwál *sardárs*. A well-grown mare can be got now for from Rs. 100 to Rs. 200, while the ordinary run of horses cost from Rs. 50 to Rs. 100. Horses are not uncommonly held in shares. One man owns, say, $\frac{1}{3}$, another $\frac{1}{4}$, and another $\frac{5}{12}$. The shares are often calculated by hoofs; one man owning half a hoof, &c. Bába Bishen Singh is said to have encouraged horse-breeding. His stallions served the *zamíndárs'* mares, and in return he used to buy the produce, if a colt, when a year or two old, at much under its value. If a mare, nothing was taken; the *zamíndár* retained her. Ponies cost from Rs. 12 to Rs. 50.

The stud farm of the 11th Bengal Lancers is at Probynabád in the Dipálpur tahsíl, some 10 miles south-west of Dipálpur itself. There are three grazing *rakhs*, attached to the stud, *viz.*, *rakh* Dhaular, area 3,301 acres near Probynábád; *rakh* Chapráli, area 1,006 acres near Okara in the Gugera tahsíl and *rakh* Jaura, area 1,000 acres, in Montgomery. In addition to these the regiment holds four estates on lease from Government, *viz.*, the Model Farm surrounding Probynábad in Dipálpur, Princeábad, Boyleganj and Chak No. 47 of the Sohág-Pára colony in Pákpattan, with a total area of 7,132 acres, of which 5,724 acres is cultivated by the aid of canal-irrigation and of 59 wells. The stud has been in existence since 1866, and the farm lands have been acquired from time to time. The regiment has sunk a large amount of capital both on stud and on purely agricultural works. The average annual number of remounts produced for the regiment is about 35. The expenses of the stud are

Chapter IV, B.

Domestic Animals.

Asses.

defrayed mainly from the agricultural profits of the farm lands which are held on very favorable terms from Government. Asses are generally kept by Kumhárs, Machhís, and Chúhras. An average male ass will cost from Rs. 8 to Rs. 12, and a good one from Rs. 15 to Rs. 16. The female will cost about Rs. 5 more; asses are put to work when between three and four years old, and work eight years. The average weight they carry is from 1½ to 2 maunds. If they belong to professional carriers, they get about 2 *sérs* each of chopped straw (*túri*) in the evening; if not, they are left to shift for themselves. The milk is not used. There are some fine white asses in the Pákpattan tahsíl, said to be descended from asses that came from Dera Gházi Khan.

Camels.

There are three kinds of camel—the *soháwa, ganda* and *hazára*. These terms seem to apply to the colour of the animal. The *soháwa* camel has long lips, medium-sized head, thick skin, and is of a brown colour. The *ganda* camel is grey, and has a large head, small mouth, and thin skin. The *hazára* camel has a small tail and is of a red colour. This is the worst of the three kinds, as it has no endurance on a journey. The *ganda* is the best. The female gives much more milk than that of the *soháwa;* the colour is good, and the strength and endurance of the *ganda* is superior. The camels of this district are of no use for riding. A good *ganda* camel costs about Rs. 100 to Rs. 120; a *soháwa* Rs. 10 less and a *hazára* Rs. 20 less. The prices of good camels are sometimes as high as Rs. 200. Outsiders generally buy male camels.

A female camel fetches on an average Rs. 20 less than the male. The camel-owners, however, depend on their profits from letting out camels as baggage animals, not on their profits from the sale of them. Considerable herds go down annually to Bhawáni and Bikanír for employment. If well treated, a camel lives 40 years. If its owner is poor, he will commence loading it at 3 years of age; if fairly off, at 4. The coupling season is Poh, Magar, Phagan, and Chetr (December to March). The period of gestation is 12 months. At 4 the female camel brings forth her first young one. She continues bearing nine or ten times, at intervals of two years. After one year the young one is weaned. Up to that period the milk is good; afterwards it is inferior. A camel will feed her young and yield 12 *sérs* of milk a day besides. The owner milks her twice a day; he milks two teats and leaves two for the young one. The milk yields curds and butter-milk, but not butter. It acts as a laxative to those not accustomed to its use. It is uncommonly good, and magnificent for disease of the spleen (*lipph*). A camel commences with carrying 3 maunds, and when full grown, carries 8. The camel is shorn in Chetr; and its hair, mixed with goats' hair, is made into ropes and *borás* (*borá*=a sack). The shearing yields about ¾ of a *sér* of hair. When the camel is at death's door, it is duly slaughtered, and there is a feast on its flesh. The Chúhra appropriates the skin, and sells it for about 8 annas to the *dabgar* or maker of large leather vessels

Age at which weaned, commences work, breeds, &c.

Milk.

Burden carried.

Hair.

Flesh.

Chapter IV, B.

Domestic Animals.

called *kuppás*, in which oil and *ghi* are carried. After the hair has been stripped off, the raw hide is placed round a hollow earthen mould. When the hide dries and hardens, the mould is broken and shaken out of the mouth of the *kuppa*, which is then complete. In a disease to which melons are subject, called *hadda*, camel's bones burned to windward of the field attacked are a fine remedy. Camels are turned out into the jungle and allowed to do for themselves. They eat almost anything; but *ák*, *dhák* and *harmal* they avoid. They are sometimes given alum and spices. A camel is called *toda* till one year old. Then *mazat* till two years old, or for one year after weaning. He is afterwards called *trihán*, *chhatar*, *doyak*, *chaugga*, *chhigga*, *nesh* and *armash*, at the commencement of his 3rd, 4th, 5th, 6th, 7th, 8th, and 9th year, respectively. After that he is full grown, and is called *únth*. The first year is divided into three parts: the first four months, when the camel is called *lihára* or *lihára toda*; the next two, when the name is changed to *mohala*; and the last six, when it becomes *kutela*. When the camel becomes a *chhatar*, his milk teeth go; and at each succeeding stage the camel gets two teeth; till when he becomes *armash*, he has his proper compliment of six incisors and four canine teeth. A female camel is called *todí* till two years old; then, till four years old, *puráp*. As soon as she has brought forth her first young one, she becomes a *dáchi*, and is afterwards called *dáchi pahlan*, *dáchi dúyán*, and so on, according to the number of young she has produced.

Food of camels.

Names of camels at different stages of growth.

Diseases of camels.

Camels are subject to many diseases and ailments. The remedies are often remarkable. However, a general remedy in all cases is to hang up a charm, or, still better, a *korán*, and drive the sick animal beneath it. The giving of alms and prayers of pious people are also very efficacious. The following are the more common diseases, with their symptoms and remedies, causes and results:—

Sat.—This is the most deadly of diseases. The only visible symptoms are trembling, sweating, and the mouth being kept open. The disease occurs at all seasons; there is no remedy; in a couple of hours after the symptoms appear the animal is dead. It is as it were struck dead; hence the name *sat*, meaning blow; it seems to be splenic apoplexy.

Zahmat.—Cause not known; occurs in hot weather; the animal coughs, ceases to eat and drink; there is a running from mouth and nose. Remedies: boil 1 *sér* of old molasses (*gur*), ¼ *sér* poppy-head (*post*), and ¼ *sér ajuáin* water; give for three or four days consecutively in the evening; or give ¼ *sér* of heated salt dissolved in water in the evening. Young animals generally escape, but the old die; it seems like rinderpest.

Hilbi occurs at any season, and is said to be due to eating unwholesome food. Throat and neck swell. The animal generally recovers in a week; the swelling is branded, or ½ *sér* of

Diseases of camels.

ghi is poured down each nostril through a tube or the spout of a *lota*, twice or thrice; or from 1 to 2 *sérs* of wheaten bread soaked in *ghi* are given every evening for a week.

Phet occurs in the rains also at commencement of the hot weather when the camels are laden with heating goods. Due in rains to noxious exhalations and attacks of mosquitoes. This is a lingering disorder, and the animal generally dies. It eats little, stays out in the sun, and becomes a mere bag of bones. Skin shrivels up. The remedies are: one *sér* of *gur* and *háliya* (*Lipidium sativum*) mixed, given every evening, or a *sér* of butter every evening; or a fermented drink made of *til* plants when the ear is forming, and *gur* or a *lota* full of butter-milk churned up with alum or *háliya*, continued till recovery. A couple of *sérs* of dry wheat should be given every day for ten or twelve days.

Sokra seems only a further stage of *pheta*; all animals attacked by *pheta* do not get it. The remedies are a decoction of roots of the *kokanber*, or a fermented drink made of equal parts of white cummins, coriander seeds and candy. About 75 per cent. of the cases terminate fatally.

Khárish, or mange, occurs in August and September, and December and January; is attributed to drinking stagnant water and getting no *lána* to eat. It lasts from two to four months, and is easily curable. The body is rubbed with sweet oil and sulphur mixed; a couple of *sérs* of onions are given every day for a fortnight, or a couple of *sérs* of mixed *gur* and bitter oil are administered daily for the same period. The whole body becomes a mass of sore; the hair comes off, the skin cracks. and blood exudes.

Símak is a swelling in the knee, hock, shoulder or ankle. It occurs in every season, and is attributed to unwholesome food. The animal raises the limb affected, and cannot walk and ceases to eat. Bleeding and branding are the remedies. A cure is generally effected.

Barr.—This is a dangerous disease; about half the animals attacked die. It generally occurs in the latter half of the year after August, and is said to be caused by taking off the saddle before the animal has got cool; the symptoms are like some noticed in rinderpest; all four legs get rigid; the animal falls down, shivers, raises its head, and ceases to eat and drink. As treatment, a line is branded all round the body; or ½ *sér gúgal (Bdellium)*, 1 *tola* of opium, ½ *sér* cloves, 1 *sér* candy, 2 *sérs* of sweet oil, and a dozen or so of fowl's eggs are mixed up and given at once. The animal is wrapped up and kept out of cold and windy places.

Gathar is a swelling containing matter on the inside on the hind legs. It lasts a month or so. Cause is not known. Rarely fatal. May occur at any time. Besides branding, the remedy is to give a hot drink of boiled camel's milk and turmeric every evening for a week.

Chapter IV, B.

Domestic Animals.

Diseases of camels.

Bel is another dangerous disease. Few escape. It may occur at any time, and is said to be caused by the animal not getting the condiments it requires. A swelling of the rectum and of the whole body up to the hump is the most conspicuous symptom. The remedies adopted are branding in the form of a double cross over the backbone and a drench of 4 *sérs* camel's milk boiled with 1 *sér háliya* and 1 *sér* old *gur*.

Akra occurs in November and December. Front legs get stiff, and are moved with difficulty; attributed to eating dry *táhli* leaves, which is hardly correct, as there are no *táhli* leaves anywhere in the jungle. The animal generally gets well in Baisákh (April); *gur* is given daily, or a drink made of the ashes of the burnt skull of a horse mixed with stale water; this seems a sort of rheumatism. *Akra* means simply stiff.

Chandri or *Chháliyán*.—This is an eruption of boils rarely fatal. Occurs at any time. Cause is unknown. Black pepper and *ghi*, mixed, are given; or *masar (ervum lens)* boiled with salt and red pepper. The boils are opened with a needle or sliced off with a knife. In very bad cases branding is resorted to.

Rasaula.—This is a large swelling like a goitre on the neck. On being opened it is found to contain blood; some say hair. At the beginning of the hot weather a boil forms under the back part of the pack-saddle; this heals about the end of the hot season after bursting. Owing to it camel-men do not care to be employed during the very hot months.

Súl, Rik.—Young camels for a couple of months after birth are liable to two diseases. One is *súl*, or colic. Few animals are attacked, if taken care of; but if attacked, they generally die. There is no remedy. The other is *rik*, which seems to be excessive purging. This is rarely fatal. A mixture of *khángar** boiled with 2 *tolás* of rice and 1 *tola* of *bhang* (dried leaves of *Cannabis sativa*) is given every evening.

Of these diseases, *khárish* is said to be contagious, *sat* and *zahmat* infectious, and the others neither. It must be remembered that some of the above names may represent the same disease in different stages.

Cows.

The cows of the Rávi are considered much superior to those of the Sutlej, as they yield considerably more milk. A cow calves during the tenth month of pregnancy, generally in January and February, or May and June. She commences calving when four years old, and, as a rule, produces four calves at intervals of from 18 months to 2 years. In places where the grass is uncommonly good, she will have as many as five calves.

Food.

As soon as she has calved, a mixture of one *sér* of *gur* and two *chittáks* of soap is stuffed down her throat to aid in the expulsion of the placenta *(jer)*. For two or three days afterwards she gets every evening two *sérs* of wheat soaked in water till it swells

* *Khángar* is the milk of an animal shortly before she runs dry.

Chapter IV, B.

Domestic Animals.

Milk.

(*ghunggani*), with two or three *chittáks* of *gur*. When not in milk, a cow is left to shift for herself pretty much, going out with the cattle of the village to graze. However, when in milk, if her owner is fairly off, and she has not many rivals, she will get some boiled cotton-seed (*varenva*), about 1¼ *sér* per diem in Poh, and in Jeth and Hár as much ground gram or barley soaked in water; and will, in other respects, be treated as owner's bullocks, sharing with them and the buffaloes the oil-cake (*khal*) he may possess. As a rule, a cow is well off if she gets some chopped straw in addition to what she can pick up in the fields. The calf is weaned when one year old. For six months after calving the supply of milk is good; it then falls off, and deteriorates. Cows are milked twice a day, morning and evening. The quantity of milk at each milking depends on the season being in proportion to the length of the day or night. On an average a cow gives four *sérs* of milk per diem or between three and four quarts. This is very little; but the animals are not fed well. This is a point on which the people are very chary of corect information; milk is not usually sold, as there is no demand. In odd places there may be some demand, and then the price will be about 16 *sérs* the rupee. The people drink as much milk as they want, and turn the rest into butter or *ghi*. The morning's milk is placed in the *dúdh kárhni*, and simmers all day long. In the evening it is poured into another vessel and mixed with the evening's milk, and an acid substance, called *jág*, or in default of that, some wheaten bread is put into it to cause coagulation. In the morning it is churned. The butter is usually sold to persons who make it into *ghi*; the butter-milk (*lassi*) is used at home; 24 *sérs* of milk will yield 14 *chittáks* of butter, which will give 9 to 10 *chittáks* of *ghi*. This is good considering the bad food of the cows. In buying cows, the points looked to are the fineness of the hair, the thin skin, heavy hind-quarters and slight fore-quarters. The size is looked to as a test of what the calves will be. If in milk, the cow is milked; she should not be savage, given to kicking or butting; nor should she allow only one person to milk her. In the former case she is called *khátar*, in the latter *hathal* Another trick cows have is only letting themselves be milked just after the calf has been sucking, and then only for a short time, so that the calf has to be brought back again. Such a cow is called, *pherwán dojh-wáli* (*pherwán*, again; *dojh*, milking). The udder should be broad and stiff, the teats long and soft.

Points of a cow.

Points looked to in buying bullocks.

In buying bullocks the points looked to are the fitness of the animal for work. This is tested by putting it to plough work at a well, &c. If it does well, its appearance is scrutinized. The eyes should be large and the ears small; the chest should be broad; the neck in front of the hump massive, so as to give a good support to the plough; the legs should be strong, hoofs broad, pasterns short. The hair and skin should be soft and fine; the tail long and thin. The colour is also looked to. White and grey are good colours; reddish brown is fair;

Chapter IV, B.

Domestic Animals.

Cost of bullocks.

Working age.

Emasculation.

Food.

red bad, and black worst of all. A bullock should have good horns, as a man should have a good moustache, according to the saying, *mard muchhel, bail singel;* but connoisseurs are not agreed as to what a good horn is. Bullocks cost from Rs. 20 to Rs. 100. A very fair average bullock can be got for Rs. 50. His work is generally light if continuous. A bullock is put to work when four, and will work eight years if taken care of In castrating bullocks, the knife is not used, as it is considered dangerous, people not being acquainted with the method to be adopted. The operation is effected by repeated blows of a small stick. It is generally carried out when the young bull is 2½ years old, in Phagan or Chetr. If before this age, the animal grows up a weed. Bullocks are fed four times a day, in the morning and evening, at noon and before the owner goes to bed. They very seldom get any grain, if ever; but they may come in for some raw cotton-seed (*varenvan*) in Poh. Twice a month, except in Hár and Jeth, some salt is rubbed into their mouths; and the same is done in respect of cows and buffaloes. A bullock will eat from 12 to 15 *sérs* of broken straw per diem, or about double that quantity of green fodder. Its food consists chiefly of broken straw of sorts, turnips, *charri, jowár* (grown as fodder), green wheat, and dry *jowár* stalks. Its food during the year, commencing with Chetr or the middle of March, may be taken to be as follows :—

Chetr.—Green wheat, *methra,* carrots (rare).

Baisákh.—Wheat straw; dry *túri;* grazes in stubble-fields.

Jeth.—*Túri* mixed with *chari,* sown early in Baisákh. *China* straw.

Hár.—*Túri.* If there has been rain, the bullocks are turned out to graze where there is grazing waste available in convenient proximity to the wells.

Sáwan-Bhádon.—Graze, as before. If there has been no rain, *túri* or *chari* or *china,* sown in Jeth and kept over, is given.

Asu.—*Kangni* straw or *chari* sown in Sáwan.

Kátik.—*Chari* sown in Sáwan, or straw of *china* sown in Bhádon. Bullocks also graze in stubble-fields.

Maghar.—*Chari* or *china* straw. Also rice straw, if available.

Poh.—*Túri* mixed with green wheat. Tops of turnips.

Mágh.—*Túri* and turnips (roots).

Phagan.—Green wheat, turnips, and *methra* at the end of the month.

Túri is dry broken straw of wheat or barley. Of course a man may feed his bullocks any way he pleases; but as a rule, they are fed much as shown above; turnips and green wheat are often given especially when still young, mixed with

Chapter IV, B.

Domestic Animals.

túri. It is not uncommon on the Rávi to turn the cattle out into the young fields of gram, *massar*, &c., to graze.

Names of cows and bullocks.

Like camels, cows and bullocks have different names at different stages of their growth. They are, however, very simple. The general name for cattle is *mál.* The following are the names in use :—

Name of Cow.	*Name of Bullock or Bull.*
Vachhi, till 1 year old.	*Vachha*, till 1 year old.
Wairki, „ 2½ „ „	*Wairka*, „ 2½ „ „
Dhandp, „ she calves.	*Vauhr*, „ 4 „ „
Gái (also *gao*, on Rávi) after calving.	*Bail* or *sanh*, after 4 years of age.

There are other names according to the number of teeth or the kind of teeth they have, *viz.* :—

Name of Cow.	*Name of Bull or Bullock.*	*Period of life.*	
Khiri ...	*Khira* ...	Till 2 years of age.	Animal has only milk teeth.
Dondi ...	*Donda* ...	From 2 to 3 years of age.	„ „ two teeth (incisors).
Chauggi ...	*Chaugga* ...	„ 3 „ 4 „ „	„ „ four „
Chhiggi ...	*Chigga* ...	After 4 years of age.	„ „ six teeth.

Buffaloes, males.

Male buffaloes are not in much request in Montgomery; they are employed in places in the Sandal *Bár* where the wells are deep, and also in ploughing up the rice fields along the Deg. They are very strong, but they feel the heat very much and die soon. This is expressed in the saying .—

Jhote nún gah ; budhi nún rah.

Mard nún chakki ; ghore nún chatti.

Cháre ráh kuráh.

or "for a buffalo to thresh ; for an old woman to travel ; for a man to grind corn ; for a horse to carry the pannier of an ass : all four ways (of doing things) are bad ways." Male buffaloes are generally eaten when young. If they escape, they are sold to men of the Manjha and Shekhupura. They cost from Rs. 15 to Rs. 50. The average price is about Rs. 30. A buffalo commences to work at the same age as a bullock. A female buffalo costs from Rs. 25 to Rs. 90. A fairly good one will cost Rs. 50, while the price of a very good one may go up to Rs. 120. The way milch-buffaloes are fed and treated is much the same as that adopted towards cows; as more valuable, they are taken more care of; and being bigger, they require more food than cows. A buffalo calves when five years of age after eleven months' gestation, generally in Hár or Sáwan. She will produce six calves in all, at intervals of two years. Buffaloes are generally milked only once a day ; they give about half as much milk again as a cow ; and the milk yields about ⅓ more butter than the same quantity of cow's milk. A buffalo continues in good milk for nine or ten months. The names of buffaloes seem to differ on the Rávi and Sutlej. The general name for a female buffalo is

Female buffaloes.

Chapter IV, B.

Domestic Animals.

Female buffaloes.

majh and *maính*, respectively. The Sutlej names are as follows :—

Male.		*Female.*		*Period during which so-called.*
Kata or *Kat*	...	*Kati*	...	Till weaned—*i. e.*, 1 year of age.
Jhotra or *Jhota*	...	*Jhoti*	...	From 1 year of age to 2 years of age.
Tirnána	...	*Trihán*	...	" 2 years " " " 3 " " "
Sandah	...	*Garhap*	...	" 3 " " " " 5 " " "
"	...	*Mainh*	...	After 5 years of age.

On the Rávi the *jhota* stage lasts till 2½, and the *trihána* stage is not recognized. The names, according to teeth possessed, are the same for buffaloes as for cows and bullocks.

Hides.

When cows, bullocks and buffaloes die, they are made over to the Chubras and Mochís. They use the skin for their own purposes, or sell them to travelling dealers. In Gugerá tahsíl the owners of the cattle are said sometimes to sell them; but this is not the custom elsewhere. The dealers are Khojas of Lahore, Kasúr, and Ferozepore; or Chamárs of Ludhiána and even Umballa. The hides of cows and bullocks sell for from Re. 1-8-0 to Rs. 4, and those of buffaloes from Rs. 2 to Rs. 6-8-0 a piece. The leather of Jhámra and Lundíanwála in Gugera is spoken well of locally.

Trade in cattle.

The district breeds all the cattle it requires. Except in the Gugera tahsíl, sales of cattle are not extensive, there large numbers of quite young bulls are sold to merchants from the Bagri country, bullocks are sold to people of the Manjha, and buffalloes to those of Shekhupura. Labanas of Lahore and Amritsar also buy young buffaloes in this district for carriage. From Pákpattan a certain number of bullocks go to the Manjha country and buffaloes to the fairs at Amritsar and elsewhere.

Diseases of cattle.

Horned cattle are subject to quite as many diseases as camels. Many are common to both classes of animals, and also attack horses, sheep and goats. The more important ailments will now be noticed. Unless specially mentioned, the remarks apply to cows, bullocks, and buffaloes, and to them only.

Sat.—This is anthrac fever. It usually occurs in or just after the rains, and is caused by half-starved cattle suddenly obtaining an abundance of nutritious food in which they indulge to excess. Large gaseous swellings, as much as a foot in diameter, appears on the back, hind-quarters or fore-quarters. Sometimes there are swellings in the mouth. There is no remedy. If a mullah can be got to charm the animal some good may be done. Cutting a piece off the ear is another device. But almost every animal attacked dies within 24 hours.

Pír, also called *Máta Sítla* and *Sihál.* This is cow-pox. It is more fatal with buffaloes than with kine. Of the latter about half recover; there is no remedy. The sick animal is generally kept apart from the others. The cause of the disease is not known. It occurs at all seasons. The crisis comes on in 8 or 9 days. The chief symptoms are a running from the eyes, nose, and mouth; blisters form, and the dung has a most offensive odour.

Ghotu, or malignant sore-throat, occurs at all seasons. Cause not known. No remedy. Sometimes a portion of one ear is cut off, probably as a counter-irritant. The symptoms are well-marked. The neck swells; the animal gasps and breathes with difficulty; there is a rattling in the throat, and foaming at the mouth. The animal almost invariably dies, and usually within 24 hours.

Barr.—This is a rather dangerous disease, as about half those attacked die. It seems to be megrims; the characteristic sign is that the animal attacked turns round and round several times till it falls. The remedy is to brand all round the body, commencing at the nose, and going down the back under the tail and up the belly. It is attributed to getting a chill. As it usually occurs in Bhádon and Assu (middle of August to middle of October), it may be due to the same cause as *sat, viz.*, half-starved animals gorging themselves with rich food.

Phiphri —Cows and bullocks when attacked mostly recover; buffaloes generally succumb. As its name implies, this is a disease of the lungs; though some insist it is a swelling of the spleen. The cause is not known; but it has been observed to follow after a chill. The symptoms are heavy breathing with cough, and a falling out of condition. The disease may last as long as six months; and is said to end fatally in five days sometimes. It seems to be pleuro-pneumonia. The remedies adopted are branding under either shoulder or along the backbone; or 1 *sér* of *ghi* and 4 *chittáks* of ground pomegranate peel are mixed and given every evening to a buffalo, or half that amount to a cow or bullock, generally for three days running only.

Táo.—In this disease, which usually lasts as long as the animal lives, but is rarely fatal, the symptoms are a thick staring coat; the animal keeps its mouth open and gasps; it seeks cool places and lies down in water whenever it can. *Táo* generally appears about the beginning of the rains. The cause is unknown. Some say buffaloes are not attacked. The remedy is a decoction of young *kikar* leaves, or some butter mixed with a medicinal substance called *ras*; it seems a very rare disease.

Bhukni, or scouring; occurs at all seasons; cause is not known, but some say heat; some say eating unsuitable food, such as *gharni* grass when green. The disease consists in constant passing of watery evacuations. *Bhukni* means a piece of bamboo stem between two joints, sometimes used as water-pipe. The reason of the name of the disease is obvious. It is a deadly disease, most animals attacked dying. But some deny this. It is said to last as long as 8 days violently. No remedy is practised, but coarsely-ground *jowár* and butter-milk, or coagulated milk and *máín* (galls of the tamarisk), or *gur* and onions, are recommended.

Chapter IV, B.

Domestic Animals.

Diseases of cattle

Munhkhur, or foot and mouth disease, seems to occur at all seasons. The cause is not known; but some attribute it to a bird, called *mahára*, pecking at the cleft of a hoof of the animal. Others scoff at this explanation. Blisters form in the mouth and on the feet; and the animal loses its appetite; the disease lasts about 10 days. It is rarely fatal. The parts affected are washed with warm water; and sometimes bread made of gram or *masúr*, with some salt and butter, is administered.

Lág occurs in the rains; and is attributed to the use of river waters, or eating grass that has grown in stagnant river water. The disease is not mortal generally. The symptoms are coughing, swelling of the neck, purging, loss of appetite. Milch cattle dry up. The remedies are: sweet oil, one *sér* per diem at intervals of 4 or 5 days, parched gram, or *chína* flour, or some salt. The disease lasts a couple of months, till the buffalo gets *khún* grass wet with dew, and other cattle *jowár* stalks.

Wáo is palsy or paralysis; when a human being is attacked, it is called *jhola*. It usually occurs at the commencement of the cold weather, and is due to a chill. The ankles swell, the coat stares, the animal moves very little, and eats little. The hindquarters are usually affected. Slight branding is sometimes, but rarely, tried. *Ghi* mixed with oil and turmeric, or oil and *til*, are given.

Hada and *motra* seem to be bag and blood spavins. Branding and bleeding, and the application of boiling butter-milk to the swelling, are practised. The last is stated to cure the disease in three days. Hot spices and arsenic pills are said to be given as tonics.

Vil and *dháh* or *tag* seem to be the same disease; but the name *vil* is applied to it when it attacks cows and bullocks, and *tag* or *dháh* when buffaloes are affected. *Tag* is used on the Rávi, and *dháh* on the Sutlej. It mostly occurs at the commencement of the cold weather, and is attributed to the animal getting a chill. It is rarely fatal. In *vil* there is a running at the mouth, the ears grow cold, the legs stiffen, the teeth chatter, and the coat stares. The only remedy really used is putting the animal into the sun; its mouth is also kept open with a *munj* rope; onions are sometimes given; and by some a grasshopper (*tidda*) now and then is considered useful. The animal generally gets well in 12 hours, but may be sick for four days. The symptoms in *dháh* are nearly the same as in *vil*, but the part affected is the back. Any pressure there makes the animal at once fall down. Hence the name, which is derived from *dhána*, to knock down. The duration of the attack is the same as that of *vil* The disease may become chronic. The remedy is to keep the animal warm and well wrapped up so as to excite perspiration. At the same time give warm spices; salt should be put under the clothing. If the disease is of old standing, bleed at the head or tail, or at the back, and rub in opium. Both *dháh* and *vil* seem to be forms of rheumatism.

Diseases of cattle.

Angyári is a swelling of the udder. The swelling lasts 3 or 4 days. It is supposed to be due to the animal having eaten some heating substance. It occurs at all seasons; but mostly in the early part of the rains. If the issue is favourable, the cow or buffalo commences giving milk as usual; if not, she never gives any more, not even if she should calve again. Butter, half a *sér* for a cow, and double that for a buffalo, is stuffed down her throat for four or five days running. A coating of earth taken from a rat's hole and applied to the udder is considered beneficial, when the swelling commences. *Angyári* means a small boil.

Ogu is a disease of buffaloes only. It occurs at any season. The cause is not known. It generally ends in death. The belly swells; the dung and urine are suppressed. Unless this can be remedied, the animal dies in a few hours. The favourite remedy is to make it sit down in water. Butter and *ghi* are given.

Diseases of horses.

Horses are attacked by *phiphri, barr, wáo, hada, motra.* Also by *ogu* and *bhúkni*, according to some; and by *ghotu*, called in their case *khunák*. They also get *kanár* or catarrh. The great remedy for this is burning blue cloth in a *lota* and making the animal inhale the smoke. Ground ginger is blown through a tube into the nostrils. There are several other remedies. This disease is not glanders usually. It is never fatal. But as glanders and catarrh are not unlike, the term *kanár* would probably be used in a case of glanders. *Khúb* seems the same as *khunák*.

Sheep.

The sheep of this district are usually white with brown heads. Quite white sheep are not uncommon; but black are rare. The usual time of tup is August and September, and the lambs are dropped in February; sometimes the autumn is preferred for lambing. The ewe is then one year old. She will give one lamb for each of the next four years; sometimes more than one lamb is dropped; in this case both are weakly.

Milk.

The lamb is allowed all the milk for two months, after that only half, or even less, for about three months more. The ewe gives milk well for four months, and altogether for six. The milk is used as such, or made into butter and *ghi*. It is not sold as milk; but *ghi* makers buy the butter at the same price, or at a little less than that of cows and buffaloes. Sheep are milked between the legs, not at the side, as cattle; the yield is about 3 *chittáks* per diem. One *sér* of milk produces $\frac{2}{3}$ to 1 *chitták* of butter. Sheep are sheared twice a year, in Chetr (middle of March to middle of April) and Kátik (middle of October to middle of November). They are first washed. The outturn of the former shearing is from 3 to 5 *chittáks*, of the latter 4 to 9 *chittáks*. The average yearly outturn is, perhaps, 12 *chittáks*. The wool (*ún*), obtained in the

Wool and skin.

Chapter IV, B.

Domestic Animals.

Wool and skin.

autumn is yellow, while the spring wool is white; the yellow wool is the cheaper of the two. The wool of the back and upper parts is good; that of the legs, belly, and throat inferior. The price of wool varies very much It averages about Rs. 20 per maund. The fleeces are sold to traders of Fázilka, Kasúr or Ferozepore. The skins are sold to wandering traders at from 1½ to 2½ annas each. They generally are taken on camels to Lahore, Amritsar or Fázilka. The skins are used for shoes, musical instruments, and bags for keeping money, clothes, flour, &c. Untanned sheep-skins are called *khalrí;* after tanning *mesha.* The flesh of sheep is extensively consumed. Sheep have also different names according to the stage of their growth. Till six months old a ram is called *lela,* and a ewe *leli;* after 12 months the former is known as *chhathra,* and the latter as *bhed.* Between the ages of 6 and 12 months there is a dispute; some say the ram is called *bodhar* and the ewe *gharáp;* others divide the period into two portions of three months each, during which the ram is called *sassa* and *chhathra* and the ewe *gharápi* and *gharáp,* but *sassa* seems properly a name applied to any well-grown lamb. According to their teeth sheep are known as:—

Khiri, till milk teeth are replaced, about 15 or 18 months after birth.
Pakka khira; pakki khiri. A few months before next stage.
Donda when animal has only 2 teeth, till about 2 years of age.
Changa " " " 4 " " 2½ "
Chhigga " " " 6 " after 2½ "

Goats.

With reference to their teeth, goats are called by the same names, except that the *pakka-khira* stage is not recognized. Goats, too, are more precocious, and so each stage ends six months sooner than with sheep Till six months old, a he-goat is known as *pathora,* a she-goat as *pathori.* The former then becomes a *bakra,* the latter a *kharap;* till one year old when she is called *bakri;* goats kid in Chetr and Baisákh (middle of March to middle of May), or in Kátik and Magar (middle of October to middle of December) once a year. The period of gestation is six months. They generally have one kid at a time, and will produce 7 or 8 altogether.

Milk, hair and skin.

Goats are milked twice a day; they give about 14 to 20 *chittáks* of milk. Till one month after birth the kid gets all the milk; then for another month, half; then it is weaned. The supply of milk is good for four months. For making butter the milk is bad, yielding only ½ *chitták* of butter for each *sér* of milk. Goats are sheared in Chetr, Baisákh or Hár. Their hair is called *jat.* Its price averages about Rs. 5 or Rs. 6 per maund. The yield of one goat ranges from 3 to 6 *chittáks.* The *jat* is sold to *kumhárs,* camel-men, or *banyas.* It is made into ropes, *koras, chhatis* and floor-cloths of shops, called *tappar* (sack-cloth). The skins of goats are disposed of in the same way as those of sheep. They fetch from four annas to Re. 1 undressed. They are used for water-bags (*mashak*), as well as the purposes for which sheep-skins are used.

Chapter IV, B.

Domestic Animals.

Sheep and goats; food; quality; sales.

Goats and sheep get nothing to eat but what they can pick up in the jungle; they do not get any salt. Shortly before kidding, a goat gets some oil or *ghi* for a few days if in bad condition. The sheep of this district are of poor quality. The wool is coarse. The climate is too arid and the country too inhospitable for much improvement to be probable. Large numbers of young sheep are sold annually to travelling dealers, who take them to the up-country districts; a sheep costs from Re. 1 to Rs. 3; a goat from Re. 1 to Rs. 5.

Diseases of sheep and goats.

Sheep and goats suffer from *sat, ghotu, pir, munkhur, phiphri* and *angyárí*, diseases described in pages 168, 169, 170 and 171. For the first four there is no remedy. Incantations, though useful to those not attacked, are of no avail to those afflicted. *Sat* and *ghotu* end in rapid death; scarcely any animal dies of *pir* or *munhkhur*. The last is caused by the *mahára*. In a case of *phiphri*, branding the nose and ears or scalding them with hot milk, the first Sunday after the new moon, is tried. Pomegranate rind and *ghi* are given to the sick animal. Few die.

Sokra occurs usually in the rains. It it rarely fatal. The legs swell, and the animal becomes quite thin—in fact dries up; hence the name. Branding the swellings, and doses of sweet and bitter oil, or embrocations of the juice of the *ák*, are the remedies adopted.

Pánilág or *rik* is attributed to the same cause as *lág*, a disease of cows, &c. The symptoms are the same. Fish oil obtained by boiling down the fish called *makni* is administered. A diet of *kíkar* branches or *chari* is said to be efficacious. It is generally a fatal disease. It seems to be "rot."

Rat is said to be a most deadly disease; none escape, if attacked. There is no remedy. The chief symptom is the passing of bloody urine. *Rat* means blood. This is the disease known as red-water. It occurs usually early in the rains. It seems almost unknown on the Sutlej, but the Rávi people are acquainted with it.

Tret is the disease called *barr* in the case of cattle. It occurs at the same time, and the symptoms are the same, but it is rarely mortal. The remedy adopted is branding either across the face or along the backbone near the tail. In the latter case opium is rubbed into the spot cauterized.

Sawattan or *savittal*, also called *zardoi*, seems to be hepatitis. The symptoms are yellow eyes, discoloured urine, and constipation. It is a rare disease, and occurs about August and September. It is attributed to the use of new grass and hot water. Death commonly results. There are really no remedies; but goat's milk diluted with water, or sometimes butter, is given.

Gada and *pán* are the itch; the former term is applied to sheep, the latter to goats. Sheep are washed with a decoction of *ukhán* leaves and *sajji*, or sweet oil or *sajji* mixed with

Chapter IV, C.

Occupations, Industries, and Commerce.

Diseases of sheep and goats.

cow-dung is rubbed over them. Goats are rubbed over with a mixture of bitter oil and sulphur, and get curds or sweet oil to drink.

Hung or *hungan* attacks goats, and is usually fatal. The coat stares; the animal ceases to eat and drink; the ears hang down; and there is a cough. These are not very distinguishing symptoms. The remedy is incantation. As the principal part of the ceremony is feasting the miracle-working *fakir* on a healthy goat, and the sick one rarely recovers, the remedy seems worse than the disease.

Tilphati seems to be rupture of the spleen, judging from is name. It is very rare, and usually fatal. Sheep and goats are attacked generally about the beginning of the cold weather. There is no remedy.

Aphar occurs at all times. It is said to be never fatal, and to last a few hours. The stomach swells; and the animal falls down. There is constipation.

Súl is a very similar disease. *Aphar* means a swelling of the stomach, that being filled with wind; and *súl* is said to mean colic.

Sericulture.

An interesting account of an experiment in sericulture made by Mr. Peake at Gugera in 1863 is given at pages 176-77 of *Punjab Products*. The experiment held out every promise of success; but was perforce abandoned in 1864 on the transfer of the head-quarters of the district from fertile Gugera to the desolate and barren wastes of the civil station of Montgomery.

SECTION C.—OCCUPATIONS, INDUSTRIES AND COMMERCE.

Occupations of the people.

Table No. XXIII shows the principal occupations followed by males of over 15 years of age as returned at the Census of 1891. The figures are practically meaningless, as the classification of occupations is based on an European and not on a native model, and the differentiation of occupations is not nearly so complete as that contemplated by the table. Reference should be made to Chapter XII of the Census Report. The figures in Table No. XXIII may be summarized as follows :—

	Per cent.
Agricultural ...	68
Pastoral ...	8
Domestic servants ...	3
Artisans ...	10
Food and drink ...	4
Unskilled labour ...	1
Government service, Civil ...	2
Do. do. Military ...	...
Religious teachers, fakirs and mendicants, &c. ...	3
Commerce and transport ...	...
Others ...	1
Total ...	100

Chapter IV, C.

Occupations, Industries, and Commerce.

More detailed figures for the occupations of both males and females will be found in Table XVII B and abstract No. 90 of the Census Report of 1891. The figures for female occupations, however, are exceedingly incomplete.

Principal industries and manufactures.

Table No. XXIV gives statistics of the cotton ginning and pressing factories of the district as they stood in 1897. No statistics are available for the other industries of the district; nor would they be likely to be reliable if there were. Coarse cotton cloth is woven in most villages for home use. The fisheries of the district have already been described at page 30.

Mr. Lockwood Kipling, Principal of the Lahore School of Art, kindly furnished the following note on some of the special industries of the district for the former edition of the Gazetteer :—

Lac-turnery, Pákpattan.

"The most notable industry of the Montgomery district is the lac-turnery of Pákpattan. There are several families who send out a variety of toys, boxes, spring wheels, charpoy legs, &c., to all parts of the Punjab. The wood used is chiefly *bhán*, locally *obhán* (*Populus euphratica*)—the black or Lombardy poplar, a soft, light, easily-worked wood, containing no resin, and not liable to the attacks of insects, all which are essential points. Nothing could be simpler in principle than the craft of the *Kharádi*, while his *lathe* is a perfect example of the many Indian contrivances which produce wonderful results with the most elementary and apparently inadequate means. The varnish, which is produced by pressing what is virtually a stick of coloured sealing-wax against a rapidly revolving wooden object, has been found by the experience of generations to resist dust, damp, and excessive heat and dryness better than any known paint, and it is used on all articles of domestic use which can be turned on the *lathe*. If this fine coating could be as cheaply applied to flat surfaces it would be of immense use. But this essentially simple art is capable of almost infinite variations. Though there are few towns in which it is not wrought in some fashion, there are some which, like Pákpattan, enjoy a special reputation. The work from this town, though strongly resembling that of Sindh, with which province the south-west of the Punjab has some noticeable affinities, may be recognised by the use of a rich, mottled purple alternating with bands of black, on which delicate floral borders and diapers appear to be painted in red and green. This ornament is, however, produced in a manner analogous to the Sgraffito of Italian architectural decoration. Coats of different colours are super-imposed on the surface, and the pattern is produced by scratching through these with a sharp stylus. Thus, a red flower is made by scratching through the black and green films; for the leaves, the black only is cut away, exposing the green; and for a white line all three are cut through to the white wood. This is obviously work requiring great delicacy of hand and long practice. The articles made at, Pákpattan, besides objects for native use, are tea-poys, toys, flower-stands, plateaux, chessmen, work-boxes, &c. The workmen are Muhammadans.

Cotton-weaving—Pákpattan.

Calico-printing—Kot Kamália.

"The cotton-waving of Pákpattan, though not of striking importance, is of good quality; and chequered *kh-s* fabrics with *lungis*, *chautahis*, and other varieties in common native use, are here strongly and neatly woven. At Kot Kamália very good cotton-printing is done. The characteristics of this work are brightness of colour, and a certain quaintness and rudeness of pattern, which usually shows a good deal of white ground. Some *dindiwárs* (a better word than our dado), printed with archaic figures of horsemen, were sent to the Punjab Exhibition. Scarves, *abras* and other articles are also made, and the work has a considerable reputation.

Reed baskets.

"Among merely domestic crafts, reed basket work, which, though almost universal in the Punjab, is better done at Gugera in the Montgomery district than elsewhere, may be here mentioned. The *chháj* or winnowing basket remarkable for its strength and lightness and perfect adaptation to its purpose, would seem to have been the original, as it is the staple article. The *tíli* or fine upper stalks of *múnj* (*Saccharum munja*) are neatly worked in rows tied to strengthening bars of stouter reed and bamboo with strips of fresh goat-skin, which is sometimes used in larger pieces to strengthen the corners. Baskets for domestic purposes are some.

Chapter IV, C.

Occupations, Industries, and Commerce.

times adorned with tufts of coloured wool, while mats, *punkahs*, and fancy baskets are worked over with lozenge-shaped crossings of parti-coloured worsted with cowries sewn on the borders. A large basket with a well-fitting cover is much used for keeping feminine gear. *Chamars* and *chuhras* are said to be the most expert workers in a craft for which gipsies all over the world seem to have a special affinity. They are also frequently employed in sifting and winnowing wheat."

Sajji.

The following account of the manufacture of *sajji* is taken, after necessary corrections, from page 86 of *Punjab Products*:—

"*Sajji* is produced from two different plants which grow spontaneously in brackish soil in the *bár* tracts of the Bári and Rechna Doábs, called *kangan khár* and *goru lána*, the last yielding inferior, and the first superior, *sajji*. The *kangan khár* plant yields the best alkali. The pure *sajji* from this plant is called *lota sajji*, and the residue mixed with ashes is called *kangan khár sajji*. The other plant yields only a dirty and inferior substance known as *bhútni sajji*, devil's soda. This is black in colour, and sold in pieces like lumps of ashes.

"The process is as follows:—The shrubs ripen about October, and the process of making *sajji* is carried on throughout October, November, December and January. The first step is to cut down the plants with a wooden scythe called *talwár*. They are then allowed to lie on the ground in heaps to dry. When perfectly inflammable, a pit in the ground is dug in a hemispherical shape, about six feet in circumference and three deep, at the bottom of which one or more inverted *tinds*, or earthen vessels, are buried, having small holes pierced in their upper portions; the holes are kept closed at the commencement of operations. A fire is kindled, and the dry plants placed in the pit, with the aid of a *sangi*, or pitchfork, and the fire is kept fed with the dry plants till all is burned. During the process of burning a liquid substance is formed, which runs down into the *tinds* below the fire. After all the liquid has run through into the *tind*, the residue is stirred up with a stick called *mashad*, which has a round flat piece of wood at the end like a ladle or a *ghorla*—*i.e.*, a piece of wood cut green from the tree to prevent its burning. Great care must be taken during the above process that no water is allowed to be put on the fire, otherwise the whole mass would blow up, and endanger the lives of those manufacturing it. After the residuary mass has been stirred in the manner described it is covered over with earth. It cools in three or four days, but can be taken out when wanted. The *bhútni sajji* is made in the same manner as the above, but from the shrub called *goru lána*. When the earth is removed, the substance is found in a solid rocky state; it is then broken out with a tool called *waddn*, or wooden crowbar. Then the *tinds* that are underneath are also removed, and being broken, the contents are taken out. The residuary mass in the pit is crude dirty potash, but that which is found inside the *tinds* is clean and free from ashes, &c.; it is called *lota sajji*, because found in the *tind* or *lota*.

"The proportion produced of *kangan* and *bhútni sajji* is four *sérs* from a maund of the plant, or one-tenth: and of the *lota sajji*, one *sér* in a maund, or $\frac{1}{40}$th part.

"The growing plants are much valued for camel-grazing. The market price of *bhútni sajji* is from Re. 1 to Re. 1-8 per maund. *Lota sajji* commands a much higher price, and sells at Rs. 8 a maund. The expense attending the manufacture, *viz.*, cutting, stocking, and lifting, is about 4 annas per maund. The workmen who cut the plants get 2 annas a day, the burners take 3 annas, and there is one man to superintend. *Lota sajji* is principally used as a medicine on account of its high price. *Kangan khár sajji* is used in washing and dyeing with madder and *kasumbha*; it is used also for making soap, and in the process of purifying sugar, and in paper-making. The castes principally employed in the manufacture of *sajji* are *chuhras*, *dhobis*, Nunaris, and a few Aroras, but there is no necessary distinction or superstition on the point."

Up to 1893 a license fee of Rs. 2 per pit (*toá*) used to be levied for the manufacture of *sajji*. At present no licenses for the manufacture of *sajji* cut on the Government waste are given: the object being to preserve a sufficient amount of the *lána* plant for the grazing of camels.

Course and nature of trade.

There are no statistics available for the general trade of the district. The exports and imports of food-grains have already

Chapter IV, C.

Occupations, Industries, and Commerce.

Course and nature of trade.

been noticed at page 153, and a list of fairs given at page 74. The exports of the district consist principally of wheat in considerable quantities, a very little rice and gram, a large amount of cotton and cotton seed, a good deal of wool and hides, much *ghi, máin* and oilseeds. The production and export of *sajji* is now much less than it used to be. No cloth is now exported. The imports consist of *jowár* and *bájra,* some rice, *gur,* sugar, salt, cloth, European and country oil, hardware, fruits and dyes. Some wheat is imported from the Chenáb Colony into the Rávi tahsíls. A little gram is imported in times of scarcity. Exports and imports are now almost entirely carried by rail. Camel carriage is mostly confined to the limits of the district. Wheat goes mainly to Karáchi for export to Europe ; gram to Lahore or Multán ; cotton to Karáchi and Bombay for European consumption ; wool to Karáchi, some of it stopping at Multán to be pressed ; cotton seeds to Ferozepore, Bhatinda and the Rohi country ; hides to Múltán, Lahore, Kasúr and Amritsar ; *ghi* to Lahore, Amritsar, Multán and Sukkar, *máin* to Amritsar and Bhawáni ; *til* and oilseeds chiefly to Karáchi. *Jowár* and *bájra* are imported from Sirsa, Bhatinda and the Rohi country, and occasionally from Sindh ; rice from Baháwalpur and Muzaffargarh ; *gur* and country sugar from Amritsar, Batála, Jullundur and the North-Western Provinces ; loaf-sugar from Europe ; salt from Shahpur ; the finer kinds of cloth from Amritsar and Delhi ; the cheaper kinds from Karáchi ; country oil from Ludhiána and Ferozepore, and European oil from Karáchi ; brass vessels from Jhang ; iron and iron goods from Lahore and Multán ; fruits from Lahore and Multán ; indigo from Multán. Very few powindahs now visit the district.

Chief trading towns.

The only trading towns of the district are Kamália and Pákpattan ; some trade is also carried on at Montgomery. The exports of Kamália consist chiefly of cotton, *ghi* and wool ; those of Pákpattan of cotton, wheat, wool and oilseeds, and those of Montgomery of wheat and oilseeds. Basirpur and Atári in the Dipalpur tahsíl aad Boyleganj in Pákpattan are large villages in which there is a good deal of local trade. Pákpattan used to have a considerable trade in cloth ; very little is now made there, and none is exported beyond the district except the *lungis* of 700 and 1,000 threads to a breadth, and *dohars* of all kinds which are much esteemed, and find a ready sale in Amritsar, Lahore, and Multán. A considerable quantity of the products of the local looms is disposed of at the annual fair in the first week of the Muharram. Most of the yarn used comes from England.

Pákpattan weavers.

There are two castes of weavers at Pákpattan, the one called Bhakri the other Paoli. The difference between them is that the women of the former class weave, those of the latter consider it a disgrace to do so. The women of both castes, but especially those of the Paoli, prepare the web, at which they make about one pice for every mile they go backwards and forwards. There are now 224 looms at work. The numbers of persons engaged are as follows :—

Chapter IV, D.

Prices, Weights and Measures, and Communications.

Pákpattan weavers.

Paolis, 100 men, 60 women and 30 boys; Bhakhris, 80 men, 40 women and 30 boys. Thread is spun by women, who are paid in kind. They get 1½ to 2 *sers* of cotton, and give back one *ser* of thread, but this method of payment is less common than it was. Twenty *sers* of cotton are carded for one rupee. Pákpattan has also a high reputation for its lacquered work. Good blankets are made at Málka Hans. Kabula does some little trade in *ghi* with Amritsar. It is not possible to do more than guess at the value of the trade of the district. Judging from a few isolated facts, Mr. Purser was, in 1874, inclined to think it about 10 lakhs per annum. It is now no doubt much more.

SECTION D.—PRICES, WEIGHTS AND MEASURES AND COMMUNICATIONS.

Prices, wages, rent-rates, interest.

Table No. XXVI gives the retail *bázár* prices of commodities for the last thirty-three years. The wages of labour are shown in Table No. XXVII, and rent-rates in Table No. XXI; but both sets of figures are probably of doubtful value. Rent rates have already been discussed at page 100.

Village prices of agricultural staples.

Mr. Purser gave the following statement showing the average quinquennial price of cotton, *jowár*, rice, *kangni*, *chína*, wheat and gram, in the towns of Dipalpur and Hujra from 1838 to 1871. These prices were taken from the books of the *karárs*, and represent dealings between them and the cultivators. The *karárs* fix the prices twice a year in Hár and Kátik. The average price is the average of prices prevailing at both seasons in both towns. These towns were selected as being in the chief agricultural part of the district:—

Year.	Cotton (raw).			*Jowar.*			Rice (unhusked).			*Kangni.*			*China.*			Wheat.			Gram.		
	M.	S.	C.	M.	S.	C.	M.	S.	C.	M.	S.	C.	M.	S.	C.	M.	S.	C.	M.	S.	C.
Average of four years, 1838-1841.	0	18	12	0	31	6	0	28	0	0	38	0	0	31	13	0	31	10	0	39	10
Average of five years, 1842-46.	0	18	0	1	6	9	0	34	5	2	8	3	1	32	13	1	3	3	1	14	0
Average of five years, 1847-51.	0	18	5	0	38	8	1	4	6	1	20	9	1	7	6	1	0	0	1	10	8
Average of five years, 1852-56.	0	24	11	1	8	8	1	13	11	2	11	3	1	26	8	1	7	8	1	34	8
Average of five years, 1857-61.	0	15	0	1	0	12	3	39	8	1	24	6	1	10	6	1	4	9	1	25	6
Average of five years, 1862-66.	0	11	[illegible]	0	35	3	0	37	9	1	8	9	1	0	0	0	36	3	1	11	11
Average of five years, 1867-71.	0	12	1	0	20	5	0	25	13	0	34	0	0	27	0	0	21	11	0	35	11
Average, 1842-1856	0	20	5	1	4	8	1	4	2	2	0	0	1	22	4	1	3	9	1	16	5
Average, 1857-1871	0	12	12	0	32	1	0	34	5	1	9	2	0	39	2	0	27	0	1	7	9
Average, 1842-1871	0	16	8	0	39	5	0	39	3	1	24	9	1	10	11	0	35	4	1	11	15

Chapter IV, D.

Prices, Weights and Measures, and Communications.

Recent rise in prices.

The statement below shows the prices in *sérs* per rupee of agricultural produce assumed for the purposes of assessment in the recent settlement.

	Gugera and Montgomery.	Dipálpur and Pákpattan.
	Sérs.	Sérs.
Rice (unhusked)	28	29
Maize	...	24
Jowár	28	30
Kangni	...	37
China	...	37
Moth	...	30
Másh	...	25
Múng	...	26
Til	12	12
Cotton (uncleaned)	12	12
Wheat	22	24
Barley	...	38
Gram	30	34

The following table gives some information regarding the course of the village prices of the chief agricultural staples in the Sutlej tahsíls during the currency of the revised settlement :—

Chapter IV, D.

Prices, Weights and Measures, and Communications.

Recent rise in prices.

1		2		3		4		5		6		7		8	9	10
Name of crop.		Average village prices in sérs per rupee, 1864 to 1873.		Prices assumed at last settlement in sérs per rupee.		Average village prices in sérs per rupee. 1874 to 1878.		1874 to 1883.		1884 to 1893.		1874 to 1893.		Prices now sanctioned in sérs per rupee.	Percentage—column 6 on column 2.	Percentage—column 8 on column 4.
		S.	Ch.	S.	Ch.	S.	Ch.	S.	Ch.	S.	Ch.	S.	Ch.	Sérs.		
Rice ...	Dipálpur	20	0	40	7	29	13	27	12	26	15	27	5	20	+7·6	+2·8
	Pákpattan	23	14	32	0	30	0	27	6	23	14	25	10		...	+3·4
Maize ...	Dipálpur	35	0	30	13	45	3	42	8	31	15	37	3	34	+9·6	+32·9
	Pákpattan	...		31	8	...		...		30	1	30	1		...	...
Jowár ...	Dipálpur	28	14	30	13	34	7	28	13	22	11	25	12	30	+27·2	+14·8
	Pákpattan	26	13	38	12	20	2	28	9	24	15	26	12		+7·5	−2·0
Til ...	Dipálpur	12	7	17	12	14	5	14	4	10	2	12	3	12	+22·8	+10·2
	Pákpattan	13	4	20	12	13	8	14	5	10	9	12	7		+25·4	+12·5
Cotton ...	Dipálpur	11	9	17	5	11	15	11	13	10	2	10	15	12	+14·2	−·5
	Pákpattan	11	3	14	2	12	9	12	8	11	0	11	12		+1·1	+4·7
Wheat ...	Dipálpur	28	10	40	7	29	6	25	3	21	3	23	3	24	+35·1	+22·4
	Pákpattan	26	10	38	10	27	3	23	8	20	14	22	3		+27·5	+13·3
Barley ...	Dipálpur	45	3	61	13	46	9	39	0	34	4	36	10	38	+31·9	+22·5
	Pákpattan	37	8	37	8	49	8	36	15	31	1	32	5		+16	−2·8
Gram ...	Dipálpur	42	10	54	9	45	8	38	9	31	11	35	2	34	+34·5	+33·8
	Pákpattan	34	13	48	0	35	11	33	7	29	14	31	10		+16·5	+4·9
Average ...	Dipálpur	...		...		...		...		...		...		...	+20·8	+19·6
	Pákpattan	...		...		...		...		...		...			+21	+9·3

Chapter IV, D.

Prices, Weights and Measures, and Communications.

Recent rise in prices.

The actual all-round rise of prices during the 30 years, 1864-93, was 30 per cent. in Dipálpur and 21 per cent. in Pákpattan. At the beginning of the period prices were considerably higher in the latter than in the former tahsíl.

Mr. Purser wrote as follows :—

"In 1871 Mr. Roe, the Settlement Officer, gave it as his opinion that the increase in price of late years has arisen from a diminished supply, and not from an increased demand. I have lived in the *pargannah* during the whole time that these high prices prevailed, and I know, from what I have seen with my own eyes, that the condition of the agriculturists has been one, not of prosperity, but of very great distress. It would also seem at first sight that the construction of a railway right through the heart of the district must have greatly benefited the people. No doubt it would have done so, had the agriculturists had any surplus produce to export ; but as they had barely sufficient for their own consumption, the opening up of new markets was practically useless. In fact, in one way the railway has injured them ; for it has led to a much stricter conservancy of the Government jungle ; formerly the *zamíndárs* obtained all the wood they required free or almost free. Now they have to pay for it, and get it with difficulty ; besides this the subordinate conservancy establishment greatly increases their indirect taxation."

Value of land.

Table XXXII gives statistics of the areas of land sold and mortgaged up to the expiration of the last settlement. The following figures based on assessment statements show the progress in the value of land including cultivated and uncultivated in the Sutlej tahsíls. Similar figures are not available in the case of tahsíls Gugera and Montgomery :—

Tahsil.	Price per acre.				Mortgage money per acre.				
	1873-82.	1883-92.	1893-96.	1872-96.	Before 1871-72.	1873-82.	1883-92.	1893-96.	1872-96.
	Rs. a. p.	Rs. a. p.	Rs. a. p.	Rs. a. p.	Rs. a. p.	Rs. a. p.	Rs. a. p.	Rs. a. p.	Rs. a. p.
Dipálpur	8 11 1	13 13 2	20 13 9	12 11 7	6 8 0	13 7 8	12 6 3	15 15 8	12 8 2
Pákpattan	3 15 2	8 5 6	21 3 7	7 14 0	2 15 1	5 15 9	8 11 11	10 2 10	8 6 3

The following statement shows the total areas transferred during the four years 1894-95 to 1897-98 inclusive, with the resulting price and mortgage-money per acre :—

Tahsíl.	Area sold in acres.	Price in rupees.	Price per acre.	Area mortgaged in acres.	Mortgage-money.	Mortgage-money per acre.
		Rs.	Rs. A. P.		Rs.	Rs. A. P.
Gugera	2,155	45,687	21 3 2	5,670	70,751	12 7 8
Montgomery ...	3,330	65,459	19 10 6	5,866	71,643	12 3 5
Dipálpur	10,140	1,86,041	18 5 7	17,701	2,79,965	15 3 1
Pákpattan	9,500	1,13,156	11 14 7	6,069	77,293	12 11 9
Total District ...	25,125	4,10,343	16 5 4	35,306	4,99,652	14 2 5

Chapter IV, D.

Prices, Weights and Measures, and Communications.

Value of land.

The quality and class of land varies so much and the prices and mortgage-money returned are so often fictitious that general rates for price and mortgage-money per acre have but little real meaning. On this subject Mr. Purser wrote in 1874:—

"The low value of land in this district, except where canal-irrigation is available, is shown by the difficulty of getting farmers, as well as by the low price at which land is sold and mortgaged. In Pákpattan it was found that 12,878 acres, paying a revenue of Rs. 3,156, or annas 3-11 per acre, had been sold for Rs. 18,646. This gave the price per acre as Re. 1-2-0, and per rupee of revenue as Rs. 5-14-7. The mortgaged area as 9,687 acres assessed at Rs. 2,272, or annas 3-9 per acre. The mortgage-money amounted to Rs. 19,081, or Re. 1-15-6 per acre, and Rs. 8-6-5 per rupee of revenue. In Dipálpur, 15,749 acres sold realized Rs. 26,421, or Re. 1-10-10 per acre, and Rs. 6-1-11 per rupee of revenue. The revenue was Rs. 4,319, falling at annas 4-5 per acre. The area mortgaged was 12,028 acres assessed at Rs. 2,964, being at the rate of Rs. 3-11 per acre. The mortgage-money amounted to Rs. 30,353, equal to Rs. 2-8-5 per acre, and Rs. 10-3-7 of Government revenue. If it is considered that these prices include not only money paid for the land, but also the cost of wells and other property attached to the land, the very low value of land is at once apparent. More money can be got by mortgaging land than by selling it. It may be that the land mortgaged is more valuable than that sold; but this fact may also be explained by the difficulty of obtaining tenants, and the dread of becoming responsible for payment of the revenue. When land is sold, the buyer becomes responsible for the revenue, and he has to make his arrangements for cultivating the land; but in the case of mortgages, the mortgagor remains, as a rule, responsible for the revenue, and continues to cultivate the land himself, or exerts himself to have it cultivated."

The figures given above, taken for what they are worth, show that the value of land increased enormously, more especially in Pákpattan, during the term of the revised settlement.

Measure of weight.

Except in towns, the Government maund and *sér* are not employed in the purchase and sale of grain. A measure of capacity is used, and not one of weight. This measure is the *topa*, and its size varies in different parts of the district. The weight of a *topa* of wheat in each locality is shown in a map attached to Mr. Purser's settlement report. There are 10 different *topas*, and the weight varies from 1 *sér*, 4 *chittáks* to 3 *sérs*, 4 *chittaks*. An attempt is being made to introduce a uniform *topa* for the whole district. The divisions and multiples of the *topa* are the *paropi*, *pái*, *man*, *kharwár*, and *máni*:—

4 paropis	... =	1 topa.
4 topas	... =	1 pái.
4 páis	... =	1 man (maund).
10 mans	... =	1 kharwár.
12½ mans	... =	1 máni.

The *kharwár* is used on the Rávi and the *máni* on the Sutlej. The native *man* then is of a fluctuating value according to locality, and one great difficulty in obtaining information concerning yield of crops, amount of seed grain, &c., is the uncertainty as to what *topa* the informant is alluding to. To make matters worse, there are two ways of using the *topa*. In one called *chhara*, when the *topa* has been filled, nothing is added with the hand; and in the second, called *bharti*, the *topa* is heaped up with the hands. *Topas* are round measures. They are usually made of *ukán* or *karíl*, sometimes of *kikar*. The differences in the value of the *topa* are due to the country

Chapter IV, D.

Prices, Weights and Measures, and Communications.

having been split up into numerous petty states, the ruler of each of which set up his own *topa*, partly to assert his independence, and partly, it would seem, at least occasionally, to cheat the *zamíndárs* under him.

Measures of length and area.

The *karam* is 5½ feet long. The current scale of square measure is :—

9 square karams	... =	1 kán.
20 káns or marlas	... =	1 kanál.
8 kanáls	... =	1 ghumáo

The *ghumáo* is thus equal to one acre, the *kanál* to half a rood, and the *kán* to a square perch. In measuring distance a term in common use is *sadpandh* (from *sad*, voice, and *pandh*, distance) ; it represents the distance at which a man's voice can be heard in the jungle, and may be roughly estimated as a mile.

Communications.

The figures in the margin show the communications of the district as returned in the quinquennial Administration Report for 1896-97 ; while Table No. XLVI shows the distances from place to place as authoritatively fixed for the purpose of calculating travelling allowance. Table No. XIX gives the area taken up by Government for communications.

Communications.		Miles.
Navigable rivers	Sutlej	104
	Rávi	139
Railways ...	... ...	82
Metalled roads ...	...	...
Unmetalled roads	...	1,003

Rivers.

The Sutlej is navigable for country craft throughout its course in this district, but the Rávi is generally too low for this in the cold weather. There is practically no river traffic. The ferries and the distances between them are shown below, following the downward course of each river :—

Rivers.	Stations.	Distance in miles.	Remarks.
Rávi ...	Qilla Bhama Singh ...	...	Ferry.
	Faridábád	5	Do.
	Majháni	5	Do.
	Jhando	1	Do.
	Pir Aly	6	Do.
	Mári	6	Ferry and mooring place.
	Khái	6	Ferry.
	Alam Sháh	1	Do.
	Mehr Shahána ...	3	Do.
	Qatab Shahána ...	3	Do.
	Hakim ke Kathya ...	8	Do.
	Muhammad Shah ...	7	Do.
	Chicháwatni	8	Bridge of boats and mooring place.
	Kikrí Patrí	11	Ferry.
Sutlej...	Moháua Fordwáh ...	...	Ferry and mooring place.
	Shekhuke	8	Do.
	Bhila Maleke	6	Do.
	Ahloke	8	Do.
	Malkána	6	Do.
	Bhallu	8	Do.
	Sahnwáli	6	Do.
	Bhuk	8	Do.
	Mádhu	7	Do.
	Jamlera	5	Do.

Chapter IV, D.

Prices, Weights and Measures, and Communications.

Railways.

The North-Western Railway from Lahore to Multán runs through the district along the high central ridge, with stations at Satghara, Okára, 9 miles, Gamber, 8 miles, Yusafwála, 9 miles, Montgomery, 7 miles, Harappa, 12 miles, Chicháwatni, 7 miles, Kassowal, 10 miles.

Roads.

There are no metalled roads; but as there is no wheel traffic, the want is not felt. The district is traversed in all directions by fine broad unmetalled roads, some of which were cut through the jungle at the expense of the people, after the unsuccessful insurrection of 1857.

The principal roads are :—(1) The Customs line road, running from Jamlera on the Multán border, nearly parallel to the Sutlej through Pákpattan and Haveli to Rohela Ghát, opposite Fázilka, in the Sirsa district. (2) The Lahore and Multán trunk road, running close to the Rávi, on the left bank of the river. Traffic on this road has greatly decreased since the opening of the railway in 1865 ; many of the *seráis* along it are in bad condition and others have been closed altogther. But the road itself is in very fair order. (3) The road leading from Jhang, *viá* Kamália, Harappa, Kabír, and Pákpattan to the Sutlej. Speaking of it, Captain Elphinstone says :—

"Numerous caravans of merchants from Afghánistán frequent this route during the cold weather. They seldom dispose of their merchandise in the district, but, as far as I could ascertain, this road is generally selected by merchants who are anxious to arrive at their principal mart, Delhi, without the delay which would otherwise attend the unpacking of their wares at intermediate stations."

(4) The road from Harappa through Montgomery, Dipálpur and Basírpur to the ferry at Rohela Ghát. (5) The road from Pákpattan to Chunián, passing near Dipálpur and through Shergarh. (6) The road from Jhang through Gugera and Satghara to Wán Rádhárám, running thence to Ferozepore. (7), (8) and (9). The roads connecting Montgomery and Pákpattan, and Gugera and Pákpattan and Gugera and Dipálpur.

Bridges.

There is now no bridge of boats over the Rávi, the one at Chicháwatni has been abolished. The Nikki is bridged on all the main roads. There are bridges over the Khánwah canal at Hujra, Dipálpur, Nathu Shah, and Kacha Pakka. There is a bridge over the Upper Sohág Canal at Gáma Waghra, near Basírpur, and a foot bridge at Shah Nawázkhanwála. There are bridges over the Lower Sohág-Pára Canal at Amira Tejeka, Haveli and Káliwál and on the Dipálpur-Pákpattan and Montgomery-Pákpattan roads. The state of the roads in canal-irrigated tracts is far from satisfactory. The roads are traversed by deep water-courses, the owners of which have either constructed no bridges, or have laid down a few crooked branches of trees, with slight twigs and leaves filling up the interstices, and have thrown earth over the whole. As soon as the twigs rot, the unwary traveller runs a good chance of breaking his neck, at the same time that his horse breaks the bridge and his own leg. If the canals ran all the year round, this state of things would soon be altered. But in the cold weather, when officers are out in camp, the water-courses are dry, and the sides are sloped down ; or else the water-course is filled up ; and so the intolerable nuisance these ditches become in the hot weather is not properly appreciated.

Chapter IV, D.

Prices, Weights and Measures, and Communications.

Sarais, rest-houses and encamping grounds.

The district is not well provided with *seráis*. But the traffic is so slight that this want is little felt. There are rest-houses affording accommodation to European travellers in all important places. The accommodation is at present in most cases far from good.

The following table shows the principal roads of the district, together with the halting places on them, and the conveniences for travellers to be found at each :—

Route.	Halting places.	Distance in miles.	Conveniences for travellers.					
			Encamping ground.	Supply house.	Serai.	District rest-house.	Dák bungalow.	Police rest-house.
Multán to Lahore ...	Doburji	...	1	1	...	...	...	...
	Chicháwatni village ...	13	1	1	...	...	...	1
	Harappa do ...	13	1	1	1	...	...	1
	Muhammadpur ...	11	1	1	...	...	...	...
	Kaure Shah	9	1	1	...	...	...	...
	Núr Shah	3	...	...	...	1	...	...
	Akbar	7	1	1	...	1	...	...
	Mirak	15	1	1	...	...	...	...
	Chúchak	10	1	1	...	...	...	1
Jhang to Chichá-watni Railway Station.	Rajána	...	...	...	1	...	...	1
	Kamália	11	1	...	1	...	...	1
	Chicháwatni Railway Station	13	...	...	1	...	1	...
Montgomery to Dipálpur	Montgomery	...	1	1	1	...	1	...
	Rúkullan	15	...	...	...	1	...	...
	Dipalpur	18	1	...	1	1	...	1
Gugera to Jhang.	Gugera	...	...	...	...	1	...	...
	Bahlak	7	1	...	1	...	...	1
Gugera to Fázilka.	Gugera	...	...	...	...	1	...	...
	Okára	14	...	...	1	1	...	...
	Kálasan	8	...	...	1	...	...	...
	Dipálpur	8	1	...	1	1	...	1
	Basírpur	13	...	...	1	1	...	...
Pákpattan to Montgomery.	Pákpattan	...	...	...	2	1	...	...
	Núrpur	14	...	...	1	1	...	...
	Montgomery	15	1	1	1	...	1	...
Akbar to Ferozepore.	Akbar	...	1	1	...	1	...	...
	Satghara	13	1	...	1	...	...	1
Jamlera to Fázilka Customs road.	Jamlera	...	...	...	...	...	...	...
	Tibbi	9	1	...	...	...	...	1
	Pákpattan	24	...	...	2	1	...	...
	Haveli	20	...	...	1	...	...	1
	Jaimal Bazideka ...	19	...	...	...	...	...	...

Chapter IV, D.

Prices, Weights and Measures, and Communications.

Serais, rest-houses and encamping grounds.

There are also unmetalled roads from Chicháwatni to Pákpattan by Kabír, 44 miles ; from Chicháwatni to Jamlera on the Sutlej, *viá* Sheikh Fázil, 45 miles ; from Montgomery to Tibbi, *viá* Kabír and Kabula, 36 miles ; Hujra to Haveli, 24 miles ; Hujra to Atári 16 miles, Hujra to Wán Rádharám *viá* Shergarh, 17 miles ; Gugera to Saiadwála, 17 miles, and on to Bucheke, 17 miles, and Lahore.

There are no fixed halting stations on these roads. The road from Gugera to Jhang crosses the Rávi by a *ghát* at Mári. Good unmetalled roads run along the Khánwah, Upper Sohág and Lower Sohág-Pára canals. On the former there is a rest-house at Dipálpur, on the Upper Sohág rest-houses at Gudar Malkana, Táhir Kalán, 19 miles, Ladhewál, 12 miles, and Bunga Hayát, 17 miles, and on the Lower Sohág-Pára at Lálu Gudar Shahamad, 10 miles ; Haveli, 10 miles; Kalewal ; 13 miles, Chanwat, 17 miles; Jewan Shah, 11 miles, and Kaliána. In addition to those already mentioned there are district rest-houses at Shergarh and at Jandraka on the Gugera-Saiadwála road, and police rest-houses at Nautheh, Kiliánwála, Saiadwála, Bucheke, Hujra, Atári, Tibbi and Kabír. The two dàk bungalows are completely furnished and provided with servants. The district and police rest-houses are generally poorly furnished ; some of them have washing and cooking utensils, but no servants. The police rest-houses are small and very undesirable residences in the hot weather. The canal rest-houses are well and substantially built and comfortably furnished.

Post Offices.

There are 30 Imperial Post Offices—at Montgomery, Kamália, Chicháwatni, Tibbi, Harappa, Pákpattan, Chak Bába Khem Singh, Basírpur, Hujra, Dipálpur, Gugera, Chúchak, Saiadwála, Bucheke, Shergarh, Chicháwatni town, Jethpur, Atári, Jandraka, Faridabád, Okára, Boyleganj, Haveli, Shahnawáz, Fatehpur, Satghara, Jakhar, Chak Ahmedabad, Kabula and Malka Háns. All the post offices have money order offices. The Savings Bank offices are at Montgomery, Dipálpur, Gugera, Kamália Okára, Pákpattan, Chicháwatni, Chúchak, Tibbi and Atári.

Telegraph.

A line of telegraph runs along the whole length of the railway with a telegraph office at each station, also one from Montgomery to Pákpattan and one from Chicháwatni to Jhang with an office at Kamália.

CHAPTER V.

ADMINISTRATION AND FINANCE.

SECTION A.—GENERAL ADMINISTRATION.

Chapter V, A.

General Administration.

Executive and Judicial.

The executive administration of the Montgomery District is under the control of the Commissioner of Lahore; the judicial under that of the Divisional and Sessions Judge of Multán. The ordinary head-quarters staff of the district consists of a Deputy Commissioner and two Extra Assistant Commissioners. It is quite inadequate for the needs of the district, and a proposal is under consideration for strengthening it by the addition of another officer. Each tahsíl is in charge of a Tahsíldár assisted by a Náib. The village Revenue Staff is shown in the margin according to proposals lately submitted. There is only one Munsif in the district stationed at Montgomery, whose jurisdiction extends to the whole district. The statistics of civil and revenue litigation for the last five years are given in Table No. XXXIX.

Tahsíl.	Kanúngos.	Patwarís and Assistants.
Montgomery ...	3	41
Gugera	3	49
Dipalpur ...	4	82
Pákpattan ...	3	52
Total ...	13	224

Criminal, Police and Jails.

The Honorary Magistrates of the district are—

(*i*) Bába Khem Singh, K. C. I. E., who has 3rd class criminal and civil powers in his *jágir* villages in the Dipálpur tahsíl.

(*ii*) A Bench consisting of Sardár Buta Singh, zaildár, Báwa Uttam Singh, Muhammad Shahbáz Khan and Muhammad Amin Khan, who sit at Dipálpur exercising 3rd class criminal powers within the limits of the police *thánás* of Dipálpur, Haveli and Atári.

(*iii*) A Bench consisting of Lála Bhág Rái and Sheikh Muhammad Hussain, who sit at Pákpattan and exercise 2nd class criminal powers in certain portions of the Pákpattan tahsíl. Lála Bhág Rái also exercises 3rd class civil powers. The Police force is controlled by a District Superintendent of Police. There is one police zaildár in the district; he has charge of 24 villages and gets an allowance of Rs. 150 per annum. The strength of the force is 465, namely, 444 district and 21 municipal. In addition to this force there are 5 daffadárs and 21 chaukidárs, whose rates of pay are as follows :—Daffadárs Rs. 4, 5, 6, and 7 per mensem each; chaukidárs Rs. 3, 4 and 5

Chapter V, A.

General Administration.

per mensem each. There are also 25 police trackers, *viz.*, 1 sergeant 3rd grade, at Rs. 12 per mensem and 24 constables, 1st grade, at Rs. 7 per mensem each.

Criminal, Police and Jails.

The *thánas* or principal police jurisdictions and the *chaukís* or police outposts are as follows:—

TAHSIL MONTGOMERY—*Thánás.*—Montgomery, Harappa, Chichawatni, Kamáliá and Killianwálá. *Chaukís.*—Kaure Shah, Doburji, Rajána.

TAHSIL PAKPATTAN—*Thánas.*—Pákpattan, Tibbi and Kabír. *Chaukís.*—Núrpur and Jamlerá.

TAHSIL DIPALPUR—*Thánas.*—Dipálpur, Hujra, Atári and Haveli.

TAHSIL GUGERA—*Thánas.*—Gugera, Báhlak, Saiadwála, Bucheke, Chúchak, Okára. *Chaukís*—Merak, Satghara.

There is a cattle pound at each *thána* except Kamália and Pákpattan, and also at *chaukís* Kaure Sháh, Satghara, Jamlera and Núrpur. These are under the control of the police. The pounds at Kamália and Pákpattan are under the Municipal Committees. The district lies within the eastern circle, under the control of the Deputy Inspector-General of Police, at Lahore. The Sadar station adds to its other distinctions that of containing the largest Central Jail in the Province, from all parts of which convicts are received. The District and Central Jails are combined. The area is 48 acres. It contains accommodation for 1,600 prisoners, but the actual number of inmates at present is much more than this.

Table No. XL gives statistics of criminal trials, Table No. XLI of police inquiries, and Table No. XLII of convicts in jail for the last five years. The Giloi Biluches of the village of Giloi in the Montgomery tahsíl were declared a criminal tribe under Act XXVII of 1871 in May 1895. At the end of 1897 there were 64 adult males on the register.

Revenue, Taxation and Registration.

The gross revenue collections of the district for the last 14 years, so far as they are made by the Financial Commissioner, are shown in Table No. XXVIII, while Tables Nos. XXIX XXXV, XXXIV and XXXIII give further details for land-revenue, excise, income-tax, and stamps respectively. Table No. XXXIIIA shows the number and situation of Registration Offices. There are no central distilleries. The cultivation of the poppy is forbidden in this district.

Table No. XXXVI gives the income and expenditure from district funds. The District Board consists of 32 members, of whom 8 are *ex-officio* and the rest nominated by the Deputy Commissioner. The *ex-officio* members are the Deputy Commissioner, Civil Surgeon, both Extra Assistant Commissioners and all the Tahsíldárs. The President is the Deputy Commissioner, and the Secretary, the Senior Extra Assistant Commissioner. There are now no Local Boards.

Chapter V, A.

General Administration.

Revenue, Taxation and Registration.

Table No. XLV gives statistics for municipal taxation, while the municipalities themselves are noticed in Chapter VI. The income from Provincial properties for the last five years is shown below :—

Source of income.	1892-93.	1893-94.	1894-95.	1895-96.	1896-97.
	Rs.	Rs.	Rs.	Rs.	Rs.
Ferries with boat-bridges ...	3,400	4,050	3,769	4,668	5,731
Do. without do.	5,111	5,382	6,315	9,516	8,318
Staging bungalows, &c. ...	44	67	77	50	33
Encamping-grounds	...	...	...	...	...
Cattle-pounds	3,529	4,038	4,086	4,187	3,824
Nazúl properties...	...	...	...	...	...
Total ...	12,084	13,537	14,247	18,421	17,906

The ferries, bungalows, and encamping-grounds have already been noticed at pages 183—186 and cattle-pounds at page 188. There are no *nazúl* properties in this district from which any income is realized.

Figures for other Government estates are given in Table No. XVII, and they and their proceeds are noticed in Section B of this Chapter, in which the land-revenue administration of the district is treated of.

Statistics of land revenue.

Table No. XXIX gives figures for the principal items and the totals of land-revenue collections since 1886-87. Table No. XXXI gives details of balances, remissions and agricultural advances for the last fourteen years ; Table No. XXX shows the amount of assigned land-revenue ; while Table No. XIV gives the areas upon which the present land-revenue of the district is assessed. Further details as to the basis, incidence, and working of the current settlement will be found in the succeeding section of this Chapter.

Education.

Table No. XXXVII gives figures for the Government and aided, high. middle and primary schools of the district. There is one high school in the district, at Montgomery itself ; there are Anglo-Vernacular Middle schools at Kamália and Dipálpur, and vernacular Middle schools at Saiadwála, Hujra and Pákpattan. There are 24 primary schools ; at Harappa and Jhakhar in the Montgomery tahsil ; Jandraka, Satghara, Sadr Gugera, Faridábád, Kammán, Okára and Bucheke in the Gugera tahsil ; Shergarh, Shahnawáz, Basírpur, Kaler Mamand, Jethpur, Haveli, Dhuliáná and Mustafábád in the Dipálpur tahsil ; Malka Háns, Chak Bedi, Kabula, Boyleganj, Chak Mahdi Khan and Kaliána in the Pákpattan tahsil. In addition to the above there are 8 *zamíndári* schools ; at Núr Sháh and Murád ke Kathya in the Montgomery tahsil ; Bámán Bála in the Gugera tahsil ; Báhripur, Kandúwálá Serái, Atári, and Kúeke

Chapter V, A.

General Administration.

Education.

Baháwal in the Dipálpur tahsil; Pakka Sidhár in the Pákpattan tahsil; they are maintained from district funds. There is one girls' school in the district at Montgomery.

Besides these there is no kind of school in the district. The district lies within the Lahore Circle, and is in charge of the Inspector of Schools at Lahore. Table No. XIII gives statistics of education collected at the Census of 1891, and the general state of education has already been described at page 75.

Dispensaries.

Table No. XXXVIII gives separate figures for the last five years for each of the dispensaries of the district, which are situated at Montgomery, Kamália, Pákpattan, Tibbi, Dipálpur, Sháhnawáz, Sayadwála and Gugera. The first is in the immediate charge of an Assistant Civil Surgeon; the rest in that of Hospital Assistants. They are all under the general control of the Civil Surgeon. There is no leper asylum, lunatic asylum, or lock hospital in this district. The Civil Surgeon at Montgomery has civil charge of the station, and is also in charge of the Central Jail. The inspection of outlying dispensaries vaccination and sanitation is carried out by the Assistant Civil Surgeon.

The Montgomery dispensary was established in 1865; it is situated in the outskirts of the town of Montgomery, and is capable of accommodating 15 in-door sick—10 males and 5 females. The buildings consist of a female ward, a male ward, operation room and Assistant Surgeon's and servants' quarters. In the centre is the dispensary and store-room, and a garden for vegetables. The establishment consists of one Assistant Surgeon in charge, one compounder, one dresser, one paid apprentice compounder and menials.

The sick treated consist chiefly of Government officials and their families, and people from the town. The surrounding country being barren and uncultivated, there are very few agricultural patients.

The average daily attendance for last year (1897) was as follows:—In-door 7·49 men, 1·43 women, 1·09 children; out-door 44·67 men, 13·25 women, 24·90 children. The institution is supported partly by municipal and partly by district funds.

Kamália dispensary in the town of Kamália, a rather large one, is capable of accommodating 8 in-door sick—4 males and 4 females. It has a large out-door attendance, consisting in great part of people from the surrounding cultivated country; it seems well appreciated by the inhabitants. The buildings consist of a male and a female ward, a dispensing house, and quarters for the establishment; within the enclosure there is a large garden for fruits and vegetables. The establishment consists of one Hospital Assistant in charge, a compounder, one dresser and menials. The average attendance last year (1897) was: in-door 3·35 men, 0·42 women, and 0·27 children; and out-door: 33·57 men, 11·22 women, and 29·65 children. The institution is supported partly by municipal and partly by district funds.

Chapter V, A.

General Administration.

Dispensaries.

Pákpattan dispensary is capable of accommodating 12 in-door sick—8 males and 4 females; and has a large out-door attendance. The establishment consists of one Hospital Assistant in charge, a compounder, and menials. The average attendance last year (1897) was: in-door 4·01 men, 0·97 women, 0·18 children; and out-door 34·93 men, 12·52 women, and 26·28 children. The institution is supported partly by municipal and partly by district funds.

Tibbi dispensary was established in 1894. It has no separate accommodation for in-door sick. At the recommendation of the Deputy Commissioner, however, in-door patients who diet themselves are allowed to be kept in a spare room which is capable of accommodating three patients. The establishment consists of one Hospital Assistant, one compounder and menials. The average daily attendance last year (1897) was: in-door 0·86 men, 0·09 women, 0·02 children; and out-door: 16·02 men, 8·24 women, and 9·14 children. The institution is supported by district funds, and Rs. 300 per annum local subscription.

Dipálpur dispensary is capable of accommodating 12 in-door patients—8 males and 4 females. The establishment consists of one Hospital Assistant in charge, one compounder, one dresser, and menials. The average attendance last year (1897) was: in-door 5·89 men, 1·85 women, 0·49 children; and out-door: 40·77 men, 13·27 women, and 26·50 children. The institution is supported partly by municipal and partly by district funds.

Shahnawáz dispensary was established in 1891. The founder is a retired native military officer, Shahnawáz Khan, Khan Bahadur, who supplied quarters free, and invested a sum of Rs. 6,000 from the interest on which the pay of the Hospital Assistant is met. The rest of the expenditure is met from district funds, Shahnawáz Khan, however, rendering extra pecuniary help from time to time. The institution is not capable of giving any in-door relief. The establishment consists of one Hospital Assistant, one compounder, and menials. The average daily attendance last year (1897) was 19·26 men, 5·38 women, and 6·74 children.

Saiadwala dispensary was established in 1884. It is located at the old tahsíl building, and is capable of accommodating 10 in-door sick—6 males and 4 females. The establishment consists of one Hospital Assistant, one compounder, and menials. The average daily attendance last year (1897) was: in-door 3·71 men, 0·89 women, 0·13 children; and out-door 23·02 men, 11·28 women, and 17·52 children. The institution is supported by district funds with a local subscription of Rs. 84 per annum.

Gugera dispensary is capable of accommodating 5 in-door sick—3 males and 2 females. The establishment consists of a Hospital Assistant, a compounder, and menials. The average attendance last year (1897) was: in-door 2·47 men, and 0·81 women, and 0·38 children; and out-door: 17·20 men, 5·0 women,

Chapter V, B.

Land and Land Revenue.

Ecclesiastical.

and 9·23 children. The institution is supported by district funds.

There is a small church at Montgomery capable of seating about 70 persons. No Chaplain is posted here; but the Chaplain of Lahore visits the station occasionally.

Head-quarters of other Departments.

The North-Western Railway runs through this district. The head officers of this line are the Traffic Manager and the District Traffic Manager, stationed at Lahore and Multán respectively.

The Katora, Khánwah, Upper Sohág and Lower Sohág-Pára Canals are in charge of the Executive Engineer, Upper Sutlej Division, Inundation Canals, whose head-quarters are at Montgomery. They are under the control of the Superintending Engineer, Bári Doáb Circle, who is stationed at Amritsar. The road between Lahore and Multán, north of Montgomery, is in charge of the District Committee. The Executive Engineer, Provincial Division, Multán, is in charge of the public buildings of the district, and is subordinate to the Superintending Engineer at Lahore. There are no military buildings in this district. The telegraph lines and offices attached to the North-Western Railway are controlled by the Telegraph Superintendent at Lahore, and the Post Offices by the Superintendent of Post Offices at Multán. There is no Customs staff in this district. The forests are under the control of the Deputy Conservator of Forests, Montgomery division.

SECTION B.—LAND AND LAND REVENUE.

The Sikh revenue system.

During the Sikh monarchy this district was held either by important chiefs revenue-free, in return for certain feudal services rendered by them, or was farmed out to *ijárádárs*. The latter paid a fixed sum to Government, and made their own arrangements with the villages included in their farm. The *ijárádár* either sub-let part of his farm to others, or managed the collection of the revenue himself through agents or *kárdárs*. Till Sáwan Mal's time the system of *kan* or appraisement of the crop was the one generally followed. The calculation of the produce involved a good deal of haggling, and the amount entered was usually the result of a compromise. The produce due on account of revenue having been decided, it might be taken in cash or in kind. *Khálsa* revenue was invariably taken in cash. In other words, the cultivator had to buy from the Government agent the Government share of the produce, commonly at something over the market price. *Jágírdárs* very often took their share in kind. In the *kharíf* harvest, money was generally taken, and grain in the *rabi*. The proprietors of a village were allowed a share of the Government produce as *inám*. The amount varied very much. It depended on the agreement made by the *kárdár*. One yoke was released out of a number agreed on. If one yoke was released for every six existing, the proprietors got

Chapter V, B.

Land and Land Revenue.

The Sikh revenue system.

one-sixth of the Government grain as *inám jog*. Besides this, the proprietors got one or more wells or a share in a well, according to the size of the village, exempted from payment of revenue. This exemption was known as *inám-taraddudána*, and was a reward for exertion in the extension of cultivation. The conditions of the grant determined who was to enjoy it, occasionally the tenants also got an *inám*, generally one-eighth of the Government share. The proprietors collected from the tenants either by actual division of the crop, or according to the Government demand, in kind or cash. And when it was customary to take *málikána*, they got it in addition. Fixed cash assessments on a whole village were not made, but sometimes a well would be leased for a fixed sum; and isolated wells in the jungle were so leased, as a rule. The usual rate was Rs. 10 to Rs. 12; but a good well would pay Rs. 20. Sáwan Mal very frequently practised *batái* or actual division of the crop. *Munshis* or *mutsaddis* under the *kárdárs* put *thápis* to watch the stacked grain of every 5 or 6 wells. If the *thápis'* seal was found broken the cultivator was fined. The crop was then divided, and Sáwan Mal took the value of his share in cash. As far as can be ascertained, the system of *ináms* has ceased now entirely. The landowners who have taken the place of the Government have abandoned it. As regards Government, the *lambardári* allowance of 5 per cent. on the revenue represents the *inám* granted formerly to the proprietors.

Zabti crops.

Zabti crops paid so much per *kanál*, or were sold standing when the *kárdár* took his share of the price; or were treated as ordinary *nijkári* crops. The usual *zabti* rates were Rs. 8 per acre for tobacco, and Rs. 6 to Rs. 8 for the first year's cotton, and half that for the second year's crop from the same roots. It may be as well to say that these rates mean nothing, for if the fundamental principle of the Sikh system was, that the Government should take as much as ever it could, as often as it could, and wherever it could, the principle that a spade should on no account be called a spade was only second in importance to it, and was much more rarely violated. The advantages of this were, that the people were made to believe that great favours were being bestowed on them, while they were being taxed as heavily as possible; and that the subordinate officials were able to plunder the Government to their heart's content, as no one knew what their accounts meant. Thus a man would be charged Rs. 5 for 6 *kanáls* of cotton. The generous *kárdár* remitted half as *inám*, and then added Rs. 4-1-6 on account of extra cesses.

Abwáb or extra cesses.

These extra cesses or *abwáb* were levied both in kind and cash. The former class appears to have amounted to one-fourth or one-fifth of the Government share of wheat, and one-sixth of the inferior grains. The cash payments were generally according to a fixed scale. The more important of these extra cesses were the following: *nazar kánjan*, *sardár thánádár*, *topkhána*, *sarráfi*, *chilkána*, *jamábandi* and *khurák*. The *nazar kánjan*

Chapter V, B.

Land and Land Revenue.

Abwáb or extra cesses.

was a tax of Rs. 2 on each *kámil* well and derives its name from the upper cross-beam of a well. A *kámil* well was one with 8 yokes of bullocks; and a proportionate allowance was made for every yoke wanting to make up this number. The cess for the *sardár thánadár* was levied at varying rates as the *kárdár* saw fit. Of course, the *thánadár* did not get it. The cess *topkhána* was probably meant to aid in keeping up the Sikh artillery; it amounted to Rs. 2 per cent. on each *pakka* well. *Sarráfi* was levied at different rates, and was supposed to defray the cost of testing the money paid as revenue. *Chilkána* was a charge of one-half anna in the rupee on all cash payments except those made on account of *khurák, sarráfi* and *tirni*. The Sikhs had several sorts of rupees. The Nának Shahi, struck in S. 1884-85, was the final standard coin. Sixteen English rupees were worth fifteen Nának Shahi rupees. The other rupees were the Hari Singhia or Kashmír rupee, worth 8 annas in the rupee less than that of 1884-85; the rupee of 1837, worth one anna in the rupee less; the Morán Shahi rupee and that of 1860, worth Rs. 2 per cent. less, and the rupee of 1870 and 1872, worth 1 per cent. less. *Chilkána* was levied to make up the difference between the value of the standard and other rupees. It seems to have been taken on all kinds of rupees. The *jamábandi* was a charge for preparing the revenue roll. The *kárdár* charged what he pleased. *Khurák* was a cess of 4 annas on each well, and was expended in feeding the *káchhus* or measurers. Besides these items, one-half anna was charged for each sheep or goat as *tirni*, but cows and buffaloes were not taxed. *Káma* was a cess levied on artisans and *ahtráfi* on shop-keepers; the rates varied from Re. 1 to Rs. 2-4 on each shop. The principal *abwáb* levied in kind were *Akáli, kharch Brahmin, moharáná* and *chúngi*. The first amounted to 6 *topas* per well, and seems to have been originally intended for the support of the Amritsar Akális.* The *Brahmin, moharáná*, and *chúngi* cesses amounted altogether to $5\frac{1}{4}$ *paropis* in each *man* of the Government share. It does not appear for what these were originally contrived nor what *moharáná* means.

Green fodder.

The cultivators were allowed to grow green fodder as tenants are now. The *kárdár* used to claim his kanál at each harvest per well; this was known as *khírá*. He either took the *khírá*, or made the cultivator give him grain in exchange at the rate of 16 to 20 *mans* per acre. The *kárdár's man* consisted of 16 *topas*, of $2\frac{1}{2}$ *sérs* each. The *sér* weighed 92 rupees.

Transit duties.

Transit duties, called *laga*, were levied on merchandize coming in or going out of a town, whether sold or not. The rates varied, and were, as a rule, fixed with reference to the carriage employed; so much for each camel-load, donkey-load, &c. The right to collect this duty was farmed. The *kárdár* was not the *ex-officio* collector. But he sometimes managed to collect some-

---

* *Kharch* was a charge at the rate of 2 *topas* in the *man* on the Government share of the grain. It was collected to defray the cost of dividing the crops. It is still taken.

Chapter V, B.

Land and Land Revenue.

thing for himself under this head from the cultivators. This tax corresponds to the present *chúngi*.

Revenue of a well

It is almost impossible to make out what the Sikhs really used to get from a well. But in settled tracts they seem to have been able to extract between Rs. 50 and Rs. 60 from an average well. Of course the Sikh *kárdárs* looked after the revenue in a very different way to that in which an over-worked *tahsíldár* can, and the cultivators were assisted by the revenue officials much more than they are now. A man who did not exert himself got a very broad hint that if he did not cultivate as much land as was expected, he would have to make way for some one who would. If a man had more land than he could manage, the ruling power never hesitated about making a portion over to another, and gave no compensation. Then the people had to pay only a small amount when the season was bad and so managed to pull along under burdens which would break them down completely now.

The first and second summary settlements are thus described by Captain Elphinstone in paras. 95 and 96 of his report :—

The first summary settlement.

"The first summary settlement was based on the papers of the former Sikh *kárdárs*. Mr. Cocks, C. S., who superintended this work, having no other data to guide him, naturally fell into some errors as to the capabilities of the different villages. His assessment for the whole district amounted to Rs. 3,70,819,—a sum which could probably have been realised without difficulty from this district if it had been more equally distributed. But the Sikh returns, which formed the ground-work of his assessment, were eminently defective for this purpose, for the following reasons :—1*st*, a system of favouring certain villages and *zamindárs* universally prevailed under the Sikh rule; 2*nd*, the authority of the Government in that portion of the district owned by the Jat tribes was by no means very secure, and the revenue demand was therefore not strictly enforced for political reasons; and 3*rd*, the amount of produce obtained by *batai* on *sailáb* lands in good seasons by no means represents the amount in cash which could be reasonably demanded from such tracts for a series of years. The sudden fall in prices also, which took place after annexation, and the scarcity of money occasioned by the constant remittances down-country of a large army of foreigners stationed in the Punjab, seriously affected the resources of the people. As, notwithstanding all these adverse circumstances, the reductions given at the time of the second summary settlement were by no means very considerable, the *jama* of Mr. Cocks' Settlement may be said to have been rather moderate.

Second summary settlement.

"The second summary settlement was commenced by Major Marsden in 1852, and amounted altogether to Rs. 3,23,099-12-10, including *jagirs*. The collections and balances of this settlement form the chief basis of the present revised assessment. The data by which Major Marsden was guided were necessarily somewhat imperfect, but his local knowledge obtained by inspecting personally nearly every estate, and the reliable information he contrived to elicit from *zamindárs* and former officials, enabled him to adjust the demand with a considerable degree of fairness. In *parganah* Gugera especially the relative equity with which the *jamas* had been distributed was very remarkable. Changes, however, subsequently took place which materially affected the condition of various parts of the district. In *parganah* Hujra the alterations on the Khánwah Canal reduced one circle of villages to about one-half of their former cultivation, and greatly enhanced the prosperity of others, which previously had derived no benefit from the canal. In *parganah* Gugera, the *sailab* of the Rávi gradually diminished in the whole tract north of the *sadr* station; and in *parganah* Pákpattan a similar change occurred in a portion of the *sailab* land. *Jagir* estates were not brought under assessment, as the *jagirdárs* continued to realise by *batai*. No modification was made in the assumed value at which they had been estimated at annexation. I mention this circumstance, because the reductions of *jama* now

Chapter V, B.

Land and Land Revenue.

Second summary settlement.

apparent in two *parganahs*, are in great part made up of alterations in the assessment of these *jagír* estates, their original or estimated values having been found, without exception, far above their present capabilities. In addition to the returns of former collections and balances, Major Marsden was aided by rough measurements conducted through the agency of the *tahsildárs* and *kánúngos*. No attempt was made to record separate fields or other details of cultivation, and the whole process had very little pretension to accuracy, but it was, no doubt, often useful as a means of comparison with other sources of information."

The correct figures for the assessment of the first and second summary settlements, excluding *jágírs*, were as follows by tahsíls :—

Tahsil.	First summary settlement.	Second summary settlement.
	Rs.	Rs.
Montgomery	76,144	60,309
Gugera	76,411	76,412
Dipálpur	1,75,571	1,33,063
Pákpattan	40,157	42,693
Total ...	3,68,283	3,12,477

The regular settlement.

In 1852, Mr. Vans Agnew was sent to Hujra to commence the regular settlement. He submitted a report on the assessment of tahsíl Hujra, in which he proposed a fluctuating revenue for canal and *sailába* lands.

Assessment of canal lands.

In the Sikh times the Khánwah and Lower (Kuhna) Soháɡ Canals supplied certain villages in this district with water. It was not till 1843 that any water-rate was levied. The rate then imposed was one anna per *kanál* on crops that came to maturity, and applied only to the Khánwah. Under English rule this rate was continued. At first a farm used to be given of this tax, and yielded on an average Rs. 9,000 to Rs. 10,000 annually. The charge was extended to the Lower Soháɡ. Mr. Vans Agnew in 1855 thus described his proposed method of fluctuating assessment :—

"I have fixed two *jamas* for every village, the one upon all *barrah* or well lands, which can be cultivated without the aid of inundation from the rivers or canals, to be *permanent*, and to be considered the fixed demand until the expiry of the period of settlement ; and the other upon all *sailába* to be *variable* and under the name of *ábiána* in canal lands, and of river *sailába jama* in those subject to the influence of the Sutlej, to fluctuate with the uncertain inundation, and to be annually revised."

The variable rates proposed were, per acre, Re. 1-11 in Dipálpur, Re. 1-8 in Hujra, and annas 12 in Basirpur *chaks*. Along the river they ranged from Re. 1-10 to annas 6 per acre. This scheme was suggested on account of the uncertainty of the

Chapter V, B.

Land and Land Revenue.

Assessment of canal lands.

river inundations and canal water supply. As regards the canals, Mr. Vans Agnew wrote :—

"The irrigation they afford is uncertain and constantly varying. Firstly in the aggregate annual volume of water they carry. Secondly, in the quantity of water they supply to each village. Thirdly, in the time when they yield that supply. Fourthly, in consequence of their being in a transition state fresh arrangements of the canal officers continually altering the direction of the water supply."

His proposals were unfortunately rejected. The Financial Commissioner, in 1856, thus laid down the principle to be adopted :—

"In the river *sailáb* lands a moderate assessment which the proprietors could be able to pay in ordinary years; in the canal villages, a division of the demand between land rent and *ábiána* in such proportion as to represent with proximate correctness their relative values, the assessment at the same time being fixed at so moderate an amount that no reduction of *ábiána* should become necessary in ordinary years."

Assessment data.

The principle, in short, apparently was that the *ábiána* was to be remissible on failure of canals by the district officers on their own authority; the *mál* was to be collected whether the canals failed or not. Early in 1856, Captain Elphinstone was placed in charge of the settlement. He assessed the whole district. "From the estimated gross produce per acre, the proprietor's share, varying from one-half to one-sixth, was deducted, and after allowing 25 per cent. for extra expenses and 10 per cent. for the loss of conversion into cash, two-thirds of the remainder were assumed as the Government demand and entered as produce rates." Wells in tracts where cultivation mainly depended on them, were divided into three classes : "the 1st class consisted of *pakka* wells with six and eight yokes and an area of from 30 to 50 acres of well-land; the 2nd class of wells with four or five yokes and from 20 to 30 acres of well-land; and the 3rd class with a less number of yokes than four, and a very limited extent of irrigated area."

Assessment circles or *chaks*.

The *parganahs* were divided into assessment circles or *chaks* chiefly with reference to "the nature of the irrigation, and, to some extent, * * *, the peculiarities of soil and productiveness which prevailed in different tracts."* As cash rents did not exist, the revenue rates were calculated in the following manner. The villages in each *chak*, which were generally admitted to have been fairly assessed, were selected; and the Settlement Officer satisfied himself that general opinion was correct. The cultivated area of these villages was divided into classes according to the prevailing mode of irrigation, as *sailába*, *cháhi*, *nahri*, and *báráni*. The relative value of these classes was ascertained from the *zamíndárs*. In tahsíl Gugera, *báráni* was valued at one-half *cháhi*, in Pakpattan and Hujra at not more than one-fifth or one-sixth. The total *jamas* were next distributed over the classes of land according to the ascertained relative value of the latter. The average rate per acre, thus obtained for each class in the standard estates, was applied to

Revenue rates.

* These assessment circles, with the rates adopted, are shown in a map attached to Mr. Purser's Settlement Report.

Chapter V, B.

Land and Land Revenue.

Soil-rates.

the same class in the other estates, and the *jama* thus obtained constituted the revenue rate *jama* of each village. Soil-rates were not fixed, partly because the returns of soils were inaccurate, and partly because productiveness depends but little here on the natural qualities of the soil itself. The fact of the soil being good or bad was, however, kept in view in assessing the individual villages.

Canal assessment.

The villages irrigated by the inundation canals in the Sutlej tahsíls were assessed in the prescribed manner. Captain Elphinstone described the process thus :—" In the canal villages the demand has been divided between land and water rent ; and the relative value has usually been assumed as bearing to each other the proportion of 2 to 3." A few villages were exempted from the system of fixed *ábiána* and in their case and in the case of land coming under irrigation subsequently to settlement the customary rate of 8 annas per acre was to be charged.

Financial result of the Regular Settlement.

The assessment of the regular settlement by tahsíls was as follows :—

Tahsíl.	*Assessment.*
	Rs.
Gugera	71,032
Montgomery...	85,925
Dipálpur	1,34,578
Pákpattan	47,530
Total ...	3,39,065

This was inclusive of *ábiána* and Rs. 24,198 and Rs. 580 canal *ábiána* in tahsíls Dipálpur and Pákpattan, respectively. Since the second summary settlement 20 villages paying a revenue of Rs. 4,082 had been transferred from Lahore to the Gugera district. Their *jamas* are included in the above total. The regular settlement did not work satisfactorily. The revenue imposed by it was not heavy ; but the settlement did not get fair play. It had been sanctioned for 10 years with effect from Kharíf 1857, and at the end of that period the condition of part of the district was so bad that it was considered advisable to commence the revised settlement at once.

The principal changes in the circumstances of the district and their causes are noted below. The following table compares the number of villages and the areas of the regular settlement of 1857 with the state of things as ascertained at the revised settlement of 1871-72 :—

Chapter V, B.

Land and Land Revenue.

Financial result of the Regular Settlement.

Name of tahsil.		Number of villages.	AREA IN ACRES.								
			Muaf.	Barren or waste.	Culturable.	Lately thrown out of cultivation.	Cultivated.				Total area.
							Irrigated.	Sailaba.	Barani.	Total.	
Gugera ...	1857	370*	1,877	19,341	121,987	13,222	39,033	37,762	8,976	85,771	242,108
	1871-72	549	819	26,387	144,514	20,659	36,852	21,471	8,056	66,379	258,758
Montgomery ...	1857	271*	1,544	10,455*	100,701*	8,718	18,456	67,721	2,504	88,681	210,100
	1871-72	493	1,287	16,506	130,591	16,882	16,646	41,850	1,134	59,630	224,896
Pákpattan ...	1857	360*	1,002	22,804	136,694	32,281	38,737	13,499	6,144	58,380	251,161
	1871-72	512	552	32,636	182,512	23,071	33,423	9,802	6,079	49,304	288,075
Dipálpur ...	1857	452*	3,366	23,344	228,784	25,282	119,307	37,603	19,266	176,176	456,052
	1871-72	612	2,053	47,699	229,526	33,689	170,645	9,289	9,629	189,563	502,530
District Total ...	1857	1,153*	7,799	75,944	588,166	79,503	215,533	156,585	36,890	409,008	1,160,420
	1871-72	2,166	4,711	123,228	687,143	94,301	257,566	82,412	24,898	364,876	1,274,259

* These figures are doubtful.

Chapter V, B.

Land and Land Revenue.

Financial result of the Regular Settlement.

From this it appears that the number of villages had increased by one-half and the total area by 113,839 acres, or nearly 10 per cent. The irrigated area had increased by 42,033 acres, or 19·5 per cent. On the other hand, there had been a falling off of—

74,173 acres, or 47·4 per cent. in the *sailába* cultivation;
11,992 „ „ 32·5 „ of *baráni* cultivation; and of
44,132 „ „ 10·8 „ of total cultivation.

The causes of these changes were :—(1) Grants of waste land and location of new estates on them; (2) Extension of the inundation canals; (3) Failure of the river inundations; (4) Bad seasons. The punishment inflicted in the Mutiny (see page 49) no doubt affected the prosperity of some of the villages; and particularly of the Joya estates on the lower Sutlej.

Changes in population.

Before considering these causes the changes in the population of the different tahsils may be noticed. The census of 1854 showed the population to be 308,020. Adding 3,304 on account of villages received, and deducting 1,826 on account of villages transferred, there remain 309,496 persons as the former population. The following table shows its distribution and the subsequent changes :—

Name of tahsil.	Population.		Increase.	
	Formerly.	By Census of 1868.	Number.	Percentage.
Gugera	81,067	95,410	14,343	17·7
Montgomery	72,940	76,453	3,513	4·8
Pákpattan	53,208	57,735	4,527	8·5
Dipálpur	102,281	129,839	27,558	27·0
District Total ...	309,496	359,437	49,941	16·13

The population remained stationary in the cis-Rávi *sailába* tracts of Montgomery, and in the well-irrigated Shergarh circle in Dipálpur; otherwise there was a general falling off in the *sailába* tracts, and a considerable increase in the well-irrigated and canal circles. The increase in the parts of Dipálpur and Pákpattan irrigated by the canals was especially large. It was in these parts that most of the grants alluded to above had been made.

Grants of waste lands. Injurious results.

These grants were allotments of Government waste lands. They were made either to men of the district or to outsiders who were supposed to have claims on Government. In the former case they were scarcely ever of large extent. The area allowed was 50 acres if the applicant proposed to sink a single-wheeled well, and 100 acres if a double-wheeled well was to be constructed. In the latter case, the grants were rarely small, but ranged from 500 to several thousand acres. Sinking wells

Chapter V, B.

Land and Land Revenue.

Grants of waste lands. Injurious results.

was quite a secondary consideration here. These applicants would have turned up their noses at land where canal-irrigation was not available. What they wanted was a nice bit of low-lying land, with a *jama* of a few annas an acre, and as much canal water at 8 annas an acre as they chose; and they generally got it. Of course, they would not cultivate themselves, so they had to look out for tenants, and the simplest—indeed the only—way to get tenants was to decoy them away from the old established villages. To get an advance of money, to be under the protection of a man on good terms with the district officers, to have fine new land and lots of canal-water with rent below the average, were great things for the tenants; and so he left his old landlord to shift for himself and settled with the grantee. No wonder things looked very well at first. There was an increase of revenue and an apparent increase of cultivation. It was not long, however, before the mischief that was being done was perceived. The migratory character of the tenant population has already been noticed at page 98. From the earliest days of our rule it had been a subject of anxiety to the revenue officers, and had repeatedly been brought to the notice of the authorities Still grants were made, till in a district where barely one-third of the area within village limits was under the plough, about 113,000 acres more were added to the lands clamouring for cultivators to till them. When the injurious effect of these new grants on the older villages became clear, it was proposed to remedy them, not by stopping the grants, but by putting heavy burdens in the shape of revenue, and price of timber cleared away, on the lessees. But there was a mania for acquiring land in those days; and land anywhere near the canal would have been taken on any terms. So this plan had little success in stopping applications. It succeeded, however, in ruining the applicants. The supply of water in the canals was not unlimited; and the later comers found it more difficult to get any; the land near the canal had been appropriated, and more unfavourably situated plots had to be accepted. The little capital of the applicants was swallowed up in paying an exorbitant revenue, instead of being spent in sinking wells and making the land yield some return. In 1872, the Punjab Government directed that in future grants should be made only in special cases and after reference to Government. On inquiry during settlement operations in 1874 it appeared that 182 estates were lying uncultivated, or more than one estate in every twelve. Of these, 102 were new grants. A few of the grants were then resumed on the lessees refusing to take up the new *jamas*. There were then 1,953 wells lying idle, which could have been brought into use at a small cost, and would have given employment to 9,765 cultivators and 11,718 yoke of bullocks.

Extension of the inundation canals.

The great demand for land was, no doubt, chiefly caused by the extension of the inundation canals, and the enormous profits made by those who were lucky enough to have land within the influence of the new supply of water thus provided, which was

Chapter V, B.

Land and Land Revenue.

Failure of the Lower Soház Canal.

freely distributed at 8 annas an acre, no matter what crop was grown. While the Khánwah and the Upper Soház Canals were being extended, and the people on their banks were, in most places, making their fortunes, the villages on the lower (*kuhná*) Sohág were being ruined. Their case is instructive, and shows how light *jamas* are no certain guard against deterioration. At the regular settlement, 26 villages on this canal were assessed at Rs. 3,613 *mál* and Rs. 1,209 *ábiána*. The cultivated area was 9,363 acres. In 1860-61, Rs. 20 per cent. were taken off the *mál jama* and added to *ábiána*. This did no good. In 1866 the cultivated area had fallen to 2,652 acres, and a new assessment became necessary. The revenue was reduced 33 per cent. and the *abiána* made fluctuating. Even in 1874 many of these villages were in bad condition.

Failure of *sailab.*

It is, however, unlikely that the extension of the canals or the grants of waste lands would have done any serious mischief anywhere had the *sailáb* not failed. If the *sailáb* were to re-visit the river villages, all the well-irrigated villages would break down at once. All the cultivators would be off to the rivers. The tenants in canal villages would hesitate at first, but if the *sailáb* showed signs of permanency, they would go too. Canal water is simply *sailáb* under more or less control, with advantages and disadvantages due to this control. On the canal, as a rule, only autumn crops can be raised and brought to maturity with canal water; cultivators have to pay for this water and to assist in clearing out the water-courses. On the river they escape the labour and payment, and can raise the more valuable spring crops. And in addition, the lands along the river offer better grazing grounds than do the more inland tracts. In 1871, when the Khánwah failed, and there was an unusual amount of *sailáb* on the river-banks in the one village of Dipálpur 70 tenants abandoned their holdings and settled in river villages. The nature of the seasons has already been discussed at page 21.

Rise in prices.

The great rise in prices, which had taken place in this district as well as elsewhere, deserved the most attentive consideration. Where rents are not paid in cash, but in kind, without any reference to the money value of the share received by the landlord, the rise or fall in prices is even more important to the person fixing a money assessment than it is in tracts where cash rents are the rule. The figures have been given already at page 178. The period of 15 years, from 1842 to 1856, may be looked on as that the prices of which would have been regarded at the settlement of 1857; and the second period, from 1856-71, as subsequent to that settlement. The percentage of rise, in the second period, of average prices over those of the first period is as regards—

Cotton	...	37 per cent.	China	...	37 per cent.
Jowár	...	28 „ „	Wheat	...	37 „ „
Rice	...	22 „ „	Gram	...	15 „ „
Kangni	...	30 „ „			

Chapter V, B.

Land and Land Revenue.

Rise in prices.

On this point Mr. Purser wrote in 1874 :—

"Another question which arises is, whether the landlord's share of the produce is large or smaller now than it used to be. Of course, the decrease in cultivated area causes the actual income of the landlords to be smaller; but does the income in kind now enjoyed by the proprietors bear the same proportion to that they enjoyed at last settlement as the present cultivated area does to the area then cultivated? I think, if anything, it is less. More fodder has to be grown than formerly; for cultivation has to a great extent forsaken the rivers where natural fodder was abundant, and has increased in the inland part of Dipálpur, where pasturage is scanty. Again the productive powers of the land cannot have been improved by ten or twelve years' more cropping. And the new grants have tended to reduce the share of the produce obtained by the proprietors. No doubt, canal cultivation has to a considerable extent been substituted for *sailáb* and *báráni* cultivation. Probably the canal is superior to the *sailáb*; though usually the *kharif* cannot hold its ground against the *rabi*; the change, as regards the *báráni* cultivation is certainly for the better. In any case, as regards this matter, there is nothing to warrant an increase of assessment."

Revision of settlement, 1874 A.D.

In 1868 the revised settlement was commenced under the superintendence of Mr. (now Sir Charles) Roe, who assessed the Gugera and Montgomery tahsíls. In 1870 Mr. Purser was put in charge, who completed the work, and reported upon it in 1874. Owing to the fact that the assessment was made by two different officers, and that changes were introduced during the operation in the system of settlement, the processes and results cannot be presented in as compact a form as is possible in the case of most other districts. But the following paragraphs, taken from the final report by Mr. Purser, give the most important facts. Pages 156 to 219 of that report contain most detailed accounts of the several assessment circles, of their condition at settlement, and of their past history, and of the basis and nature of the assessment of each.

Rávi tahsíls. Revenue rates.

The system of entirely fixed assessments was maintained in the Rávi tahsíls at the revised settlement. The revenue rates on which the assessments were based consisted—

(1) Of a lump *ábiána* per well in use which varied from Rs. 8 to Rs. 12 in different circles; (2) a rate on all land under cultivation (*i.e.*, cropped at the time of measurement) which ranged from 8 annas to Re. 1 per acre; (3) a rate on all new fallow of 4 annas or 6 annas per acre.

Tahsíl Gugera. Assessment circles.

The assessment circles into which Mr. Roe divided the Gugera tahsil were—

Cis-Rávi.—(1) Bet Purána Gugera—land depending mainly on *sailáb* from the Rávi, and lying next the Montgomery *parganah*.

(2) Bet Urár—land depending mainly on *sailáb* from the Rávi, and lying next the Lahore district.

(3) Shumáli Ganji—high *bangar* land depending entirely on wells; adjoining Bet Urár, but further inland.

(4) Ganji Khás } containing only a few scattered wells
(5) Ganji Janúbi } in the *bar*.

Trans-Rávi.—(1) Bet Pár—the *sailáb* of the Rávi.

(2) Cháhi Pár—lands lying between the Deg and Rávi.

(3) Deg—lands watered by the Deg.

(4) Sandal Bár—containing scattered wells.

Chapter V, B.

Land and Land Revenue.

Tahsíl Gugera. Assessment.

The table below shows Mr. Roe's assessment of tahsil Gugera. The initial demand shown in the last column was to be increased after ten years by Rs. 4,294. Taking the tahsil as a whole, there was an immediate reduction of Rs. 3,681, or 4·7 per cent. on the demand for 1870-71. Extra cesses reduced the decrease little more than one per cent, while the addition of local rates made the actual result an enhancement of the burden on the land—

Name of *chak.*	*Jama* of 1870-71.	*Estimates.*				*Proposed by Settlement Officer.*	*Fixed by Settlement Commissioner.*
		Tahsildar's.	Produce.	Plough.	Rate.	Initial.	Initial.
	Rs.	Rs.	Rs.	Rs.	Rs.	Rs.	Rs.
Bet Purána Gugera	18,656	16,670	22,492	16,950	18,069	16,808	17,423
Bet Urar ...	12,874	13,306	14,538	13,122	11,645	11,948	12,697
Shumáli Ganji ..	6,244	6,129	8,025	7,320	5,118	5,894	6,193
Total Cis-Rávi ..	37,773	36,105	15,055	37,392	34,832	34,450	36,313
Bet Pár ...	21,744	20,845	22,861	20,378	16,105	18,845	19,815
Deg ..	7,041	7,277	9,747	8,512	6,638	6,578	7,027
Cháhi Pár ...	4,595	5,037	6,235	4,536	3,875	4,300	4,540
Sandal Bár ..	477	450	457	450	399	397	430
Total Trans-Rávi	33,857	33,899	39,320	23,874	27,017	30,120	31,812
Total ...	71,630	70,004	84,375	71,266	61,849	64,570	68,125
Scattered Wells.							
Bet Purána Gugera	1,191	1,041	1,705	2,080	1,710	1,043	1,138
Shumáli Ganji ..	1,823	1,689	2,537	2,148	963	1,548	1,625
Ganji Khás ...	165	60	50	64	43	150	160
Ganji Janúbi ...	109	109	359	264	135	107	109
Deg ...	1,681	1,750	2,955	2,792	1,413	1,670	1,721
Cháhi Pár ...	149	160	292	174	200	159	160
Sandal Bár ..	1,343	1,372	1,997	2,770	960	1,286	1,312
Total Wells ..	6,401	6,181	9,595	10,292	5,366	5,963	6,225
Total *Parganah* ...	78,032	76,185	94,270	81,558	67,215	70,533	74,350

Tahsíl Montgomery. Assessment circle.

The assessment circles into which tahsil Montgomery was divided are thus described by Mr. Roe, in allusion to Mr. Elphinstone's division into four circles, consisting respectively of the *sailáb* and *cháhi* lands on either side of the river:—

"A re-arrangement has been made of the assessment circles. In the alluvial or Bet *chaks*, as they are now called, it was found by experience that at each end of the *parganah* the estates were superior to those in the middle; accordingly on the Gugera side, the Bet Núr Shah circle, and on the Multán side, the Bet Chichawatni circle, were marked off. Each of these circles contain lands on both sides of the river. The alluvial land in the centre forms two more Bet *chaks*, the trans-Rávi the Bet Pár *chak*, and the cis-Rávi the Bet Harappa. As regards the well *chaks*, all the trans-Rávi wells lying beyond the Bet *chaks* have been formed as before into one assessment circle, which is called the Sandal Bár circle. On this side of the Rávi, the former *cháh—cháhi*—Harappa has been divided into three circles, the wells being grouped according to their situation with reference to the high ridge of the Ganji Bár; those lying to the north of this ridge forming the Ganji Shumáli *chak*; those to the south, the Ganji Janúbi, and those on the ridge itself, the Ganji Khás. These *chaks* are merely a continuation of the Gugera *chaks* of the same name."

Tahsíl Montgomery. Assessment.

The table below shows Mr. Roe's assessment. Taking the tahsil as a whole, there was a decrease in the initial assessment of Rs. 6,219, or 7 per cent., which extra cesses reduced to 3·5 per cent. But the demand was to be increased by Rs. 4,677 after ten years.

Chapter V, B.

Land and Land Revenue.

Tahsíl Montgomery. Assessment.

Name of chak.	Demand of 1870-71.	Estimates.					New Initial.
		Tahsíldár.	Ex. Assist. Commr.	Plough.	Produce.	Rate.	
	Rs.	Rs.	Rs.	Rs.	Rs.	Rs.	Rs.
1. Bet Núr Shah	30,067	30,137	28,270	22,787	33,545	24,794	28,461
2. Bet Chíchawatni ...	4,999	5,310	5,300	8,469	6 384	6,476	5,357
3. Bet Harappa	17,340	17,622	20,020	25,200	24 310	19,384	18,597
4. Bet Pár	26,035	23,914	20,377	23,598	15,987	14,858	19,814
5. Ganji Shumáli	2,647	2,729	2,745	3,682	2,644	2,393	2,810
6. Ganji Janúbi	509	548	480	678	640	375	540
7. Sandal Cháhi	2,339	2,353	2,370	2,120	2,495	2,055	2,153
8. Ganji Khás	238	278	391	132	74	106	223
Total ...	84,174	82,883	79,953	86,660	86,079	70,341	77,955

Assessment of canal lands in the Sutlej tahsíls.

Before assessing the two Sutlej tahsils, Dipálpur and Pákpattan, in respect of the land revenue, it was necessary to decide the rates which were to be paid by the people for canal water, and the principles on which these rates were to be fixed and collected. The system adopted at the regular settlement described at pages 196 and 197 had not worked satisfactorily. The people had no object in economising water; and they wasted it. It was found that many villages were paying next to nothing for their water. The canal tracts were not bearing anything like a fair share of the public burdens. And the revenue credited to the canals was far from equalling the expenditure incurred in keeping them up. It was also known that the prosperity of the canal tracts depended entirely on the canals; and that if the canals were abandoned, the country would relapse into jungle. It was therefore only fair that the canal rates should be raised. A good deal of correspondence took place on the subject; and the result was the adoption of the main principle of Mr. Vans Agnew's scheme. Each village was to be assessed at a sum which would represent what it could fairly pay from its natural products, *báráni* and well cultivation. This was to be fixed land revenue. Besides this fixed *jama*, villages taking canal water were to pay for it separately. The area irrigated was to be ascertained by annual measurements, and the rates of charge were to vary with the crops grown. If the crops did not come to maturity owing to the failure of the canal, no *ábiána* was to be paid. In case of partial failure of crops, partial remissions might be made. Lands irrigated by lift were to pay half the rates fixed for lands irrigated by flow. The amount payable each year was to be announced to the

Chapter V, B.

Land and Land Revenue.

Assessment of canal lands in the Sutlej Tahsíls.

lambardârs by the canal officer. The proposed arrangement was sanctioned with some modifications. No portion of the fluctuating revenue was to be credited as proposed to the canal departments; but there were to be "three sub-heads under the general head of land revenue. Under the first of these sub-heads will be shown the fixed *báráni* assessment, or the rate which would be leviable on unirrigated land; under the second the fixed assessment on lands irrigated by wells; while under the third sub-head will be shown the fluctuating revenue derived from lands irrigated by canals. This last will be the amount which the irrigation department will be entitled to show in their administration departmental accounts as the financial result of the canals under their charge." The rates adopted are given below.

Assignments of canal revenue.

Jágírdárs were to receive the whole revenue of their villages credited under the first two sub-heads, and one half of that shown under the third sub-head, the other half representing approximately what would elsewhere be separately charged as water-rate. As regards cesses, it was decided that the people in this tract should only pay at half the ordinary rates for the—

Extra cesses on canal revenue.

(1) *Patwári's* cess,
(2) *Lambardár's* cess,
(3) *Ala lambardár's* cess,
(4) *Zaildár's* cess,

and that Government should contribute out of land revenue an amount equal to that paid by the people. Formerly only the *patwári's* cess was realized on the *ábiána jama*, fixed or fluctuating. Subsequently the local cess also was charged on the fixed *ábiána*. This rule was to apply to *jágír* villages also. The other authorized cesses were to be paid on, and over and above, the entire Government demand by the occupants of land.

Water-rates.

The rates sanctioned in 1874 were for five years only; revised rates were sanctioned by the Government of India with effect from the *kharíf* crop of 1880, and continued in force up to Kharíf 1897; they were as follows:—

Class.	Crop.	Rate per acre.	Class.	Crop.	Rate per acre.
		Rs. A.			Rs. A.
I	Rice	3 0	III.—*contd.*	*Kangni*	1 2
	Gardens			*China*	
	Chillies (red pepper)			*Sowánk*	
II	Cotton	2 0		*Mash*	
	Melons			*Moth*	
	Sugarcane			Indigo	
	Til			Turmeric	
	Hemp			All other *kharíf* crops not otherwise mentioned	
III	Indian corn (*makkai*)	1 2	IV	All *rabi* crops	0 14
	Bajra			Plantations	
	Múnj			Vegetables	
	Jowar		V	Fallow land	0 10
	Charri			Lands ploughed but not sown	
				Grasses	

NOTE.—The above rates were for *flow* irrigation. Irrigation by *lift* was charged at half the above rates.

Chapter V, B.
Land and Land Revenue.
Water-rates.

As a rule, the *rabi* crops can get only one watering, which is not sufficient to bring them to maturity, and recourse is had to well irrigation; on this account the rate was fixed low. On the same principle the light rate on sugarcane is explained.

In actual practice remissions for failed crops have been allowed only in the *kharíf;* the canals not being responsible for the ripening of the *rabi* crops.

Canal management.

A brief description of the arrangements for irrigation from the Sutlej Inundation Canals may conveniently be given here. On the Khánwah and Upper Sohág Canals there is but little irrigation by *jhallárs,* but a good deal on the Lower Sohág-Pára in Dipálpur. If a village wants canal water it has to apply for an opening into the canal. This opening is called a *muhana.* In fixing the position of the opening the people are guided by the fact that the country slopes down from north to south and from east to west. Water-courses are always called *chhárs,* but really there are two kinds, the *chhár* and the *takki.* The size of the opening of the *takki* is half that of the *chhár.* The brick opening of a *chhár* is 2 feet broad by 4 feet high; that of a *takki* was 1 foot broad by 4 feet high. Thus a *takki* gets about half as much water as a *chhár.* But it was found that it was not possible to clean out an opening only 1 foot broad and perhaps 15 feet long; so the opening was made 2 feet square. This ingenious arrangement gave a *takki* almost as much water as a *chhár.* When applying for an opening the estimated cost of making the brick head has to be deposited with the canal officer, who makes the head and refunds any balance there may be. The land required for the water-course from the canal to the irrigating village is obtained by agreement or under the Act. It has hitherto been the custom for it to remain the property of the original owners, who take the trees and spontaneous products on the banks of the water-course, and have a right of re-entry on the *chhár* being abandoned, while the irrigators have a right of occupation in the land transferable with the land irrigated from the water-course. When a *chhár* is owned by more than one village, the water is divided according to the expenditure incurred by each. Each village is entitled to a certain number of turns or *varis* lasting 24 hours each or fractions of such period. The village nearest the canal gets the first turn, the next village the second and so on; but if the supply is short, the length of the *vári* may be reduced; and a village losing its turn is entitled to get the first turn when the canal runs again. The expenditure of each village is usually distributed equally over the wells, and then the wells share equally in the irrigation; or it is distributed according to the shares held in the village, and each man receives his share of the irrigation according to his payments. The well nearest the canal has the first turn. Turns last from 6 to 24 hours; but may be less, if there is a short supply. The shares in the irrigation belonging to each well are distributed according to the shares held in the well. As

Chapter V, B.

Land and Land Revenue.

regards clearances, the canal department cleans out the canals and the main distributing channels (*rájwáhs*) and the brick openings. The people have to effect the clearances of their *chhárs*.

Silt clearances.

As a great deal of silt is brought down, the *chhárs* have usually to be cleared out two or three times in the year. The owners are responsible for the first clearance; but the tenants have to join in the others, on getting two meals a day. Only the first mile of the *chhár* requires much clearing out. *Chhárs* are commonly cleaned by *ors* or *ods*, who here seem to be professional navvies. The usual payment averages 3 annas per hundred cubic feet. And the cost of clearance may be put at 10 annas per acre irrigated. The canal officer distributes the water among the *chhárs* as he sees fit. Many of these *chhárs* are long and winding, and much water is wasted in them by evaporation and percolation. Their number is also needlessly large, for each village prefers, and in the past has been allowed to have, a separate water-course instead of one joint one shared with other villages. Efforts are being made by the canal officers to remedy this state of things which in principle is decidedly objectionable.

Tahsíl Dipálpur. Assessment circles.

The assessment circles into which Mr. Purser divided Dipálpur are thus described by him :—

"Lieutenant Elphinstone's 5 assessment circles were :—1st, the river *chak* or villages benefitting from the overflow of the Sutlej; 2nd, *chak* Basírpur, or tract between the Khánwah canal and river *sailáb*; 3rd, *chak* Hujra, or villages irrigated by the upper portion of the Khánwah canal; 4th, *chak* Dipálpur irrigated by the southern portion of the Khánwah; 5th, *chak* Shergarh, a circle of villages irrigated by wells in the north-western part of the *parganah*. The villages transferred from Chunián were not included in any of those circles. At the present settlement the river *chak* was broken up into two circles, the Sutlej *chardi* and Sutlej *lahandi*. There is much more *baráni* and less *sailába* cultivation (in the former), and the population is more purely Wattu than in the latter. The Bet *chahi* circle corresponds closely with the Basírpur *chak*. There are many new estates in it, and a considerable area is irrigated by the two Sohág canals. But the mainstay of the cultivation is well-irrigation. There is a large proportion of Wattu villages in this tract. The Naya Nahri *chak* consists of new estates and some of the transferred Pákpattan villages, at the end of the Khánwah canal. Khatrís, Kambohs, Aroras and Arains predominate here. The Purana Nahri *chak*, so called to distinguish it from the newer circle, corresponds to the former Hujra and Dipálpur *chaks*. Most of the estates are owned by the same tribes as in the Naya Nahri *chak*, but the agriculturists out-number the traders here while the contrary is the case as regards the new circle. In both these *chaks* there is much *rakand* soil. Elsewhere *gasra* is more common. The Shergarh *chak* has been retained. Another *chak*, the Ganji Janúbi, has been formed out of some of the Pákpattan villages and new grants in the western corner of the tahsíl. This *chak* is undeveloped; water is much deeper from the surface than in Shergarh; the agricultural population consists chiefly of Kambohs and Arains. There are some Aroras. In Shergarh most of the estates are owned by Sayads. The Chunian villages have been incorporated with the *chaks* adjoining them."

Tahsíl Dipálpur. Rates and assessments.

Mr. Purser thus described the rates and assessments of the Dipálpur tahsil :—

Chapter V, B.

Land and Land Revenue.

Tahsíl Dipalpur. Rates and assessments.

" The rates adopted in the non-canal tracts were :—

Name of *chak*.	Plough rate.	Revenue Rates.		
		On wells.	On cultivation.	On *jadid*
Sutlej *lhandi*	Rs. 7	Rs. 10	As. 12	As. 4
Sutlej *chardi*	„ 7	„ 10	„ 10	„ 4
Shergarh	„ 5	„ 10	„ 8	„ 4
Ganji Janúbi	„ 5	„ 10	„ 6	„ 4

" In the canal *chaks* the rates adopted were :—(1) A *banjar* rate of one anna on each acre of culturable and *jadid* of the *málguzari* area. (2) A *báráni* rate of eight annas on each acre of *báráni* cultivation. (3) A well rate of Rs. 50 on each double-wheeled well, and Rs. 30 on each single-wheeled well in the Purána Nahri *chak;* of Rs. 45 and Rs. 25 on double and single-wheeled wells, respectively, in the Bet Cháhi *chak ;* and of Rs. 40 and Rs. 22-8 in the Naya Nahri *chak*, on the same classes, respectively, of wells. The points considered in fixing these rates were the depth of water from the surface, the number of yokes, the character of the agricultural tribes, and the date of construction of the wells, as regards the likelihood of trenching on capital or not.

Proposed revenue rate *jama*.

" The demand at sanctioned rates amounted to Rs. 1,15,050-8-0 made up thus :—

	Rs.	A.	P.
Purana nahri	47,390	1	0
Bet chahi	34,064	12	0
Naya nahri	3,027	11	0
Sultej lhandi	14,906	0	0
Sutlej chardi	9,600	0	0
Shergarh	4,813	0	0
Gunji janúbi	1,249	0	0

Canal revenue.

" The canal revenue was in future to fluctuate. So only an estimate of its amount could be made. Our return showed in the whole tahsíl 59,146 acres of *nahri* and 35,120 acres of *chahi-nahri* land. A total of 94,266 acres benefited from the canals. The canal returns showed an average irrigation of about 10,000 acres less. In my report on the new system of assessing canal lands, I assumed the canal area at 60,000 acres, cultivated with the different crops in the proportion given by Mr. Palmer, the Superintending Engineer. The estimated income was Rs. 1,02,312 on 60,000 acres. I retained this estimate, because I anticipated a considerable falling-off at first in canal cultivation, owing to the new and increased rates, and a permanent falling-off in the area under the highly taxed rice, which would cause a reduction in the income, even if the place of rice were taken by another crop, though the measurements would have warranted a more sanguine estimate.

Estimated results of new rates.

" The estimated results of the new assessments were a net increase of Rs. 63,390, and may be shown thus :—

	Rs.
Present fixed land revenue	1,09,287
Present fixed *ábiána*	37,106
Fluctuating *ábiána*	7,579
Present revenue	1,53,972
Proposed fixed revenue	1,15,050
Estimated fluctuating revenue	1,02,312
Estimated revenue	2,17,362
Increase	63,390

Chapter V, B.

Land and Land Revenue.

Jamas actually announced.

Progressive *jamas*.

"The *jamas* actually announced differed somewhat from those proposed. The total revenue announced was Rs. 1,16,031, giving an increase over the proposed *jama* of Rs. 981. A reduction of Rs. 954 beyond the estimate had to be given in the Sutlej *chardi chak*. Progressive *jamas* amount to Rs. 391 after 5 years; Rs. 3,659 after 10 years; Rs. 76 after 15 years. The *kámil jama* then will be Rs. 1,20,157, a net increase of Rs. 10.742-1-0 over the revenue of S. 1930 (A.D. 1873-74). Progressive *jamas* are caused chiefly by the non-expiry of the periods of lease of new grants.

Cesses.

"The cesses have been increased by Rs. 2-8-0 per cent. as in Pákpattan, and, besides, the *patwaris*' pay has been fixed at a uniform rate of Rs. 5 per cent. It averaged formerly Rs. 4-4-0 per cent. The cesess now amount to Rs. 20-12 per centum."

Tahsíl Pák Pattan, Assessment circles.

The assessment circles into which Mr. Purser divided tahsíl Pákpattan are described in the following extract :—

"Lieutenant Elphinstone divided the tahsíl into four assessment circles or *chaks:* the *nahri*, consisting of villages within the influence of the canal; the *cháhi*, consisting of inland villages. completely out of the influence of the canal or river; the *sailába*, a narrow strip along the Sutlej; and the *mashmúla sailába*, a group of villages near the centre of the tahsíl, between the *sailaba* and *cháhi chaks*, which occasionally got some *sailáb*, and in which the soil was kept moist by the vicinity of the river. These divisions were practically maintained at the present Settlement; for though the *sailaba chak* was divided into two circles, the Sutlej *chardi* and *lhandi*, and the *cháhi* was divided into the *mutafarrik* and *bángar cháhi chaks*; yet, in both cases, the differences in the sub divisions were not such as to call for different revenue rates. The *chaks* formed at the present settlement were the *nahri*; the Sutlej *chardi* and *lhandi*; the *bet cháhi*, corresponding to the old *mashmúla sailába*; the *bángar cháhi* forming the eastern portion of the old *cháhi chak*; while the western portion was represented by the *mutafarrik cháhi* circle. I do not think the Bet Chahi *chak* derives any benefit now from the river. The soil in the *bangar cháhi chak* is rather inferior to that in the *mutafarrik cháhi chak*, but water is 9 feet nearer the surface. In the Sutlej *lhandi* circle the people are mostly Joyas; in the Sutlej *chardi* circle Wattús. The former is not so settled as the latter, and has better grazing grounds."

Tahsíl Pákpattan. Rates and assessments.

The assessment of tahsíl Pákpattan is thus described by Mr. Purser :—

"For revenue rates I assumed the following :—

Name of chak.	Plough rates.	Revenue Rates. On wells.	Revenue Rates. On cultivation.		Revenue Rates. On *jadid*.	Rate at which revenue rate jama falls on cultivated acre.		
	Rs.	Rs.	A.	p.	A.	Rs.	a.	p.
Nahri	7	10	10	0	4	0	15	4
Sutlej lhandi ...	7	10	12	9	4	1	0	3
Sutlej chardi ...	7	10	12	0	4	0	15	1
Bet cháhi ...	6	12	8	0	4	1	0	4
Bángar chahi ...	5	10	6	0	4	0	14	6
Mutafarrik cháhi	5	10	6	0	4	1	0	7

"In the following form are shown the principal *jamas* considered in assessing with the rates at which they fall on the area of cultivation :—

Tahsil Pakpattan.
Rates and assessment.

Name of chak.	At former rates on cultivation.		At ½ gross produce.		At ½ net assets.		At proposed plough-rates.		At rates of rent roll of S. 1928.		At proposed revenue rates.	
	Jama.	Rate.	Jama.	Rate.	Jama.	Rate.	Jama.	Rate.	Jama.	Rate.	Jama.	Rate.
	Rs.	Rs. a. p.	Rs.	Rs. a. p.	Rs.	Rs. a. p.	Rs.	Rs. a. p.	Rs.	Rs. a. p.	Rs.	Rs. a. p.
Nahri	5,629	0 13 0	9,875	1 7 1	6,784	0 15 1	6,209	0 14 6	5,894	0 13 9	6,543	0 15 4
Sutlej lhandi	8,175	0 14 0	12,127	1 4 9	8,378	0 14 4	9,982	1 1 0	10,941	1 2 9	9,466	1 0 3
Sutlej chardi	8,284	0 15 5	11,310	1 5 1	7,273½	0 15 1	10,703	1 3 11	8,907	1 0 7	8,121	0 15 1
Bet cháhi	11,814	0 12 5	22,464	1 7 7	14,247½	0 14 3	15,372	1 0 2	16,483	1 1 4	15,524	1 0 4
Bángar cháhi	3,263	0 9 2	7,639	1 5 5	4,397½	0 12 4	6,275	1 1 7	4,548	0 12 9	5,159	0 14 6
Mutafarrik cháhi ...	2,814	0 12 6	5,697	1 9 4	3,476½	0 15 5	4,525	1 4 1	4,422	1 3 8	3,728	1 0 7
Total ...	40,059	0 13 0	69,112	1 6 5	44,556½	0 14 5	53,066	1 1 2	51,195	1 0 7	48,541	0 15 9

Chapter V, B.

Land and Land Revenue.

"The *jamas* in the canal circle do not include the *abiana* it was proposed to take in future. The revenue rates submitted for sanction gave a decrease of Rs. 2,654 on the rent-roll of A.D. 1871-72, or about 5 per cent. These proposals were sanctioned for all the circles, except the *nahri*, by His Honor the Lieutenant-Governor. As regards the *nahri* circles, orders were issued to adopt the plan proposed for the Dipálpur canal tracts and already described. The rates finally adopted in the *nahri* circle were one anna per acre on culturable and *jadid*, annas 8 per acre on *barani* cultivation, and Rs. 40 on each double-wheeled well, and Rs. 20 on each single-wheeled well.

Revenue finally assessed.

"In this final assessment I did not go so low as the revenue rate *jama;* but assessed the tahsil at Rs. 50,353, being a reduction of Rs. 1,772 on the rent-roll of S. 1929. In the *nahri* circle the introduction of the new system of canal rates resulted in a decrease of Rs. 521, instead of an increase of Rs. 649 given by the revenue rates first proposed. This reduction is merely nominal, and will be more than made up by the increased *abiana.* The following new cesses were imposed :—

			Rs.	A.	P.	
Zaildar's cess	at	... ...	1	0	0	per cent.
Ala lambardar's cess	"	... ...	1	0	0	"
Postal cess	"	... ...	0	8	0	"

The local cess at Rs. 6-4 per cent. was already in force.

Progressive *jamas* : canal revenue.

"After five years the present revenue will increase by Rs. 184, and after 10 years, by Rs. 968, on account of progressive *jamas.* One main reason for this future increase is, that at present the leases of some of the new grants have not expired. The returns show 4.674 acres irrigated by canals. These would pay now about Rs. 2,400 *abiana.* In future they will pay about Rs. 7,000. So the new assessments, as a whole, result in a net increase of actual revenue of nearly Rs. 3,000."

Final result of assessment.

The actual result of the assessment of the four tahsíls is given below. As regards the Rávi tahsíls, the decrease refers to the rent-roll of S. 1927 (A.D. 1870-71); as regards Pákpattan, to that of S. 1929 (A.D. 1872-73); and the increase, as regards Dipálpur, to that of S. 1930 (A.D. 1873-74) :—

Name of tahsil.	Former jamas.	New jamas.	Initial decrease.	Initial increase.	Progressive income after 5 years.	Progressive income after 10 years.	Progressive income after 15 years.	Kanil jamas.	Final decrease.	Final increase.
Gugera	78,027	74,450	3,577	...	773	3,521	.	78,744	...	717
Montgomery	84,171	77,955	6,219	..	627	1,050	..	82,632	1,542	...
Pakpattan	52,125	50,353	1,772	..	184	965		51,505	620	...
Dipálpur	1,09,415	1,16,031		6,616	391	3,650	76	1,20,157	..	10,742
Total ...	3,23,711	3,18,789	11,568	6,616	1,975	12,198	76	3,33,038	2,162	11,459

The result was an initial net decrease of Rs. 4,952 with a final net increase of Rs. 9,297. The new *jama* fell at the rate of annas 14 per acre on the cultivated area as shown in the completed returns. The *jama* of the regular settlement, as given in the printed report, was Rs. 3,03,520 exclusive of *ábiána.* This fell at the rate of annas 11-9 per acre on the cultivated area of 409,059 acres given in the same statement.

Period of settlement.

The assessments of the Gugera and Montgomery tahsíls were sanctioned for a term of 20 years, from Kharíf 1871-72. Mr. Roe stated that he considered the assessments "decidedly high as they had been fixed, not on present cultivation, but on what it was hoped that cultivatien would be." The assessments of the Dipálpur and Pákpattan tahsíls were sanctioned for a term of 20 years, from Kharíf 1873-74.

Chapter V, B.

Land and Land Revenue.

Introduction of fluctuating assessment into Ravi *tahsíls.*

Shortly after the introduction of the revised settlement changes in river inundation began to take place in the Rávi tahsils. Early in 1879 the Financial Commissioner marched through part of the Rávi riverain. He found widespread distress due to the failure of *sailáb* and to the consequent desertion of tenants, and many estates expressed a wish for the introduction of fluctuating assessments. In October 1879 Mr. Purser was deputed to the district to frame proposals for the reduction of a system of fluctuating assessment in the Rávi riverain villages. After some modification of his proposals the system sanctioned by Government in 1880 was as follows:—

(a) A fixed assessment at from 1 to 1½ annas per acre on all cultivated and culturable land.

(b) An *ábiána* of Rs. 10 per well in use during the year.

(c) Fluctuating crop rates as under :—

(1) Jhallári crop Rs. 1-10-0 per acre.

(2) All crops on lands newly brought under cultivation for the first two years, 12 annas per acre.

(3) All other crops Re. 1-8-0 per acre.

Crops irrigated by wells were in addition to the *ábiána* to pay rates (2) or (3). Subsequently the *abiáná* was reduced to Rs. 6 or Rs. 7 per well according to the depth of water level. In Gugera 17 and in Montgomery 50 estates accepted the above system of fluctuating assessment in the early part of 1880. Between that year and 1885 modifications were constantly introduced. Early in 1881 Sir James Lyall while marching through the tract found that the *ábiána* rate in some cases pressed heavily on the wells, and that the uniform crop rates of Re. 1-8-0 per acre pressed unduly on the inferior kharíf crops. Consequently in 1882 Government sanctioned the abolition of the *ábiána* rate and the adoption of the following revised rates :—

	Per acre. Rs.	a.	p.
Dofasli	2	4	0
Cháhi and Jhallári	1	10	0
Sailába	1	8	0
New cultivation, and *til*, *moth*, *múng*, *mash* and *rawan*	0	12	0

It was also directed that when more than one-third of a crop sown on flooded or unirrigated land failed, a proportionate remission should be given.

In 1883, on the recommendation of the Financial Commissioner, Government sanctioned the reduction of the fixed charge on

Chapter V, B.

Land and Land Revenue.

Introduction of fluctuating assessment into Rávi tahsils.

cultivated and culturable areas in villages paying *tirni* to a rate from 9 pies to one anna per acre; the *cháhi* and *jhallári*, and the *sailáb* rates being at the same time reduced to Re. 1-8-0 and Re. 1-6-0 per acre, respectively. It was also directed that half rates were to be charged on crops irrigated by new wells for five years, and by old wells restored for two years, from the date of the starting of the well. In 1884 the Financial Commissioner (Colonel Davies) after marching through the Rávi riverain authorized the reduction of the rate for the fixed assessment of the culturable area to 9 pies per acre and sanctioned the following reduced crop rates for the fluctuating assessment:—

	Per acre. Rs.	a.	p.
Cháhi and jhallári	1	4	0
Sailába	1	0	0
Dofasli	2	0	0
New cultivation	0	8	0

In February 1887 it was decided that the fixed assessment on cultivated and culturable area should be abolished, that all new cultivation should be charged at 8 annas per acre for the past two years, and all other cultivation at one rupee per acre; that all crops harvested or cut for fodder should be charged, *dofasli* crops were to be exempted. Crops, if irrigated by new wells, were to be assessed at half rates for five years, if by old restored wells, for two years. This system was to be applied to all estates then under fluctuating assessment, with a discretion to extend it to any other estates which might apply thereafter for its application to them. Up to and inclusive of 1885-86, 67 estates in the Rávi tahsíls were under fluctuating assessment. In subsequent years their number was as follows up to 1892-93, the end of the term of the revised settlement:

Year.	*No. of estates under fluctuating assessment.*
1886-87	120
1887-88	152
1888-89	252
1889-90	257
1890-91	262
1891-92	262
1892-93	264

The relief given by the system of fluctuating assessment as finally adopted may be gauged from the following figures:—

Tahsil.	No. of estates under fluctuating assessment in 1892-93.	Fixed assessment of revised settlement.	Average annual fluctuating assessment, 1889-90 to 1892-93
	Rs.	Rs.	Rs.
Gugera	99	33,163	14,857
Montgomery	165	52,161	16,306
Total ...	264	85,324	31,163

Chapter V, B.

Land and Land Revenue.

Introduction of fluctuating assessment into Rávi tahsils.

Excluding the 264 estates mentioned above, in the remainder of the Rávi tahsils the system of wholly fixed assessment was maintained up to the expiry of the revised settlement in 1892-93. Collections appear to have been difficult and remissions fairly frequent. Their assessment in 1892-93 stood as follows:—

Tahsil.	Fixed.	Fluctuating.	Total.
	Rs.	Rs.	Rs.
Gugera	45,856	18,860	64,716
Montgomery	32,838	24,067	56,905
Total ...	78,694	42,927	1,21,621

Changes in the Sutlej tahsils.

In the Sutlej tahsils the new Sohág Pára Colony established in the years 1888-91 was, except for the payment of a fixed *malikána* of Re. 1 per 10 acres, placed under wholly fluctuating assessment. Consolidated land revenue and canal water-rates per acre of crop were sanctioned by Government of India in 1887. They were as follows:—

Crop.		Land revenue.			Water-rate.			Total.		
		Rs.	a.	p.	Rs.	a.	p	Rs.	a.	p.
Canal irrigated	Rice	0	4	0	3	0	0	3	4	0
	Other *kharif* crops ...	0	4	0	1	12	0	2	0	0
	All *rabi* crops	0	12	0	1	0	0	1	12	0
All crops not irrigated by the canal ...		0	12	0	...			0	12	0

For crop failures in the *kharif* harvest proportionate remissions of the above rates were to be given; as regards the *rabi* rates it was decided in 1890 that in holdings provided with wells remissions might be given if the *rabi* crops failed entirely, and remissions in proportion to outturn in seasons of decided failure of winter rains. *Rabi* crops receiving irrigation from new wells were to be charged 6 annas in place of 12 annas per acre land-revenue. The average annual demand for land-revenue assessed on the colony during the five years ending 1895-96 under the above system was Rs. 16,986 after deducting the remissions of half *rabi* rates on crops irrigated by new wells. The demand for water-rates and *malikána* during the same period averaged Rs. 44,654 and Rs. 6,518, respectively. The assessment of the Sutlej tahsils immediately before revision was

Chapter V, B.

Land and Land Revenue.

Changes in the Sutlej tahsíls.

as follows. The fixed assessments are those of 1896-97 and 1897-98 for Dipálpur and Pákpattan respectively; the fluctuating is for 1897-98 :—

Tahsíl.	Fixed.	Fluctuating.	Total.
	Rs.	Rs.	Rs.
Dipálpur	1,32,886	2.748	1,35,634
Pákpattan	65,973	21,752	87,725
Total ...	198,859	24,500	2,23,359

For a detailed account of the progress of the district during the term of the revised settlement reference may be made to the assessment reports and the final report of the recent settlement.

Revision of settlement, 1892-99: Rávi tahsíls.

In the original plan of operations under which the recent revision of the settlement of the district was carried out it was decided that the district should be dealt with piecemeal; the two Rávi tahsils being taken up first and on their completion those on the Sutlej. The re-settlement of the Rávi tahsíls was commenced at the end of 1891 under the superintendence of Mr. Douie, Deputy Commissioner. He left the district in February 1892. In November of the same year Mr. Kennedy, as Deputy Commissioner, took charge of the settlement, and carried out the re-assessment of the two Rávi tahsíls. Only a very partial re-measurement of the tract was considered necessary.

Assessment circles.

The Montgomery tahsíl was divided into three assessment circles, *viz.*, the Bet, or riverain tract, and the Sandal and Ganji Bár circles to the north and south of the riverain tract, respectively. In the Gugera tahsíl the riverain tract was divided into two circles, the Bet Urár on the south and the Bet Pár on the north of the Rávi; there was also a Sandal Bár and a Ganji Bár circle as in Montgomery; and in addition the tract traversed by the Deg Nála, between the Sandal Bár and the Bet Pár circle, was formed into the Deg circle.

System of assessment.

For the Bet circles the system of assessment adopted was to impose a fixed demand on wells and the lands attached to them, and fluctuating rates on mature crops grown outside well areas. In the Bár and Deg circles the assessment was wholly fixed except that crops irrigated from the Deg canal were put under fluctuating assessment. A certain amount of fixed demand was imposed on the waste in all circles except the Deg. It was also decided that in all circles the fixed assessment on wells which should become unfit for use should be remitted, and that new wells should be assessed after certain periods of exemption.

Chapter V, B.

Land and Land Revenue.

New assessment.

The new assessment imposed by Mr. Kennedy from Rabi 1894 is compared below with the previous one; which in the case of the Bet circles was the average of the four years, 1889-90 to 1892-93, and in the others that of 1892-93 :—

Tahsíl.	Assessment circle	Previous assessment.	New Assessment.			Increase.	Percentage of increase.
			Fixed.	Fluctuating (estimate).	Total.		
		Rs.	Rs.	Rs.	Rs.	Rs.	Rs.
Montgomery.	Bet	45,697	36,050	37,703	73,753	28,056	61
	Sandal Bár ...	932	1,175	...	1,175	243	28
	Ganji Bár ...	1,543	1,728	...	1,728	185	12
	Total ...	48,172	38,953	37,703	76,656	28,484	59
Gugera.	Bet Urár ...	19,285	16,605	14,723	31,328	12,043	62
	Bet Pár ...	21,350	21,114	14,061	35,175	13,825	65
	Total Bet circle	40,635	37,719	28,784	66,503	25,868	63
	Deg	9,700	12,520	972	13,492	3,792	39
	Sandal Bár ...	1,701	1,881	...	1,881	180	10
	Ganji Bár	8,769	10,592	...	10,592	1,823	21
	Total ...	60,805	62,712	29,756	92,468	31,663	52
Total Rávi tahsils ...		1,08,977	1,01,665	67,459	1,69,124	60,147	55

Revision of new assessments.

The announcement of Mr. Kennedy's assessments produced considerable discontent in the Gugera and Montgomery tahsíls, and led to a certain amount of agitation. In October 1894 it was decided that so far as the Bet circles were concerned, they should be revised by Mr. Fagan, who had succeeded Mr. Kennedy as Deputy Commissioner, and was also in charge of the settlement of the Sutlej tahsíls, The revision was completed in January 1896. It was decided that the system originally adopted should, as far as possible, be adhered to. The fixed assessments on the well areas were reduced and revised on the basis of the area of crops: which it was estimated that the wells of individual estates could mature in the year without the aid of river water; any area of mature crops actually grown on well areas in excess of such estimated area being liable to fluctuating assessment at a rate uniform for all crops, which varied in different tracts from Re. 1 to Re. 1-4-0 per acre. A purely fluctuating assessment was retained for crops outside well areas; such crops were divided into three classes; the rates for which were, respectively, Re. 1-8-0, Re. 1-2-0 and Re. 0-12-0 per acre; superior crops, such as rice, cotton, *til*, wheat, were put in the first class, medium crops, *jowár*, maize, barley and gram in the second, and others in the third. The fixed assessments on waste were retained, but were considerably reduced. The results of the revision as compared with those of Mr. Kennedy's assessment were as follows :—

Chapter V, B.

Land and Land Revenue.

Revision of new assessments.

1	2	3	4	5	6	7	8	9	10	11
Tahsíl.	Assessment circle.	Average demand of previous four years, 1889-90 to 1892-93.	Mr. Kennedy's assessment. As announced. Fixed.	Mr. Kennedy's assessment. As announced. Fluctuating (estimate).	Mr. Kennedy's assessment. As announced. Total.	Assessment as revised. Fixed.	Assessment as revised. Fluctuating, estimated on areas of 1894-95.	Assessment as revised. Total assessment.	Increase or decrease. Column 9 on column 3 with percentage.	Increase or decrease. Column 9 on column 6.
		Rs.	Rs.	Rs.	Rs.	Rs.	Rs.	Rs.	Rs.	Rs.
Gugera ...	Bet Urár	19,285	16,605	14,723	31,328	12,448	19,213	31,661	+12,376 +64%	+333
	Bot Pár	21,350	21,114	14,061	35,175	15,053	11,422	26,475	+5,125 +24%	—8,700
	Total ...	40,635	37,719	28,784	66,503	27,501	30,635	58,136	+17,501 +43%	—8,367
Montgomery,	Bet	45,697	36,050	37,703	73,753	22,391	37,761	60,152	+14,455 +32%	—13,601
	Total two tahsíls ...	86,332	73,769	66,487	1,40,256	49,892	68,396	1,18,288	31,956 +37%	—21,968

Chapter V, B.

Land and Land Revenue.

Revision of new assessments.

The actual fluctuating assessments imposed since the revision have been as follows:—

				Rs.
1.	Estimated at revision		...	68,396
2.	As actually assessed, Kharif-Rabi	1895-96	...	19,952
3.	Ditto ditto	1896-97	...	18,959
4.	Ditto ditto	1897-98	...	56,644
	Average of three years ...		...	31,852

The average has been so much below the estimate because 1895-96 and 1896-97 were abnormally bad years for *sailáb*. That of 1897-98 was much better, but still below average. Suspensions of the fixed demand under the new assessment had to be extensively given in the Rávi tahsíls in the years 1895-96 and 1896-97, and to some extent in 1897-98. At the end of the latter year the amount under suspension was Rs. 17,168.

Revision of settlement, 1892-99: Sutlej tahsíls.

The re-settlement of the Sutlej tahsíls was commenced at the beginning of 1894, and lasted till February 1899. It was conducted by Mr. Fagan. Though only a very partial re-measurement had been contemplated in the original plan of operations it was in practice found needful to re-measure and re-map every estate in both tahsíls.

Assessment circles.

Each tahsíl was divided into four assessment circles which followed generally the existing natural sub-divisions; they were (*i*) a *bár* or upland circle; (*ii*) the canal-irrigated tract divided into two circles, *viz.*, the Khánwah and the Sohág in Dipálpur and the Khánwah-Sohág and Sohág-Pára in Pákpattan; (*iii*) a Bet or riverain circle.

Half net assets.

The theoretically estimated half-net assets of the two tahsíls are shown in the following table:—

DIPALPUR.		PAKPATTAN.		BOTH TAHSILS.	
Assessment circle.	Half net assets.	Assessment circle.	Half net assets.	Tract.	Half net assets.
	Rs.		Rs.		Rs.
Bár	9,065	Bár	9,274	Bár ...	18,339
Khánwah	91,335	Khánwah-Sohág,	13,256		
Sohág ... ... Sohág-Pára colony	1,20,103 5,095	Sohág-Pára ... Sohág-Pára colony.	43,542 49,849	Canal...	3,23,180
Total Sohág circle	1,25,198	Total Sohág-Pára circle.	93,391		
Bet	31,456	Bet	73,773	Riverain	1,05,229
Total ...	2,57,054	Total ...	1,89,694	...	4,46,748

Chapter V, B.

Land and Land Revenue.

System of assessment adopted.

The main features of the system of assessment adopted for the Sutlej tahsíls were as follows:—(*i*) A fixed assessment was imposed on each estate based on the average area of well-irrigated and *báráni* cultivation. In cases where the waste area was large a certain amount of fixed demand was imposed on it also; (*ii*) all lands which receive canal-irrigation will be charged harvest by harvest with occupier's rates on the mature crop area, the rates varying with the class of crops and being liable to quinquennial revision. Such lands will also be assessed with a canal-advantage land-revenue rate on the area sown without reference to the success or failure of the crop, *dofasli* area being exempt. Both occupiers' rates and canal-advantage rate will be assessed whether the land receives well-water in addition to canal-irrigation or not. The present occupier's rates, introduced from Rabi 1898, are—

Crops.	*Rate per acre.* Rs.	a.	p.
Rice, gardens, pepper	3	4	0
Cotton, sugarcane, melons, *til*, hemp	2	4	0
All other *kharif* crops	1	4	0
All mature *rabi* crops, plantations, vegetables ...	1	0	0
Failed *rabi* crops and grasses	0	8	0

The canal-advantage (land-revenue) rate varies from assessment circle to assessment circle, the limits being 7 annas and Re. 1 per acre in Pakpattan, and 8 annas and 12 annas in Dipálpur; (*iii*) all *sailáb* and *ábi* (*jhallári*) cultivation which does not receive well irrigation will be subject to a fluctuating assessment imposed on the area of crops matured. The rates sanctioned for this assessment are as follows:—

Tahsíl.	*Assessment circle.*	*Class of cultivation.*		*Rate per acre.* Rs.	a.	p.
Dipálpur	Bet	Sailáb	Superior...	1	6	0
			Inferior ...	0	14	0
		Abi	... ...	0	12	0
Pákpattan	Bár ... ... Soház Pára .. Bet	Sailáb	Superior...	1	8	0
			Inferior ...	0	14	0
		Abi	... ...	0	14	0

Superior crops are rice, *til*, cotton, wheat and tobacco; inferior crops comprise all others. *Dofasli* crops are not charged except that if a superior crop follows an inferior one as *dofasli*, the difference between the superior and inferior rates is assessed on the former. The occasional cultivation which takes place on small areas in the Khánwáh and Soház circles of Dipálpur on the Ganji and Mokal spills from the Lahore district will be assessed on area sown, whether the crop matures or fails, at Re. 1 per acre for *sailáb* and 8 annas per acre for *ábi* cultivation. *Sailáb* and *abi* cultivation in all circles, if irrigated by wells under fixed assessment, will be exempt from fluctuating assessment.

New assessment.

The following table exhibits the results of the re-assessment of the Sutlej tahsils:—

Chapter V, B.
Land and Land Revenue.
New assessment.

Name of tahsíl.	Name of assessment circle.	Revenue prior to revision. Amount.	Revenue prior to revision. Incidence per acre on cultivated soil area by new measurement.	Demand at sanctioned rates.	Revenue actually assessed. Fixed. Initial.	Fixed. Deferred on protective well leases.	Fixed. Total.	Estimated fluctuating.	Total assessment.	Incidence per acre on cultivated soil area by new measurement.	Increase on revenue before revision. Amount.	Increase on revenue before revision. Percentage.
		Rs.	Rs. a. p.	Rs.	Rs.	Rs.	Rs.	Rs.	Rs.	Rs. a. p.	Rs.	
Dipálpur.	Bár	7,707	0 7 9	9,108	7,681	479	8,160	811	8,971	0 9 0	1,264	16
	Khánwah	52,866	0 8 1	74,049	36,170	2,160	38,330	36,631	74,961	0 11 6	22,095	42
	Sohág	53,269	0 6 9	96,506	45,546	4,544	50,090	46,476	96,566	0 12 0	43,297	81
	Bet	21,792	0 10 10	26,833	9,629	1,355	10,984	16,063	27,047	0 13 5	5,255	24
	Total ...	1,35,634	0 7 9	2,06,496	99,026	8,538	1,07,564	99,981	2,07,545	0 11 10	71,911	53
Pákpattan.	Bár	5,988	0 6 10	7,619	5,659	127	5,786	2,824	8,610	0 9 11	2,622	44
	Khánwah-Soháy	8,333	0 7 4	10,630	5,042	288	5,330	6,043	11,373	0 10 0	3,040	36
	Soháy-Pára	35,745	0 6 9	73,212	18,076	5,034	23,110	52,868	75,978	0 14 5	40,233	113
	Bet	37 659	0 10 11	57,788	13,840	1,018	14,858	44,029	58,887	1 1 1	21,228	56
	Total ...	87,725	0 8 2	1,49,249	42,617	6,467	49,084	1,05,764	1,54,848	0 14 5	67,123	76
	Total two tahsíls ...	2,23,359	0 7 11	3,55,745	1,41,643	15,005	1,56,648	2,05,745	3,62,393	0 12 10	1,39,034	62

Chapter V, B.

Land and Land Revenue.

New assessment.

The revenue prior to revision is, in the case of Dipálpur, that of 1896-97 except as regards the Sohág-Pára colony (included in the Sohág-Pára circle) for which it is that of 1897-98, amounting to Rs. 2,748; in the case of Pákpattan it is that of 1897-98. With the exception of the colony the new assessments were introduced into the Dipálpur tahsíl with effect from Rabi 1898 and into Pákpattan from the following *kharíf*. In the colony they were introduced from Rabi 1899. A good deal of opposition to the new assessments was shown in Dipálpur, but practically none in Pákpattan. In both cases they are certainly moderate and special care has been taken not to press too heavily on well-irrigated cultivation.

Results of re-assessment for the whole district.

The results of the re-assessment for the whole district are as follows:—

Tahsíl.	Revenue in years prior to revision.	Revised Assessment. Fixed. Initial.	Deferred on wells.	Total.	Estimated fluctuating.	Total assessment.	Increase. Amount.	Percentage.
	Rs.	Rs.	Rs.	Rs.	Rs.	Rs.	Rs.	
Gugera ...	64,716	49,993	2,362	52,355	30,635	82,990	18,274	28
Montgomery	56,905	23,971	923	24,894	37,761	62,655	5,750	10
Dipálpur ...	1,35,634	99,026	8,538	1,07,564	99,981	2,07,545	71,911	53
Pákpattan ...	87,725	42,617	6,467	49,084	1,05,764	1,54,848	67,123	76
Total district	3,44,980	2,15,607	18,290	2,33,897	2,74,141	5,08,038	1,63,058	47

In the case of the Rávi tahsíls the revenue prior to revision is that of 1892-93, the revised fixed assessment is as it stood in 1897-98, and the fluctuating assessment is that estimated at Mr. Fagan's revision in 1894-96.

Period of settlement.

The assessment of the Rávi tahsíls, Gugera and Montgomery will probably run for 10 years, from Kharíf 1895 in the case of the Bet circles and from Rabi 1894 in the case of the others. Excluding the Sohág-Pára colony, the term of settlement in the Sutlej tahsíls will probably be 20 years, from Rabi 1898 in Dipálpur and from Kharíf 1898 in Pákpattan. In the case of the colony it will be 10 years from Rabi 1899.

Revenue instalments.

The dates on which the *kists* or revenue instalments now fall due are, for the *kharíf* harvest, January 15th in all tahsils: for the *rabi* harvest July 15th in the Rávi tahsils and July 1st in Dipálpur and Pákpattan. The usual proportions of instalments of fixed revenue in all parts of the district except the Bet and Deg

Chapter V, B.
Land and Land Revenue.
Cesses.

circles of Gugera, are one-fourth in the *kharíf* and three-fourths in the *rabi;* in the Bet and Deg circles they are two-fifths in the *kharíf* and three-fifths in the *rabi.*

The future rate of the Patwári cess has not yet been finally fixed, but if the proposals which have been made are accepted, the cesses which will be imposed on and in addition to land-revenue, fixed and fluctuating, inclusive of canal advantage, will be as follows:—

	Rate per cent. Rs.	a.	p.
Patwári	7	13	0
Lambardári	5	0	0
Local rate	10	6	8
Total ...	23	3	8

Assignments of land-revenue.

Table No. XXX gives details as to land-revenue assignments for the year 1896-97 prior to the introduction of the revised assessments in the Sutlej tahsíls. The following statement shows the portion of the new fixed assessments of the district which is assigned:—

Detail.	Gugera.	Montgomery.	Dipálpur.	Pákpattan.	Total district.
	Rs.	Rs.	Rs.	Rs.	Rs.
Total fixed assessment	52,355	24,894	1,07,564	49,084	2,33,897
Released in perpetuity	142	308	7,260	...	7,710
„ for life or lives	487	69	2,120	7	2,683
For maintenance of institutions	582	100	772	739	2,193
Total assigned ...	1,211	477	10,152	746	12,586

The chief individual assignees are Bába Khem Singh K. C. I. E., the fixed revenue of whose *jágír* is Rs. 3,616, of which half is for three lives, including his own and half in perpetuity; Bábás Deva Singh, Uttam Singh and Parduman Sing, his nephews, and sons of Bába Sampuran Singh, who enjoy Rs. 2,289 fixed revenue in perpetuity; and the Patháns of Wendla, Farídpur *jágír*, Kariwála, Nawankot and Farídpur-Sohág, whose fixed *jágír* is Rs. 2,061 in perpetuity after payment of one-fourth *nazarána*. The chief institutions which enjoy assignments are the shrine of Bába Faríd at Pákpattan with a fixed *jágír* of Rs. 729, and the Derah at Bhuman Shah with one of Rs. 1,075. It has been proposed that all assignees shall enjoy one-third of the canal-advantage assessment imposed on the assigned lands, and that such of them as would be entitled to owner's rate under current rules shall enjoy the remaining two-thirds also.

Chapter V, B.

Land and Land Revenue.

Government lands, forests, &c.

Table No. XVII deals with the area and income of Government lands; Table No. XVIII gives the area of the reserved forests while table No. XIX shows the area of land acquired by Government for public purposes. The forests, both reserved and unclassed, have already been noticed at pages 154 to 159. Over 2,400 square miles of Government waste land (unclassed forests) are under the control of the Deputy Commissioner, while the area in charge of the Forest Department is 847 square miles, of which 760 square miles are unclassed forests and 87 square miles are reserves.

The income from the unclassed forests consists of the fixed *tirni* assessment which in 1897-98 stood at Rs. 1,41,330, and out of which Rs. 27,844 is credited to the Forest Department on account of the unclassed area under its control; *tirni* on cattle brought in for grazing from other districts; the annual sum paid for collecting *máín* (the galls of the *ukán* tree); price of wood cut on permit; *kásht-báráni* assessment for single harvest cultivation and other items. The average annual income excluding *tirni* for the five years ending 1897-98 from the unclassed area under the control of the Deputy Commissioner was Rs. 22,448. Further particulars regarding forest administration will be found in the Final Settlement Report.

Lessees of Government waste lands.

The area held from Government on long leases is as follows:—

	Acres.
Gugera	5,144
Montgomery	3,836
Dipálpur	39,392
Pákpattan	27,004
Total ...	75,376

The figures exclude the Sohág-Pára colony. Nearly all the leases were given during the currency of the last settlement. The question of the treatment of leased lands was dealt with in the recent settlement. In the Rávi tahsíls purchase on favourable terms was allowed in a few cases, but in nearly all the others the leases were renewed with or without modification of terms. No orders have as yet been passed regarding this matter in the Sutlej tahsils. Sale at a reasonable price, after deducting cost of improvements, &c., has been proposed in a good many cases, and at favourable rates in those where this was provided for by the lease. In other cases renewal of the leases has been proposed.

Grants of waste land.

Grants of waste land are now made either on single harvest leases or on leases for longer periods. In the former case the cultivation, known as *kásht-báráni*, is assessed at uniform rates on the area of mature crops.

The rates at present are:—

Assessment circle.	*Rate per acre.* Rs.	a.	p.
Bet circle	1	8	0
Deg circle	1	4	0
Other circles	1	0	0

In the Sutlej tahsíls if canal water is given to such cultivation both canal-advantage and occupier's rates are charged in addition to the above. The Government waste tracts in which *kásht-bárání* cultivation may be permitted or long leases given has been much restricted under recent orders in view of future extensions of irrigation from Government canals.

Chapter V, B.

Land and Land Revenue.

Tirni.

Intimately connected with the land revenue is the *tirni* or grazing tax. This tax is an inheritance from the Sikhs, and the object of it appears to have been to make professional cattle-breeders, who did not otherwise contribute to the expenses of the State, share in the burdens of the rest of the population. Agricultural cattle were exempt from taxation, and so were cows and buffaloes, the property of *boná fide* cultivators. Sheep and goats were, however, always taxed. Up to last settlement, only camels, buffaloes, sheep and goats paid *tirni* in this district. Captain Elphinstone recommended that cows should be taxed. They were taxed. The main excellence of the Sikh system, that the cattle of cultivators were exempted from taxation, was lost sight of. In process of time even agricultural bullocks came to be taxed. In 1857-58 the *tirni* income amounted to a little under Rs. 32,000. In 1872-73 the income was Rs. 1,08,009, of which sum about one *lákh* is due to *tirni* proper, and the rest to leases of *kokanber*, grass, *múnj* and *sajji*, which were formerly shown separately. In 1881-82 it amounted to Rs. 1,48,000. The system in force up to 1870-71 involved periodical counting of the cattle of all the villages of the district. But only those villages whose cattle actually grazed in the Government jungle paid *tirni*. If, however, any cattle of non-*tirni*-paying villages were found in the jungle all the cattle had to pay double rates. In 1870-71 the Government waste lands were divided into blocks or *tirni mahals* which were leased annually, and farmers were left to make their own arrangements with people grazing cattle in their blocks. The farmers were allowed to charge at certain fixed rates for each head of cattle grazing, *viz.* :—

	Rs.	a.	p.		Rs.	a.	p.
Male camel ...	1	0	0	Female buffalo ...	1	0	0
Female camel ...	1	8	0	Cow ...	0	8	0
Male buffalo ...	0	8	0	Sheep or goat ...	0	1	0

Plough bullocks no longer paying *tirni*. These rates were by no means excessive, considering the great profits yielded by cattle. But it was found that this system led to so much oppression and extortion, and the contractors became so obnoxious to the people, that their lives were hardly safe when they ventured among the grazing community to enumerate the cattle. Consequently in 1879 the system of employing contractors was discontinued, and fees were collected by Government officials on the enumeration of cattle effected for each village or locality, the rates remaining unchanged. In 1882 it was found that the *tirni záildárs* gave little or no assistance, and all were dismissed, save a very few of the best men. In that year the Afghán war drew about 7,000 camels from the district; the enumeration was purposely not made too strictly; and the numbers thus arrived at were under orders of Government; and in order to avoid annoyance caused by annual enumeration, accepted for a period of five years. This, of course, only applied to the inhabitants

Chapter V, B.
Land and Land Revenue.
Tirni.

of the district, and not to nomad tribes or to people from neighbouring districts, whose only object in coming is probably to evade paying *tirni* dues in their own villages. Some of the large stock-owners are very independent, and almost always evade enumeration of their animals by distributing them among dependants, or by driving them across the boundary of the district. The total *tirni* demand for the year 1885-86 was Rs. 1,54,979, but of this Rs. 27,731 was remitted and Rs. 24,871 was suspended. In 1886-87 the Multán system of *tirni* assessment in a modified form was introduced into the district. The main feature of the system was that each *tirni*-paying village or grazing hamlet (*rahná* or *jhok* of the *bár*) contracted to pay a fixed annual sum as *tirni* for a period of five years. The assessment of this sum was made by the Deputy Commissioner for each village or grazing hamlet and was based on the application of certain rates to the number of *tirni*-chargeable cattle belonging to the village as ascertained partly by estimate and partly by enumeration carried out in 1885-86. The rates used were those in force previously, except that cows were charged 6 annas instead of 8 annas per head. Bullocks were exempted. A few estates which had not paid *tirni* before were assessed at half rates, and a good many which had no Government waste available for grazing near them were exempted from assessment. The *tirni* demand for the year 1886-87 under the new assessment was Rs. 1,12,188; and the average annual demand for the five years was estimated at Rs. 1,13,006. It was intended that the fixed *tirni* assessment of each village should be distributed each year over all the cattle of the village at rates for each class of animal proportionate to the rates which were used in framing the assessment.

The quinquennial assessment expired in March 1891, and the demand had then risen to Rs 1,24,368. A fresh quinquennial assessment was made, the demand being raised by 13 per cent. to Rs. 1,40,843. This assessment is still in force; the demand under it in 1897-98 was Rs. 1,41,330. The collection of *tirni* on cattle brought in for grazing from other districts is farmed separately and in 1897-98 it yielded Rs. 5,675. No cesses are charged on *tirni*, but out of the collections 8 per cent. is credited to the district fund, 3 per cent. to the Patwári fund and 5 per cent. is paid to lambardárs. Large suspensions of *tirni* demand have been given in recent years. They have been as follows :—

	Rs.
1895-96	10,944
1896-97	11,986
1897-98	37,194 (proposed).

CHAPTER VI.

TOWNS AND MUNICIPALITIES.

Chapter VI.

Towns and Municipalities.

General statistics of towns.

At the Census of 1891, all places possessing more than 5,000 inhabitants, all municipalities, and all head-quarters of districts and cantonments were classed as towns. Under this rule the following places were returned as the towns of the district :—

Tahsil.	Town.	Persons.	Males.	Females.
Montgomery	Kamália	7,490	3,910	3,580
Ditto	Montgomery	5,159	3,505	1,654
Pákpattan	Pákpattan	6,522	3,378	3,144

The distribution by religion of the population of these towns and the number of houses in each are shown in Table No. XLIII, while further particulars will be found in the Census Report in Tables Nos IV and V. The remainder of this chapter consists of a detailed description of each town, with a brief notice of its history, the increase and decrease of its population, its commerce, manufactures, municipal government, institutions, and public buildings ; and statistics of births and deaths, trade and manufactures, wherever figures are available.

Kamálía town.

The town of Kamália, generally known as Kot Kamália, lies 8 miles north-west of the Rávi on an isolated mound upon the bank which marks the northern limits of the river's excursions, and contains a population of 7,490 souls. It is situated in a flat country, which for some distance round is well populated, and a few fruit and flower gardens surround the town. The town is traversed by a single *bázár* from east to west. The streets are, as a rule, well paved, and though many of them are narrow and crooked, the drainage, and indeed the sanitary arrangements generally, are fairly good. The water-supply is obtained from wells dug within and without the town. The principal building of antiquarian interest is a *masjid* within the town, built at the time of the Kharral chief Khán Kamál.

Kamália is a very ancient town. General Cunningham* identifies it as one of the towns of the Malli taken by Alexander in

* Ancient geography of India, 208-210.

Chapter VI.

Towns and Municipalities.

Kamália town.

his invasion of India. An account of the campaign against the Malli has been given elsewhere.† The modern town was founded in the fourteenth century by a Kharral chief named Khán Kamál, from whom it derives its name, and whose descendants still occupy it. The site, however, has been undoubtedly occupied from a much earlier period, as is testified by an ancient mound of burnt brick ruins, adjoining the modern town; and its situation so exactly fits in with the narrative of Arrian, that its identification with the town of the Malli may probably be accepted as correct. General Cunningham mentions a tradition to the effect that the old town was overthrown by a king from the west, at the same time as Shorkot. He also suggests a connection between the name Kamalia and that of the Malli. After the annexation of the province, the town made a great start into prosperity, a brisk trade in the produce of the lowlands of the Rávi springing up. It was much thrown back by the systematic plunder effected by the insurgent tribes in 1857, who held it for a whole week and sacked it most completely. The inhabitants had time to secrete much of their property before the attack was made, but their loss, nevertheless, must have been very serious. Upon the restoration of order, ample compensation was made to them, and the town has now quite recovered its former prosperity. The opening of the North-Western Railway added immensely to the commercial importance of the town. The road which passes from Chícháwatni to Jhang and onwards to Dera Ismáil Khán is the main road of traffic with Jhang.

The municipality of Kamália was first constituted on 29th July 1868. It is now a municipality of the second class. The committee consists of 12 members, of whom 2 are *ex-officio*, 2 nominated and 8 elected. The Tahsíldár of Montgomery is the President. The *ex-officio* members are the Tahsíldar and the Hospital Assistant. Table No. XLV shows the income of the municipality for the last eleven years It is chiefly derived from octroi levied at different rates on the value of goods brought within municipal limits. Indigo and hides are exempt from municipal duty, and wheat, so far as it is produced within municipal limits, is also excluded from taxation. Kamália is a place of considerable commerce; collecting grain from surrounding villages and the adjacent parts of Jhang, *gur* and sugar from Amritsar and Jullundur, cloth from Karáchi, Delhi and Amritsar. The exports are chiefly cotton, *ghi* and wool. The area round the town is irrigated by *chhárs* known as the *ghark* and *gharakna*, constructed at the time of Gholam Mohammad Khán, a descendant of a Kharral chief, Kamál Khán. As noticed in Chapter I, their management has been taken over by the District Board and considerable improvements have been effected. The figures given on the next page show the total imports within municipal limits for the last five years. Further information will be found in the Trade Reports.

† See Gazetteer of the Multán district.

Chapter VI.

Towns and Municipalities.

Kamália town.

Imports of Kamália.

1	2						3	4				5	6			7	8			9
Year.	Articles of food or drink for men or animals.							Articles of fuel, lighting and washing.				*	Drugs, gums, spices and perfumes.				Piece-goods and other textile fabrics and manufactured articles of clothing and dress.			
	Grain.	Refined sugar.	Unrefined sugar.	Ghí.	Other articles.	Total.	Animals for slaughter.	Oil.	Oilseeds.	Other articles.	Total.	Building materials.	Drugs, gums and spices.	Perfumes.	Total.	Tobacco.	All cotton, silk, satin, woolen, hair, pashmina and other cloth.	Other articles not cloth.	Total.	Metals.
	Mds.	Mds.	Mds.	Mds.	Mds.	Mds.	Rs.	Mds.	Mds.	Mds.	Mds.	Rs.	Rs.	Rs.	Rs.	Mds.	Rs.	Rs.	Rs.	Rs.
1892-93	13,392	1,115	3,200	503	50,639	98,849	1,509	138	564	2,185	2,887	5,691	5,200	181	5,393	230	54,179	2,459	56,638	2,875
1893-94	92,140	1,102	3,698	532	62,428	159,900	1,661	179	1,080	3,485	5,344	8,030	6,367	285	6,652	481	63,701	6,430	70,131	7,419
1894-95	43,804	1,134	3,961	506	63,506	112,911	1,888	16	1,024	2,250	3,290	11,584	7,808	160	7,968	525	72,400	2,133	74,533	7,267
1895-96	44,920	1,021	4,538	314	43,937	94,760	1,656	146	768	13,614	14,528	14,000	10,884	226	11,110	729	64,340	9,345	73,685	7,266
1896-97	33,904	1,173	3,878	314	104	72,373	1,584	176	469	23,402	24,047	15,068	4,032	224	4,256	250	59,033	2,133	62,066	4,600

Chapter VI.

Towns and Municipalities.

Kamália town.

The principal institution is the town school; the other buildings of importance are five *dharmsálas*, also a *samádh* (shrine) of Bhaí Prem Dás, a *shiválá* of Báwa Gobindgir, and a *thákar dawárá* of Báwa Mangal Dás, with a good well and some trees around it; *thâná*, post office, dispensary, municipal committee house, and a *saráí*. This town was formerly the head-quarters of a *tahsíl*, but in 1855 the head-quarters were removed to Harappa and subsequently to Montgomery. The population, as ascertained at the enumerations of 1868, 1875, 1881 and 1891, is shown in the margin.

Limits of enumeration.	Year of Census.	Persons.	Males.	Females.
Whole town ..	1868	5,695	3,109	2,586
	1881	7,594	4,282	3,312
	1891	7,490	3,910	3,580
Municipal limits	1868	5,695	...	..
	1875	5,900	...	...
	1881	7,594	...	...
	1891	7,490	...	...

It is difficult to ascertain the precise limits within which the enumerations of 1868 and 1875 were taken; but the details in the margin, which give the population of suburbs, throw some light on the matter. The figures for the population within municipal limits according to the Census of 1868 are taken from the published tables of the Census of 1875; but it was noted at the time that their accuracy was in many cases doubtful. The Deputy Commissioner in the district report on the Census of 1881 thus explained the increase of population:—"Owing to a change "in the course of the Rávi (which formerly ran some 12 miles "from the town) and to new land deposited in the neighbourhood, "the lands of Kamália have of late been abundantly inundat"ed, and the new deposits and the additional fertility have attracted "a large influx of cultivators." The constitution of the population by religion, and the number of occupied houses are shown in Table No. XLIII. Details of sex will be found in Table No. V of the Census Report of 1891.

Town or suburb.	Population.		
	1868.	1881.	1891.
Kamália town ...	4,842	6,692	7,490
Thatha Fatehpur	390	528	
Do Dulman Toya	463	374	

Montgomery town.

Montgomery is a small place of 5,159 inhabitants, and lies on the North-Western Railway, midway between Lahore and Multán. The town was founded in 1865 by Mr. Blyth, then Deputy Commissioner of Gugera district; the head-quarters of the district being transferred to it from Gugera in order to be on the line of rail and for the more easy provision of medical and spiritual privilges to its European inhabitants. The spot where it stands was then occupied by the small village of Sáhíwál, and is about 27 miles south of Gugera. It received its present name by way of a somewhat dubious compliment to Sir Robert Montgomery, then

Chapter VI.

Towns and Municipalities.

Montgomery town.

Lieutenant-Governor of the Punjab. The town lies in the midst of a sterile plain unbroken by vegetation and covered with saline efflorescence, and the surrounding scenery, desolate beyond description, harmonises well with the rows of empty shops and houses which an intelligent people has declined to inhabit. The town itself is a collection of *kacha* native houses without a wall ; and the four sides of the town are open towards the jungle or *bár*. It has two *bázárs* (Blyth-Ganj and Ford-Ganj ; the streets are wide, but except one not paved. The chief buildings in this town are district court, police office, sessions-house police-lines, *thána* and *tahsíl* (combined), munsiff's court, dispensary, central jail, church, dak-bungalow, and post-office. There is also an encamping-ground with a *sarái* and a good well. There are a few other *pakka* houses in the station for European residents. In the words of the *Imperial Gazetteer* the situation of the station is almost unequalled for dust, heat and general dreariness. The Municipal Committee is of the second class and consists of 12 members, of whom 3 are *ex-officio*, one nominated and 8 elected. The Deputy Commissioner is the President. The *ex-officio* members are, the Deputy Commissioner, the Assistant Surgeon and the District Inspector of Schools. Its income for the last 11 years is shown in Table No. XLV, and is derived from octroi levied on the value of goods imported for consumption within municipal limits. The town has little or no trade, and is in fact nothing but the head-quarters of the district staff. The population, as ascertained at the enumerations of 1868, 1875, 1881 and 1891 is shown below :—

Limits of enumeration.	Year of census.	Persons.	Males.	Females.
Whole town	1868	2,413	1,879	534
	1881	3,178	2,131	1,047
	1891	5,159	3,505	1,654
Municipal limits	1868	2,416	...	...
	1875	2,588	...	...
	1881	3,178	...	...
	1891	5,159	...	...

It is difficult to ascertain the precise limits within which the enumerations of 1868 and 1875 were taken ; but the details in the margin, which give the population of suburbs, throw some light on the matter. The figures for the population within municipal limits, according to the Census of 1868, are taken from the published tables of the Census of 1875 ; but it was noted at the time that their accuracy was in many cases doubtful. The constitution of the population by religion, and the number of occupied houses are shown in Table No. XLIII. Details of sex will be found in Table No. V of the Census Report of 1891.

Town or suburb.	Population.		
	1868.	1881.	1891.
Montgomery town	1,297	1,926	2,830
" Civil lines	1,116	1,232	1,521

Chapter VI.

Towns and Municipalities.

Dipálpur town. Description.

Dipálpur is a small place of 3,707 inhabitants, situated about 17 miles from the Okárah railway station, and 20 miles north of the river Sutlej. In 1870 the *tahsíl* head-quarters were transferred from Hujra to Dipálpur, where there was no *tahsíl*. It is no longer a town within the Census description as its Municipal Committee was abolished in 1886-87; but some description of it may be given. The place used before the extension of railways to be frequented by traders from Dera Ismail Khan and other places towards the frontier, on account of the main road from Okárah to Fázilka passing through that place. The town itself is an unpretentious collection of *kacha* and *pakka* native houses surrounded by an old wall with three gates, one *Thattayári* towards the east, *Multáni* towards the west, and the third *Shumáli Darwáza* towards the north. The important buildings in the town are the temple of Lálu-jas-ráj, where an annual fair is held in the month of Mágh; an old *masjid*, built at the time of Khán Khánán, Wazír of Sháh Jahán, Emperor of Delhi; and a tomb of Imám Sháh, where also an annual fair is held. It has two *bázárs*, well paved, the main street of one passing from east to west and of the other from the middle of the first *bázár* towards the north. There is no grain market in the town. The other buildings are a *tahsil* and *thâná*, post-office, school-house, *lambarkhána* dispensary, *sarai*, district rest-house and canal bungalow. There is also an encamping ground with a well on it. The land around the town is irrigated by the Khánwah canal, which runs a short distance to the south of the town. Formerly the place was a small agricultural village, but the transfer of the head-quarters of the *tahsil* here from Hujra has increased the importance of the place, besides adding much to the public convenience.

Dipálpur is a very old city indeed. It is said to have been founded by one Sri Chand, after whom it was called Srínagar. Sri Chand had no children. His priest, Chandar Mani, stood on one leg for 5 months and 27 days; after which the goddess Devi gave him her two sons, Bhím and Lalu-jas-raj. He brought them to Dipálpur and two of Sri Chand's wives adopted them. One day on the way to the temple they indulged in a game of tip-cat. The cat struck one of Sri Chand's wives, who expressed in vigorous language her opinion that they ought to be swallowed up by the earth. Almost immediately Bhím disappeared in the ground, and Lalu-jas-ráj went after him. Chandar Mani had just time to catch him by the lock of hair at the back of his head (*choti*) before he vanished. He then directed that every Khatri of the Khanna sub-division should offer up his *choti* in that place before marriage, and so should other tribes when making vows. He then disappeared. This legend, and the old name of the town, may have some bearing on the question of who were the Oxudrakae (Ancient Geography of India, page 214). But it is incredible that the Káthias should ever be allies of the Khatrís. The present name of the town is said to be derived from Dipa, one of Rája Sálváhan's sons, who re-founded the town. Risálu, another son, lived at Dhaular some miles to the west. The love adventures of his queen Kokilán and Rája Hodi are still sung by Mirásis.

Chapter VI.

Towns and Municipalities.

Dipálpur town. Description.

There are, however, several other stories concerning the name Dipálpur. According to General Cunningham,* "the foundation of the place is attributed to Rája Deva Pála, whose date is unknown." Another tradition is to the effect that the town was founded by one Bija Chand, a Khatri; that it was originally called Sripur, after the son of the founder, Sri Chand, and that subsequently a Rája, by name Har Singh surrounded it with a wall and changed its name to Dipálpur. This tradition also mentions no date. The antiquity of the town, however, is clearly established. General Cunningham remarks that "the interior surface on which the houses are now built is on a level with the terreplein of the ramparts. The old coins, also, which are found there in great numbers, show that Dipálpur was in existence as early as the time of the Indo-Scythians." Being thus persuaded of the ancient origin of the town, General Cunningham is "inclined to identify it with the Daidala of Ptolemy, which was on the Sutlej, to the south of Labokla and Amakatis or Lahore and Ambakápi.† In the 14th century the emperor Firoz Tughlak frequently visited the town, his hunting excursions extending in this direction from the neighbourhood of Sirsa and Hissár.‡ He is said to have erected a large mosque outside the city, and drawn a canal from the Sutlej for the irrigation of its lands. It is repeatedly mentioned by the early Muhamadan historians, and must have retained some of its importance in the time of the emperor Bábar, who says, speaking of the garden he laid out at Kábul, "in the year in which I defeated Bihár Khan and conquered the countries of Lahore and Dipálpur."

At the time of Taimúr's invasion the town was second only to Multán in size and importance, and was popularly said to possess 84 towers, 84 mosques, and 84 wells. At present it is nearly deserted, there being only one inhabited street running between the two gates. In shape, it is a square of nearly 1,600 feet, with a projection 500 feet square at the south-east quarter. To the south-west there is a high ruined mound, connected with the town by a bridge of three arches which is still standing; and from its high and commanding position, General Cunningham is inclined to believe that popular tradition is right in affirming this mound to be the remains of a citadel. To the south and east there are also long mounds of ruins, which are doubtless the remains of suburbs. The existing ruins, including the citadel and suburbs, occupy a space ¾ mile in length by ½ mile in breadth, or 2½ miles in circuit. But in its flourishing days the town must have been much larger, as the fields to the east are strewn with brick right up to the banks of the Khánwah canal, near which was situated the mosque built by Fíroz Sháh, Tughlak. This extension of the town beyond the walls may also be inferred from the fact that the people of Dipálpur, on Taimur's invasion, sought refuge in Bhatner, which they would not have done had their

* Ancient Geog., i, pp. 213-14.

† Ancient Geography, i, p. 214. As to Ambakápi, see Gazetteer of Gujránwála district. In an earlier publication (Arch. Rep., i, p., 140) General Cunningham suggests the identity of Daidala with Delhi.

‡ See Gazetteer of the Hissár district.

Chapter VI.
Towns and Municipalities.
Dipálpur town. Description.

own city been defensible.* The complete decay of the town in modern times is probably to be attributed to the drying up of the old Biás. It is said that many of the inhabitants migrated, after the failure of the river, to Haidarabad in the Dakkhan, and large numbers of Khatrís in Sindh and Kach assert Dipálpur to be their original home. Improvements made in the Khánwah canal after annexation have to a certain extent revived the prosperity of the town as a local trade centre.

The most noticeable feature in the modern town is the shrine of Bába Lálu-jas-ráj, a saint much venerated by Khatrís of the three highest classes—Khanna, Kapúr and Marotra. The male children of these classes throughout the greater part of the province are taken to this shirne in or about their tenth year for the purpose of dedication to the saint. The ceremony consists in shaving the child's head, after which the lock upon the top of the head (*choti*) is considered sacred, and may never afterwards be shaved or cut. Other classes besides those mentioned resort to the shrine for the same purpose, but only in fulfilment, generally, of a special vow, the saint being by no means universally venerated. The sacred days upon which the ceremony can be performed are the Sundays in the month of Mágh. The attendance in the course of the month averages about 11,000. The town is the chief seat of the Khatrís. It has a very bad reputation as regards the honorableness of its inhabitants. The following verse expresses this :—

Shor Shoron, te kúr Lahoron, jhagra Chinioton ;
Peo putr te chuglhi kare, Dipalpur de koton.

Which implies that Shorkot is the place for uproars, Lahore for falsehood, and Chiniot for quarrelling, and the town of Dipálpur is the place where the father tells tales on his son. All the houses in Dipálpur are built of brick. The streets are narrow, the old walls are tumbling in ; the bastions were pulled down on annexation. Altogether the place has a desolate look. It is decidely unhealthy and the water is very bad for drinking purposes.

Pák Pattan town. Description.

The town of Pák Pattan lies in north latitude 30·21′, and east longitude 73·25′, and contains a population of 6,522 souls. The town itself is situated on an eminence of about 40 feet in height at a distance of about 8 miles from the right bank of the river Sutlej. The country round is fairly well wooded. There is no wall round the town but extensive suburbs stretch from its foot for some distance. Towards the east about half a mile from the town the *tahsíl* and *thána* offices are situated. The town is traversed by six main streets running from north to south and from east to west. These are all well paved, and though many of them are narrow and crooked, the drainage and indeed the sanitary arrangements generally are fairly good. The water is obtained from wells dug within and outside the town. The principal building of antiquarian interest is the shrine of Bába Sheikh Faríd-ud-dín Sáhib Shakar Ganj, with a few cloisters around it (see below). The principal institution is the town school. The other buildings are the *tahsíl*, *thána*, post-office, *sarái* and rest-house.

* General Cunningham, Anc. Geog., *i*, p. 213.

Chapter VI.

Towns and Municipalities.

Pák Pattan town. Description.

The municipality of Pák Pattan was first constituted in July 1868. It is now a municipality of the second class; the committee consists of 12 members, of whom 2 are *ex-officio*, 2 nominated and 8 elected. The Tahsíldár is the President. The *ex-officio* members are the Tahsíldár and the Hospital Assistant. Table No. XLV shows the income of the municipality for the last 11 years. It is chiefly derived from octroi levied at different rates on the value of goods brought within municipal limits. Indigo and hides are exempt from municipal duty, and wheat, so far as it is produced within municipal limits, is excluded from taxation. Pák Pattan is a place of considerable commerce, collecting wheat, pulses, cotton and oil seeds from surrounding villages, *gúr* and sugar from Amritsar, Jullundur and the North-Western Provinces, cloth pieces from Amritsar, Delhi and Karáchi, *majith* and fruits from Afghánistán. The exports from the town are cotton, wheat, wool, oil-seeds.

The figures below show total imports within municipal limits for the last five years. Further information will be found in Trade Reports. The manufactures are unimportant, consisting chiefly of lacquered wood-work and coarse checquered silk (see Mr. Kipling's note at page 175).

Chapter VI.

Towns and Municipalities.

Pák Pattan town. Description.

Imports of Pák Pattan.

Year		2						3	4				5	6			7	8			9
		Articles of food or drink for men or animals.							Articles of fuel, lighting and washing.					Drugs, gums, spices and perfumes.				Piece goods and other textile fabrics and manufactured articles of clothing and dress.			
		Grain.	Refined sugar.	Unrefined sugar.	Ghi.	Other articles.	Total.	Animals for slaughter.	Oil.	Oilseeds.	Other articles.	Total.	Building materials.	Drugs, gums and spices.	Perfumes.	Total.	Tobacco.	All cotton, silk, satin, woolen, hair, pashmina and other cloth.	Other articles not cloth.	Total.	Metals.
		Mds.	Mds.	Mds.	Mds.	Mds.	Mds.	Rs.	Mds.	Mds.	Mds.	Mds.	Rs.	Rs.	Rs.	Rs.	Mds.	Rs.	Rs.	Rs.	Rs.
1892-93	...	32,706	1,056	...	358	16,672	50,792	5,248	73	1,381	6,595	8,052	3,010	6,381	227	6,611	139	57,800	1,000	58,800	6,635
1893-94	...	50,688	1,154	...	44	16,756	69,046	7,552	352	1,478	7,291	9,121	3,581	7,536	512	8,018	210	69,600	1,600	71,200	10,666
1894-95	...	61,480	1,254	...	526	18,685	81,945	7,296	409	1,074	9,654	11,137	5,600	5,376	224	5,600	612	67,400	2,400	69,800	8,724
1895-96	...	64,372	1,224	...	618	18,472	84,686	7,452	436	1,048	5,432	6,916	6,816	6,412	258	6,670	772	68,100	3,600	71,700	9,642
1896-97	...	66,482	1,148	...	579	8,496	76,705	5,056	352	400	2,688	3,440	16,576	2,368	512	2,880	596	44,100	3,200	44,300	8,533

Chapter VI.

Towns and Municipalities.

Pák Pattan town Description.

Pák Pattan, anciently Ajudhan, is recognized by General Cunningham as one of the towns of the people variously mentioned by Alexander's historians and other classical writers as Ohydrakæ, Sydrakæ, Sudrakæ, Surakousæ, and Hydarkæ,* whose country extended up the Sutlej, to the north of that of the Malli, a people in conjunction with whom they are always mentioned:—

"The place has always been one of some importance. It was for centuries the principal ferry of the Sutlej. Here met the two great Western roads from Dera Gházi Khán and Dera Ismáil Khán—the first *via* Mankhera, Shorkot and Harrapa, the second *via* Multán. At this point the great conquerors Mahmúd and Taimur, and the great traveller Ibn Batuta. crossed the Sutlej. The fort is said to have been captured by Sabuktagin in A. H. 367, or A. D. 977-78, during his plundering expedition in the Punjab; and again by Ibrahím Ghaznavi, in A. H. 472, or A. D. 1079-80. On the invasion of Taimur, the mass of people fled to Bhatner, and the few people that remained were spared by that ruthless barbarian out of respect for the famous saint Faríd-ud-dín Shaker Ganj, whose shrine is at Ajudhan."

It is to this Faríd-ud-din, familiarly and better known as Bába Faríd, that the name of Pák Pattan, or "ferry of the pure one," is ascribed. *See* footnote to page 27, Chapter II. He is one of the most famous saints of northern India, and to him is attributed the conversion of the whole southern Punjab to Muhammadanism. It is said that in his progress through the Punjab the saint was opposed at Ajudhan by a Hindu Jogi, Birnáth, whom, however he conquered and subsequently converted under the Muhammadan title of Pir Kamál. The town thenceforth became his principal residence. "By continual fasting, his body is said to have become so pure that whatever he put into his mouth to allay the cravings of hunger, even earth and stones, was immediately changed into sugar, whence his name of Shakar-Ganj, or sugar-store.† This miraculous power is recorded in a well-known Persian couplet:—

"*Sang dar dast O guhar gardad,*
"*Zahar dar kám O shakar gardad:.*"

which may be freely rendered:—

"Stones in his hands are changed to money (jewels),
And poison in his mouth to honey (sugar).

From another memorial couplet, we learn that he died in A. H. 664, or A. D. 1265-66, when he was ninety-five lunar years of age. But as the old name of Ajudhan is the only one noted by Ibn Batuta in 1334 and by Taimur's historian in A. D. 1397, it seems probable that the present name of Pák Pattan is of comparatively recent date. It is perhaps not older than the reign of Akbar, when

---

* See Gazetteer of the Multán district.

† Another version of the story is that the saint, when hungry, used to tie a wooden cake (*chapatti*) or a bunch of wooden dates to his stomach, and that this composed his sole nourishment for thirty years. The truth of the story is vouched for by the preservation of the identical cake and dates to this very day. They are kept at his shrine at Pák Pattan, and are objects of reverence and worship to the faithful.

Chapter VI.

Towns and Municipalities.

Pák Pattan town. Description.

the saint's descendant, Mír-ud-din, revived the former reputation of the family by the success of his prayers for an heir to the throne.* The sanctity of the town and of its shrine is acknowledged far beyond the boundaries of the Punjab, even in Afghánistán and Central Asia, and pilgrims are constantly flocking to it. The principal festival is at Muharram, when crowds that have been estimated at between fifty and sixty thousand are collected at the shrine. The festival lasts from the first to the fifth day of the Muharram. On the afternoon and night of the last two days takes place the characteristic ceremony of the festival. There is a narrow opening in a wall adjoining the shrine, 5 feet by 2½ in size, called "the gate of paradise;" and whosoever during the prescribed hours can force his way through this passage is assured hereafter a free entrance into paradise. Special arrangements are made by the district authorities for the control of the crowd of pilgrims and for their orderly passage through the gate. The stream flows on ceaselessly all night until the early hours of the morning. Women are not allowed to pass through. The lineal descendants of the saint are still represented at the shrine of which they are the managers and guardians. They enjoy a reputation for the utmost sanctity. They commonly receive the honorific appellation of Dewáns. The present head of the family is twenty-eighth in descent from Bába Faríd. He enjoys a handsome revenue grant *júgír* from the British Government, in addition to the revenues of the shrine itself, which are considerable. A list of the lineal representation of Bába Faríd is given below. Bába Faríd himself arrived at Pákpattan in H. 584 and died in H. 664. His successors were—

	Name.	Date of succession.		Name.	Date of succession.
1.	Badr-ud-dín	H. 664	16.	Muhammad Dín ...	H. 1019
2.	Ala-ud-dín	668	17.	Muhammad Ashraf	1057
3.	Muaf-ud-dín	722	18.	Muhammad Saiyad	1090
4.	Fazl-ud-dín	738	19.	Muhammad Yusuf	1120
5.	Manohar	755	20.	Muhammad ...	1135
6.	Núr-ud-dín	805	21.	Muhammad Ghulám Rasúl	1179
7.	Baháwaldín	823	22.	Muhammad Yár ...	1223
8.	Muhammad	855	23.	Sharf-ud-dín ...	1243
9.	Ahmad	879	24.	Allah Jowáya ...	1261
10.	Ataulla	901	25.	Abdurrahmán ...	1300
11.	Muhammad	918	26.	Said Muhammad ...	1304
12.	Ibrahím	940	27.	Abdurrahmán ...	1307
13.	Táj-ud-dín	982	28.	Fatteh Muhammad	1307
14.	Faizulla	1008	29.	Said Muhammad ...	1311
15.	Ibrahím	1010			

The right to the guardianship of the shrine has of late years been subject to legal vicissitudes. Litigation began in 1898, after the death of Dewán Allah Jowaya. Abdul Rahmán, the uncle of the deceased, succeeded to the *gaddi*, but Said Muhammad, the daughter's son of Dewán Allah Jowaya, sued for it and obtained a decree under which he was installed in 1888. An appeal was preferred by Pir Abdul Rahmán to the Chief Court, in which he

* General Cunningham, Anc. Geog., i, p. 218.

Chapter VI.

Towns and Municipalities.

Pák Pattan town. Description.

succeeded and was accordingly installed. Said Muhammad made a further appeal to the Privy Council, but before any decision was passed, Pir Abdul Rahman died and was succeeded by his son Fatteh Mohammad. Said Muhammad's appeal to the Privy Council was accepted and Fatteh Muhammad had to vacate the *gaddi*, which was taken by Said Muhammad, the present incumbent or Sijjadá Nashin (as he is called) of the shrine.

Population and annual statistics.

The population, as ascertained at the enumerations of 1868, 1875, 1881 and 1891 is shown in the margin. The constitution of the population by religion, and the number of occupied houses are shown in Table No. XLIII. Details of sex will be found in Table No. V of the Census Report of 1891.

Limits of enumeration.	Year of Census.	Persons.	Males.	Females.
Whole town ...	1868	6,086	3,264	2,822
	1881	5,993	3,160	2,833
	1891	6,522	3,378	3,144
Municipal limits ...	1868	6,086	...	...
	1875	5,723	...	...
	1881	5,993	...	...
	1891	6,522	...	...

STATISTICAL TABLES

APPENDED TO THE

GAZETTEER

OF THE

MONTGOMERY DISTRICT.

(INDEX ON REVERSE).

STATISTICAL TABLES.

Table No. II, showing DEVELOPMENT.

1	2	3	4	5	6	7	8	9	10	11
DETAILS.	1853-54.	1858-59.	1863-64.	1868-69.	1873-74.	1878-79.	1883-84.	1888-89.	1893-94.	1896-97.
Population	...	...	...	360,415	...	426,529	426,529	426,529	499,521	499,521
Cultivated acres	...	...	...	538,240	420,957	357,622	365,975	433,024	556,181	338,333
Irrigated acres	...	...	...	225,195	328,915	347,809	275,793	301,698	29,136	310,642
Do. (from Government works)	...	...	...	66,495	101,837	78,827	84,702	110,670	394,801	144,625
Assessed land revenue, rupees	...	...	...	326,785	320,761	317,362	207,287	292,542	370,739	336,364
Revenue from land, rupees	...	...	...	283,073	458,364	295,208	276,532	250,146	248,760	274,036
Gross revenue, rupees	...	...	...	414,220	526,150	685,831	618,584	711,552	818,444	618,252
Number of kine	...	...	...	226,225	241,760	260,636	249,316	212,801	157,887	152,745
Do. sheep and goats	...	...	...	270,407	272,159	469,766	426,162	407,960	469,790	458,683
Do. camels	...	...	...	7,912	11,748	1,737	10,874	6,583	8,838	10,288
Miles of metalled roads	...	...	...	} 941	...	...	..	...	5	5
Do. unmetalled roads	...	...	...		1,052	1,007	1,054	1,054	1,003	1,003
Do. railways	...	...	...	84	82	82	82	82	82	82
Police staff	...	...	526	584	513	497	466	485	540	465
Prisoners convicted	845	841	920	1,592	1,850	1,264	1,049	1,624	1,885	2,510
Civil suits, number	2,480	1,518	1,513	2,699	4,065	2,945	3,118	4,750	3,979	4,248
Do. value in rupees	99,832	97,084	101,181	116,826	172,859	219,618	289,771	376,532	287,027	251,295
Municipalities, number	...	...	...	...	3	5	5	3	3	3
Do. income in rupees ...	...	..	...	7,837	10,548	10,719	20,182	19,090	28,430	26,621
Dispensaries, number of	...	...	...	1	1	5	5	6	7	8
Do. patients	...	...	...	2,599	3,672	22,158	24,639	23,761	50,312	56,791
Schools, number of	...	...	30	40	22	27	30	33	37	40
Do., scholars	...	...	961	1,266	1,321	1,343	1,573	1,705	1,918	1,950

Table No. III, showing RAINFALL.

1	2	3	4	5	6	7	8	9	10	11	12	13	14	15	16	17	18	19	20	21	22	23	24	25	26	27	28	29	30	31	32	33
Rain-gauge station.	Annual Rainfall in tenths of an inch.																															
	1866-67.	1867-68.	1868-69.	1869-70.	1870-71.	1871-72.	1872-73.	1873-74.	1874-75.	1875-76.	1876-77.	1877-78.	1878-79.	1879-80.	1880-81.	1881-82.	1882-83.	1883-84.	1884-85.	1885-86.	1886-87.	1887-88.	1888-89.	1889-90.	1890-91.	1891-92.	1892-93.	1893-94.	1894-95.	1895-96.	1896-97.	Average.
Montgomery	42	50	72	239	100	80	92	73	94	14	208	88	187	50	116	114	122	107	118	83	80	90	64	91	136	88	174	84	82	131	92	103
Gugera	62	76	47	92	38	44	55	70	81	98	84	116	121	88	64	197	124	70	74	83	69	81	86	111	190	51	118	140	86	75	110	90
Dipálpur	67	112	99	111	40	45	112	60	75	172	120	60	42	8	54	106	137	118	36	31	78	113	103	37	116	81	113	107	107	72	115	90
Pákpattan	36	86	62	178	74	34	120	56	94	90	88	100	92	52	78	136	73	67	94	35	77	85	75	15	132	63	120	132	76	88	61	84

Table No. III A, showing RAINFALL at HEAD-QUARTERS.

1	2	3
	Annual Average.	
Months.	Number of rainy days in each month, 1867 to 1897.	Rainfall in tenths of an inch in each month, 1867 to 1897.
January ...	3	20
February ...	2	20
March ...	2	10
April ...	2	4
May ...	2	10
June ...	3	20
July ...	7	80
August ...	7	60
September ...	2	30
October ...	...	...
November ...	...	...
December ...	1	10
1st October to 31st December ...	1	10
1st January to 31st March ...	7	50
1st April to 30th September ...	23	204
Whole year ...	31	264

Table No. III B, showing RAINFALL at TAHSIL STATIONS.

1	2	3	4	5
	Average fall in tenths of an inch from 1892-93 to 1896-97.			
Tahsil Stations.	1st October to 31st December.	1st January to 31st March.	1st April to 30th September.	Whole year.
Montgomery ...	4	23	73	100
Gugera ...	2	29	48	79
Dipálpur ...	2	14	85	101
Pákpattan ...	1	21	72	94

Table No. IV, showing TEMPERATURE.

1	2	3	4	5	6	7	8	9	10
	May.			July.			December.		
YEAR.	Maximum.	Mean.	Minimum.	Maximum.	Mean.	Minimum.	Maximum.	Mean.	Minimum.
1886-87	114·3	91·0	67·2	111·8	93·2	74·2	81·1	58·5	33·4
1887-88	115·6	91·6	70·2	106·1	93·4	77·2	82·6	59·0	36·4
1888-89	116·6	91·9	63·3	111·6	94·8	75·2	79·3	59·5	39·2
1889-90	113·8	91·1	68·2	112·3	94·3	76·2	81·3	61·0	40·8
1890-91	120·9	92·9	64·8	107·9	93·1	75·1	73·8	56·1	38·8
1891-92	115·9	88·1	67·2	120·4	95·9	74·1	81·3	59·0	35·3
1892-93	118·9	94·6	63·8	117·4	94·3	77·6	77·8	56·4	33·3
1893-94	114·4	90·7	64·5	106·4	91·3	76·1	79·3	59·8	38·3
1894-95	116·9	94·6	70·5	107·9	91·8	70·5	84·3	56·8	35·5
1895-96	121·9	97·5	66·0	112·4	94·6	73·0	79·3	58·7	38·5
1896-97	118·4	95·4	73·0	112·4	95·5	69·5	82·0	56·5	31·5

Table No. V, showing the DISTRIBUTION of POPULATION.

1	2	3	4	5	6
		DETAIL OF TAHSIL.			
DETAIL.	District.	Montgomery.	Gugera.	Dipálpur.	Pákpattan.
Total square miles (1896-97)	5,586	1,749	1,525	986	1,326
Cultivated, square miles	620	31	81	334	174
Culturable, square miles	3,878	1,211	1,022	569	1,076
Square miles under crops (average of 1892-93 to 1896-97)	773	77	107	371	218
Total population	499,521	93,648	113,447	180,455	111,971
Urban population	19,171	12,649	...	...	6,522
Rural population	480,350	80,999	113,447	180,455	105,449
Total population per square mile	87	54	74	187	85
Rural population per square mile	83	47	74	187	80
Towns and villages.					
Over 10,000 souls	...	...	...	...	...
5,000 to 10,000	3	2	...	...	1
3,000 to 4,999	3	...	1	2	...
2,000 to 2,999	5	2	1	1	1
1,000 to 1,999	58	7	13	27	11
500 to 999	190	31	34	86	39
200 to 499	469	77	104	173	115
Under 200	1,139	201	395	227	316
Total	1,867	320	548	516	483
Occupied houses — Towns	2,763	1,672	...	...	1,091
Occupied houses — Villages	74,483	11,974	18,496	27,171	16,842
Resident families — Towns	4,033	2,598	...	...	1,435
Resident families — Villages	94,447	21,008	27,931	30,050	15,458

Table No. VI, showing the MIGRATION.

1	2	3	4	5	6	7	8	9
			Males per 1,000 of both sexes.		Distribution of Immigration by Tahsils.			
Districts.	Immigrants.	Emigrants.	Immigrants.	Emigrants.	Montgomery.	Gugera.	Dipálpur.	Pákpattan.
Hissár	1,291	280	511	657	256	20	611	404
Rohták	109	2	658	1,000	50	...	29	30
Gurgáon	49	16	612	400	18	...	31	...
Delhi	144	37	583	992	32	6	54	52
Karnál	97	51	381	1,000	10	25	14	48
Umballa	87	30	621	567	42	7	26	12
Simla	...	5	...	600	...	...	...	...
Kángra	130	4	631	750	65	8	9	48
Hoshiárpur	372	46	793	391	120	47	85	120
Jullundur	603	52	642	500	173	31	216	183
Ludhiána	402	26	754	634	106	40	48	208
Ferozepore	6,419	10,066	485	556	140	150	4,803	1,326
Mooltan	2,592	7,230	543	580	1,266	62	419	845
Jhang	4,566	2,445	564	580	1,692	1,865	498	511
Lahore	16,558	16,9[illegible]	483	511	927	4,105	8,989	2,537
Amritsar	2,978	450	619	624	319	184	986	1,489
Gurdáspur	610	92	628	771	162	99	237	112
Gujrát	218	55	702	709	59	29	76	54
Gujránwála	1,159	1,957	609	578	162	569	292	136
Siálkot	1,089	60	698	722	239	146	479	225
Shahpur	184	56	571	643	72	59	36	17
Jhelum	147	25	762	560	57	34	24	32
Ráwalpindi	210	27	676	852	43	25	13	129
Hazára	26	1	730	1,000	17	2	...	7
Pesháwar	77	11	792	818	33	6	9	29
Kohát	12	7	833	1,000	12	...	...	...
Bannu	85	19	882	842	32	...	38	15
Dera Ismail Khan	104	27	721	815	43	13	17	31
Dera Gházi Khan	36	47	861	745	23	...	2	11
Muzaffargarh	107	171	673	643	46	23	20	18
Biloch Trans-frontier	...	...	...	..	...	...	...	...
Punjab States	5,825	17,258	526	549	175	89	2,170	3,391
Punjab, part unspecified	8	...	625	...	...	...	...	8
Kashmír and India outside the Punjab ...	1,950	...	699	...	444	138	870	498
Asiatic countries	97	...	918	...	18	12	35	32
England	14	...	857	...	14	...	...	...
Other European countries	2	...	1,000	...	2	...	...	...
Africa	...	...	...	...	...	...	...	...
America	2	...	1,000	...	2	...	...	...
Australia	...	...	...	...	...	...	...	...
At Sea	...	...	...	...	...	...	...	...

Table No. VII showing RELIGION and SEX.

1	2	3	4	5	6	7	8	9
	DISTRICT.			TAHSILS.				
DETAIL.	Persons.	Males.	Females.	Montgomery.	Gugera.	Dipálpur.	Pákpattan.	Villages.
Persons	499,521	...	...	93,648	113,447	180,455	111,971	480,350
Males	...	269,613	...	51,965	60,952	96,517	60,179	[258,820
Females	...	...	229,908	41,683	52,49:	83,938	51,792	221,530
Hindús	121,481	65,354	56,127	21,750	22,330	46,862	30,539	113,480
Sikhs	16,032	9,256	6,776	1,515	3,295	6,534	4,688	15,371
Jains	...	...	...	...	..	...	..	...
Budhists	...	...	...	...	...	...	..	...
Zoroastrians	...	..	...	...	...	...	...	..
Musalmáns	361,923	194,953	166,970	70,301	87,822	127,056	76,744	351,495
Christians	85	50	35	82	...	3	...	4
Others and unspecified ...	...	...	...	...	...	...	...	...
European and Eurasian Christians	72	41	28	69	...	3	...	...

Table No. VIII showing LANGUAGES.

1	2	3	4	5	6
		Distribution by Tahsils.			
Languages.	District.	Montgomery.	Gugera.	Dipalpur.	Pakpattan.
Urdu ...	36	17	...	1	18
Punjabi	497,152	92,964	113,343	179,550	111,325
Pashto	135	62	9	31	33
Mooltani	112	48	15	11	38
Hindgi	253	11	10	30	202
Hindustáni	1,270	386	70	678	136
Sindhi	16	7		9	
Kashmíri	9	8	...	1	...
English	66	66	...	...	...
Persian	3	2	...	1	...
Bágri ...	176	10	...	112	54
Marwári	163	3	...	17	143
Púrbi ...	95	59	...	14	22
Telegu	1	1	...	...	...
French	1	1	...	...	...
Goanese	3	3	...	...	...
Total ...	499,521	93,648	113,447	180,455	111,971

Table No. IX showing MAJOR CASTES and TRIBES.

1	2	3	4	5	6	7	8	9	10	11	12
		TOTAL NUMBER.			MALES AND FEMALES BY RELIGION.						
Serial No. in Census, 1881, Table No. VIII A.	CASTE OR TRIBE.	Persons.	Males.	Females.	Hindus.	Sikhs.	Jains.	Musalmáns.	Christians.	Parsis.	Proportion per mille of population.
	Total Population	490,521	269,613	220,908	121,461	16,032	...	361,923	55	...	1,000
1	Jat	45,694	24,846	20,848	2,663	2,159	...	40,842	...	...	91
2	Rájpút	66,923	36,746	30,177	1,163	177	.	65,583	.	...	134
12	Awán	1,935	1,049	886	87	...	...	1,848	...	..	4
7	Arain	27,924	14,489	13,435	.	...	...	27,924	.	...	56
17	Sheikh	5,241	2,702	2,449		.	.	5,241		...	10
3	Brahman	3,493	1,993	1,500	3,485	8	...	...	.	...	6
24	Sayad	4,997	2,589	2,408	..	...	...	4,997	..	.	10
35	Faqírs ...	4,354	2,478	1,876	146	3	...	4,205	...	...	9
21	Nai	7,831	4,198	3,633	13	.	..	7,818	.	..	15
25	Mirási	11,023	[illegible]	5,039	...	...		11,023	...	...	22
18	Biloch	16,241	8,609	7,632	...	.	...	16,241	...	...	33
16	Khatri	5,547	2,883	2,664	3,930	1,617		.	...	...	11
33	Kamboh	16,074	8,866	8,108	13,261	244	.	1,449	...	...	34
77	Kharal	21,973	12,094	9,879	74	22		21,877	...	...	44
10	Arora	57,418	31,321	26,097	51,191	6,227		..	...	...	115
14	Khoja	9,111	1,743	1,368	...	..	...	9,111	...	...	18
4	Chuhra ...	30,478	16,407	14,071	22,577	132	...	7,769	...	...	61
51	Mahtam	14,061	7,490	6,571	7,173	2,344		4,544	...	...	28
28	Machhi	19,405	10,332	9,073	...	..	...	19,405	.	...	39
9	Juláha	22,429	12,120	10,309	.	...		22,429	...	...	45
22	Lohár	4,261	2,269	1,993	3	...	.	4,261	...	...	9
11	Tarkhán	11,662	6,522	5,140	464	873	...	10,325	...	...	23
13	Kumhar	20,083	10,759	9,324	548	168		19,367	...	...	40
32	Dhobi	5,331	2,804	2,527	..	.	...	5,331	...	...	11
23	Teli	2,309	1,332	977	.	...	..	2,309	...	...	5
30	Sunár	4,192	2,244	1,948	1,535	355	...	2,302	...	...	8
37	Mughal	2,730	1,361	1,369	..	..	...	2,730	...	...	6
58	Khokhar	8,577	4,481	4,096	...	16	...	8,561	...	...	17
19	Mochi	15,583	8,330	7,253	...	...	...	15,583	...	...	31

Table No. IX A showing MINOR CASTES and TRIBES.

1	2	3	4	5
Serial No. in Census (1881).	Caste and Tribe.	Persons.	Males.	Females.
6	Pathán	1,578	950	628
36	Chhímba	2,702	1,406	1,296
37	Mughal	2,730	1,361	1,369
38	Qassáb	6,582	3,676	2,906
40	Jogi	442	322	120
14	Banya	103	72	31
52	Labána	52	39	13
42	Malláh	5,841	3,024	2,817
26	Kashmíri	83	45	38
48	Bharái	2,122	1,137	985
5	Chamár	174	108	66
53	Bairági	203	133	70
56	Kalál	739	396	343
61	Darzi	403	220	183
62	Bhat	66	34	32
15	Jhínwar	277	195	82
67	Lilári	357	212	145
49	Barwála	66	38	28
70	Ulama	491	249	242
72	Sánsi	534	307	227
64	Changar	722	381	341
85	Od	968	493	475
117	Pakhiwára	60	42	18
104	Parácha	265	116	149
8	Gujar	462	280	182
46	Dogar	275	125	150
94	Banjára	127	46	81
80	Bázígar	2,571	1,179	1,392
76	Nungar	418	307	111
99	Kori	269	221	48
110	Rangrez	307	159	148
27	Ahír	95	63	32
141	Bhand	83	56	27

Table No. X showing CIVIL CONDITION.

1	2	3	4	5	6	7	8
		SINGLE.		MARRIED.		WIDOWED.	
	DETAIL.	Males.	Females.	Males.	Females.	Males.	Females.
Actual figures of all religions.	All religions	162,200	108,978	95,510	96,127	11,897	24,803
	Hindus	38,613	25,832	23,614	23,959	3,127	6,390
	Sikhs	5,072	2,886	3,726	3,206	458	684
	Jains	...	...	...	...	...	...
	Musalmans ...	118,450	80,241	68,151	68,940	8,312	17,780
	Budhists	...	...	...	...	...	...
	Christians	31	10	10	10	...	3
	Parsis	...	...	...	...	...	...
Distribution of every 10,000 souls of each age.	All ages	162,206	108,978	95,510	96,127	11,897	24,803
	0—9	5,707	7,057	9	27	6	6
	10—14	1,568	1,056	84	300	15	11
	15—19	1,196	514	621	1,642	178	120
	20—24	616	87	1,109	1,700	317	228
	25—29	406	39	1,618	1,909	543	533
	30—39	314	23	2,777	2,458	1,505	1,874
	40—49	135	11	1,830	1,151	1,957	2,148
	50—59	93	8	1,289	485	2,728	2,529
	60 and over	65	5	711	228	2,791	2,256

Table No. XI showing BIRTHS and DEATHS.

1	2	3	4	5	6	7	8	9	10
	TOTAL BIRTHS REGISTERED.			TOTAL DEATHS REGISTERED.			TOTAL DEATHS FROM		
YEARS.	Males.	Females.	Persons.	Males.	Females.	Persons.	Cholera.	Small-pox.	Fever.
1887	7,002	6,206	13,208	4,777	4,057	8,834	73	247	6,208
1888	8,654	7,630	16,284	5,544	4,776	10,320	...	553	7,162
1889	10,362	9,009	19,371	7,421	6,574	13,995	1	966	8,224
1890	9,806	8,556	18,362	7,880	6,965	14,854	18	268	8,923
1891	9,182	8,301	17,483	6,401	5,663	12,064	97	103	7,316
1892	9,697	8,455	18,152	15,438	13,454	28,892	3,076	336	16,692
1893	8,322	7,273	15,595	8,033	6,622	*14,655	159	130	9,705
1894	11,597	10,310	21,907	7,333	6,274	13,607	...	229	6,557
1895	11,958	10,799	22,757	5,774	5,004	10,778	—	227	4,626
1896	11,170	10,380	21,550	6,323	5,739	12,062	45	2,068	4,536
1897	10,494	9,562	20,056	5,075	5,503	11,538	...	473	5,528

Table No. XI A showing MONTHLY DEATHS from ALL CAUSES.

1	2	3	4	5	6	7	8	9	10	11	12
Months.	1887.	1888.	1889.	1890.	1891.	1892.	1893.	1894.	1895.	1896.	1897.
January	812	851	1,698	1,330	1,197	2,264	2,228	1,852	1,239	1,884	792
February	507	629	1,333	1,041	839	1,395	1,431	1,400	858	1,083	578
March	552	564	1,088	820	649	1,115	1,069	1,148	880	1,002	628
April	476	512	993	690	518	1,326	807	1,025	784	878	606
May	567	594	1,022	861	791	2,664	1,018	1,221	851	1,074	772
June	600	649	938	853	925	2,681	913	942	718	1,015	786
July	553	657	795	651	1,003	1,290	646	692	671	963	776
August	684	674	661	733	783	1,003	792	767	700	841	757
September	651	680	882	1,984	766	2,388	828	749	592	720	839
October	1,138	1,145	1,364	2,134	1,037	5,097	1,205	1,070	883	816	1,338
November	1,102	1,478	1,611	2,067	1,406	4,438	1,786	1,275	1,006	856	1,908
December	1,042	1,857	1,610	1,684	2,150	3,161	1,932	1,457	1,596	924	1,758
Total ...	8,834	10,320	13,995	14,854	12,064	28,892	14,655	13,607	10,778	12,062	11,538

Table No. XI B showing MONTHLY DEATHS from FEVER.

1	2	3	4	5	6	7	8	9	10	11	12
Months.	1887.	1888.	1889.	1890.	1891.	1892.	1893.	1894.	1895.	1896.	1897.
January	586	666	1,195	826	750	1,729	1,719	1,151	622	1,007	333
February	422	487	917	617	499	961	1,064	838	414	455	241
March	370	372	681	467	380	678	721	503	385	325	270
April	337	361	538	354	300	595	529	424	336	270	268
May	375	391	478	481	433	735	574	499	337	310	329
June	377	432	437	501	550	650	557	398	287	318	283
July	302	353	339	343	579	436	427	271	263	267	294
August	391	373	290	360	451	447	466	284	240	296	272
September	435	390	468	1,200	388	1,481	442	312	228	240	351
October	865	826	801	1,296	567	3,350	708	497	345	329	781
November	952	1,140	1,041	1,353	856	3,206	1,167	619	386	334	1,130
December	796	1,391	1,039	1,125	1,563	2,421	1,331	761	783	365	1,023
Total ...	6,208	7,182	8,224	8,923	7,316	16,692	9,705	6,557	4,626	4,536	5,528

Table No. XII showing INFIRMITIES.

1	2	3	4	5	6	7	8	9
	Persons of unsound mind or insane.		Blind.		Deaf and Dumb.		Lepers.	
	Males.	Females.	Males.	Females.	Males.	Females.	Males.	Females.
All religions ... ... { Total	160	85	930	737	311	154	25	6
All religions ... ... { Villages	156	84	896	698	299	150	24	6

Table No. XIII showing EDUCATION.

1		2	3	4	5
		MALES.		FEMALES.	
		Under instruction.	Can read and write.	Under instruction.	Can read and write.
All religions	Total	3,537	16,381	140	274
	Villages	2,715	14,319	92	212
Hindús		2,078	12,129	33	80
Sikhs		274	1,528	6	24
Jains		...	.	...	...
Budhists		...	.	..	...
Musalmáns		1,173	2,693	95	150
Christians		12	31	6	20
Pársís		..	...	..	..
Montgomery		961	4,370	59	106
Gugera		746	3,272	21	36
Dipálpur		1,071	5,518	44	101
Pákpattan		759	3,221	16	31

Table No. XIV showing DETAIL of SURVEYED and ASSESSED AREA.

1	2	3	4	5	6	7	8	9	10	11	12
	CULTIVATED.				UNCULTIVATED.						
	Irrigated.										
YEAR.	By Government works.	By private individuals.	Unirrigated.	Total cultivated.	Grazing lands.	Culturable.	Unculturable.	Total uncultivated.	Total area assessed.	Gross assessment.	Unappropriated culturable waste, the property of Government.
	Acres.	Acres.	Acres.	Acres.	Acres.	Acres.	Acres.	Acres.	Acres.	Rs.	Acres.
1886-87	138,756	169,806	100,045	438,297	540,171	2,611,767	148,267	3,300,205	3,590,235	3,31,400	1,518,345
1887-88	134,839	187,200	111,321	433,426	539,212	2,747,250	150,487	3,436,949	3,719,898	3,28,781	1,527,360
1888-89	145,064	193,499	104,502	443,065	541,202	2,555,086	152,371	3,248,659	3,539,353	3,18,670	1,519,458
1889-90	156,786	184,178	118,000	458,964	548,006	2,429,233	154,571	3,131,810	3,430,203	3,33,059	1,552,014
1890-91	133,749	221,585	161,988	517,322	547,800	2,377,175	149,470	3,074,403	3,442,306	3,44,665	1,547,403
1891-92	169,717	182,366	94,639	466,722	547,809	2,431,514	152,121	3,131,444	3,446,045	3,41,106	1,547,908
1892-93	220,136	165,065	161,380	556,181	550,007	2,354,947	151,821	3,056,775	3,401,135	3,70,917	1,546,006
1893-94	193,060	160,031	163,809	516,900	540,978	2,370,010	156,008	3,067,506	3,427,897	4,23,547	1,503,727
1894-95	198,541	158,144	164,812	516,497	530,303	2,362,878	166,557	3,058,828	3,418,768	4,07,885	1,501,685
1895-96	197,831	156,131	63,420	417,382	540,781	2,440,812	128,178	3,127,771	3,410,975	4,08,731	1,501,732
1896-97	197,948	155,759	42,812	396,519	594,353	2,481,004	112,787	3,180,184	3,472,806	4,16,530	1,501,005
Tahsíl details for 1896-97—											
Montgomery	...	31,125	16,722	19,643	350,012	774,756	58,372	1,225,510	683,910	24,250	580,254
Gugera	...	30,160	12,310	51,842	182,708	654,016	30,175	1,109,122	708,705	53,606	464,224
Dipálpur	100,434	48,304	5,820	218,931	2,239	304,180	3,957	185,473	1,212,035	211,314	79,585
Pákpattan	97,514	46,110	7,060	111,103	52,734	680,042	20,283	609,029	868,216	127,354	431,002

Table No. XV—showing VARIETIES of TENURE held direct from GOVERNMENT during the year ending Rabi 1897.

1	2	3	4	5	6	7	8	9	10	11	12	13	14
		Montgomery.						Gugera.					
Description of villages according to revenue paid by them.	Tenure.	Number of estates.	Number of villages.	Number of holders or share-holders.	Gross area.	Average area of each estate.	Average assessment of each estate.	Number of estates.	Number of villages.	Number of holders or share-holders.	Gross area.	Average area of each estate.	Average assessment of each estate.
					Acres.	Acres.	Rs.				Acres.	Acres.	Rs.
Villages paying Rs. 5,000 to Rs. 50,000.	1. Zamindári	...	...	...	...	...	...	...	...	...	...	...	...
	2. Pattidári and Bhaiachára	...	...	...	...	...	...	...	...	...	...	...	...
Villages paying Rs. 100 to Rs. 5,000.	1. Zamindári	11	11	276	15,093	1,900	2,137	8	8	112	5,590	1,034	1,485
	2. Pattidári and Bhaiachára	167	167	13,725	158,180	17,565	56,832	177	182	11,113	225,737	50,780	60,874
Villages paying less than Rs. 100.	1. Zamindári	25	25	372	10,757	557	652	36	36	450	11,307	1,095	1,652
	2. Pattidári and Bhaiachára*	51	51	3,091	32,163	10,301	13,851	93	93	2,675	31,570	4,688	6,138
	Leases from Government without right of ownership.	8	8	220	6,039	1,771	2,552	8	8	64	2,516	285	565
	Total	265	265	17,687	222,232	32,277	76,327	322	327	14,414	276,810	57,888	70,694

ADDENDA.

A.—Holdings included in the above held wholly or partially free of revenue, viz.:—	3	4	5	6	7	8	9	10	11	12	13	14
1. In perpetuity free of conditions	...	...	28	940	...	218	...	...	2	975	125	...
2. Do. subject to conditions	...	...	39	4,202	...	247	...	...	41	602	222	...
3. For life or lives	...	...	16	301	...	92	...	...	14	4,671	799	...
4. At pleasure of Government	...	...	...	...	...	...	...	...	1	502	87	...
5. Up to the time of settlement	...	...	...	...	...	...	...	...	...	...	...	...
Total of these holdings	...	...	83	5,515	...	557	...	...	58	6,740	1,233	...
B.—Lands included in the above of which the ownership is encumbered by usufructuary mortgages	...	...	1,647	Total 36,877	Of which cultivated. 5,989	...	...	...	1,781	Total 28,397	Of which cultivated. 7,738	...

Table No. XV—showing VARIETIES of TENURES held direct from GOVERNMENT during the year ending Rabi 1897—*concluded.*

Description of villages according to revenue paid by them.	Tenure.	15	16	17	18	19	20	21	22	23	24	25	26	27	28	29	30	31	32
		Dipalpur.						Pakpattan.						Total District.					
		Number of estates.	Number of villages.	Number of holders or share-holders.	Gross area.	Average area of each estate.	Average assessment of each estate.	Number of estates.	Number of villages.	Number of holders or share-holders.	Gross area.	Average area of each estate.	Average assessment of each estate.	Number of estates.	Number of villages.	Number of holders or share-holders.	Gross area.	Average area of each estate.	Average assessment of each estate.
					Acres.	Acres.	Rs.				Acres.	Acres.	Rs.				Acres.	Acres.	Rs.
Villages paying Rs. 5,000 to Rs. 50,000.	1. Zamindári	...	...	...	...	...	...	...	...	...	...	...	...	...	...	...	...	...	...
	2. Pattidári and Bhaiachára ...	...	...	...	...	...	...	...	...	...	...	...	...	...	...	...	...	...	...
Villages paying Rs. 100 to Rs. 5,000.	1. Zamindári	69	67	680	98,351	47,373	10,098	85	85	952	109,118	38,044	23,329	175	174	1,026	228,158	89,041	47,220
	2. Pattidári and Bhaiachára ...	234	220	6,705	324,200	183,035	67,068	115	116	4,080	166,222	62,274	32,182	693	690	35,722	870,300	313,600	240,576
Villages paying less than Rs. 100.	1. Zamindári	57	60	901	42,084	18,461	8,852	57	57	657	20,304	6,502	2,001	205	176	2,380	84,002	26,705	14,000
	2. Pattidári and Bhaiachára ...	59	38	1,070	30,017	11,203	6,947	60	66	1,500	24,952	8,903	3,707	209	246	8,845	118,702	35,246	30,046
	Leases from Government without right of ownership.	41	35	527	47,184	22,682	14,784	61	61	1,353	90,570	85,257	22,207	118	112	2,161	146,306	79,005	40,109
	Total	460	420	9,510	541,930	282,754	1,38,272	384	384	8,617	413,220	171,730	84,407	1,400	1,402	50,537	1,454,170	544,010	3,78,700
ADDENDA.																			
A.—Holdings included in the above held wholly or partially free of revenue, *viz.* :—																			
1. In perpetuity free of conditions ...		...	...	32	23,104	...	6,243	...	...	1	1,451	...	150	...	...	63	28,470	...	6,730
2. Do. subject to conditions		...	...	34	11,820	...	2,004	...	...	9	2,588	...	772	...	...	123	10,392	...	3,845
3. For life or lives ...		...	...	26	9,210	...	2,502	...	...	11	26	...	15	...	...	67	14,111	...	3,409
4. At pleasure of Government ...		...	...	4	22	...	5	...	...	6	341	...	26	...	...	16	865	...	118
5. Up to the time of settlement ...		...	...	...	...	...	...	...	...	...	...	...	...	...	...	...	...	...	...
Total of these holdings ...		...	...	96	40,150	...	11,354	...	...	29	4,406	...	963	...	...	269	62,947	...	14,107
																	Total	Of which cultivated.	
B.—Lands included in the above of which the ownership is encumbered by usufructuary mortgages.		...	...	...	...	...	...	...	...	...	...	...	...	...	...	3,711	123,910	31,130	...

Table No. XVI—showing the CULTIVATING OCCUPANCY of LAND for the year ending Rabi 1897.

1		2	3	4	5	6	7	8	9	10	11
Details.		Tahsil Montgomery.		Tahsil Gugera.		Tahsil Dipalpur.		Tahsil Pakpattan.		Total of the District.	
		Number of holdings.	Area.	Number of holdings.	Area.	Number of holdings.	Area.	Number of holdings.	Area.	Number of holdings.	Area.
Total cultivated area		10,946	32,277	20,565	57,887	31,368	215,705	13,920	119,185	76,709	425,054
Area cultivated by owners		3,508	11,101	5,475	19,191	2,488	22,203	1,333	18,096	12,801	70,891
Area cultivated by tenants free of rent, or at nominal rent ...		173	520	333	251	590	929	223	633	1,319	2,339
Area cultivated by tenants paying rent. With right of occupancy.	Paying at revenue rates, with or without málikána.	716	1,009	920	1,138	417	1,587	4	5	2,057	3,739
	Paying other cash rents	30	86	12	32	40	109	...	...	82	227
	Paying in kind, with or without an addition in cash.	307	629	409	829	1,085	5,559	83	200	1,884	7,277
Area cultivated by tenants paying rent. Without right of occupancy.	Paying at revenue rates, with or without málikána.	257	339	666	1,157	132	526	161	1,664	1,216	3,686
	Paying other cash rents	63	139	95	303	220	808	14	82	398	1,332
	Paying in kind, with or without an addition in cash.	5,892	18,148	12,655	31,986	26,390	183,984	12,102	98,445	57,039	335,563
Area cultivated by tenants paying rent.	Total held by tenants paying rents	7,265	20,350	14,757	38,415	28,290	192,573	12,364	100,456	62,676	351,824

Table No. XVI—showing the CULTIVATING OCCUPANCY of LAND for the YEAR ending RABI 1897—*concld.*

		1	2	3	4	5	6	7	8	9	10	11
		DETAILS.	TAHSIL MONTGOMERY.		TAHSIL GUGERA.		TAHSIL DIPALPUR.		TAHSIL PAKPATTAN.		TOTAL OF THE DISTRICT.	
			Area.		*Area.*		*Area.*		*Area.*		*Area.*	
			Irrigated.	Unirrigated.	Irrigated.	Unirrigated.	Irrigated.	Unirrigated.	Irrigated.	Unirrigated.	Irrigated.	Unirrigated.
Detail of rents and area on which paid by tenants-at-will.	Rents in kind.	1. Zabti rents	...	...	...	...	79	...	9	...	88	...
		2. Half produce or more	1,470	8,805	1	99	163	11	581	...	2,215	8,918
		3. Two-fifths and less than half	243	2,058	1,681	2,307	101	58	...	58	4,037	4,541
		4. One-third and less than two-fifths ...	3,928	395	2,836	4,319	2,262	2,006	2,009	10,369	20,609	17,089
		5. Less than one-third	1,174	75	17,616	5,677	170,848	8,430	11,583	8,987	254,517	23,169
		6. By fixed amount of produce	...	...	350	7	23	...	64,819	...	373	7
		7. Total area under rents in kind	6,815	11,333	22,517	12,409	173,476	10,508	79,031	19,414	281,839	53,724
	Cash rents	8. Total paying at revenue rates, with or without málikána	205	134	704	453	420	106	1,586	78	2,015	771
		9. Total paying other cash rents	119	20	114	189	797	11	80	2	1,110	222
		10. Total cash rents paid on area entered in column 9.	475	...	398	311	2,380	...	266	...	3,519	311

Table No. XVII—showing GOVERNMENT LANDS.

1	2	3	4	5	6	7	8	9
Tahsil.	Number of estates.	Total acres.	Acres held under cultivating leases.		Remaining acres.			Average yearly income from 1892-93 to 1896-97.
			Cultivated.	Uncultivated.	Under Forest Department.	Under other Departments.	Under Deputy Commissioner.	
								Rs.
Whole District	359	2,269,140	60.709	116,287	541,529	3,266	1,547,349	1,34,0[illegible]8
Montgomery	51	893.938	2,614	4,268	301.584	2,497	582,975	...
Gugera	70	710,506	4,306	1,431	239,945	769	464,055	...
Dipálpur	131	138,383	18,927	35,032	...	...	84.424	...
Pákpattan	107	526,313	34,862	75,556	...	...	415,895	...

Table No. XVIII—showing AREA of GOVERNMENT RESERVED FORESTS.

1	2	3	4
Tahsíl.	Name of Forest.	Area in acres.	Remarks.
Gugera	Sayadwála	4,958	
"	Kamán	2,264	
"	Kohla	1,190	
"	Chaukián	1,566	
"	Satghara	2,077	
"	Bíbípur	864	
"	Bagiána	1,470	
"	Okára	4,097	
"	Gashkauri	4,024	
	Total ...	22,510	
Montgomery	Burj Jewa Khan	4,554	
"	Núr Sháh	3,445	
"	Aliwál	1,228	
"	Montgomery	4,280	
"	Muhammadpur	1,748	
"	Mirdád	3,405	
"	Dád Fatiána	1,072	
"	Harappa	1,945	
"	Kalera	4,561	
"	Darsána	1,663	
"	Ranjit Singh	5,877	
	Total ...	33,278	
	Grand Total ...	55,788	

Table No. XIX—showing LAND ACQUIRED by GOVERNMENT.

1	2	3	4
Purpose for which acquired.	Acres acquired.	Compensation paid in rupees.	Reduction of revenue in rupees.
Roads	978	3,932	82
Canals	3,865	26,552	458
State Railways	110	588	45
Guaranteed Railways	...	...	...
Miscellaneous	115	500	23
Total	5,068	31,572	608

Table No. XX—showing AREA under CROPS.

1	2	3	4	5	6	7	8	9	10	11	12	13	14	15	16	17
Years.	Total.	Rice.	Wheat.	Jowár.	Bájra.	Maize.	Barley.	Gram.	Moth.	Poppy.	Tobacco.	Cotton.	Indigo.	Sugarcane.	Vegetables.	Miscellaneous.
1876-77	480,174	7,870	263,494	28,020	172	2,512	21,802	61,010	6,068	94	651	15,836	6	113	1,423	58,303
1877-78	398,410	9,031	208,561	26,285	57	1,541	28,667	64,123	2,083	44	1,390	21,004	2	160	2,704	40,911
1878-79	271,031	8,241	151,573	24,166	338	1,598	12,579	11,048	758	60	1,343	29,178	11	100	2,000	20,060
1879-80	352,263	20,490	183,442	21,423	223	1,031	22,177	21,100	1,579	80	1,039	28,067	1	100	1,981	48,474
1880-81	371,749	19,047	201,290	21,211	306	2,723	16,005	21,844	1,513	46	1,280	23,472	3	176	2,248	57,677
1881-82	403,156	16,209	194,906	36,527	309	4,944	14,006	24,153	1,072	83	1,636	20,462	...	163	2,041	65,802
1882-83	405,770	8,690	214,308	31,553	342	4,735	13,975	40,204	690	70	1,399	15,621	...	172	2,006	71,515
1883-84	370,030	7,122	194,346	38,745	473	4,970	13,064	38,010	1,045	78	1,069	14,169	...	192	4,746	51,908
1884-85	370,930	11,338	205,237	41,832	511	5,041	14,729	19,350	958	89	1,281	18,067	10	205	3,954	52,739
1885-86	361,725	13,210	153,126	44,720	810	4,937	12,615	18,231	16,321	167	1,031	19,338	26	323	4,870	71,975
1886-87	352,086	14,287	130,246	47,721	522	2,790	16,021	17,360	23,206	128	1,316	26,407	32	236	2,164	61,172
1887-88	423,502	13,350	166,806	45,182	556	5,034	16,608	38,781	23,562	152	2,180	37,034	20	192	2,100	81,660
1888-89	420,157	10,088	183,652	40,168	862	7,014	14,722	27,100	22,292	100	2,111	28,158	45	194	4,118	68,004
1889-90	483,585	17,014	185,901	55,820	1,707	6,394	11,414	10,239	10,468	59	1,402	34,015	42	157	1,630	81,324
1890-91	489,784	10,656	220,039	50,416	2,720	7,021	17,771	33,773	21,005	58	2,004	31,511	4	122	5,910	85,176
1891-92	463,003	15,715	205,118	43,105	2,020	8,202	14,202	47,965	18,838	58	1,119	28,422	1	790	3,402	73,200
1892-93	567,127	11,823	229,383	62,346	2,565	13,620	16,254	72,482	20,135	55	2,301	37,276	1	303	5,533	93,044
1893-94	525,538	21,043	231,629	34,947	1,570	11,656	12,371	50,578	19,670	40	2,057	46,862	18	530	1,762	61,736
1894-95	502,505	11,860	237,066	33,677	568	7,527	6,670	46,613	8,463	80	2,098	40,020	1	341	407	106,500
1895-96	370,891	10,700	140,018	12,202	531	5,867	7,503	19,469	7,150	32	1,631	41,137	2	418	1,713	122,246
1896-97	480,153	9,905	130,665	12,284	2,327	6,653	12,082	15,420	930	51	1,464	40,410	25	648	1,320	147,063
Names of Tahsils.	**Tahsil averages for the six years from 1891-92 to 1896-97.**															
Montgomery	49,463	10	18,017	3,246	63	70	861	8,872	13	2	258	1,715	1	41	59	15,635
Gugera	68,026	4,541	21,170	5,375	538	1,123	4,141	6,057	182	37	361	2,796	2	61	424	21,818
Dipálpur	237,307	7,807	105,226	24,298	203	5,018	5,287	16,432	1,443	11	801	19,928	...	143	411	50,380
Pákpattan	139,483	1,107	58,593	11,757	474	2,396	1,152	12,040	48	7	317	12,478	3	139	241	38,731
Total	494,969	13,465	203,006	44,676	1,278	8,607	11,441	43,401	1,686	57	1,737	36,917	6	384	1,135	126,573

Table No. XXI—showing AVERAGE RENT RATES and YIELD PER ACRE.

Average of rents commonly agreed upon by tenants-at-will for

Tahsil.	Cháhi Lands. Cash.	Cháhi Lands. Kind.	Nahri Lands. Cash.	Nahri Lands. Kind.	Cháhi Abi Lands. Cash.	Cháhi Abi Lands. Kind.	Abi Lands. Cash.	Abi Lands. Kind.	Sailáb Lands. Cash.	Sailáb Lands. Kind.	Báráni Lands. Cash.	Báráni Lands. Kind.
	Rs. A.	Per cent.	Rs. A.	Per cent.	Rs. A.	Per cent.	Rs. A.	Per cent.	Rs. A.	Per cent.	Rs. A.	Per cent.
Montgomery	8 0	33—25	...	50—33	...	...	...	50—33	...	17—25 33	...	33
Gugera	12 0	25—30	...	20—25 33	...	...	...	20—25	12 0	20—25 33	...	25—33
Dipálpur	...	20—25	...	25—33	...	...	...	25—33	...	25—33	...	17—20 33
Pákpattan	...	25	...	25	...	...	...	25	...	25	...	25
Average	10 0	20—25 33	...	20—25 33—50	..	...	...	20—25 33—50	12 0	17—20 25—33	...	17—20 25—33

Yield in standard sers per acre of principal crops.

Crop.	Irrigated.	Unirrigated.
Rice (in husk)	600	...
Maize	350	...
Jowár	250	100
Cane (gur)	...	...
Cotton (uncleaned) ...	200	80
Wheat	360	200
Barley	440	200
Gram	280	200
Pulses of both harvests	140	100

Table No. XXII—showing NUMBER of STOCK.

1	2	3	4	5	6	7	8	9	10	11
	Whole district for the years						Tahsils for the year 1896-97.			
Kind of Stock.	1871-72.	1876-77.	1882-83.	1887-88.	1892-93.	1896-97.	Montgomery.	Gugera.	Dipálpur.	Pákpattan.
Cows and bullocks	226,225	241,760	260,636	213,629	303,067	265,571	50,205	45,019	97,171	73,176
Buffaloes	...	...	...	42,132	52,468	75,449	15,780	16,668	30,124	12,877
Young stock calves or buffalo calves ...	...	...	...	...	...	61,831	9,344	6,762	30,534	15,191
Horses	1,600	1,375	472	5,386	6,966	8,762	890	1,167	4,445	2,260
Ponies	35	4,125	866							
Mules	...	...	...	...	...	96	7	18	71	...
Donkeys	4,995	4,995	6,951	14,759	20,740	25,540	3,007	3,075	11,665	7,193
Sheep and goats	270,407	272,159	469,766	392,412	462,301	455,686	114,187	96,250	116,725	128,524
Pigs	...	...	...	...	...	...	...	...	...	...
Camels	7,012	11,748	1,737	6,859	7,395	12,730	6,128	1,981	2,874	1,806
Carts	...	32	70	265	440	328	26	39	126	137
Ploughs	29,909	40,275	40,792	41,294	60,261	53,230	4,746	8,633	24,570	15,281
Boats	44	61	48	72	89	100	31	11	50	8

Table No. XXIII—showing OCCUPATIONS of MALES.

1	2	3	4	5	6
			MALES ABOVE 15 YEARS OF AGE.		
Class.	Order.	Sub-order and occupations.	Towns.	Villages.	Total.
		Total population ...	7,810	144,450	152,260
		Occupation specified	4,258	111,563	115,821
A.—Government	I and III—6	Civil Administration	481	1,865	2,346
	II and III—7	Army	2	372	374
B.—Pastoral and agricultural.	V.—Agriculture	Landowners 10/30 to 32 and 34	236	1,880	2,125
		Tenants 10/33	...	...	...
		Labourers 11/35 and 36	258	20,227	20,485
		Other miscellaneous 12 and 13/37 to 42	654	55,077	55,731
	IV.	Pastoral 8 and 9/10 to 29	157	9,126	9,283
C.—Personal service	VI.	Personal and household service 14 to 16/43 to 55	443	3,081	3,524
	VII.—Food and drink	Dealers in milk, butter and ghi 17/56 to 58	98	414	512
		Dealers in fish 17/62 and 63	...	5	5
		Fowl and egg dealers 17/60	...	...	...
		Butchers and roast-meat shopkeepers 17/59 and 61	...	7	7
		Dealers in grain and flour 18/64 to 68	55	1,151	1,206
		Fruit and vegetable sellers 18/69 and 70	37	37	74
		Grocers and general shopkeepers 19/83	24	109	133
		Other dealers and manufacturers of food and drink 19/71 to 82 & 84 to 86	290	2,590	2,880

D.—Preparation and supply of material substances.	XII.—Textile fabrics ...	Dealers in wool and fur 38/144 to 158	11	40	51
		Workers in silk 30/159 to 162	...	1	1
		Do. in cotton 10/163 to 175	5	77	82
	XIII.—Metals and precious stones.	Do. in gold, silver and precious stones 13/187 to 198	132	1,825	1,957
		Do. in other metals 44 to 46/199 to 207	463	7,127	7,590
	XV.—Wood and cane leaves.	Do. in timber and wood 10/212 to 217	93	596	689
		Do. in canework 50/218 to 226	240	1,385	1,625
	XVII.—Leather, horn and grease.	Do. in leather 53/214 to 217	3	35	38
E.—Commerce, transport and storage.	XIII.—Commerce ..	Bankers and Bank Managers 54/248	2	6	8
		Money-lenders 54/249	...	8	8
		Bill discounters 54/250	...	8	8
		Money changers and testers 54/251	...	8	8
		Cashiers and accountants 54/252	...	30	30
		General merchants 54/253	...	3	3
F.—Professional.	XX.—Learning and artistic professions.	Religious teachers and ministers 63 (a)/287 to 295	39	3,196	3,235
		Fakirs and mendicants 63 (b) and 76 (b)/296 to 298 and 318	59	441	500
G.—Indefinite and Independent.	XXII.—Indefinite ..	Unskilled labour 74/336 to 340	430	120	550
	XXIII.—Independent of work.	Pensioners 77 (a)/349 to 351	46	707	753

Table No. XXIV, showing MANUFACTURES.

1	2	3	4	5	6	7	8	9	10	11	12	13	14	15	16	17	18	19
	Silk.	Cotton.	Wool.	Other fabrics.	Paper.	Wood.	Iron.	Brass and copper.	Buildings.	Dyeing and manufacturing of dyes.	Leather.	Pottery, common and glazed.	Oil-pressing and refining.	Pashmina and shawls.	Carpets.	Gold, silver and jewellery.	Other manufactures.	Total.
Number of mills and large factories	...	4	...	...	...	...	...	...	...	...	...	...	...	...	...	...	...	4
Number of private looms or small works ...	...	...	...	...	...	...	...	...	...	...	...	...	...	...	...	...	...	...
Number of workmen in large works. Male	...	147	...	...	...	...	...	...	...	...	...	...	...	...	...	...	...	147
Number of workmen in large works. Female	...	94	...	...	...	...	...	...	...	...	...	...	...	...	...	...	...	94
Number of workmen in small works or independent artisans.	...	...	...	...	...	...	...	...	...	...	...	...	...	...	...	...	...	...
Value of plant in large works, in rupees ...	...	...	...	...	...	...	...	...	...	...	...	...	...	...	...	...	...	...
Estimated annual outturn of large works, in rupees.	...	5,00,000 (approximately.)	...	...	...	...	...	...	...	...	...	...	...	...	...	...	...	...

Table No. XXV showing RIVER TRAFFIC.

1	2	3	4	5	6
Trade.		Principal Merchandise carried.	Average duration of voyage in days.		Distance in miles.
From	To		Summer or floods.	Winter or low water.	
		Nil.			

Table No. XXVI, showing RETAIL PRICES.

1	2		3		4		5		6		7		8		9		10		11		12		13		14		15		16	
	Number of Sers and Chittacks per Rupee.																													
Year.	Wheat.		Barley.		Gram.		Indian-corn.		Jowár.		Bájra.		Rice (fine).		Urd (dál).		Potatoes.		Cotton (cleaned).		Sugar (refined).		Ghi (cow's).		Firewood.		Tobacco.		Salt (Lahori).	
	Srs.	Chs.	Srs.	Chs.	Srs.	Chs.	Srs.	Chs.	Srs.	Chs.	Srs.	Chs.	Srs.	Chs.	Srs.	Chs.	Srs.	Chs.	Srs.	Chs.	Srs.	Chs.	Srs.	Chs.	Srs.	Chs.	Srs.	Chs.	Srs.	Chs.
1864-65	24	4	29	14	29	11	0	0	14	15	0	0	5	9	16	13	...	...	2	5	..	...	2	1	208	9	6	8	...	...
1865-66	18	13	23	7	21	9	0	0	16	9	0	0	6	4	16	5	...	0	2	13	0	0	1	10	211	8	7	...	0	0
1866-67	21	8	29	3	30	4	0	0	16	15	0	0	7	5	17	7	...	0	2	5	0	0	1	7	149	5	6	14	0	0
1867-68	16	15	24	8	22	3	0	0	16	15	0	0	7	7	15	4	...	0	2	15	0	0	1	7	149	5	6	11	0	0
1868-69	14	3	17	4	25	14	0	0	9	3	0	0	6	6	9	1	...	0	2	11	0	0	1	5	119	5	7	10	0	0
1869-70	9	6	10	13	10	7	0	0	11	4	13	5	5	2	10	4	...	0	2	2	0	0	1	8	111	15	8	15	0	0
1870-71	14	7	20	0	18	2	0	0	16	1	15	8	6	5	13	1	...	0	2	3	0	0	1	8	149	5	5	14	0	0
1871-72	16	8	25	8	20	0	18	0	20	0	22	0	7	0	13	0	9	0	2	12	2	0	1	8	160	0	8	0	9	0
1872-73	21	0	28	0	21	0	20	0	24	0	28	0	6	0	14	0	10	0	2	12	2	4	1	8	160	0	7	0	8	0
1873-74	19	0	26	0	26	0	0	0	25	0	24	0	6	0	15	0	8	0	3	0	3	0	1	12	160	0	6	0	8	0
1874-75	21	0	28	0	31	0	0	0	...	0	0	0	6	0	18	0	13	0	3	0	2	12	1	12	180	0	8	0	9	0
1875-76	19	0	25	0	26	0	0	0	28	0	25	0	6	0	18	0	12	0	2	12	3	0	1	3	180	0	8	0	9	8
1876-77	31	0	50	0	44	0	0	0	30	0	0	0	8	0	18	0	16	0	2	8	3	0	1	10	160	0	8	0	9	0
1877-78	18	0	26	0	23	0	0	0	...	0	18	0	6	8	10	0	12	0	2	8	3	4	1	8	200	0	8	0	9	0
1878-79	12	0	16	0	14	0	14	0	14	0	13	4	4	8	7	0	10	0	2	12	2	8	1	8	160	0	8	0	9	0
1879-80	13	0	18	0	16	0	0	0	17	0	...	0	7	0	10	0	10	0	2	12	2	8	1	6	200	0	8	0	10	0
1880-81	13	12	18	0	17	0	17	0	18	0	...	0	5	0	13	0	12	0	2	3	2	4	1	6	200	0	5	0	10	4

Table No. XXVI, showing RETAIL PRICES—*concluded.*

Number of sers and chittaks per rupee.

1	2		3		4		5		6		7		8		9		10		11		12		13		14		15		16	
Year.	Wheat.		Barley.		Gram.		Indian-corn.		Jowár.		Bájra.		Rice (fine).		Urd (dál).		Potatoes.		Cotton (cleaned).		Sugar (refined).		Ghi (cow's).		Firewood.		Tobacco.		Salt (Lahori).	
	Srs.	Chs.	Srs.	Chs.	Srs.	Chs.	Srs.	Chs.	Srs.	Chs.	Srs.	Chs.	Srs.	Chs.	Srs.	Chs.	Srs.	Chs.	Srs.	Chs.	Srs.	Chs.	Srs.	Chs.	Srs.	Chs.	Srs.	Chs.	Srs.	Chs.
1881-82	15	0	20	0	24	0	20	0	25	0	24	0	5	0	14	0	10	0	2	8	2	4	1	9	200	0	5	0	10	0
1882-83	21	0	32	0	33	0	26	0	32	0	0	0	5	0	13	0	12	0	3	...	2	12	1	11	200	0	6	0	12	0
1883-84	18	0	28	0	33	0	26	0	28	0	0	0	6	0	16	0	9	0	2	12	2	12	1	9	200	0	6	0	12	0
1884-85	17	0	24	0	22	0	16	0	16	0	16	0	10	0	0	0	13	0	2	8	2	12	1	9	200	0	6	0	12	0
1885-86	17	0	25	0	33	0	20	0	16	0	16	0	10	0	16	0	10	0	2	8	2	11	1	8	200	0	5	8	11	8
1886-87	19	0	23	12	31	0	19	0	16	0	15	0	10	0	15	8	10	0	3	7	2	10	1	8	200	0	5	8	11	8
1887-88	19	0	23	12	33	0	18	8	16	0	15	0	11	0	16	0	11	0	2	8	2	10	1	5	200	0	6	0	12	0
1888-89	18	0	23	12	33	0	18	0	16	0	15	0	11	0	16	0	11	0	2	8	2	8	1	4	200	0	6	0	11	8
1889-90	16	0	21	8	30	0	17	0	15	0	14	0	11	0	16	0	10	0	2	8	2	10	1	5	200	0	6	0	11	8
1890-91	19	0	19	0	30	0	15	0	15	0	14	0	10	8	12	0	11	0	2	8	1	15	1	5	180	0	5	8	12	0
1891-92	17	0	20	0	29	8	16	0	14	0	15	0	10	12	10	0	9	0	2	8	2	0	1	4	180	0	6	0	10	11
1892-93	16	0	18	8	29	0	16	0	14	0	14	8	11	0	8	8	10	0	1	14	2	0	1	3	100	0	6	0	11	0
1893-94	15	0	18	0	26	0	15	0	15	0	14	0	10	0	8	0	8	0	2	0	2	0	1	4	130	0	6	0	12	0
1894-95	14	0	15	8	25	7	15	0	13	0	14	0	9	0	10	0	9	0	2	8	2	8	1	2	140	0	7	0	12	8
1895-96	13	0	15	8	25	0	14	0	13	0	13	0	9	0	8	12	6	0	2	0	2	8	1	0	170	0	6	8	12	0
1896-97	13	0	16	0	25	0	14	8	14	8	14	0	9	0	8	0	7	0	2	0	2	8	1	5	160	0	7	0	12	0

Table No. XXVI, showing PRICE of LABOUR.

1	2	3	4	5	6	7	8	9	10	11	12	13
Year.	Wages of labour per day.				Carts per day.		Camels per day.		Donkeys per score per day.		Boats per day.	
	Skilled.		Unskilled.									
	Highest.	Lowest.	Highest.	Lowest.	Highest.	Lowest.	Highest.	Lowest.	Highest.	Lowest.	Highest.	Lowest.
	Rs. a. p.	Rs. a. p.	Rs. a. p.	Rs. a. p.	Rs. a. p.		Rs. a. p.		Rs. a. p.		Rs. a. p.	Rs. a. p.
1873-74	0 8 0	0 4 0	0 3 0	0 2 0	2 0 0		0 8 0		2 8 0		10 0 0	2 0 0
					Rs. a. p.	Rs. a. p.	Rs. a. p.	Rs. a. p.	Rs. a. p.	Rs. a. p.		
1878-79	0 8 0	0 6 0	0 4 0	0 3 0	2 0 0	1 0 0	0 8 0	0 3 0	3 12 0	2 8 0	10 0 0	2 0 0
1883-84	0 10 0	0 6 0	0 4 0	0 3 0	1 6 0	0 14 0	0 13 0	0 4 0	3 2 0	2 1 0	3 13 0	1 12 0
1884-85	0 10 0	0 6 0	0 4 0	0 3 0	1 6 0	0 14 0	0 13 0	0 4 0	3 2 0	2 1 0	3 13 0	1 12 0
1885-86	0 10 0	0 6 0	0 4 0	0 3 0	1 6 0	0 14 0	0 13 0	0 4 0	3 2 0	2 1 0	3 13 0	1 12 0
1886-87	0 10 0	0 6 0	0 4 0	0 3 0	1 6 0	0 14 0	0 13 0	0 4 0	3 2 0	2 1 0	3 13 0	1 12 0
1887-88	0 10 0	0 6 0	0 4 0	0 3 0	1 6 0	0 14 0	0 13 0	0 4 0	3 2 0	2 1 0	3 13 0	1 12 0
1888-89	0 10 0	0 8 0	0 4 0	0 3 0	1 0 0	0 14 0	0 8 0	0 7 0	3 12 0	3 12 0	2 8 0	1 8 0
1889-90	0 10 0	0 8 0	0 4 0	0 3 0	0 8 0	0 7 0	0 8 0	0 7 0	3 12 0	3 12 0	2 8 0	1 8 0
1890-91	0 10 0	0 8 0	0 4 0	0 3 0	0 8 0	0 7 0	0 8 0	0 7 0	3 12 0	3 12 0	2 8 0	1 8 0
1891-92	0 10 0	0 8 0	0 4 0	0 3 0	0 8 0	0 7 0	0 8 0	0 7 0	3 12 0	3 12 0	2 8 0	1 8 0
1892-93	0 10 0	0 8 0	0 4 0	0 3 0	0 8 0	0 7 0	0 8 0	0 7 0	3 12 0	3 12 0	2 8 0	1 8 0
1893-94	0 12 0	0 8 0	0 5 0	0 4 0	0 8 0	0 7 0	0 8 0	0 6 0	2 8 0	1 14 0	2 0 0	1 8 0
1894-95	0 12 0	0 8 0	0 5 0	0 4 0	0 8 0	0 7 0	0 8 0	0 6 0	2 8 0	1 14 0	2 0 0	1 8 0
1895-96	0 12 0	0 8 0	0 5 0	0 4 0	0 8 0	0 7 0	0 8 0	0 6 0	2 8 0	1 14 0	2 0 0	1 8 0
1896-97	0 12 0	0 8 0	0 5 0	0 4 0	0 8 0	0 7 0	0 8 0	0 6 0	2 8 0	1 14 0	2 0 0	1 8 0

Table No. XXVIII, showing REVENUE COLLECTED.

1	2	3	4	5	6	7	8	9
					Excise.			
Year.	Fixed land revenue.	Fluctuating and miscellaneous land revenue.	Tribute.	Local rates.	Spirits.	Drugs.	Stamps.	Total collections.
	Rs.	Rs.		Rs.	Rs.	Rs.	Rs.	Rs.
1886-87 ...	2,93,731	3,32,818	...	65,918	3,639	6,839	41,261	7,41,236
1887-88 ...	3,04,765	3,60,926	...	70,834	2,112	8,410	45,411	7,22,458
1888-89 ...	2,52,931	3,39,625	...	60,368	1,738	7,219	49,671	7,11,552
1889-90 ...	2,52,561	3,00,962	...	60,642	1,063	6,344	48,989	6,70,561
1890-91 ...	2,56,265	2,79,779	...	58,024	9,878	6,578	43,047	6,53,571
1891-92 ...	2,61,135	3,58,147	...	65,152	12,150	7,691	46,257	7,50,532
1892-93 ...	2,63,280	3,83,245	...	71,634	14,559	8,785	42,684	7,84,187
1893-94 ...	2,49,016	4,32,098	...	62,472	15,393	10,850	48,585	8,18,444
1894-95 ...	2,42,173	3,78,234	...	71,540	15,949	12,165	49,245	7,69,306
1895-96 ...	2,64,920	2,35,620	...	63,672	15,395	12,412	47,772	6,39,791
1896-97 ...	2,74,036	2,19,779	...	52,726	8,407	12,520	50,784	6,18,252

Table No. XXIX, showing REVENUE DERIVED FROM LAND.

1	2	3	4	5	6	7	8	9	10	11	12	13
			FLUCTUATING REVENUE.					MISCELLANEOUS REVENUE.				
								Grazing dues.				
YEAR.	Fixed land revenue demand.	Fluctuating and miscellaneous land revenue collections.	Revenue of alluvial lands.	Revenue of waste lands brought under assessment.	Water-advantage revenue.	Fluctuating assessments of river lands.	Total fluctuating land revenue.	By enumeration of cattle.	By grazing leases.	Sale of wood by rakhs and forests.	Sajji.	Total miscellaneous land revenue.
	Rs.	Rs.	Rs.	Rs.		Rs.	Rs.	Rs.	Rs.	Rs.	Rs.	Rs.
1886-87	2,70,695	2,17,149	2,532	220	...	1,10,132	1,31,021	...	70,393	1,560	40	86,128
1887-88	2,62,804	3,35,652	1,408	7,008	...	1,76,132	2,25,537	...	94,810	8,600	35	1,10,115
1888-89	2,53,299	3,29,050	2,341	12,087	...	1,72,965	2,30,404	...	84,341	6,764	71	98,556
1889-90	2,55,680	2,99,060	5,717	12,526	...	1,34,977	1,91,200	...	83,154	10,915	...	1,07,770
1890-91	2,58,899	2,79,193	4,611	10,175	...	1,07,139	1,75,636	...	84,598	2,449	...	1,03,557
1891-92	2,64,606	3,56,864	3,778	13,000	...	1,58,400	2,01,314	...	95,250	906	2,461	1,55,545
1892-93	2,66,872	3,82,727	1,794	...	...	1,78,285	2,40,009	...	95,312	1,614	6,257	1,40,658
1893-94	2,69,186	4,21,303	1,143	...	...	1,72,874	3,03,220	...	93,439	4,577	1,118	1,21,137
1894-95	2,68,006	3,73,453	918	...	...	1,51,495	2,57,833	...	91,331	2,768	812	1,15,620
1895-96	2,64,920	2,67,475	1,180	6,671	...	1,07,738	1,70,118	...	61,439	16,974	372	91,357
1896-97	2,74,036	2,36,482	821	551	...	1,30,104	1,87,642	...	26,989	10,005	247	48,840
TAHSIL TOTALS FOR 6 YEARS 1891-92 TO 1896-97.												
Montgomery	1,56,690	3,04,761	...	40	...	...	1,52,508	...	1,01,251	22,665	6,144	1,52,253
Gugera	2,23,953	2,74,641	18	272	...	...	1,63,207	...	90,247	627	1,037	1,11,434
Dipálpur	6,32,954	7,67,383	2,640	971	...	6,56,054	6,69,201	...	78,652	1,380	1,693	98,182
Pákpattan	3,29,513	3,37,715	3,198	5,936	...	93,442	1,81,972	...	98,301	3,256	Included in Montgomery tahsil.	1,55,743
Total	13,43,110	16,84,500	5,850	7,228	...	7,49,490	11,66,858	...	3,68,451	27,928	8,874	5,17,612

Table No. XXX, showing ASSIGNED LAND REVENUE.

1	2	3	4	5	6	7	8	9	10	11	12	13
	TOTAL AREA AND REVENUE ASSIGNED.								DISTRIBUTION OF AREA AND JAMA.			
TAHSIL	*Village.*		*Fractional portion of village.*		*Plots.*		*Total.*		*In perpetuity free of conditions.*		*In perpetuity subject to conditions.*	
	Area.	Jama.	Area.	Jama.	Area.	Jama.	Area.	Jama.	Area.	Jama.	Area.	Jama.
	Acres.	Rs.	Acres.	Rs.	Acres.	Rs.	Acres.	Rs.	Acres.	Rs.	Acres.	Rs.
Montgomery	601	87	4,062	115	881	353	5,517	555	949	218	4,202	255
Gugera	5,850	982	611	109	276	156	6,737	1,247	975	125	1,486	509
Dipálpur	21,058	5,012	13,310	3,789	1,803	262	36,171	9,063	15,471	4,662	10,950	1,880
Pákpattan	3,861	820	...	...	601	158	4,462	978	...	...	4,054	922
Total District ...	31,373	6,901	17,983	4,013	3,561	929	52,917	11,813	17,395	5,005	20,782	3,566

Table No. XXX, Showing ASSIGNED LAND REVENUE—*concluded.*

	14	15	16	17	18	19	20	21	22	23	24	25	26	27
	DISTRIBUTION OF AREA AND JAMA—*concld.*								NUMBER OF HOLDERS.					
TAHSIL.	*For life or lives.*		*At pleasure of Government.*		*For term of Settlement.*		*Pending orders of Government.*		In perpetuity free of conditions.	In perpetuity subject to conditions.	For life or lives.	At pleasure of Government.	For term of Settlement.	Pending orders of Government.
	Area.	Jama.	Area.	Jama.	Area.	Jama.	Area.	Jama.						
	Acres.	Rs.	Acres.	Rs.	Acres.	Rs.	Acres.	Rs.						
Montgomery	306	82	...	...	...	...	...	...	40	26	15	...	...	...
Gugera	3,774	526	502	87	...	...	...	...	2	42	12	1	...	...
Dipálpur	9,567	2,516	183	5	...	...	...	...	8	43	23	5	...	...
Pákpattan	21	15	387	41	...	...	...	...	...	3	6	8	...	...
Total District ...	13,668	3,139	1,072	133	...	...	...	...	50	114	56	14	...	...

Table No. XXXI, showing BALANCES, REMISSIONS and TAKAVI.

1	2	3	4	5
	BALANCES OF LAND REVENUE IN RUPEES.			
YEAR.	Fixed revenue.	Fluctuating and miscellaneous revenue.	Reductions of fixed demand on account of bad season, deterioration, &c., in rupees.	Takávi advances in rupees
1886-87	98,473	21,295	63	65,722
1887-88	43,827	13,787	15,655	84,444
1888-89	43,827	13,787	21,650	23,702
1889-90	3,502	5,595	11,727	82,200
1890-91	3,365	745	2,237	...
1891-92	2,767	478	4,561	13,490
1892-93	3,488	585	2,966	...
1893-94	3,649	8,196	3,500	12,900
1894-95	20,680	4,894	2,815	10,738
1895-96	41,224	22,313	2,544	5,731
1896-97	80,190	41,449	1,210	14,781

Table No. XXXII, showing SALES and MORTGAGES of LAND up to end of LAST SETTLEMENT.

1	2	3	4	5	6	7	8	9	10
	Area mortgaged, in Acres.			Area sold, in Acres.			Total area transferred, in Acres.		
Name of Tahsil.	To old agriculturists.	To new agriculturists.	Total.	To old agriculturists.	To new agriculturists.	Total.	To old agriculturists.	To new agriculturists.	Total.
Montgomery	25,708	19,086	44,794	Not available.		10,588	Not available.		55,382
Gugera	15,742	10,494	26,236	14,298	9,828	24,126	30,010	20,322	50,362
Dipálpur	21,853	18,160	40,013	35,713	11,230	46,943	57,566	29,390	86,956
Pákpattan	8,059	10,564	18,623	18,726	7,156	25,882	26,785	17,720	44,505
Total District	71,362	58,304	129,666	Not available.		107,539	Not available.		237,205

Table No. XXXIII, showing SALE of STAMPS and REGISTRATION of DEEDS.

1	2	3	4	5	6	7	8	9	10	11	12	13
	Income from sale of Stamps.				Operations of the Registration Department.							
	Receipts, in rupees.		Net income, in rupees.		Number of deeds registered.				Value of property affected, in rupees.			
Year.	Judicial.	Non-judicial.	Judicial.	Non-judicial.	Touching immoveable property.	Touching moveable property.	Wills, money obligations and miscellaneous.	Total of all kinds.	Immoveable property.	Moveable property.	Money obligations and miscellaneous.	Total of all kinds.
1887-88	33,468	11,943	29,757	11,337	317	7	167	521	2,25,202	4,554	50,109	2,79,865
1888-89	39,663	11,511	38,767	10,904	317	1	154	472	2,26,116	209	26,467	2,53,122
1889-90	36,000	11,682	35,021	13,968	378	3	174	555	2,91,902	4,223	35,780	3,31,905
1890-91	32,663	12,802	30,783	12,261	354	3	134	491	2,41,835	2,121	16,719	2,60,978
1891-92	34,024	13,860	33,042	13,214	467	1	169	637	2,81,870	1,379	21,971	3,05,230
1892-93	30,808	13,851	29,525	13,150	417	121	10	548	2,78,421	...	18,262	2,96,683
1893-94	37,314	13,054	36,216	12,369	432	158	10	600	3,56,826	...	35,073	3,91,899
1894-95	38,056	12,807	37,089	12,156	498	149	11	658	3,36,453	...	22,896	3,59,349
1895-96	36,454	13,596	34,852	12,920	578	162	12	752	3,14,110	...	23,240	3,37,350
1896-97	37,331	12,918	33,718	12,468	804	235	10	1,049	4,42,672	...	29,036	4,71,708

Table No. XXXIII A, showing REGISTRATIONS.

1	2	3	4	5	6	7
Name of Registration Office.	Number of Deeds registered.					
	1895-96.			1896-97.		
	Compulsory.	Optional.	Total.	Compulsory.	Optional	Total.
Registrar, Montgomery	7	...	7	13	...	13
Sub-Registrar, Montgomery	21	10	31	48	28	76
Joint Sub-Registrar, Montgomery tahsíl ...	10	1	11	15	...	15
Ditto Kamália	171	97	268	185	126	311
Sub-Registrar, Dipálpur	42	15	57	74	40	114
Joint Sub-Registrar, Dipálpur, tahsíl ...	83	45	128	152	68	220
Sub-Registrar, Gugera	74	12	86	70	21	91
Ditto Pákpattan	88	57	145	45	24	69
Joint Sub-Registrar, Pákpattan tahsíl ...	9	10	19	105	35	140
Total District ...	505	247	752	707	342	1,049

Table No. XXXIV, showing INCOME TAX COLLECTIONS for the years 1886-87 to 1896-97.

1	2	3	4	5	6	7	8	9	10	11	12	13	14	15
Year.	Number of persons assessed in each class and grade.											Total number of persons assessed.	Total amount of fees.	Number of villages in which persons are assessed.
	Class I.					Class II.								
	Rs. 30,000	Rs. 10,000	Rs. 5,000	Rs. 2,500	Rs. 2,000	Rs. 1,750	Rs. 1,500	Rs. 1,250	Rs. 1,000	Rs. 750	Rs. 500			
1886-87	...	...	2	22	10	19	34	36	56	130	531	840	14,568	288
1887-88	...	...	2	22	12	19	33	37	56	129	531	811	15,379	330
1888-89	...	...	2	22	12	19	34	38	57	133	528	845	14,375	349
1889-90	...	...	6	22	19	19	35	39	71	174	536	924	16,397	338
1890-91	...	...	6	22	20	20	38	52	88	188	509	943	17,160	355
1891-92	...	...	6	25	24	21	37	59	96	208	528	1,004	18,507	350
1892-93	...	...	7	21	20	30	34	62	106	214	527	1,021	18,735	365
1893-94	...	...	8	19	30	32	49	70	127	234	557	1,126	21,210	366
1894-95	...	...	5	20	26	37	49	75	112	217	575	1,146	21,257	380
1895-96	...	...	2	23	33	31	42	82	149	220	571	1,159	21,580	381
1896-97	...	...	3	23	36	25	46	78	116	222	538	1,117	21,252	381
Tahsíl details for 1896-97—														
Montgomery	...	..	1	5	6	10	12	21	44	66	155	300	5,772	71
Gugera	...	...	...	3	10	5	9	18	35	11	99	220	4,268	76
Dipálpur	...	...	1	9	9	6	11	24	33	52	150	295	5,777	123
Pákpattan	...	...	1	6	11	4	14	15	31	63	154	302	5,135	111

Table No. XXXV—showing EXCISE STATISTICS.

1	2	3	4	5	6	7	8	9	10	11	12	13	14	15
		Fermented Liquors.				Intoxicating Drugs.						Excise revenue from		
		Number of Retail shops.		Consumption, in gallons.		Number of Retail Licenses.		Consumption, in maunds.						
Year.	Number of Central Distilleries.	Country spirits.	European liquors.	Rum.	Country spirits.	Opium.	Other drugs.	Opium.	Charas.	Bhang.	Other drugs.	Fermented liquors.	Drugs.	Total.
								Md. S. C.	Md. S. C.	Md. S. C.				
1891-92	1	28	3	698	...	31	31	20 31 7	4 7 8	81 16 8	...	12,150	7,998	20,148
1892-93	1	30	1	725	...	31	31	20 24 6	3 28 11	80 19 6	...	14,559	9,012	23,571
1893-94	1	31	2	403	...	34	31	17 36 13	4 15 10	71 36 9	...	15,393	11,082	26,475
1894-95	1	32	1	127	991	34	31	20 35 6	5 15 2	61 28 8	...	15,949	12,362	28,311
1895-96	...	31	1	107	1,201	34	31	22 28 9	5 26 0	72 17 0	...	15,400	12,417	27,817
1896-97	...	31	1	115	1,056	34	31	22 33 10	5 37 0	21 25 6	...	15,367	12,805	28,172
Total ...	...	193	9	2,175	3,250	31	31	125 33 3	29 9 15	439 23 5	...	88,818	65,676	154,494
Average ...	...	32	2	363	542	6	6	21 0 0	5 0 0	73 0 0	...	11,803	10,946	25,749

Table No. XXXVI—showing DISTRICT FUNDS.

1	2	3	4	5	6	7	8	9	10	11	12
Year.	Annual Income in Rupees.			Annual Expenditure, in Rupees.							
	Provincial rates.	Miscellaneous.	Total Income.	Establishment.	District post and arboriculture.	Education.	Medical.	Miscellaneous.	Contribution from Local to Provincial.	Public Works.	Total Expenditure.
1892-93	55,004	7,650	62,654	2,447	2,798	10,638	8,813	2,188	9,372	11,277	47,533
1893-94	55,956	11,340	67,296	2,344	2,831	11,560	8,808	2,703	10,033	21,166	59,034
1894-95	58,893	9,838	68,731	2,399	3,276	11,402	9,075	2,496	11,335	35,095	75,738
1895-96	56,181	11,186	67,367	2,455	5,849	11,054	9,668	3,085	10,555	36,670	79,931
1896-97	46,787	7,273	54,060	2,721	6,804	13,198	9,840	6,255	8,500	21,853	69,270

Table No. XXXVII—showing GOVERNMENT and AIDED SCHOOLS.

1	2	3	4	5	6	7	8	9	10	11	12	13	14	15	16	17	18	19	20	21
Year.	High Schools.						Middle Schools.						Primary Schools.							
	English.				Vernacular.		English.				Vernacular.		English.				Vernacular.			
	Government.		Aided.		Government.		Government.		Aided.		Government.		Government.		Aided.		Government.		Aided.	
	Schools.	Scholars.	Schools.	Scholars.	Schools.	Scholars.	Schools.	Scholars.	Schools.	Scholars.	Schools.	Scholars.	Schools.	Scholars.	Schools.	Scholars.	Schools.	Scholars.	Schools.	Scholars.
Figures for Boys.																				
1885-86	...	...	...	...	...	...	1	190	...	...	2	350	...	...	...	...	27	1,033	...	...
1886-87	...	...	...	...	...	...	1	182	...	...	2	304	...	...	...	...	27	1,046	...	...
1887-88	...	...	...	...	...	...	1	185	...	...	2	375	...	...	...	...	29	996	...	...
1888-89	...	...	...	...	...	...	1	183	...	...	2	395	...	...	...	...	30	1,127	...	...
1889-90	...	...	...	...	...	...	1	205	...	...	2	314	...	...	...	...	33	1,251	...	...
1890-91	...	...	...	...	...	...	2	424	...	...	1	183	...	...	...	...	33	1,371	...	...
1891-92	...	...	...	...	...	...	3	490	...	...	1	131	...	...	...	...	33	1,185	...	...
1892-93	...	...	...	...	...	...	3	476	...	...	1	183	...	...	...	...	33	1,142	...	...
1893-94	...	...	...	...	...	...	3	470	...	...	1	206	...	...	...	...	33	1,142	...	...
1894-95	...	...	...	...	...	...	3	474	...	...	1	194	...	...	...	...	35	1,218	...	...
1895-96	...	...	...	...	...	...	3	526	...	...	2	368	...	...	...	...	34	1,111	...	...
1896-97	1	242	...	...	...	...	2	261	...	...	2	353	...	...	...	...	34	1,094	...	...
Figures for Girls.																				
1885-86	...	...	...	...	...	...	...	...	...	...	...	...	...	...	...	...	2	46	...	...
1886-87	...	...	...	...	...	...	...	...	...	...	...	...	...	...	...	...	2	44	...	...
1887-88	...	...	...	...	...	...	...	...	...	...	...	...	...	...	...	...	2	47	...	...
1888-89	...	...	...	...	...	...	...	...	...	...	...	...	...	...	...	...	2	39	...	...
1889-90	...	...	...	...	...	...	...	...	...	...	...	...	...	...	...	...	1	23	...	...
1890-91	...	...	...	...	...	...	...	...	...	...	...	...	...	...	...	...	1	24	...	...
1891-92	...	...	...	...	...	...	...	...	...	...	...	...	...	...	...	...	1	35	...	...
1892-93	...	...	...	...	...	...	...	...	...	...	...	...	...	...	...	...	1	39	...	...
1893-94	...	...	...	...	...	...	...	...	...	...	...	...	...	...	...	...	1	45	...	...
1894-95	...	...	...	...	...	...	...	...	...	...	...	...	...	...	...	...	1	47	...	...
1895-96	...	...	...	...	...	...	...	...	...	...	...	...	...	...	...	...	1	44	...	...
1896-97	...	...	...	...	...	...	...	...	...	...	...	...	...	...	...	...	1	54	...	...

Table No. XXXVIII—showing the WORKING of DISPENSARIES.

1	2	3	4	5	6	7	8	9	10	11	12	13	14	15	16	17	18
		NUMBER OF PATIENTS TREATED.															
		Men.							Women.							Children.	
Name of Dispensary.	Class of Dispensary.	1891.	1892.	1893.	1894.	1895.	1896.	1897.	1891.	1892.	1893.	1894.	1895.	1896.	1897.	1891.	1892.
Montgomery	Second class ...	4,424	5,194	4,905	6,098	5,498	5,168	6,585	864	1,130	1,118	1,361	1,206	1,064	1,720	1,550	2,206
Kamália	Do. ...	5,114	5,208	5,674	5,290	4,350	4,248	4,223	1,933	1,832	1,918	2,257	1,591	1,605	1,410	3,520	3,260
Pákpattan	Do. ...	3,845	4,810	4,095	4,733	4,483	4,773	5,037	951	1,319	1,145	1,273	1,085	1,184	1,692	1,210	1,765
Tibbi	Do. ...	...	...	...	2,681	2,383	2,280	2,353	...	...	...	906	843	831	1,120	...	...
Dipálpur	Do. ...	4,465	4,767	5,057	5,538	5,135	5,202	5,299	1,310	1,263	1,484	1,734	1,655	1,849	1,801	1,493	1,050
Shah Nawáz Khan ...	Third class ...	520	2,058	2,006	2,028	2,064	2,874	2,937	176	803	498	550	690	798	818	137	677
Sayadwála	Second " ...	3,533	3,905	4,065	4,850	4,679	4,014	3,920	1,614	1,790	1,690	2,080	2,200	1,901	1,702	1,728	1,079
Gugera	Do. ...	4,281	4,578	3,918	4,194	3,356	3,088	2,873	1,403	1,497	1,292	1,191	1,092	968	767	1,570	1,475

Table No. XXXVIII—*continued.*

1	2	19	20	21	22	23	24	25	26	27	28	29	30	31	32	33	34
		NUMBER OF PATIENTS TREATED.															
		Children—concluded.					*Total patients.*							*Indoor patients.*			
Name of Dispensary.	Class of Dispensary.	1893.	1894.	1895.	1896.	1897.	1891.	1892.	1893.	1894.	1895.	1896.	1897.	1891.	1892.	1893.	1894.
Montgomery	Second class ..	1,815	2,009	1,833	1,914	2,893	6,847	8,530	7,888	9,168	8,537	8,086	11,198	218	244	287	307
Kamália	Do. ...	2,755	2,533	2,726	3,566	2,968	10,573	10,300	10,347	10,080	8,667	9,419	8,631	166	208	179	187
Pákpattan	Do. ...	1,302	1,550	1,633	1,774	2,663	6 012	7,934	6,542	7,556	7,181	7,731	9,395	211	190	177	206
Tibbi	Do. ...	...	715	753	871	1,241	...	...	...	4,302	3,979	3,982	4,723	...	...	...	...
Dipálpur	Do. ...	1,568	2,272	2,389	2,698	2,812	7,268	7,080	8,109	9,544	9,179	9,789	9,912	271	287	305	304
Shah Nawáz Khan ...	Third class ...	501	523	573	724	891	833	4,438	3,605	4,001	4,233	4,396	4,646	...	...	...	...
Sayadwála	Second „ ...	1,745	2,181	2,259	2,103	2,298	6,870	7,743	7,506	9,111	9,344	8,018	8,010	...	142	228	206
Gugera	Do. ...	1,161	960	1,115	1,314	1,163	7,251	7,550	6,371	6,354	5,561	5,370	4,803	220	199	109	11

Table No. XXXVIII—*concluded.*

1	2	35	36	37	38	39	40	41	42	43	44
Name of Dispensary	Class of Dispensary.	Number of Patients treated.			Expenditure in Rupees.						
		Indoor patients—*concld.*									
		1895.	1896.	1897.	1891.	1892.	1893.	1894.	1895.	1896.	1897.
Montgomery	Second class .	280	253	279	1,957 7 10	2,323 1 2	3,560 12 5	4,040 2 5	4,030 3 7	4,016 6 9	4,613 7 0
Kamália	Do. ...	170	151	143	1,183 6 2	1,135 2 9	1,555 15 9	1,840 6 7	1,721 15 1	1,444 6 10	1,044 13 11
Pákpattan	Do. ...	151	155	163	1,525 4 4	1,754 0 9	1,478 1 2	1,407 5 11	1,665 14 9	1,403 15 8	1,375 9 9
Tibbi	Do. ...	55	67	40	...	...	...	5,260 10 10	1,529 10 1	877 0 1	1,268 3 7
Dipálpur	Do. ...	291	270	289	1,184 10 2	1,775 4 3	1,319 12 10	1,435 6 1	1,725 7 6	1,723 4 9	1,456 13 6
Shah Nawáz Khan ...	Third class ...	...	...	...	557 1 5	6,688 9 11	796 13 10	714 1 2	924 2 10	1,000 13 5	1,000 5 10
Sayadwála	Second „ ...	242	201	176	1,402 4 8	1,438 6 5	2,482 8 11	1,275 8 0	1,793 6 2	1,694 3 10	1,588 3 1
Gugera	Do. ...	97	92	71	1,072 9 2	954 8 10	916 15 10	4,230 5 8	1,290 9 2	1,183 13 1	1,076 1 3

Table No. XXXIX—showing CIVIL and REVENUE LITIGATION.

1	2	3	4	5	6	7	8	9
Year.	Number of Civil suits concerning.				Value of suits concerning.			Number of Revenue cases.
	Money or movable property.	Rent and tenancy rights.	Land and revenue and other matters.	Total.	Land.	Other matters.	Total.	
					Rs.	Rs.	Rs.	
1891	3,137	...	1,105	4,242	56,033	2,28,386	2,84,419	4,245
1892	2,858	...	1,709	4,567	61,048	2,13,877	2,74,925	5,157
1893	3,768	13	198	3,979	5,10,290	4,79,190	9,89,480	5,244
1894	4,206	93	106	4,405	2,66,900	4,34,640	7,01,540	5,378
1895	3,818	17	198	4,033	61,420	5,51,270	6,12,690	4,156
1896	4,060	19	169	4,248	61,850	5,37,250	5,99,100	4,578
1897	3,563	83	77	3,723	29,200	4,25,540	4,54,740	5,160

Table No. XL—showing CRIMINAL TRIALS.

	1	2	3	4	5	6	7	8	9	10	11	12
	Details.	1887.	1888.	1889.	1890.	1891.	1892.	1893.	1894.	1895.	1896.	1897.
Persons tried.	Brought to trial	2,871	3,979	2,815	3,124	4,795	3,666	5,782	4,850	3,865	4,627	5,729
	Discharged	502	749	568	622	1,875	1 429	2,200	1,775	1,502	2,296	2,348
	Acquitted	148	110	225	356	318	545	635	398	387	464	359
	Convicted	1,978	2,687	1,049	1,278	1,210	1,621	1,987	1,650	1,885	1,646	2,510
	Committed or referred	30	22	19	57	10	14	21	12	15	55	39
	Died or escaped or transferred	2	1	3	1	3	5	6	2	3	10	12
	Remaining under trial	211	410	951	810	379	49	933	1,013	73	156	461
Cases disposed of.	Summons cases (Regular)	504	637	519	750	598	689	745	638	549	415	418
	" " (Summary)	5	2	4	9	12	10	17	10	8	7	10
	Warrant cases (Regular)	822	735	619	726	648	725	838	735	618	629	738
	" " (Summary)	...	...	...	1	2	1	2	1	...	1	1
	Total cases disposed of	1,331	1,374	1,172	1,486	1,260	1,425	1,602	1,384	1,175	1,052	1,167
Number of persons sentenced to	Death	1	2	1	3	1	2	4	3	2	4	3
	Transportation for life	2	3	4	2	2	4	5	4	7	9	...
	" for a term	...	1	2	3	2	2	1	...	...	1	2
	Penal servitude	...	...	...	...	...	...	...	...	...	...	...
	Fine under Rs. 10	537	238	319	821	510	860	915	738	647	850	799
	" Rs. 10 to rupees 50	219	110	206	204	308	305	210	319	218	231	368
	" " 50 to " 100	9	7	5	8	6	6	10	5	3	2	3
	" " 100 to " 500	...	...	...	4	2	2	3	1	...	...	...
	" " 500 to " 1,000	1	..	1	...	...	1	1	...	...	...	...
	Over rupees 1,000	...	...	...	...	...	...	...	...	...	...	...
	Imprisonment under 6 months	248	210	198	375	406	410	610	538	398	521	610
	" 6 months to 2 years	319	415	279	201	194	209	307	210	248	165	115
	" over 2 years	18	20	16	9	5	6	15	10	11	15	18
	Whipping	51	30	48	61	52	41	30	19	68	97	87
	Find sureties of the peace	7	9	5	4	6	4	10	5	30	61	50
	Recognisance to keep the peace	20	10	13	12	19	18	19	12	3	4	6
	Give sureties for good behaviour	18	15	20	16	26	22	24	50	98	149	138

Table No. XLI—showing POLICE ENQUIRIES.

1	2	3	4	5	6	7	8	9	10	11	12	13	14
Nature of offence.	Number of cases enquired into.												
	1885.	1886.	1887.	1888.	1889.	1890.	1891.	1892.	1893.	1894.	1895.	1896.	1897.
Rioting or unlawful assembly	16	19	12	16	14	32	15	16	8	10	28	27	26
Murder and attempts to murder	15	4	7	3	6	2	4	8	4	3	6	14	13
Total serious offences against the person	95	80	75	77	66	110	115	45	30	32	41	96	87
Abduction of married women	...	...	...	...	...	...	...	...	...	...	...	...	...
Total serious offences against property	330	248	258	198	177	546	443	393	280	169	307	419	423
Total minor offences against the person	20	25	11	15	26	18	17	9	8	5	3	9	7
Cattle theft	681	587	468	379	298	676	577	436	298	312	210	349	328
Total minor offences against property	543	327	308	176	110	580	469	344	446	387	208	210	198
Total cognizable offences	398	387	269	267	304	319	306	414	428	502	315	318	215
Rioting, unlawful assembly, affray	2	2	3	6	3	2	5	...	...	...	...	4	3
Offences relating to marriage	1	5	3	5	4	4	3	2	...	...	...	3	2
Total non-cognizable offences	180	172	165	150	125	180	170	60	55	46	47	75	77
Grand total of offences	2,281	1,856	1,579	1,292	1,133	2,469	2,124	1,727	1,557	1,486	1,165	1,524	1,379

Table No. XLI—*continued.*

1	15	16	17	18	19	20	21	22	23	24	25	26	27
	NUMBER OF PERSONS ARRESTED OR SUMMONED.												
Nature of offence.	1885.	1886.	1887.	1888.	1889.	1890.	1891.	1892.	1893	1894.	1895.	1896.	1897.
Rioting or unlawful assembly	55	33	38	45	29	115	117	119	75	88	139	147	134
Murder and attempts to murder	9	8	8	5	6	5	5	4	3	5	14	22	18
Total serious offences against the person	42	38	86	68	65	78	115	131	107	119	125	175	160
Abduction of married women	...	...	...	...	...	...	...	...	...	...	...	...	...
Total serious offences against property	145	110	121	106	118	215	198	226	195	135	210	228	230
Total minor offences against the person	19	21	18	26	25	14	23	11	7	13	8	27	23
Cattle theft	234	228	240	229	310	339	234	260	237	248	235	317	329
Total minor offences against property	318	219	229	307	210	217	407	346	215	110	78	85	77
Total cognizable offences	219	258	218	307	409	307	358	403	426	513	442	451	368
Rioting, unlawful assembly, affray	28	22	41	38	57	27	36	...	...	...	...	39	31
Offences relating to marriage	6	30	25	19	28	96	83	17	...	...	...	13	8
Total non-cognizable offences	7,536	2,309	1,607	1,041	877	1,299	1,310	4,532	749	918	851	678	682
GRAND TOTAL OF OFFENCES	8,641	3,276	2,631	2,191	2,134	2,712	2,886	6,049	2,014	2,149	2,102	2,182	2,060

Table No. XLI—*concluded.*

1	28	29	30	31	32	33	34	35	36	37	38	39	40
	NUMBER OF PERSONS CONVICTED.												
Nature of offence.	1885.	1886.	1887.	1888.	1889.	1890.	1891.	1892.	1893.	1894.	1895.	1896.	1897.
Rioting or unlawful assembly	48	20	31	33	18	142	45	68	55	76	65	82	73
Murder and attempts to murder	6	5	7	5	4	3	8	5	3	5	7	8	5
Total serious offences against the person	37	25	75	52	49	117	125	52	87	107	112	118	110
Abduction of married women	...	...	...	...	...	...	...	...	...	...	...	...	...
Total serious offences against property	115	103	115	93	91	204	183	126	168	115	99	88	92
Total minor offences against the person	8	14	7	19	18	10	13	...	6	10	7	6	3
Cattle theft	209	189	202	187	283	175	133	144	193	219	225	238	232
Total minor offences against property	287	173	198	289	177	213	189	182	188	88	76	67	58
Total cognizable offences	235	233	185	275	392	216	225	319	372	399	377	269	281
Rioting, unlawful assembly, affray	12	18	32	29	33	19	32	...	...	...	...	30	28
Offences relating to marriage	6	17	16	11	17	19	13	..	...	...	...	10	9
Total non-cognizable offences	5,102	1,975	1,219	833	665	344	212	819	803	810	818	517	562
GRAND TOTAL OF OFFENCES ...	6,065	2,772	2,087	1,826	1,747	1,462	1,178	1,715	1,875	1,829	1,786	1,433	1,653

Table No. XLII—showing CONVICTS in GAOL.

1	2	3	4	5	6	7	8	9	10	11	12	13	14
	Number in jail at beginning of the year.		Number imprisoned during the year.		Religion of convicts.			Previous occupation of male convicts.					
Year.	Males.	Females.	Males.	Females.	Musalmáns.	Hindus.	Budhist and Jain.	Officials.	Professional.	Service.	Agricultural.	Commercial.	Industrial.
1886-87	255	...	710	12	573	56	...	8	2	27	396	10	244
1887-88	283	3	967	11	867	109	...	13	...	5	557	9	315
1888-89	402	1	758	21	693	84	...	13	...	3	435	7	260
1889-90	615	4	683	9	601	91	...	12	4	...	430	15	207
1890-91	579	2	582	12	531	104	...	9	1	95	407	10	77
1891-92	775	3	616	12	565	63	...	10	3	83	423	1	64
1892-93	697	4	606	5	547	64	..	6	...	117	223	40	52
1893-94	738	3	740	9	665	84	...	8	..	36	479	98	61
1894-95	986	4	639	9	562	86	.	7	...	21	439	9	124
1895-96	1,268	3	657	15	593	109	...	14	3	12	508	19	105
1896-97	1,209	1	873	16	793	96	...	6	...	14	716	25	36

1	15	16	17	18	19	20	21	22	23	24	25	26
	Length of sentence of convicts.							Previously convicted.			Pecuniary results.	
Year.	Under 6 months.	6 months to 1 year.	1 year to 2 years.	2 years to 5 years.	5 years to 10 years.	Over 10 years, &c., transportation.	Death.	Once.	Twice.	More than twice.	Cost of maintenance.	Profits of convicts' labour.
											Rs.	Rs. a. p.
1886-87	150	145	60	31	...	2	2	63	12	6	15,983	6,428 0 0
1887-88	617	157	166	33	2	2	1	95	20	4	18,309	858 6 0
1888-89	435	135	159	37	4	4	1	107	12	6	25,510	2,639 13 0
1889-90	428	125	113	18	4	2	2	83	12	6	27,846	2,740 3 0
1890-91	400	138	60	12	3	11	2	99	21	6	27,630	2,076 6 0
1891-92	421	118	58	21	4	3	3	39	38	7	37,818	22,413 2 0
1892-93	401	131	65	6	3	1	2	30	2	...	40,504	22,072 9 0
1893-94	309	273	94	63	5	4	1	54	12	10	45,369	16,055 0 0
1894-95	229	259	88	63	5	1	3	63	11	8	58,174	3,982 2 0
1895-96	347	197	80	62	7	7	2	40	16	7	63,156	1,939 6 0
1896-97	399	343	82	41	8	12	4	32	21	10	36,397	2,116 10 0

Table No. XLIII—showing the POPULATION of TOWNS.

1	2	3	4	5	6	7	8	9	10
Tahsil.	Town.	Total population.	Hindus.	Sikhs.	Jains.	Mussalmáns.	Other religions.	Number of occupied houses.	Persons per 100 occupied houses.
Montgomery	Montgomery	5,159	1,864	440	...	2,774	81	582	886
	Kamália	7,490	3,701	119	...	3,670	...	1,090	687
Pákpattan	Pákpattan	6,522	2,436	102	...	3,984	...	1,091	598

Table No. XLIV—showing BIRTHS and DEATHS for TOWNS.

1	2	3	4	5	6	7	8	9	10	11	12	13
Towns.	Sex.	Total population by the census of	Total births registered during the year.					Total deaths registered during the year.				
		1891.	1893.	1894.	1895.	1896.	1897.	1893.	1894.	1895.	1896.	1897.
Montgomery ...	Males	3,505	88	77	94	61	84	64	55	107	85	60
	Females	1,654	50	56	59	52	72	40	37	35	41	41
Kamália	Males	3,910	215	213	183	171	226	187	155	116	121	183
	Females	3,580	168	188	158	156	197	139	127	99	125	165
Pákpattan	Males	3,378	110	117	119	115	127	84	105	101	83	83
	Females	3,144	96	134	122	152	89	68	83	76	77	50

Table No. XLV—showing MUNICIPAL INCOME.

1	2	3	4	5	6
Name of Municipality.	Montgomery.	Kamália.	Pákpattan.	Sayadwála.	Dipálpur.
Class of Municipality	II	II	II	III	III
1886-87	5,656	5,932	5,617	20	70
1887-88	6,444	6,188	6,236	Abolished.	Abolished.
1888-89	6,031	6,829	6,230	...	...
1889-90	6,575	6,865	6,615	...	...
1890-91	6,872	6,962	6,907	...	...
1891-92	10,621	9,058	6,523	...	...
1892-93	9,095	7,451	5,570	...	...
1893-94	11,661	9,894	6,875	...	...
1894-95	11,474	9,621	7,545	...	...
1895-96	10,779	9,405	7,781	...	...
1896-97	10,568	8,716	7,337	...	...

POLYMETRICAL TABLE OF DISTANCES

OF THE

MONTGOMERY DISTRICT

Station	Montgomery	Anbar	Attari	Ahmadabad	Bahlak	Bunga Hayat	Basirpur	Bucheke	Chechawatni	Chuchak	Chawant	Doburji	Dipalpur	Dhapai	Dhoular	Dhoulri	Gugera	Gamar	Gudbar Malkana	Garh	Harappa	Hujra	Haveli	Jamlera	Jiwan Shah	Jhamra	Jandraka	Jhabbar	Kouri Shah	Kamalia	Kassowal	Kalewal	Kalyana	Killianwala	Kamir	Lalu Gudar	Ladhewal	Mahamadpur	Mirak	Miran Shah	Moharanwala	Nurpur	Nur Shah	Nouthen	Okara	Pakpattan	Pindi Sheikh Musa	Rajana	Rasullan	Satghara	Sher Garh	Sheikh Fazal	Saidan Shah	Shahamad	Shah Yakka	Shah Nawaz	Sayadwala	Tibbi	Tahar
Montgomery
Anbar	20
Attari	37	51
Ahmadabad	46	68	89
Bahlak	32	13	61	71
Bunga Hayat	25	45	14	42	57
Basirpur	46	39	18	64	39	22
Bucheke	39	41	70	99	36	84	77
Chechawatni	26	46	83	47	47	57	72	88
Chuchak	44	25	50	85	23	69	62	26	71
Chawant	22	42	61	24	54	14	22	61	48	65
Doburji	59	69	98	60	51	70	85	85	13	94	52
Dipalpur	33	27	24	79	37	14	13	54	89	41	28	72
Dhapai	20	34	51	64	46	10	34	73	40	57	10	53	27
Dhoular	21	38	36	40	35	4	20	55	43	43	14	58	12	10
Dhoulri	22	34	57	48	33	68	68	74	15	39	44	28	55	36	48
Gugera	25	5	54	64	7	50	43	35	53	22	47	64	30	39	29	40
Gamar	15	70	48	55	29	19	37	51	41	36	37	54	24	29	14	37	15
Gudbar Malkana	59	59	9	77	60	40	16	87	85	54	56	98	26	50	40	81	53	46
Garh	15	15	67	87	14	61	56	64	34	39	37	47	43	29	37	16	20	18	64
Harappa	13	33	77	33	34	38	59	70	13	58	35	26	46	27	32	11	39	28	72	21
Hujra	45	29	16	91	43	26	12	54	71	34	40	84	12	39	27	90	36	36	17	55	58
Haveli	39	43	24	50	53	14	14	70	61	57	27	78	16	27	17	49	46	40	32	40	62	28
Jamlera	50	66	82	6	78	51	68	105	39	87	41	41	66	54	46	66	71	61	87	99	40	37	38
Jiwan Shah	29	49	58	14	61	25	48	88	29	69	13	52	43	17	28	51	54	44	68	44	31	55	34	20
Jhamra	31	12	68	71	8	56	36	82	84	23	53	59	36	45	35	38	6	22	59	22	44	42	52	74	67
Jandraka	37	78	52	85	79	74	55	23	62	10	50	76	42	72	46	49	11	34	78	32	49	61	54	83	68	79
Jhabbar	32	45	96	59	41	57	84	97	6	70	54	10	71	58	60	11	51	47	87	27	14	83	87	45	40	40	68
Kouri Shah	30	70	59	50	22	35	56	49	33	35	32	59	30	10	22	22	15	31	40	25	20	43	38	56	39	21	22	33
Kamalia	27	47	84	49	37	62	90	77	11	62	47	14	60	27	48	7	43	50	105	23	15	72	56	50	32	45	49	6	28
Kassowal	36	56	99	39	30	61	88	103	10	85	49	7	75	50	58	25	76	51	108	41	23	87	83	40	40	[illegible]	[illegible]	16	48	21
Kalewal	31	33	33	41	64	6	19	75	58	49	12	71	15	17	10	54	57	23	37	47	45	27	9	47	23	80	48	64	42	62	72
Kalyana	32	85	53	19	65	23	43	96	45	70	13	58	38	20	31	50	58	36	58	47	39	40	23	24	8	65	71	59	42	59	50	22
Killianwala	17	19	56	57	18	42	68	44	24	45	39	58	47	31	34	40	26	23	76	5	16	68	56	54	47	18	27	28	73	77	53	49	52
Kamir	16	37	66	23	48	30	56	73	21	59	16	34	38	18	24	29	41	31	83	31	18	80	42	28	13	47	53	31	26	34	34	31	21	24
Lalu Gudar	37	52	5	52	61	28	11	82	88	56	40	98	24	39	34	73	54	48	10	72	70	15	20	74	54	60	53	89	58	84	105	80	43	74	62
Ladhewal	36	34	24	50	44	11	8	74	62	48	22	75	7	13	13	58	37	24	39	54	[illegible]	77	9	56	31	43	45	66	46	69	72	9	31	53	38	21
Mahamadpur	6	19	79	46	32	31	52	59	24	42	28	50	43	20	28	19	25	21	65	12	[illegible]	55	40	52	35	31	37	24	9	23	24	38	29	11	22	63	42
Mirak	34	16	40	76	19	58	52	32	61	10	55	84	8	47	33	49	12	26	44	24	[illegible]	24	47	79	59	13	7	60	25	52	85	39	60	35	48	46	38	32
Miran Shah	18	5	57	58	15	28	46	42	37	30	44	53	33	32	26	32	8	11	53	[illegible]	[illegible]	38	47	64	47	14	20	42	8	50	54	34	51	16	34	59	35	16	24
Moharanwala	59	40	70	99	36	84	77	78	83	26	86	85	54	73	57	74	32	62	87	[illegible]	[illegible]	54	70	105	88	26	25	97	49	71	103	75	96	44	73	82	74	59	32	42
Nurpur	75	25	49	42	38	76	38	65	33	66	7	46	27	6	73	37	31	76	49	[illegible]	[illegible]	40	29	48	15	37	52	47	25	35	51	20	16	32	11	15	27	21	41	33	66
Nur Shah	13	7	59	53	14	28	41	46	39	82	35	62	35	18	35	59	72	9	80	[illegible]	[illegible]	39	49	57	42	18	24	36	3	44	45	32	30	15	29	57	33	12	22	5	48	28
Nouthen	16	21	43	35	49	10	30	65	47	47	12	55	28	4	7	38	38	11	76	[illegible]	[illegible]	82	24	41	21	38	45	43	17	45	52	15	29	34	19	40	20	25	37	21	65	8	18
Okara	25	18	40	63	21	48	29	48	49	22	45	62	16	37	78	45	12	8	42	27	[illegible]	20	32	69	41	20	26	55	20	50	59	24	45	32	39	40	23	27	15	18	48	26	18	19
Pakpattan	29	49	44	28	69	17	34	78	43	58	7	56	29	9	75	51	43	27	49	59	[illegible]	41	22	36	14	49	57	52	39	58	59	13	11	46	22	40	23	35	46	37	73	14	42	16	31
Pindi Sheikh Musa	23	9	62	63	4	36	51	44	50	25	46	47	38	29	45	26	7	17	64	10	[illegible]	42	51	36	52	11	18	37	13	22	60	40	56	16	50	62	41	28	15	6	44	38	11	31	12	44
Rajana	38	58	95	60	48	73	101	76	22	67	58	70	71	38	59	18	54	54	118	28	[illegible]	83	77	61	57	58	60	17	39	11	32	73	85	22	44	95	80	34	57	38	76	48	37	54	61	67	40
Rasullan	15	18	42	48	31	11	29	59	41	49	16	54	18	5	7	37	24	8	47	30	[illegible]	30	25	53	27	36	36	47	25	62	51	16	29	32	25	28	19	21	39	35	64	12	28	4	16	20	38	53
Satghara	33	15	40	76	79	62	39	47	59	12	59	71	26	47	28	52	12	18	41	31	[illegible]	24	42	79	86	15	12	63	28	51	69	34	55	34	49	41	33	34	7	18	37	36	20	30	10	41	18	51	42
Sher Garh	38	28	24	69	36	27	20	44	64	18	41	77	16	36	30	60	28	25	25	25	[illegible]	8	30	82	55	34	28	70	41	65	74	31	50	55	54	37	23	44	18	34	46	40	36	32	15	41	34	76	28	18
Sheikh Fazal	33	53	78	20	55	47	73	90	18	76	31	20	76	35	41	33	67	59	88	52	[illegible]	76	66	21	21	64	70	24	54	31	19	52	31	37	17	75	58	42	66	51	90	28	48	39	56	35	58	42	42	64	80
Saidan Shah	9	14	58	49	27	34	55	64	34	38	21	48	42	23	31	20	20	16	68	9	[illegible]	54	48	55	38	27	22	40	4	33	45	40	41	11	25	66	45	10	28	5	64	24	7	28	32	38	17	44	18	32	48	42
Shahamad	46	43	16	78	53	21	6	85	72	57	29	85	16	31	25	68	46	40	22	70	[illegible]	18	10	63	44	51	54	66	52	73	89	17	39	63	52	11	11	52	47	52	85	37	49	32	32	30	54	84	29	42	28	69	55
Shah Yakka	24	25	33	46	45	4	20	67	50	41	14	63	11	14	4	52	38	15	13	35	[illegible]	23	15	52	32	37	38	58	34	51	64	8	27	41	30	31	10	30	31	20	67	17	24	10	16	18	32	62	9	26	24	47	27	20
Shah Nawaz	27	28	30	49	46	4	17	67	53	41	15	66	11	17	7	55	39	17	34	38	[illegible]	23	73	55	28	38	38	59	37	54	67	7	27	44	33	28	7	33	31	29	87	20	27	15	17	18	35	65	12	26	27	50	30	17	3
Sayadwala	41	22	62	81	22	66	59	18	71	8	63	73	36	55	40	58	18	44	69	36	[illegible]	36	52	87	70	14	5	79	31	59	85	57	78	40	57	64	58	41	14	24	18	47	28	47	24	55	26	65	45	14	29	74	46	69	49	49
Tibbi	38	44	65	4	93	38	58	87	38	80	31	56	53	39	39	52	67	51	73	56	[illegible]	65	48	12	15	73	81	54	68	55	42	37	13	69	22	64	46	44	79	58	97	30	51	38	55	24	81	69	44	65	55	24	47	54	42	41	79
Tahar	46	40	11	65	50	24	3	74	72	44	39	86	15	63	29	68	43	37	44	56	[illegible]	11	17	71	51	48	72	84	44	74	88	22	46	69	53	9	13	53	38	48	74	40	47	51	29	37	51	88	32	33	19	70	50	8	22	20	56	61
Wan Radha Ram	43	29	93	75	35	34	27	24	69	14	48	82	22	43	37	65	28	28	32	48	[illegible]	15	37	71	62	31	24	75	41	70	79	38	57	52	59	44	30	49	18	38	48	47	37	38	20	48	38	[illegible]	36	16	7	89	18	35	34	34	22	62	26

PREPARED BY GHOLAM QADIR AHMAD, DISTRICT OVERSEER, OF THE MONTGOMERY DISTRICT 18-2-99.

Nasir Ahmad 3-4-99.

RAILWAY STATIONS

Station	Montgomery	Harrappa	Chichawatni	Kassowal	Gammar	Okara	Satgara	Wan Radharam
Montgomery
Harrappa	13
Chichawatni	26	13
Kassowal	36	23	10
Gammar	15	28	41	51
Okara	23	36	49	59	8
Satgara	33	46	59	69	18	10
Wan Radharam	43	56	69	79	28	20	10
Usafwala	8	19	32	42	9	17	27	37

NOTE

The Village Chichawatni is 3 Miles further from Railway Station Chichawatni

— " — Harrappa — 4 — " — " — " — Harrappa

— " — Satgara — 5 — " — " — " — Satgara

— " — Koure Shah — 3 — " — " — " Encamping Ground Koure Shah

MAP OF THE MONTGOMERY DISTRICT

SCALE 16 MILES = 1 INCH

Sgd. A. J. W. KITCHIN

DEPUTY COMMISSIONER

MONTGOMERY DISTRICT